Matt Zandstra

SAMS Teach Yourself PHP4 in 24 Hours

SAMS

A Division of Macmillan USA
201 West 103rd St., Indianapolis, Indiana, 46290 USA

Sams Teach Yourself PHP4 in 24 Hours

Copyright © 2000 by Sams Publishing

International Standard Book Number: 0-672-31804-0

Library of Congress Catalog Card Number: 99-65599

Printed in the United States of America

First Printing: June 2000

03 02 01 00 4 3 2 1

Trademarks

All terms mentioned in this book that are known to be trademarks or service marks have been appropriately capitalized. Sams Publishing cannot attest to the accuracy of this information. Use of a term in this book should not be regarded as affecting the validity of any trademark or service mark.

This publication was produced using the Advent 3B2 Publishing System.

Warning and Disclaimer

Every effort has been made to make this book as complete and as accurate as possible, but no warranty or fitness is implied. The information provided is on an "as is" basis. The author and the publisher shall have neither liability nor responsibility to any person or entity with respect to any loss or damages arising from the information contained in this book or from the use of the programs accompanying it.

ACQUISITIONS EDITOR
Jeff Schultz

DEVELOPMENT EDITOR
Scott D. Meyers

MANAGING EDITOR
Charlotte Clapp

PROJECT EDITOR
Paul Schneider

COPY EDITOR
Geneil Breeze

INDEXER
Heather McNeill

PROOFREADER
Kathy Bidwell

TECHNICAL EDITOR
Ken Jenks

TEAM COORDINATOR
Amy Patton

MEDIA DEVELOPER
Jason Haines

INTERIOR DESIGNER
Gary Adair

COVER DESIGNER
Aren Howell

COPYWRITER
Eric Borgert

3B2 DESIGN
Michelle Mitchell

3B2 LAYOUT TECHNICIAN
Susan Geiselman

Contents

About the Author

Matt Zandstra (`matt@corrosive.co.uk`) runs Corrosive Web Design (`http://www.corrosive.co.uk`) with his business partner Max Guglielmino. A compulsive scripter, he has developed software in PHP, Java, JavaScript, Perl, Lingo, and AppleScript. Matt originally graduated in philosophy and has learned his trade by reinventing wheels and then working out why they don't run straight. Matt has taught courses in HTML, JavaScript, Perl, and PHP and was a contributing author to *Dynamic HTML Unleashed*. When not coding, Matt is a committed urban cyclist, a Guinness drinker, an obsessive reader, and a writer of unpublishable short stories. One day he claims he will write a novel.

Dedication

For my father. Who would have approved.

Acknowledgments

The open source concept made both my career and this book possible. I would like to thank all those people whose voluntary efforts continue to defy the received wisdom.

Particular thanks to the PHP community, especially contributors to the PHP mailing lists whose postings revealed pitfalls, suggested techniques, and kept me amused.

From Macmillan, I would like to thank Randi Roger for suggesting me for this project as well as Jeff Schultz, Paul Schneider, and Scott Meyers for support and tolerance as deadlines loomed and panic set in.

Thanks must also go to all at Corrosive for putting up with my continued absence and my extreme vagueness on any matter not pertaining to PHP. In particular, my business partner Massimo Guglielmino, who kept the Corrosive show on the road under the usual stressful circumstances, and Dave Urmson, who took over formatting when the going got tough. Other Corrosive stars include Anisa Swaffield, Jeff Coburn, Mai Chokelumlerd, and Moira Govern.

I must also thank Small Planet (`http://www.smallpla.net`) for providing me with additional development space and allowing me to use it to play with beta software. Particular thanks to Mohammed Abba and Clive Hills, who recompiled PHP on the Small Planet system more times than we care to remember.

One of the best ways to test a tutorial text is to use it in class. Thanks to my PHP students who graciously agreed to act as guinea pigs.

Thanks also to my partner Louise and our new daughter Holly for being there, and bearing the grumpy, hunched, and obsessed character I became while writing this book.

As my social life took second place to PHP, my local became a refuge for last minute pint and proofing sessions. Thanks to Alan and Dora of the Prince Arthur for running the perfect pub.

Finally, thanks to the fishes, who cheered up a lurker.

Tell Us What You Think!

As the reader of this book, *you* are our most important critic and commentator. We value your opinion and want to know what we're doing right, what we could do better, what areas you'd like to see us publish in, and any other words of wisdom you're willing to pass our way.

You can fax, email, or write me directly to let me know what you did or didn't like about this book—as well as what we can do to make our books stronger.

Please note that I cannot help you with technical problems related to the topic of this book, and that due to the high volume of mail I receive, I might not be able to reply to every message.

When you write, please be sure to include this book's title and author as well as your name and phone or fax number. I will carefully review your comments and share them with the author and editors who worked on the book.

Fax: 317-581-4770

Email: `webdev_sams@mcp.com`

Mail: Mark Taber
Associate Publisher
Sams Publishing
201 West 103rd Street
Indianapolis, IN 46290 USA

Introduction

This is a book about PHP, the open source Web scripting language that has joined Perl, ASP, and Java on the select list of languages that can be used to create dynamic online environments. It is also a book about programming. In the space available, it is neither possible to create a complete guide to programming in PHP nor to cover every function and technique that PHP offers. Nevertheless, whether you are an experienced programmer considering a move to PHP or a newcomer to scripting, the steps in this book should provide enough information to get your journey off to a good start.

Who Should Read This Book?

This book will take you from the first principles through to a good working knowledge of the PHP4 programming language. No prior experience of programming is assumed, though if you have worked with a language such as C or Perl in the past, you will find the going much easier.

PHP4 is a Web programming language. To get the most from this book, you should have some understanding of the World Wide Web and of HTML in particular. If you are just starting out, you will still be able to use this book, though you should consider acquiring an HTML tutorial. If you are comfortable creating basic documents and can build a basic HTML table, you will be fine.

PHP4 is designed to integrate well with databases. Some of the examples in this book are written to work with MySQL, a SQL database that is free for personal use on some platforms. We include a short introduction to SQL, but if you intend to use PHP to work with databases, you might want to spend some time reading up on the subject. Numerous introductory SQL tutorials are available online. If you intend to work with a database other than MySQL, many of the examples in this book will be relatively easy to reproduce with the equivalent PHP functions designed to query your database.

How This Book Is Organized

This book is divided into four parts:

- Part 1 is an introduction to PHP4.
- Part 2 covers the basic features of the language. Pay particular attention to this section if you are new to programming.

- Part 3 covers PHP4 in more detail, looking at the functions and techniques you will need to become a proficient PHP programmer.
- Part 4 illustrates a complete self-contained example.

Part 1 contains Hours 1 through 3 and handles the information you will need to get your first script up and running:

- Hour 1, "PHP: From Home Page to Portal," describes the history and capabilities of PHP and looks at some of the compelling reasons for deciding to learn this scripting language.
- Hour 2, "Installing PHP," explains how to install PHP on a UNIX system and discusses some of the configuration options you might want to choose when compiling PHP. In this hour, we also look at PHP configuration options.
- Hour 3, "A First Script," looks at the different ways in which you can embed a PHP script in a document and create a script that writes text to the user's browser.

Part 2 comprises Hours 4 through 8. In this part, you will learn the basic components of the PHP language:

- Hour 4, "The Building Blocks," covers the basics of PHP. You will learn about variables, data types, operators, and expressions.
- Hour 5, "Going with the Flow," covers the syntax for controlling program flow in your scripts. In addition to `if` and `switch` constructs, you will learn about loops using `for` and `while` statements.
- Hour 6, "Functions," explores the use of functions to organize your code.
- Hour 7, "Arrays," discusses the array data type that can be used to hold list information. We will also look at some of the functions that PHP4 provides to manipulate arrays.
- Hour 8, "Objects," introduces PHP4's support for classes and objects. Throughout the course of the hour, we will develop a working example.

Part 3 consists of Hours 9 through 22. In this part, you will come to grips with the features and techniques of the language:

- Hour 9, "Working with Forms," introduces the dimension of user input through the mechanism of the HTML form. You will learn how to gather data submitted via a form.
- Hour 10, "Working with Files," shows you how to work with files and directories on the local machine.

- Hour 11, "Working with the DBM Functions," demonstrates PHP4's support for DBM database systems, versions of which are available on most systems.
- Hour 12, "Database Integration—MySQL," provides a brief introduction to SQL syntax and introduces the PHP4 functions that can be used to work with the MySQL database.
- Hour 13, "Beyond the Box," covers some of the details of HTTP requests and looks at PHP network functions.
- Hour 14, "Working with Dynamic Images" explores PHP's image functions. With these, you can create GIF or PNG files dynamically.
- Hour 15, "Working with Dates," covers the functions and techniques you can use for date arithmetic. We create a calendar example.
- Hour 16, "Working with Data," revisits data types and explores some more of the functions you can use to work with data in your scripts. More array functions are also covered.
- Hour 17, "Working with Strings," covers the functions that you can use to manipulate strings.
- Hour 18, "Working with Regular Expressions," introduces regular expression functions. You can use these to find and replace complex patterns in strings.
- Hour 19, "Saving State with Cookies and Query Strings," shows you some techniques for passing information across scripts and requests.
- Hour 20, "Saving State with Session Functions," extends the techniques explored in Hour 19, using PHP4's built-in session functions.
- Hour 21, "Working with the Server Environment," shows you how to call external programs from your scripts and incorporate their output into your own.
- Hour 22, "Debugging," shows you some techniques that you can use to track down problems in your code. We also examine some common errors.

Part 4 consists of Hours 23 and 24. In these, we build a working example that incorporates some of the techniques that were introduced earlier in the book.

- Hour 23, "An Example (Part 1)," creates a brief for a club listings script. We build the code that will allow users to create accounts and enter listings.
- Hour 24, "An Example (Part 2)," concludes the project, building the code for nonmembers to browse the listings and look at club profiles.

PART I

Getting Started

Hour

HOUR 1

PHP: From Home Page to Portal

Welcome to PHP! Throughout this book you will look at almost every element of the PHP language. But first you will explore PHP as a product—its history, features, and future.

In this hour, you will learn

- What PHP is
- About PHP's history
- What improvements can be found in PHP4
- Some options that add features to your PHP binary
- Some reasons you should choose to work with PHP

What Is PHP?

PHP is a language that has outgrown its name. It was originally conceived as a set of macros to help coders maintain personal home pages, and its name grew from its purpose. Since then, PHP's capabilities have been extended, taking it beyond a set of utilities to a full-featured programming language, capable of managing huge database-driven online environments.

As PHP's capabilities have grown, so too has its popularity. According to NetCraft (`http://www.netcraft.com`), PHP was running on more than 1 million hosts in November 1999. As of February 2000, that figure had already risen to 1.4 million hosts. According to E-Soft, PHP is the most popular Apache module available, beating even ModPerl.

PHP is now officially known as PHP: HyperText Preprocessor. It is a server-side scripting language usually written in an HTML context. Unlike an ordinary HTML page, a PHP script is not sent directly to a client by the server; instead, it is parsed by the PHP binary or module. HTML elements in the script are left alone, but PHP code is interpreted and executed. PHP code in a script can query databases, create images, read and write files, talk to remote servers—the possibilities are endless. The output from PHP code is combined with the HTML in the script and the result sent to the user.

How Did PHP Evolve?

The first version of PHP was created by Rasmus Lerdorf in 1994 as a set of Web publishing macros. These were released as the Personal Home Page Tools and later rewritten and extended to include a package called the Form Interpreter (PHP/FI). From a user's perspective, PHP/FI was already an attractive proposition, and its popularity grew steadily. It also began to attract interest from the developer community. By 1997, a team of programmers was working on the project.

The next release—PHP3—was born out of this collaborative effort. PHP3 was an effective rewrite of PHP, with an entirely new parser created by Zeev Suraski and Andi Gutmans, as well as differences in syntax and new features. This release established PHP as one of the most exciting server scripting languages available, and the growth in usage was enormous.

PHP's support for Apache and MySQL further secured its popularity. Apache is now the most-used Web server in the world, and PHP3 can be compiled as an Apache module. MySQL is a powerful free SQL database, and PHP provides a comprehensive set of functions for working with it. The combination of Apache, MySQL, and PHP is all but unbeatable.

That isn't to say that PHP is not designed to work in other environments and with other tools. In fact, PHP supports a bewildering array of databases and servers.

The rise in popularity of PHP has coincided with a change of approach in Web publishing. In the mid-1990s it was normal to build sites, even relatively large sites, with hundreds of individual hard-coded HTML pages. Increasingly, though, site publishers are harnessing the power of databases to manage their content more effectively and to personalize their sites according to individual user preferences.

The use of databases to store content, and of a scripting language to retrieve this data, will become further necessary as data is sent from a single source to multiple environments, including mobile phones and PDAs, digital television, and broadband Internet environments.

In this context, it is not surprising that a tool of PHP's sophistication and flexibility is becoming so popular.

At the time of this writing, PHP4 is in its final beta stage and is due for release shortly. By the time you read this book, PHP4 will be making waves!

What's New in PHP4

PHP4 introduces numerous new features that will make the programmer's life more interesting. Let's take a quick look at some of them.

- A new `foreach` statement, similar to that found in Perl, makes it much easier to loop through arrays. We will be using this for most of the array examples in this book. Additionally, a raft of new array functions have been added, making arrays easier to manipulate.
- The language now includes the `boolean` data type.
- A particularly useful feature of PHP3 was the capability to name form elements as if they were elements in an array. The elements' names and values are then made available to the code in array form. This feature has been extended to support multidimensional arrays.
- Support for object-oriented programming was somewhat rudimentary in PHP. This is significantly extended in PHP4; for example, it is now possible to call an overridden method from a child class.
- PHP4 now provides native support for user sessions, using both cookies and the query string. You can now "register" a variable with a session, and then access the same variable name and value in subsequent user requests.

- A new comparison operator (===) has been introduced that tests for equivalence of type as well as equivalence of value.
- New associative arrays containing server and environmental variables have been made available, as well as a variable that holds information about uploaded files.
- PHP4 now provides built-in support for both Java and XML.

Although these and other features significantly improve the language, perhaps the most significant change has taken place under the hood.

The Zend Engine

When PHP3 was written, an entirely new parser was created from the ground up. PHP4 represents a similar change to the scripting engine. This rewrite, though, is more significant by orders of magnitude.

Zend is a scripting engine that sits below the PHP-specific modules. It is optimized to significantly improve performance.

These changes in efficiency will ensure PHP4's continued success. Most code written for PHP3 will continue to run with no changes; however, these scripts may run up to 200 times faster!

A commercial addition to the Zend engine will be the facility for compiling PHP scripts. This will provide a further gain in performance that should leave most, if not all, competitors far behind.

Zend is built to improve performance but is also designed for increased flexibility. Communication with servers has been improved, so it will be possible to create PHP modules that work with a wider range of servers. Unlike a CGI interpreter, which sits outside a server and is initialized every time a script is run, a server module runs in conjunction with the server. This improves performance because the scripting engine does not need to be started for a PHP page to be executed.

Why Choose PHP?

There are some compelling reasons to work with PHP4. For many projects you will find that the production process is significantly faster than you might expect if you are used to working with other scripting languages. As an open source product, PHP4 is well supported by a talented production team and a committed user community. Furthermore, PHP can be run on all the major operating systems with most servers.

Speed of Development

Because PHP allows you to separate HTML code from scripted elements, you will notice a significant decrease in development time on many projects. In many instances, you will be able to separate the coding stage of a project from the design and build stages. Not only can this make life easier for you as a programmer, it also can remove obstacles that stand in the way of effective and flexible design.

PHP Is Open Source

To many people, "open source" simply means free, which is, of course, a benefit in itself. To quote from the official PHP site at `http://www.php.net/`:

> This may sound a little foreign to all you folks coming from a non-UNIX background, but PHP doesn't cost anything. You can use it for commercial and/or non-commercial use all you want. You can give it to your friends, print it out and hang it on your wall or eat it for lunch. Welcome to the world of Open Source software! Smile, be happy, the world is good. For the full legalese, see the official license.

Well-maintained open source projects offer users additional benefits, though. You benefit from an accessible and committed community who offer a wealth of experience in the subject. Chances are that any problem you encounter in your coding can be answered swiftly and easily with a little research. If that fails, a question sent to a mailing list can yield an intelligent, authoritative response.

You also can be sure that bugs will be addressed as they are found, and that new features will be made available as the need is defined. You will not have to wait for the next commercial release before taking advantage of improvements.

There is no vested interest in a particular server product or operating system. You are free to make choices that suit your needs or those of your clients, secure that your code will run whatever you decide.

Performance

Because of the powerful Zend engine, PHP4 compares well with ASP in benchmark tests, beating it in some tests. Compiled PHP leaves ASP far behind.

Portability

PHP is designed to run on many operating systems and to cooperate with many servers and databases. You can build for a UNIX environment and shift your work to NT without a problem. You can test a project with Personal Web Server and install it on a UNIX system running on PHP as an Apache module.

Summary

In this hour, we introduced PHP. You learned the history of PHP from a simple set of macros to the powerful scripting environment it has become. You found out about PHP4 and the Zend scripting engine, and how they incorporate new features and more efficiency. Finally, you discovered some of the features that make PHP a compelling choice as a Web programming language.

Q&A

Q Is PHP an easy language to learn?

A In short, yes! You really can learn the basics of PHP in 24 hours. PHP provides an enormous wealth of functions that allow you to do things for which you would have to write custom code in other languages. PHP also handles data types and memory issues for you (much like Perl).

Understanding the syntax and structures of a programming language is only the beginning of the journey, however. Ultimately, you will only really learn by building your own projects and by making mistakes. You should see this book as a starting point.

Workshop

The Workshop provides quiz questions to help you solidify your understanding of the material covered. Try to understand the quiz answers before continuing to the next hour's lesson. Quiz answers are provided in Appendix A.

Quiz

1. What did the initials PHP originally stand for?
2. Who created the original version of PHP?

3. What is the name of the new scripting engine that powers PHP?
4. Name a new feature introduced with PHP4.

Activity

1. Flick through this book to get an idea of its structure. Think about the topics covered and how they might help you with any future projects.

Hour 2

Installing PHP

Before getting started with the PHP language, you must first acquire, install, and configure the PHP interpreter. PHP is available for a wide range of platforms and works in conjunction with many servers.

In this hour, you will learn

- Which platforms, servers, and databases are supported by PHP4
- Where to find PHP and other useful open source software
- One way of installing PHP on Linux
- Some options that add features to your PHP binary
- Some configuration directives
- How to find help when things go wrong

Platforms, Servers, Databases, and PHP

PHP is truly cross-platform. It runs on the Windows operating system, most versions of UNIX including Linux, and even the Macintosh. Support is provided for a range of Web servers including Apache (itself open source and cross-platform), Microsoft Internet Information Server, WebSite Pro, the iPlanet Web Server, and Microsoft's Personal Web Server. The latter is useful if you want to test your scripts offline on a Windows machine, although Apache can also be run on Windows.

You can also compile PHP as a standalone application. You can then call it from the command line. In this book, we will concentrate on building Web applications, but do not underestimate the power of PHP4 as a general scripting tool comparable to Perl.

PHP is designed to integrate easily with databases. This feature is one of the factors that make the language such a good choice for building sophisticated Web applications. Many databases are directly supported, including Adabas D, InterBase, Solid, dBASE, mSQL, Sybase, Empress, MySQL, Velocis, FilePro, Oracle, UNIX dbm, Informix, and PostgreSQL. PHP also supports ODBC.

Throughout this book, we will be using a combination of Linux, Apache, and MySQL. All these are free to download and use, and can be installed relatively easily on a PC. You can find out more about getting Linux for your computer at `<http://www.linux.org/help/beginner/distributions.html>`. If you want to run Linux on a Power PC, you can find information about LinuxPPC at `<http://www.linuxppc.org>`.

MySQL, the database we will use in this book, can be downloaded from `<http://www.mysql.com>`. There are versions for many operating systems including UNIX, Windows, and OS/2.

On the other hand, you can easily stick with Windows, NT, or MacOS. PHP is, after all, a cross-platform scripting language.

Where to Find PHP and More

You can find PHP4 at `<http://www.php.net/>`. PHP4 is open source software, which means that you won't need your credit card handy when you download it.

The PHP WebSite is an excellent resource for PHP coders. The entire manual can be read online at `<http://www.php.net/manual/>`, complete with helpful annotations from other PHP coders. You can also download the manual in several formats.

Installing PHP4 for Linux and Apache

In this section, we will look at one way of installing PHP4 with Apache on Linux. The process is more or less the same for any UNIX operating system. You might be able to find prebuilt versions of PHP for your system, which are simple to install. Compiling PHP, though, gives you greater control over the features built in to your binary.

Before you install you should make sure that you are logged into your system as the root user. If you are not allowed access to your system's root account, you may need to ask your system administrator to install PHP for you.

There are two ways of compiling an Apache PHP module. You can either recompile Apache, statically linking PHP into it, or you can compile PHP as a Dynamic Shared Object (DSO). If your version of Apache was compiled with DSO support, it will be capable of supporting new modules without the need for recompiling the server. This method is the easiest way to get PHP up and running, and it is the one we will look at in this section.

In order to test that Apache supports DSOs you should launch the Apache binary (httpd) with the -l argument.

```
/www/bin/httpd -l
```

You should see a list of modules. If you see

```
mod_so.c
```

among them, you should be able to proceed; otherwise, you may need to recompile Apache. The Apache distribution contains full instructions for this.

If you have not already done so, you will need to download the latest distribution of PHP4. Your distribution will be archived as a tar file and compressed with gzip, so you will need to unpack it:

```
tar -xvzf php-4.0.tar.gz
```

After your distribution is unpacked, you should move to the PHP4 distribution directory:

```
cd ../php-4.0
```

Within your distribution directory you will find a script called `configure`. This accepts arguments that will control the features that PHP will support. For this example, we will include some useful command line arguments, although you might want to specify arguments of your own. We will discuss some of the `configure` options available to you later in the hour.

```
./configure  --enable-track-vars \
             --with-gd \
             --with-mysql \
             --with-apxs=/www/bin/apxs
```

The path you assign to the `--with-apxs` argument is likely to be different on your system. It is possible that you will find apxs in the same directory as your Apache executable.

After the `configure` script has run, you can run the `make` program. You will need a C compiler on your system to run this command successfully.

```
make
make install
```

These commands should end the process of PHP4 compilation and installation. You should now be able to configure and run Apache.

Some `configure` Options

When we ran the `configure` script, we included some command-line arguments that determined the features that the PHP interpreter will include. The `configure` script itself gives you a list of available options. From the PHP distribution directory type the following:

```
./configure --help
```

The list produced is long, so you may want to add it to a file for reading at leisure:

```
./configure --help > configoptions.txt
```

Although the output from this command is very descriptive, we will look at a few useful options—especially those that might be needed to follow this book.

`--enable-track-vars`

This option automatically populates associative arrays with values submitted as part of `GET`, `POST` requests or provided in a cookie. You can read more about arrays in Hour 7, "Arrays," and about HTTP requests in Hour 13, "Beyond the Box." It is a good idea to include this option when running `configure`.

--with-gd

`--with-gd` enables support for the GD library, which, if installed on your system, allows you to create dynamic GIF or PNG images from your scripts. You can read more about creating dynamic images in Hour 14, "Working with Dynamic Images." You can optionally specify a path to your GD library's install directory:

```
--with-gd=/path/to/dir
```

--with-mysql

`--with-mysql` enables support for the MySQL database. If your system has MySQL installed in a directory other than the default location, you should specify a path:

```
--with-mysql=/path/to/dir
```

As you know, PHP provides support for other databases. Table 2.1 lists some of them and the `configure` options you will need to use them.

TABLE 2.1 Some Database `configure` Options

Database	`configure` *Option*
Adabas D	`--with-adabas`
FilePro	`--with-filepro`
msql	`--with-msql`
informix	`--with-informix`
iODBC	`--with-iodbc`
OpenLink ODBC	`--with-openlink`
Oracle	`--with-oracle`
PostgreSQL	`--with-pgsql`
Solid	`--with-solid`
Sybase	`--with-sybase`
Sybase-CT	`--with-sybase-ct`
Velocis	`--with-velocis`
LDAP	`--with-ldap`

Configuring Apache

After you have compiled PHP and Apache, you should check Apache's configuration file, `httpd.conf`, which you will find in a directory called `conf` in the Apache install directory. Add the following lines to this file:

```
AddType application/x-httpd-php .php
AddType application/x-httpd-php-source .phps
```

This ensures that the PHP interpreter will parse files that end with the `.php` extension. Any files with the `.phps` extension will be output as PHP source. That is, the source code will be converted to HTML and color-coded. This can be useful for debugging your scripts.

If you want to offer to your users PHP pages with extensions more familiar to them, you can choose any extension you want. You can even ensure that files with the `.html` extension are treated as PHP files with the following:

```
AddType application/x-httpd-php .html
```

Note that treating files with the `.html` extension as PHP scripts could slow down your site, because every page with this extension will be parsed by the PHP interpreter before it is served to the user.

If PHP has been preinstalled and you have no access to the Apache configuration files, you may be able to change the extensions that will determine which files will be treated as PHP executables by including an `AddType` directive in a file called `.htaccess`. After you have created this file, the directive will affect the enclosing directory, as well as any subdirectories. This technique will only work if the `AllowOverride` directive for the enclosing directory is set to either `FileInfo` or `All`.

Although the filename `.htaccess` is the default for an access control file, it may have been changed. Check the `AccessFileName` directive in `httpd.conf` to find out. Even if you don't have root access, you should be able to read the Apache configuration files.

An `.htaccess` file can be an excellent way of customizing your server space if you do not have access to the root account. An additional way of controlling the behavior of PHP, even as a non-root user, is the `php.ini` file.

php.ini

After you have compiled or installed PHP, you can still change its behavior with a file called `php.ini`. On UNIX systems, the default location for this file is `/usr/local/lib`; on a Windows system, the default location is the Windows directory. A `php.ini` file in the current working directory will override one in the default location, so you can change the behavior of PHP on a per-directory basis.

You should find a sample `php.ini` file in your distribution directory, which contains factory settings. Factory settings will be used if no `php.ini` file is used.

The default settings should be adequate for most of the examples in this book, although you can read about some amendments you might like to make in Hour 22, "Debugging."

Directives in the `php.ini` file take the form of a directive and a value separated by an equals sign. Whitespace is ignored.

If PHP has been preinstalled on your system, you might want to check some of the settings in `php.ini`. Remember, if you are not allowed to alter this document, you can create one in your script's directory that can override the default. You can also set an environmental variable `PHPRC` that designates a `php.ini` file.

You can change your `php.ini` settings at any time, though if you are running PHP as an Apache module, you should restart the server for the changes to take effect.

short_open_tag

The `short_open_tag` directive determines whether you can begin a block of PHP code with the symbols `<?` and close it with `?>`. If this has been disabled, you will see one of the following:

```
short_open_tag = Off
short_open_tag = False
short_open_tag = No
```

To enable the directive you can use one of the following:

```
short_open_tag = On
short_open_tag = True
short_open_tag = Yes
```

You can read more about PHP open and close tags in Hour 3, "A First Script."

Error Reporting Directives

To diagnose bugs in your code, you should enable the directive that allows error messages to be written to the browser. This is on by default:

```
display_errors = On
```

You can also set the level of error reporting. We will cover the options available for the `error_reporting` directive in more depth in Hour 22. For now, however, you should set this to the following:

```
error_reporting = E_ALL & ~ E_NOTICE
```

This will report all errors but not notices that warn about potential problems with your code. Notices can interfere with some PHP techniques. This setting is the default.

Variable Directives

PHP makes certain variables available to you as a result of a `GET` request, a `POST` request, or a cookie. You can influence this in the `php.ini` file.

The `track_vars` directive creates associative arrays containing elements generated as a result of an HTTP request. This is allowed by default:

```
track_vars = On
```

The `register_globals` directive determines whether values resulting from an HTTP request should be made available as global variables. Many scripts in this book will require the following setting to be enabled:

```
register_globals = On
```

Help!

Help is always at hand on the Internet, particularly for problems concerning open source software. Wait a moment before you hit the send button, however. No matter how intractable your installation, configuration, or programming problem might seem, chances are you are not alone. Someone will have already answered your question.

When you hit a brick wall, your first recourse should be to the official PHP site at `<http://www.php.net/>`, particularly the annotated manual at `<http://www.php.net/manual>`.

If you still can't find your answer, don't forget that the PHP site is searchable. The advice you are seeking may be lurking in a press release or a Frequently Asked Questions file. Another excellent and searchable resource is the PHP Knowledge Base at `<http://www.faqts.com/knowledge-base/index.phtml>`.

Still no luck? You can find links to searchable mailing list archives at `<http://www.php.net/mailsearch.php3>`. These archives represent a huge information resource with contributions from many of the great and the good in the PHP community. Spend some time trying out a few keyword combinations.

If you are still convinced that your problem has not been addressed, you may well be doing the PHP community a service by exposing it.

You can join the PHP mailing lists at <http://www.php.net/support.php3>. Although these lists are often high volume, you can learn a lot from them. If you are serious about PHP scripting, you should certainly subscribe at least to a digest list. Once subscribed to the list that matches your concerns, you might consider posting your problem.

When you post a question it is often a good idea to include as much information as possible (without writing a novel). The following items often are pertinent:

- Your operating system
- The version of PHP you are running or installing
- The `configure` options you chose
- Any output from the `configure` or `make` commands that preceded an installation failure
- A reasonably complete example of the code that is causing you problems

Why all these cautions about posting a question to a mailing list? First, developing research skills will stand you in good stead. A good researcher can generally solve a problem quickly and efficiently. Asking a naive question of a technical list often involves a wait rewarded only by a message or two referring you to the archives where you should have begun your search for answers.

Second, remember that a mailing list is not analogous to a technical support call center. No one is paid to answer your questions. Despite this, you have access to an impressive resource of talent and knowledge, including that of some of the creators of PHP itself. A good question and its answer will be archived to help other coders. Asking a question that has been answered several times just adds more noise.

Having said this, don't be afraid to post a problem to the list. PHP developers are a civilized and helpful breed, and by bringing a problem to the attention of the community, you might be helping others to solve the same problem.

Summary

PHP4 is open source software. It is also open in the sense that it does not demand that you use a particular server, operating system, or database.

In this hour, you learned where to locate PHP and other open source software that can help you host and serve Web sites. You learned how to compile PHP as an Apache module on Linux. If you download a PHP binary for another platform, your distribution will contain step-by-step instructions. You learned some of the `configure` options that can change the features that your binary will support. You learned about `php.ini` and some of the directive it contains. Finally, you learned about sources of support. You should now be ready to come to grips with the language itself.

Q&A

Q You have covered an installation for Linux and Apache. Does that mean that this book will not apply to my server and operating system?

A No, one of PHP's great strengths is that it runs on multiple platforms. If you are having trouble installing PHP to work on your operating system or with your server, don't forget to read the files that come with your PHP distribution. You should find comprehensive step-by-step instructions for installation. If you are still having problems, review the "Help!" section earlier in this hour. The online resources mentioned there will almost certainly contain the answers you need.

Workshop

The Workshop provides quiz questions to help you solidify your understanding of the material covered. Try to understand the quiz answers before continuing to the next hour's lesson. Quiz answers are provided in Appendix A.

Quiz

1. Where can you find the PHP online manual?
2. From a UNIX operating system, how would you get help on configuration options (the options that you pass to the `configure` script in your PHP distribution)?
3. What is Apache's configuration file typically called?
4. What line should you add to the Apache configuration file to ensure that the `.php` extension is recognized?
5. What is PHP's configuration file called?

Activity

1. Install PHP on your system. If it is already in place, review your `php.ini` file and check your configuration.

HOUR 3

A First Script

Having installed and configured PHP, it is now time to put it to the test. In this hour, you will create your first script and spend a little time analyzing its syntax. By the end of the hour, you should be ready to create documents that include both HTML and PHP.

In this hour, you will learn

- How to create, upload, and run a PHP script
- How to incorporate HTML and PHP in the same document
- How to make your code clearer with comments

Our First Script

Let's jump straight in with a PHP script. To begin, open your favorite text editor. Like HTML documents, PHP files are made up of plain text. You can create them with any text editor, such as Notepad on Windows, Simple Text and BBEdit on MacOS, or VI and Emacs on UNIX operating systems. Most popular HTML editors provide at least some support for PHP.

Type in the example in Listing 3.1 and save the file, calling it something like `first.php`.

LISTING 3.1 A First PHP Script

```
1: <?php
2:     print "Hello Web!";
3: ?>
```

Figure 3.1 shows the script created in Listing 3.1 as typed into the BBEdit text editor for MacOS.

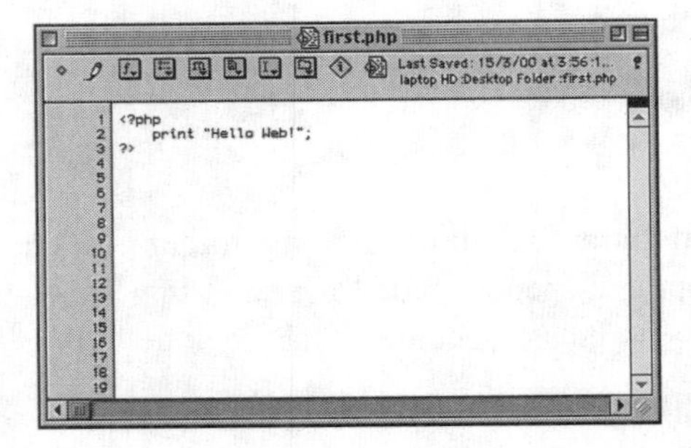

FIGURE 3.1
Your first script as created in the BBEdit text editor.

The extension to the PHP document is important because it tells the server to treat the file as PHP code and invoke the interpreter. The default PHP extension for a PHP 4 document is `.php`. This can be changed, however, by altering the server's configuration. You saw how to do this in Hour 2, "Installing PHP."

If you are not working directly on the machine that will be serving your PHP script, you will probably need to use an FTP client, such as WS-FTP for Windows or Fetch for MacOS to upload your saved document to the server.

After the document is in place, you should be able to access it via your browser. If all has gone well, you should see the script's output. Figure 3.2 shows the output from the `first.php` script.

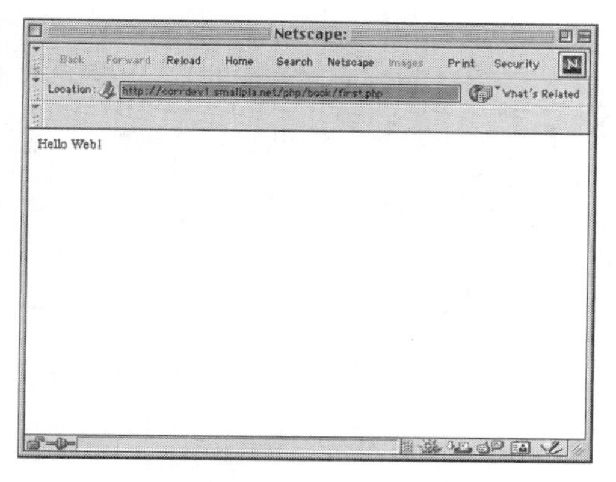

FIGURE 3.2
Success: the output from Listing 3.1.

If PHP is not installed on your server or your file's extension is not recognized, you may not see the output shown in Figure 3.2. In these cases, you probably will see the source code created in Listing 3.1. Figure 3.3 shows what happens when an unknown extension is encountered.

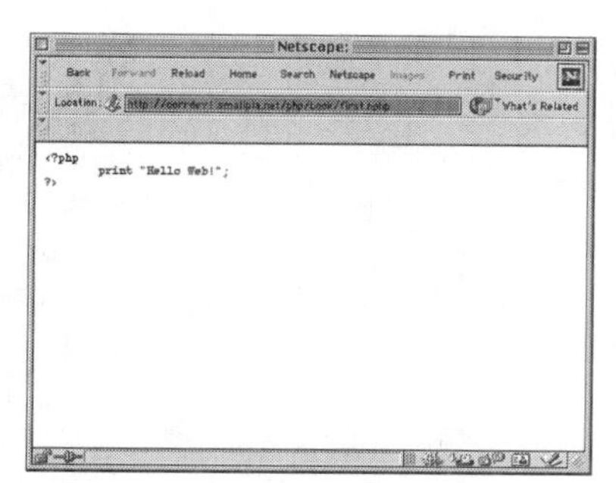

FIGURE 3.3
Failure: the extension is not recognized.

If this happens, first check the extension with which you saved your PHP script. In Figure 3.3, the document was accidentally called `first.nphp`. If the file extension is as it should be, you may need to check that PHP has been installed properly and that your server is configured to work with the extension that you have used for your script. You can read more about installing and configuring PHP in Hour 2.

Now that you have uploaded and tested your script, you can take a look at the code in a little more detail.

Beginning and Ending a Block of PHP Statements

When writing PHP, you need to inform the interpreter that you want it to execute your commands. If you don't do this, the code you write will be mistaken for HTML and will be output to the browser. Table 3.1 shows the four ways of enclosing PHP code.

TABLE 3.1 PHP Start and End Tags

Tag Style	*Start Tag*	*End Tag*
Standard tags	`<?php`	`?>`
Short tags	`<?`	`?>`
ASP tags	`<%`	`%>`
Script tags	`<SCRIPT LANGUAGE="php">`	`</SCRIPT>`

Of the tags in Table 3.1, only the standard and the script tags can be guaranteed to work on any configuration. The short and ASP style tags must be explicitly enabled in your `php.ini`. You examined the `php.ini` file in Hour 2.

To activate recognition for short tags, you must make sure that the `short_open_tag` switch is set to "On" in `php.ini`:

```
short_open_tag  =  On;
```

Short tags are enabled by default, so you would only need to edit `php.ini` if you want to disable these.

To activate recognition for the ASP style tags, you must enable the `asp_tags` setting:

```
asp_tags = On;
```

After you have edited `php.ini`, you should be able to choose from any of the four styles for use in your scripts. This is largely a matter of preference, although if you intend to work with XML, you should disable the short tags (`<? ?>`) and work with the standard tags (`<?php ?>`).

Let's run through some of the ways in which you can legally write the code in Listing 3.1. You could use any of the four PHP start and end tags that you have seen:

```
<?
print("Hello Web!");
?>

<?php
print("Hello Web!");
?>

<%
print("Hello Web!");
%>

<SCRIPT LANGUAGE="php">
print("Hello Web!");
</SCRIPT>
```


Single lines of code in PHP also can be presented on the same line as the PHP start and end tags:

```
<? print("Hello Web!"); ?>
```

Now that you know how to define a block of PHP code, take a closer look at the code in Listing 3.1 itself.

The `print()` Function

`print()` is a function that outputs data. In most cases, anything output by `print()` ends up in the browser window. A *function* is a command that performs an action, usually modified in some way by data provided for it. Data sent to a function is almost always placed in parentheses after the function name. In this case, you sent the `print()` function a collection of characters, or string. Strings must always be enclosed by quotation marks, either single or double.

Function calls generally require parentheses after their name whether or not they demand that data be passed to them. `print()` is an exception, and enclosing the data you want to print to the browser in parentheses is optional. This is the more common syntax, so we will usually omit the brackets in our examples.

You ended your only line of code in Listing 3.1 with a semicolon. The semicolon informs the interpreter that you have completed a statement.

New Term A *statement* represents an instruction to the interpreter. Broadly, it is to PHP what a sentence is to written or spoken English. A statement should usually end with a semicolon; a sentence should end with a period. Exceptions to this include statements that enclose other statements, and statements that end a block of code. In most cases, however, failure to end a statement with a semicolon will confuse the interpreter and result in an error.

Because the statement in Listing 3.1 is the final one in that block of code, the semicolon is optional.

Combining HTML and PHP

The script in Listing 3.1 is pure PHP. You can incorporate this into an HTML document simply by adding HTML outside the PHP start and end tags, as shown in Listing 3.2.

Listing 3.2 A PHP Script Including HTML

```
 1: <html>
 2: <head>
 3:     <title>Listing 3.2 A PHP script including HTML</title>
 4: </head>
 5: <body>
 6: <b>
 7: <?php
 8:     print "hello world";
 9: ?>
10: </b>
11: </body>
12: </html>
```

As you can see, incorporating HTML into a PHP document is simply a matter of typing in the code. The PHP interpreter ignores everything outside PHP open and close tags. If you were to view Listing 3.2 with a browser, as shown in Figure 3.4, you would see the string "hello world" in bold. If you were to view the document source, as shown in Figure 3.5, the listing would look exactly like a normal HTML document.

You can include as many blocks of PHP code as you need in a single document, interspersing them with HTML as required. Although you can have multiple blocks of code in a single document, they combine to form a single script. Anything defined in the first block (variables, functions, or classes, for example) usually will be available to subsequent blocks.

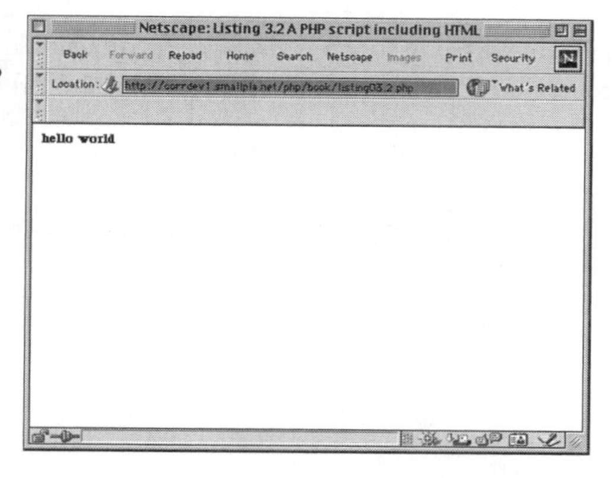

FIGURE 3.4
The output of Listing 3.2 as viewed in a browser.

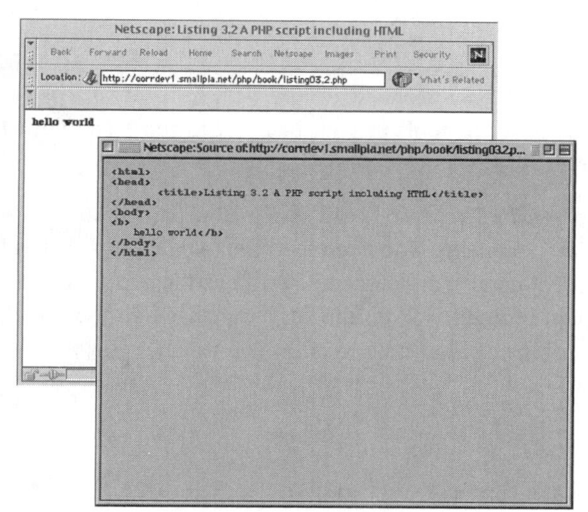

FIGURE 3.5
The output of Listing 3.2 as HTML source code.

Adding Comments to PHP Code

Code that seems clear at the time of writing, can seem like a hopeless tangle when you come to amend it six months later. Adding comments to your code as you write can save you time later on and make it easier for other programmers to work with your code.

A *comment* is text in a script that is ignored by the interpreter. Comments can be used to make code more readable, or to annotate a script.

Single line comments begin with two forward slashes (//) or a single hash sign (#). All text from either of these marks until either the end of the line or the PHP close tag is ignored.

```
// this is a comment
#  this is another comment
```

Multiline comments begin with a forward slash followed by an asterisk (/*) and end with an asterisk followed by a forward slash (*/).

```
/*
this is a comment
none of this will
be parsed by the
interpreter
*/
```

Summary

You should now have the tools at your disposal to run a simple PHP script on a properly configured server.

In this hour, you created your first PHP script. You learned how to use a text editor to create and name a PHP document. You examined four sets of tags that you can use to begin and end blocks of PHP code. You learned how to use the print() function to send data to the browser, and you brought HTML and PHP together into the same script. Finally, you learned about comments and how to add them to PHP documents.

Q&A

Q Which are the best start and end tags to use?

A It is largely a matter of preference. For the sake of portability the standard tags (<?php ?>) are probably the safest bet. Short tags are enabled by default and have the virtue of brevity.

Q What editors should I avoid when creating PHP code?

A Do not use word processors that format text for printing (such as Word, for example). Even if you save files created using this type of editor in plain text format, hidden characters are likely to creep into your code.

Q When should I comment my code?

A This is a matter of preference once again. Some short scripts will be self-explanatory to you, even after a long interval. For scripts of any length or complexity, you should comment your code. This often saves you time and frustration in the long run.

Workshop

The Workshop provides quiz questions to help you solidify your understanding of the material covered. Try to understand the quiz answers before continuing to the next hour's lesson. Quiz answers are provided in Appendix A.

Quiz

1. Can a user read the source code of PHP script you have successfully installed?
2. What do the standard PHP delimiter tags look like?
3. What do the ASP PHP delimiter tags look like?
4. What do the script PHP delimiter tags look like?
5. What function would you use to output a string to the browser?

Activity

1. Familiarize yourself with the process of creating, uploading, and running PHP scripts.

PART II

The Language

Hour

Hour 4

The Building Blocks

In this hour, you are going to get your hands dirty with some of the nuts and bolts of the language.

There's a lot of ground to cover, and if you are new to programming, you might feel bombarded with information. Don't worry—you can always refer back here later on. Concentrate on understanding rather than memorizing the features covered.

If you're already an experienced programmer, you should at least skim this hour's lesson. It covers a few PHP-specific features.

In this hour, you will learn

- About variables—what they are and how to use them
- How to define and access variables
- About data types
- About some of the more commonly used operators

- How to use operators to create expressions
- How to define and use constants

Variables

A variable is a special container that you can define to "hold" a value. A variable consists of a name that you can choose, preceded by a dollar ($) sign. The variable name can include letters, numbers, and the underscore character (_). Variable names cannot include spaces or characters that are not alphanumeric. The following code defines some legal variables:

```
$a;
$a_longish_variable_name;
$2453;
$sleepyZZZZ
```

Remember that a semicolon (;) is used to end a PHP statement. The semicolons in the previous fragment of code are not part of the variable names.

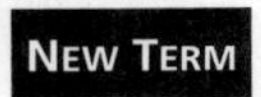

A *variable* is a holder for a type of data. It can hold numbers, strings of characters, objects, arrays, or booleans. The contents of a variable can be changed at any time.

As you can see, you have plenty of choices about naming, although it is unusual to see a variable name that consists exclusively of numbers. To declare a variable, you need only to include it in your script. You usually declare a variable and assign a value to it in the same statement.

```
$num1 = 8;
$num2 = 23;
```

The preceding lines declare two variables, using the assignment operator (=) to give them values. You will learn about assignment in more detail in the Operators and Expressions section later in the hour. After you give your variables values, you can treat them exactly as if they were the values themselves. In other words

```
print $num1;
```

is equivalent to

```
print 8;
```

as long as `$num1` contains 8.

Dynamic Variables

As you know, you create a variable with a dollar sign followed by a variable name. Unusually, the variable name can itself be stored in a variable. So, when assigning a value to a variable

```
$user = "bob";
```

is equivalent to

```
$holder="user";
$$holder = "bob";
```

The `$holder` variable contains the string `"user"`, so you can think of `$$holder` as a dollar sign followed by the value of `$holder`. PHP interprets this as `$user`.

> You can use a string constant to define a dynamic variable instead of a variable. To do so, you must wrap the string you want to use for the variable name in braces:
>
> ```
> ${"user"} = "bob";
> ```
>
> This might not seem useful at first glance. However, by using the concatenation operator and a loop (see Hour 5, "Going with the Flow"), you can use this technique to create tens of variables dynamically.

When accessing a dynamic variable, the syntax is exactly the same:

```
$user ="bob";
print $user;
```

is equivalent to

```
$user ="bob";
$holder="user";
print $$holder;
```

If you want to print a dynamic variable within a string, however, you need to give the interpreter some help. The following print statement:

```
$user="bob";
$holder="user";
print "$$holder";
```

does not print `"bob"` to the browser as you might expect. Instead it prints the strings `"$"` and `"user"` together to make `"$user"`. When you place a variable within quotation marks,

PHP helpfully inserts its value. In this case, PHP replaces `$holder` with the string `"user"`. The first dollar sign is left in place. To make it clear to PHP that a variable within a string is part of a dynamic variable, you must wrap it in braces. The print statement in the following fragment:

```
$user="bob";
$holder="user";
print "${$holder}";
```

now prints `"bob"`, which is the value contained in `$user`.

Listing 4.1 brings some of the previous code fragments together into a single script using a string stored in a variable to initialize and access a variable called `$user`.

LISTING 4.1 Dynamically Setting and Accessing Variables

```
 1: <html>
 2: <head>
 3: <title>Listing 4.1 Dynamically setting and accessing variables</title>
 4: </head>
 5: <body>
 6: <?php
 7: $holder = "user";
 8: $$holder = "bob";
 9:
10: // could have been:
11: // $user = "bob";
12: // ${"user"} = "bob";
13:
14: print "$user<br>";        // prints "bob"
15: print $$holder;           // prints "bob"
16: print "<br>";
17: print "${$holder}<br>"; // prints "bob"
18: print "${'user'}<br>";  // prints "bob"
19: ?>
20: </body>
21: </html>
```

References to Variables

By default, variables are assigned by value. In other words, if you were to assign `$aVariable` to `$anotherVariable`, a *copy* of the value held in `$aVariable` would be stored in `$anotherVariable`. Subsequently changing the value of `$aVariable` would have no effect on the contents of `$anotherVariable`. Listing 4.2 illustrates this.

LISTING 4.2 Variables Are Assigned by Value

```
 1: <html>
 2: <head>
 3: <title>Listing 4.2 Variables are assigned by value</title>
 4: </head>
 5: <body>
 6: <?php
 7: $aVariable = 42;
 8: $anotherVariable = $aVariable;
 9: // a copy of the contents of $aVariable is placed in $anotherVariable
10: $aVariable = 325;
11: print $anotherVariable; // prints 42
12: ?>
13: </body>
14: </html>
```

This example initializes `$aVariable`, assigning the value 42 to it. `$aVariable` is then assigned to `$anotherVariable`. A copy of the value of `$aVariable` is placed in `$anotherVariable`. Changing the value of `$aVariable` to 325 has no effect on the contents of `$anotherVariable`. The print statement demonstrates this by outputting 42 to the browser.

In PHP4, you can change this behavior, forcing a reference to `$aVariable` to be assigned to `$anotherVariable`, rather than a copy of its contents. This is illustrated in Listing 4.3.

LISTING 4.3 Assigning a Variable by Reference

```
 1: <html>
 2: <head>
 3: <title>Listing 4.3 Assigning a variable by reference</title>
 4: </head>
 5: <body>
 6: <?php
 7: $aVariable = 42;
 8: $anotherVariable = &$aVariable;
 9: // a copy of the contents of $aVariable is placed in $anotherVariable
10: $aVariable= 325;
11: print $anotherVariable; // prints 325
12: ?>
13: </body>
14: </html>
```

We have added only a single character to the code in Listing 4.2. Placing an ampersand (`&`) in front of the `$aVariable` variable ensures that a reference to this variable, rather than a copy of its contents, is assigned to `$anotherVariable`. Now any changes made to

`$aVariable` are seen when accessing `$anotherVariable`. In other words, both `$aVariable` and `$anotherVariable` now point to the same value.

Because this technique avoids the overhead of copying values from one variable to another, it can result in a small increase in performance. Unless your script assigns variables intensively, however, this performance gain will be barely measurable.

References to variables were introduced with PHP4.

Data Types

Different types of data take up different amounts of memory and may be treated differently when they are manipulated in a script. Some programming languages therefore demand that the programmer declare in advance which type of data a variable will contain. PHP4 is loosely typed, which means that it will calculate data types as data is assigned to each variable. This is a mixed blessing. On the one hand, it means that variables can be used flexibly, holding a string at one point and an integer at another. On the other hand, this can lead to confusion in larger scripts if you expect a variable to hold one data type when in fact it holds something completely different.

Table 4.1 shows the six data types available in PHP4.

TABLE 4.1 Data Types

Type	*Example*	*Description*
Integer	5	A whole number
Double	3.234	A floating-point number
String	`"hello"`	A collection of characters
Boolean	`true`	One of the special values `true` or `false`
Object		See Hour 8, "Objects"
Array		See Hour 7, "Arrays"

Of PHP4's six data types, we will leave arrays and objects for Hours 7 and 8.

You can use PHP4's built-in function `gettype()` to test the type of any variable. If you place a variable between the parentheses of the function call, `gettype()` returns a string representing the relevant type. Listing 4.4 assigns four different data types to a single variable, testing it with `gettype()` each time.

> You can read more about calling functions in Hour 6, "Functions."

LISTING 4.4 Testing the Type of a Variable

```
 1: <html>
 2: <head>
 3: <title>Listing 4.3 Testing the type of a variable</title>
 4: </head>
 5: <body>
 6: <?php
 7: $testing = 5;
 8: print gettype( $testing ); // integer
 9: print "<br>";
10: $testing = "five";
11: print gettype( $testing ); // string
12: print("<br>");
13: $testing = 5.0;
14: print gettype( $testing ); // double
15: print("<br>");
16: $testing = true;
17: print gettype( $testing ); // boolean
18: print "<br>";
19: ?>
20: </body>
21: </html>
```

This script produces the following:

```
integer
string
double
boolean
```

An *integer* is a whole or real number. In simple terms, it can be said to be a number without a decimal point. A *string* is a collection of characters. When you work with strings in your scripts, they should always be surrounded by double (`"`) or single (`'`) quotation marks. A double is a floating-point number. That is, a number that includes a decimal point. A boolean can be one of two special values, `true` or `false`.

4

Prior to PHP4, there was no boolean type. Although `true` was used, it actually resolved to the integer 1.

Changing Type with `settype()`

PHP provides the function `settype()` to change the type of a variable. To use `settype()`, you must place the variable to change (and the type to change it to) between the parentheses and separated by commas. Listing 4.5 converts 3.14 (a double) to the four types that we are covering in this hour.

LISTING 4.5 Changing the Type of a Variable with `settype()`

```
 1: <html>
 2: <head>
 3: <title>Listing 4.5 Changing the type of a variable with settype()</title>
 4: </head>
 5: <body>
 6: <?php
 7: $undecided = 3.14;
 8: print gettype( $undecided ); // double
 9: print " -- $undecided<br>";  // 3.14
10: settype( $undecided, string );
11: print gettype( $undecided ); // string
12: print " -- $undecided<br>";  // 3.14
13: settype( $undecided, integer );
14: print gettype( $undecided ); // integer
15: print " -- $undecided<br>";  // 3
16: settype( $undecided, double );
17: print gettype( $undecided ); // double
18: print " -- $undecided<br>";  // 3.0
19: settype( $undecided, boolean );
20: print gettype( $undecided ); // boolean
21: print " -- $undecided<br>";  // 1
22: ?>
23: </body>
24: </html>
```

In each case, we use `gettype()` to confirm that the type change worked and then print the value of the variable `$undecided` to the browser. When we convert the string "3.14" to an integer, any information beyond the decimal point is lost forever. That's why `$undecided` still contains 3 after we have changed it back to a double. Finally, we convert `$undecided` to a boolean. Any number other than 0 becomes `true` when converted to a boolean. When printing a boolean in PHP, `true` is represented as 1 and `false` as an empty string, so `$undecided` is printed as 1.

Changing Type by Casting

By placing the name of a data type in brackets in front of a variable, you create a copy of that variable's value converted to the data type specified. The principal difference between `settype()` and a cast is the fact that casting produces a copy, leaving the original variable untouched. Listing 4.6 illustrates this.

LISTING 4.6 Casting a Variable

```
1: <html>
2: <head>
3: <title>Listing 4.6 Casting a variable</title>
4: </head>
5: <body>
6: <?php
7: $undecided = 3.14;
8: $holder = ( double ) $undecided;
9: print gettype( $holder ) ; // double
10: print " -- $holder<br>";   // 3.14
11: $holder = ( string ) $undecided;
12: print gettype( $holder );  // string
13: print " -- $holder<br>";   // 3.14
14: $holder = ( integer ) $undecided;
15: print gettype( $holder );  // integer
16: print " -- $holder<br>";   // 3
17: $holder = ( double ) $undecided;
18: print gettype( $holder );  // double
19: print " -- $holder<br>";   // 3.14
20: $holder = ( boolean ) $undecided;
21: print gettype( $holder );  // boolean
22: print " -- $holder<br>";   // 1
23: ?>
24: </body>
25: </html>
```

We never actually change the type of `$undecided`, which remains a double throughout. In fact, by casting `$undecided`, we create a copy that is then converted to the type we specify. This new value is then stored in the variable `$holder`. Because we are working with a copy of `$undecided`, we never discard any information from it as we did in Listing 4.5.

4

Operators and Expressions

You can now assign data to variables. You can even investigate and change the data type of a variable. A programming language isn't very useful, though, unless you can manipulate the data you can store. Operators are symbols that make it possible to use one or more values to produce a new value. A value that is operated on by an operator is referred to as an operand.

NEW TERM An *operator* is a symbol or series of symbols that, when used in conjunction with values, performs an action and usually produces a new value.

NEW TERM An *operand* is a value used in conjunction with an operator. There are usually two operands to one operator.

Let's combine two operands with an operator to produce a new value:

```
4 + 5
```

4 and 5 are operands. They are operated on by the addition operator (+) to produce 9. Operators almost always sit between two operands, though you will see a few exceptions later in this hour.

The combination of operands with an operator to manufacture a result is called an expression. Although most operators form the basis of expressions, an expression need not contain an operator. In fact in PHP, an expression is defined as anything that resolves to a value. This includes integer constants such as 654, variables such as `$user`, and function calls such as `gettype()`. The expression (4 + 5), therefore is an expression that consists of two further expressions and an operator.

NEW TERM An *expression* is any combination of functions, values, and operators that resolve to a value. As a rule of thumb, if you can use it as if it were a value, it is an expression.

Now that we have the principles out of the way, it's time to take a tour of PHP4's more common operators.

The Assignment Operator

You have met the assignment operator each time we have initialized a variable. It consists of the single character =. The assignment operator takes the value of its right-hand operand and assigns it to its left-hand operand:

```
$name ="matt";
```

The variable `$name` now contains the string `"matt"`. Interestingly, this construct is an expression. It might look at first glance that the assignment operator simply changes the variable `$name` without producing a value, but in fact, a statement that uses the assignment operator always resolves to a copy of the value of the right operand. Thus

```
print ( $name = "matt" );
```

prints the string `"matt"` to the browser in addition to assigning `"matt"` to `$name`.

Arithmetic Operators

The arithmetic operators do exactly what you would expect. Table 4.2 lists these operators. The addition operator adds the right operand to the left operand. The subtraction operator subtracts the right-hand operand from the left. The division operator divides the left-hand operand by the right. The multiplication operator multiplies the left-hand operand by the right. The modulus operator returns the remainder of the left operand divided by the right.

TABLE 4.2 Arithmetic Operators

Operator	*Name*	*Example*	*Example Result*
+	Addition	10+3	13
-	Subtraction	10-3	7
/	Division	10/3	3.3333333333333
*	Multiplication	10*3	30
%	Modulus	10%3	1

The Concatenation Operator

The concatenation operator is a single dot. Treating both operands as strings, it appends the right-hand operand to the left. So

```
"hello"." world"
```

returns

```
"hello world"
```

Regardless of the data types of the operands, they are treated as strings, and the result always is a string.

More Assignment Operators

Although there is really only one assignment operator, PHP4 provides a number of combination operators that transform the left-hand operand as well as return a result. As a rule, operators use their operands without changing their values. Assignment operators break this rule. A combined assignment operator consists of a standard operator symbol followed by an equals sign. Combination assignment operators save you the trouble of using two operators yourself. For example,

```
$x = 4;
$x += 4; // $x now equals 8
```

is equivalent to

```
$x = 4;
$x = $x + 4; // $x now equals 8
```

There is an assignment operator for each of the arithmetic operators and one for the concatenation operator. Table 4.3 lists some of the most common.

TABLE 4.3 Some Combined Assignment Operators

Operator	*Example*	*Equivalent to*
`+=`	`$x += 5`	`$x = $x + 5`
`-=`	`$x -= 5`	`$x = $x - 5`
`/=`	`$x /= 5`	`$x = $x / 5`
`*=`	`$x *= 5`	`$x = $x * 5`
`%=`	`$x %= 5`	`$x = $x % 5`
`.=`	`$x .= "test"`	`$x = $x" test"`

Each of the examples in Table 4.3 transforms the value of `$x` using the value of the right-hand operand.

Comparison Operators

Comparison operators perform tests on their operands. They return the boolean value `true` if the test is successful, or `false` otherwise. This type of expression is useful in control structures, such as `if` and `while` statements. You will meet these in Hour 5.

To test whether the value contained in `$x` is smaller than 5, for example, you would use the less than operator:

```
$x < 5
```

If `$x` contained 3, this expression would be equivalent to the value `true`. If `$x` contained 7, the expression would resolve to `false`.

Table 4.4 lists the comparison operators.

TABLE 4.4 Comparison Operators

Operator	*Name*	*Returns True if*	*Example*	*Result*
`==`	Equivalence	Left is equivalent to right	`$x == 5`	`false`
`!=`	Non-equivalence	Left is not equivalent to right	`$x != 5`	`true`
`===`	Identical	Left is equivalent to right and they are the same type	`$x === 5`	`false`
`>`	Greater	Left is than greater than right	`$x > 4`	`false`
`>=`	Greater than or equal to	Left is greater than or equal to right	`$x >= 4`	`true`
`<`	Less than	Left is less than right	`x < 4`	`false`
`<=`	Less than or equal to	Left is less than or equal to right	`$x <= 4`	`true`

These operators are most commonly used with integers or doubles, although the equivalence operator is also used to compare strings.

Creating More Complex Test Expressions with the Logical Operators

The logical operators test combinations of booleans. The `or` operator, for example returns `true` if either the left or the right operand is `true`.

```
true || false
```

would return `true`.

The and operator only returns true if both the left and right operands are true.

```
true && false
```

would return false. It's unlikely that you would use a logical operator to test boolean constants, however. It would make more sense to test two or more expressions that resolve to a boolean. For example,

```
( $x > 2 ) && ( $x < 15 )
```

would return true if $x contained a value that is greater than 2 and smaller than 15. We include the parentheses to make the code easier to read. Table 4.5 lists the logical operators.

TABLE 4.5 Logical Operators

Operator	*Name*	*Returns True if...*	*Example*	*Result*
`||`	Or	Left or right is true	`true || false`	`true`
`or`	Or	Left or right is true	`true || false`	`true`
`xor`	Xor	Left or right is true but not both	`true || true`	`false`
`&&`	And	Left and right are true	`true && false`	`false`
`and`	And	Left and right are true	`true && false`	`false`
`!`	Not	The single operand is not true	`! true`	`false`

Why are there two versions of both the or and the and operators? The answer lies in operator precedence, which you will look at later in this section.

Automatically Incrementing and Decrementing an Integer Variable

When coding in PHP, you will often find it necessary to increment or decrement an integer variable. You will usually need to do this when you are counting the iterations of a loop. You have already learned two ways of doing this. I could increment the integer contained by $x with the addition operator

```
$x = $x + 1; // $x is incremented
```

or with a combined assignment operator

```
$x += 1; // $x is incremented
```

In both cases, the resultant integer is assigned to $x. Because expressions of this kind are so common, PHP provides some special operators that allow you to add or subtract the integer constant 1 from an integer variable, assigning the result to the variable itself. These are known as the post-increment and post-decrement operators. The post-increment operator consists of two plus symbols appended to a variable name.

```
$x++; // $x is incremented
```

increments the variable `$x` by one. Using two minus symbols in the same way decrements the variable:

```
$x--; // $x is decremented
```

If you use the post-increment or post-decrement operators in conjunction with a conditional operator, the operand will only be modified after the test has been completed:

```
$x = 3;
$x++ < 4; // true
```

In the previous example, `$x` contains 3 when it is tested against 4 with the less than operator, so the test expression returns `true`. After this test is complete, `$x` is incremented.

In some circumstances, you might want to increment or decrement a variable in a test expression before the test is carried out. PHP provides the pre-increment and pre-decrement operators for this purpose. On their own, these operators behave in exactly the same way as the post-increment and post-decrement operators. They are written with the plus or minus symbols preceding the variable:

```
++$x; // $x is incremented
--$x; // $x is decremented
```

If these operators are used as part of a test expression, the incrementation occurs before the test is carried out.

```
$x = 3;
++$x < 4; // false
```

In the previous fragment, `$x` is incremented before it is tested against 4. The test expression returns `false` because 4 is not smaller than 4.

Operator Precedence

When you use an operator, the interpreter usually reads your expression from left to right. For complex expressions that use more than one operator, though, the waters can become a little murky. First, consider a simple case:

4 + 5

There's no room for confusion, here. PHP simply adds 4 to 5. What about the next fragment?

4 + 5 * 2

This presents a problem. Does it mean the sum of 4 and 5, which should then be multiplied by 2, giving the result 18? Does it mean 4 plus the result of 5 multiplied by 2, resolving to 14? If you were to read simply from left to right, the former would be `true`. In fact, PHP attaches different precedence to operators. Because the multiplication operator has higher precedence than the addition operator does, the second solution to the problem is the correct one.

You can force PHP to execute the addition expression before the multiplication expression with parentheses:

(4 + 5) * 2

Whatever the precedence of the operators in a complex expression, it is a good idea to use parentheses to make your code clearer and to save you from obscure bugs. Table 4.6 lists the operators covered in this hour in precedence order (highest first).

TABLE 4.6 Order of Precedence for Selected Operators

<table>
<tr><th>Operators</th></tr>
<tr><td><code>++ -- (cast)</code></td></tr>
<tr><td><code>/ * %</code></td></tr>
<tr><td><code>+ -</code></td></tr>
<tr><td><code>< <= => ></code></td></tr>
<tr><td><code>== === !=</code></td></tr>
<tr><td><code>&&</code></td></tr>
<tr><td><code>||</code></td></tr>
<tr><td><code>= += -= /= *= %= .=</code></td></tr>
<tr><td><code>and</code></td></tr>
<tr><td><code>xor</code></td></tr>
<tr><td><code>or</code></td></tr>
</table>

As you can see, `or` has a lower precedence than `||` and `and` has a lower precedence than `&&`, so you could use the lower-precedence logical operators to change the way a complex test expression is read. This is not necessarily a good idea. The following two expressions are equivalent, but the second is much easier to read:

```
$x and $y || $z
( $x && $y ) || $z
```

Constants

Variables offer a flexible way of storing data. You can change their values and the type of data they store at any time. If, however, you want to work with a value that you do not want to alter throughout your script's execution, you can define a constant. You must use PHP's built-in function `define()` to create a constant. After you have done this, the constant cannot be changed. To use the `define()` function, you must place the name of the constant and the value you want to give it within the call's parentheses:

```
define( "CONSTANT_NAME", 42 );
```

The value you want to set can only be a number or a string. By convention, the name of the constant should be in capitals. Constants are accessed with the constant name only; no dollar symbol is required. Listing 4.7 defines and accesses a constant.

LISTING 4.7 Defining a Constant

```
 1: <html>
 2: <head>
 3: <title>Listing 4.7 Defining a constant</title>
 4: </head>
 5: <body>
 6: <?php
 7: define ( "USER", "Gerald" );
 8: print "Welcome ".USER;
 9: ?>
10: </body>
11: </html>
```

Notice that we used the concatenation operator to append the value held by our constant to the string `"Welcome"`. This is because the interpreter has no way of distinguishing between a constant and a string within quotation marks.

Predefined Constants

PHP automatically provides some built-in constants for you. `__FILE__`, for example, returns the name of the file currently being read by the interpreter. `__LINE__` returns the line number of the file. These constants are useful for generating error messages. You can also find out which version of PHP is interpreting the script with `PHP_VERSION`. This can be useful if you want to limit a script to run on a particular PHP release.

Summary

In this hour, you covered some of the basic features of the PHP language. You learned about variables and how to assign to them using the assignment operator. You learned about dynamic or "variable" variables. You also learned how to assign to variables by reference rather than by value. You were introduced to operators and learned how to combine some of the most common of these into expressions. Finally, you learned how to define and access constants.

Q&A

Q Why can it be useful to know the type of data a variable holds?

A Often the data type of a variable constrains what you can do with it. You may want to make sure that a variable contains an integer or a double before using it in a mathematical calculation, for example.

You explore situations of this kind a little further in Hour 16, "Working with Data."

Q Should I obey any conventions when naming variables?

A Your goal should always be to make your code both easy to read and understand. A variable such as `$ab123245` tells you nothing about its role in your script and invites typos. Keep your variable names short and descriptive.

A variable named `$f` is unlikely to mean much to you when you return to your code after a month or so. A variable named `$filename`, on the other hand, should make more sense.

Q Should I learn the operator precedence table?

A There is no reason why you shouldn't, but I would save the effort for more useful tasks. By using parentheses in your expressions, you can make your code easy to read at the same time as defining your own order of precedence.

Workshop

The Workshop provides quiz questions to help you solidify your understanding of the material covered. Try to understand the quiz answers before continuing to the next hour's lesson. Quiz answers are provided in Appendix A.

Quiz

1. Which of the following variable names is not valid?

```
$a_value_submitted_by_a_user
$666666xyz
$xyz666666
$_____counter_____
$the first
$file-name
```

2. How could you use the string variable created in the assignment expression

```
$my_var = "dynamic";
```

to create a "variable" variable, assigning the integer 4 to it. How might you access this new variable?

3. What will the following statement output?

```
print gettype("4");
```

4. What will be the output from the following code fragment?

```
$test_val = 5.4566;
settype( $test_val, "integer" );
print $test_val;
```

5. Which of the following statements does not contain an expression?

```
4;
gettype(44);
5/12;
```

6. Which of the statements in question 5 contains an operator?
7. What value will the following expression return?

```
5 < 2
```

What data type will the returned value be?

Activities

1. Create a script that contains at least five different variables. Populate them with values of different data types and use the `gettype()` function to print each type to the browser.
2. Assign values to two variables. Use comparison operators to test whether the first value is
    - The same as the second
    - Less than the second

- Greater than the second
- Less than or equal to the second

Print the result of each test to the browser.

Change the values assigned to your test variables and run the script again.

HOUR 5

Going with the Flow

The scripts created in the last hour flow only in a single direction. The same statements are executed in the same order every time a script is run. This does not leave much room for flexibility.

You now will look at some structures that enable your scripts to adapt to circumstances. In this hour, you will learn

- How to use the `if` statement to execute code only if a test expression evaluates to true
- How to execute alternative blocks of code when the test expression of an `if` statement evaluates to false
- How to use the `switch` statement to execute code based on the value returned by a test expression
- How to repeat execution of code using a `while` statement
- How to use `for` statements to make neater loops

- How to break out of loops
- How to nest one loop within another

Switching Flow

Most scripts evaluate conditions and change their behavior accordingly. The facility to make decisions makes your PHP pages dynamic, capable of changing their output according to circumstances. Like most programming languages, PHP4 allows you to do this with an `if` statement.

The `if` Statement

The `if` statement evaluates an expression between parentheses. If this expression results in a true value, a block of code is executed. Otherwise, the block is skipped entirely. This enables scripts to make decisions based on any number of factors.

```
if ( expression )
   {
   // code to execute if the expression evaluates to true
   }
```

Listing 5.1 executes a block of code only if a variable contains the string `"happy"`.

LISTING 5.1 An `if` Statement

```
 1: <html>
 2: <head>
 3: <title>Listing 5.1</title>
 4: </head>
 5: <body>
 6: <?php
 7: $mood = "happy";
 8: if ( $mood == "happy" )
 9:     {
10:     print "Hooray, I'm in a good mood";
11:     }
12: ?>
13: </body>
14: </html>
```

You use the comparison operator == to compare the variable `$mood` with the string `"happy"`. If they match, the expression evaluates to true, and the code block below the `if` statement is executed. Although the code block is wrapped in braces in the example, this is only necessary if the block contains more than one line. The following fragment, therefore, would be acceptable:

```
if ( $mood == "happy" )
    print "Hooray, I'm in a good mood";
```

If you change the value of `$mood` to `"sad"` and run the script, the expression in the `if` statement evaluates to false, and the code block is skipped. The script remains sulkily silent.

Using the `else` Clause with the `if` Statement

When working with the `if` statement, you will often want to define an alternative block of code that should be executed if the expression you are testing evaluates to false. You can do this by adding `else` to the `if` statement followed by a further block of code:

```
if ( expression )
   {
   // code to execute if the expression evaluates to true
   }
else
   {
   // code to execute in all other cases
   }
```

Listing 5.2 amends the example in Listing 5.1 so that a default block of code is executed if `$mood` is not equivalent to `"happy"`.

LISTING 5.2 An `if` Statement That Uses `else`

```
 1: <html>
 2: <head>
 3: <title>Listing 5.2</title>
 4: </head>
 5: <body>
 6: <?php
 7: $mood = "sad";
 8: if ( $mood == "happy" )
 9:     {
10:     print "Hooray, I'm in a good mood";
11:     }
12: else
13:     {
14:     print "Not happy but $mood";
15:     }
16: ?>
17: </body>
18: </html>
```

`$mood` contains the string `"sad"`, which is not equivalent to `"happy"`, so the expression in the `if` statement evaluates to false. This means that the first block of code is skipped. The block of code after `else`, therefore, is executed, and the message `"Not happy but sad"` is printed to the browser.

Using the `else` clause with the `if` statement allows scripts to make sophisticated decisions, but you currently are limited to an either-or branch. PHP4 allows you to evaluate multiple expressions in a cascade.

Using the `elseif` Clause with the `if` Statement

You can use an `if-elseif-else` construct to test multiple expressions before offering a default block of code:

```
if ( expression )
   {
   // code to execute if the expression evaluates to true
   }
elseif ( another expression )
   {
   // code to execute if the previous expression failed
   // and this one evaluates to true
else
   {
   // code to execute in all other cases
   }
```

If the first expression does not evaluate to `true`, then the first block of code is ignored. The `elseif` clause then causes another expression to be evaluated. Once again, if this expression evaluates to `true`, then the second block of code is executed. Otherwise, the block of code associated with the `else` clause is executed. You can include as many `elseif` clauses as you want, and if you don't need a default action, you can omit the `else` clause.

Listing 5.3 adds an `elseif` clause to the previous example.

Listing 5.3 An `if` Statement That Uses `else` and `elseif`

```
 1: <html>
 2: <head>
 3: <title>Listing 5.3</title>
 4: </head>
 5: <body>
 6: <?php
 7: $mood = "sad";
 8: if ( $mood == "happy" )
 9:     {
10:     print "Hooray, I'm in a good mood";
```

LISTING 5.3 continued

```
11:     }
12: elseif ( $mood == "sad" )
13:     {
14:     print "Awww. Don't be down!";
15:     }
16: else
17:     {
18:     print "Neither happy nor sad but $mood";
19:     }
20: ?>
21: </body>
22: </html>
```

Once again, `$mood` holds a string, `"sad"`. This is not equivalent to `"happy"`, so the first block is ignored. The `elseif` clause tests for equivalence between the contents of `$mood` and `"sad"`, which evaluates to `true`. This block of code is therefore executed.

The `switch` Statement

The `switch` statement is an alternative way of changing program flow according to the evaluation of an expression. There are some key differences between the `switch` and `if` statements. Using the `if` statement in conjunction with `elseif`, you may evaluate multiple expressions. `switch` evaluates only one expression, executing different code according to the result of that expression, as long as the expression evaluates to a simple type (a number, a string, or a boolean). The result of an expression evaluated as part of an `if` statement is read as either `true` or `false`. The expression of a `switch` statement yields a result that is tested against any number of values.


```
switch ( expression )
       {
       case result1:
        // execute this if expression results in result1
        break;
       case result2:
        // execute this if expression results in result2
        break;
       default:
            // execute this if no break statement
            // has been encountered hitherto
       }
```

The `switch` statement's expression is often simply a variable. Within the `switch` statement's block of code, you find a number of `case` statements. Each of these tests a value against the result of the `switch` statement's expression. If these are equivalent, then the code after the `case` statement is executed. The `break` statement ends execution of the `switch` statement altogether. If this is left out, the next `case` statement's expression is evaluated. If the optional `default` statement is reached, its code is executed.

> Don't forget to include a `break` statement at the end of any code that will be executed as part of a `case` statement. Without `break`, the program flow will continue to the next `case` statement and ultimately to the `default` statement. In most cases, this will not be the behavior that you will be expecting.

Listing 5.4 re-creates the functionality of the `if` statement example, using the `switch` statement.

LISTING 5.4 A `switch` Statement

```
 1: <html>
 2: <head>
 3: <title>Listing 5.4</title>
 4: </head>
 5: <body>
 6: <?php
 7: $mood = "sad";
 8: switch ( $mood )
 9:     {
10:     case "happy":
11:         print "Hooray, I'm in a good mood";
12:         break;
13:     case "sad":
14:         print "Awww. Don't be down!";
15:         break;
16:     default:
17:         print "Neither happy nor sad but $mood";
18:     }
19: ?>
20: </body>
21: </html>
```

Once again, the `$mood` variable is initialized to `"sad"`. The `switch` statement uses this variable as its expression. The first `case` statement tests for equivalence between `"happy"` and the value of `$mood`. There is no match, so script execution moves on to the second `case` statement. The string "sad" is equivalent to the value of $mood, so this block of code is executed. The break statement ends the process.

Using the ? Operator

The ? or ternary operator is similar to the if statement but returns a value derived from one of two expressions separated by a colon. Which expression is used to generate the value returned depends on the result of a test expression:

```
( expression )?returned_if_expression_is_true:returned_if_expression_is_false;
```

If the test expression evaluates to true, the result of the second expression is returned; otherwise, the value of the third expression is returned. Listing 5.5 uses the ternary operator to set the value of a variable according to the value of $mood.

LISTING 5.5 Using the ? Operator

```
 1: <html>
 2: <head>
 3: <title>Listing 5.5</title>
 4: </head>
 5: <body>
 6: <?php
 7: $mood = "sad";
 8: $text = ( $mood=="happy" )?"Hooray, I'm in a good mood":"Not happy but $mood";
 9: print "$text";
10: ?>
11: </body>
12: </html>
```

$mood is set to "sad". $mood is tested for equivalence to the string "happy". Because this test returns false, the result of the third of the three expressions is returned.

The ternary operator can be difficult to read but is useful if you are dealing with only two alternatives and like to write compact code.

Loops

So far you've looked at decisions that a script can make about what code to execute. Scripts can also decide how many times to execute a block of code. Loop statements are designed to enable you to achieve repetitive tasks. Almost without exception, a loop continues to operate until a condition is achieved, or you explicitly choose to exit the loop.

The `while` Statement

The `while` statement looks similar in structure to a basic `if` statement:

```
while ( expression )
      {
      // do something
      }
```

As long as a `while` statement's expression evaluates to `true`, the code block is executed over and over again. Within the block, you usually change something that affects the `while` statement's expression; otherwise, your loop continues indefinitely. Listing 5.6 creates a `while` loop that calculates and prints multiples of two.

LISTING 5.6 A `while` Statement

```
 1: <html>
 2: <head>
 3: <title>Listing 5.6</title>
 4: </head>
 5: <body>
 6: <?php
 7: $counter = 1;
 8: while ( $counter <= 12 )
 9:     {
10:     print "$counter times 2 is ".($counter*2)."<br>";
11:     $counter++;
12:     }
13: ?>
14: </body>
15: </html>
```

In this example, we initialize a variable `$counter`. The `while` statement tests the `$counter` variable. As long as the integer contained by `$counter` is smaller than or equal to 12, the loop continues to run. Within the `while` statement's code block, the value contained by `$counter` is multiplied by two, and the result is printed to the browser. Then `$counter` is incremented. This last stage is extremely important. If you were to forget to change `$counter`, the `while` expression would never resolve to `false`, and the loop would never end.

The `do..while` Statement

A `do...while` statement looks a little like a `while` statement turned on its head. The essential difference between the two is that the code block is executed before the truth test and not after it:

```
do   {
     // code to be executed
     }
     while ( expression );
```

The test expression of a `do...while` statement should always end with a semicolon.

This statement might be useful if you want the code block to be executed at least once even if the `while` expression evaluates to `false`. Listing 5.7 creates a `do...while` statement. The code block is executed a minimum of one time.

LISTING 5.7 The `do...while` Statement

```
 1: <html>
 2: <head>
 3: <title>Listing 5.7</title>
 4: </head>
 5: <body>
 6: <?php
 7: $num = 1;
 8: do
 9:     {
10:     print "Execution number: $num<br>\n";
11:     $num++;
12:     }
13:     while ( $num > 200 && $num < 400 );
14: ?>
15: </body>
16: </html>
```

The `do...while` statement tests whether the variable `$num` contains a value that is greater than 200 and smaller than 400. We have initialized `$num` to 1 so this expression returns `false`. Nonetheless, the code block is executed before the expression is evaluated, so the statement will print a single line to the browser.

The `for` Statement

You cannot achieve anything with a `for` statement that you cannot do with a `while` statement. On the other hand, the `for` statement is often a neater and safer way of achieving the same effect. Earlier, Listing 5.6 initialized a variable outside the `while` statement. The `while` statement then tested the variable in its expression. The variable was incremented within the code block. The `for` statement allows you to achieve this on a single line. This allows for more compact code and makes it less likely that you forget to increment a counter variable, thereby creating an infinite loop.

```
for ( variable assignment; test expression; variable increment )
    {
    // code to be executed
    }
```

Each of the expressions within the parentheses of the `for` statement is separated by semicolons. Usually, the first expression initializes a counter variable, the second expression is the test condition for the loop, and the third expression increments the counter. Listing 5.8 shows a `for` statement that re-creates the example in Listing 5.6, which multiplies 12 numbers by 2.

LISTING 5.8 Using the `for` Statement

```
 1: <html>
 2: <head>
 3: <title>Listing 5.8</title>
 4: </head>
 5: <body>
 6: <?php
 7: for ( $counter=1; $counter<=12; $counter++ )
 8:     {
 9:     print "$counter times 2 is ".($counter*2)."<br>";
10:     }
11: ?>
12: </body>
13: </html>
```

The results of Listings 5.6 and 5.8 are exactly the same. The `for` statement, though, makes the code more compact. Because `$counter` is initialized and incremented at the top of the statement, the logic of the loop is clear at a glance. Within the `for` statement's parentheses, the first expression initializes the `$counter` variable and sets it to 1. The test expression checks that `$counter` contains a value that is less than or equal to 12. The final expression increments the `$counter` variable.

When program flow reaches the `for` loop, the `$counter` variable is initialized, and the test expression is evaluated. If the expression evaluates to `true`, the code block is executed. The `$counter` variable is then incremented and the test expression evaluated again. This process continues until the test expression evaluates to `false`.

Breaking Out of Loops with the `break` Statement

Both `while` and `for` statements incorporate a built-in test expression with which you can end a loop. The `break` statement, though, enables you to `break` out of a loop according to additional tests. This can provide a safeguard against error. Listing 5.9 creates a simple `for` statement that divides a large number by a variable that is incremented, printing the result to the screen.

LISTING 5.9 A `for` Loop That Divides 4000 by Ten Incremental Numbers

```
 1: <html>
 2: <head>
 3: <title>Listing 5.9</title>
 4: </head>
 5: <body>
 6: <?php
 7: for ( $counter=1; $counter <= 10, $counter++ )
 8:     {
 9:     $temp = 4000/$counter;
10:     print "4000 divided by $counter is... $temp<br>";
11:     }
12: ?>
13: </body>
14: </html>
```

This example initializes the variable `$counter` to 1. The `for` statement's test expression checks that `$counter` is smaller than or equal to 10. Within the code block, 4000 is divided by `$counter`, printing the result to the browser.

This seems straightforward enough. What, though, if the value you place in `$counter` comes from user input? The value could be a minus number, or even a string. Let's take the first instance. Changing the initial value of `$counter` from 1 to -4 causes 4000 to be divided by zero as the code block is executed for the fifth time, which is not advisable. Listing 5.10 guards against this by breaking out of the loop if the `$counter` variable contains zero.

LISTING 5.10 Using the `break` Statement

```
1: <html>
2: <head>
3: <title>Listing 5.10</title>
4: </head>
5: <body>
6: <?php
7: $counter = -4;
```

LISTING 5.10 continued

```
 8: for ( ; $counter <= 10; $counter++ )
 9:     {
10:     if ( $counter == 0 )
11:         break;
12:     $temp = 4000/$counter;
13:     print "4000 divided by $counter is... $temp<br>";
14:     }
15: ?>
16: </body>
17: </html>
```

Dividing a number by zero does not cause a fatal error in PHP4. Instead, a warning is generated and execution continues.

Use an `if` statement to test the value of `$counter`. If it is equivalent to zero, the `break` statement immediately halts execution of the code block, and program flow continues after the `while` statement. Notice that we initialized the `$counter` variable outside the `for` statement's parentheses to simulate a situation in which the value of `$counter` is set according to form input or a database look up.

You can omit any of the expressions of a `for` statement, but you must remember to retain the semicolons.

Skipping an Iteration with the `continue` Statement

The `continue` statement ends execution of the current iteration but doesn't cause the loop as a whole to end. Instead, the next iteration is immediately begun. Using the `break` statement in Listing 5.10 was a little drastic. With the `continue` statement in Listing 5.11, you can avoid a divide by zero error without ending the loop completely.

LISTING 5.11 Using the `continue` Statement

```
1: <html>
2: <head>
3: <title>Listing 5.11</title>
```

LISTING 5.11 continued

```
 4: </head>
 5: <body>
 6: <?php
 7: $counter = -4;
 8: for ( ;  $counter <= 10; $counter++ )
 9:     {
10:     if ( $counter == 0 )
11:         continue;
12:     $temp = 4000/$counter;
13:     print "4000 divided by $counter is... $temp<br>";
14:     }
15: ?>
16: </body>
17: </html>
```

We have swapped the `break` statement for a `continue` statement. If the `$counter` variable is equivalent to zero, the iteration is skipped, and the next one immediately is started.

> The `break` and `continue` statements can make code more difficult to read. Because they often add layers of complexity to the logic of the loop statements that contain them, they can lead to obscure bugs. They are best used sparingly.

Nesting Loops

Loop statements can contain other loop statements. This combination is particularly useful when working with dynamically created HTML tables. Listing 5.12 uses two `for` statements to print a multiplication table to the browser.

LISTING 5.12 Nesting Two `for` Loops

```
 1: <html>
 2: <head>
 3: <title>Listing 5.12</title>
 4: </head>
 5: <body>
 6: <?php
 7: print "<table border=\"1\">\n";
 8: for ( $y=1; $y<=12; $y++ )
 9:     {
10:     print "<tr>\n";
```

LISTING 5.12 continued

```
11:     for ( $x=1; $x<=12; $x++ )
12:         {
13:         print "\t<td>";
14:         print ($x*$y);
15:         print "</td>\n";
16:         }
17:     print "</tr>\n";
18:     }
19: print "</table>";
20: ?>
21: </body>
22: </html>
```

The outer `for` statement initializes a variable called `$y`, setting its starting value to 1. It defines an expression that tests that `$y` is smaller or equal to 12 and defines the increment for `$y`. For each iteration, the code block prints a `TR` (table row) HTML element and defines another `for` statement. This inner loop initializes a variable called `$x` and defines expressions along the same lines as `for` the outer loop. For each iteration, the inner loop prints a `TD` (table cell) element to the browser, as well as the result of `$x` multiplied by `$y`. The result is a neatly formatted multiplication table.

Summary

In this hour, you learned about control structures and the ways in which they can help to make your scripts flexible and dynamic. Most of these structures will reappear regularly throughout the rest of the book.

You learned how to define an `if` statement and how to provide for alternative actions with the `elseif` and `else` clauses. You learned how to use the `switch` statement to change flow according to multiple equivalence tests on the result of an expression. You learned about loops, in particular, the `while` and `for` statements, and you learned how to use `break` and `continue` to prematurely end the execution of a loop or to skip an iteration. Finally, you learned how to nest one loop within another and saw a typical use for this structure.

Q&A

Q Must a control structure's test expression result in a boolean value?

A Ultimately, yes, but in the context of a test expression zero, an undefined variable, or an empty string will be converted to `false` for the purposes of the test. All other values will evaluate to `true`.

Q Must I always surround a code block in a control statement with brackets?

A If the code you want executed as part of a control structure consists of only a single line, you can omit the brackets.

Q Does this hour cover every kind of loop there is?

A In Hour 7, "Arrays," you encounter the `foreach` statement, which enables you to loop through every element in an array.

Workshop

The Workshop provides quiz questions to help you solidify your understanding of the material covered. Try to understand the quiz answers before continuing to the next hour's lesson. Quiz answers are provided in Appendix A.

Quiz

1. How would you use an `if` statement to print the string `"Youth message"` to the browser if an integer variable, `$age`, is between 18 and 35? If `$age` contains any other value, the string `"Generic message"` should be printed to the browser.
2. How would you extend your code in question 1 to print the string `"Child message"` if the `$age` variable is between 1 and 17?
3. How would you create a `while` statement that prints every odd number between 1 and 49?
4. How would you convert the `while` statement you created in question 3 into a `for` statement?

Activities

1. Review the syntax for control structures. Think about how these techniques will help you in your scripting.
2. Review the section on the ternary operator. What distinguishes it from the control structures covered in the rest of the chapter? Why might it be useful?

HOUR 6

Functions

Functions are the heart of a well-organized script, making code easy to read and reuse. No large project would be manageable without them.

Throughout this hour, we will investigate functions and demonstrate some of the ways in which they can save you from repetitive work. In this hour, you will learn

- How to define and call functions
- How to pass values to functions and receive values in return
- How to call a function dynamically using a string stored in a variable
- How to access global variables from within a function
- How to give a function a "memory"
- How to pass data to functions by reference

What Is a Function?

You can think of a function as a machine. A machine takes the raw materials you feed it and works with them to achieve a purpose or to produce a product. A function accepts values from you, processes them, and then performs an action (printing to the browser, for example) or returns a new value, possibly both.

If you needed to bake a single cake, you would probably do it yourself. If you needed to bake thousands of cakes, you would probably build or acquire a cake-baking machine. Similarly, when deciding whether to create a function, the most important factor to consider is the extent to which it can save you from repetition.

A function, then, is a self-contained block of code that can be called by your scripts. When called, the function's code is executed. You can pass values to functions, which they will then work with. When finished, a function can pass a value back to the calling code.

A *function* is a block of code that is not immediately executed but can be called by your scripts when needed. Functions can be built-in or user-defined. They can require information to be passed to them and usually return a value.

Calling Functions

Functions come in two flavors—those built in to the language and those you define yourself. PHP4 has hundreds of built-in functions. The very first script in this book consisted of a single function call:

```
print("Hello Web");
```

`print()` is not a typical function in that it does not require parentheses in order to run successfully.

```
print(("Hello Web");
```

and

```
print "Hello Web";
```

are equally valid. This is an exception. All other functions require parentheses, whether or not they accept arguments.

In this example, we called the `print()` function, passing it the string `"Hello Web"`. The function then went about the business of writing the string. A function call consists of the function name, `print` in this case, followed by parentheses. If you want to pass information to the function, you place it between these parentheses. A piece of information passed to a function in this way is called an argument. Some functions require that more than one argument be passed to them. Arguments in these cases must be separated by commas:

```
some_function( $an_argument, $another_argument );
```

`print()` is typical in that it returns a value. Most functions give you some information back when they've completed their task, if only to tell whether their mission was successful. `print()` returns a boolean, therefore.

The `abs()` function, for example, requires a signed numeric value and returns the absolute value of that number. Let's try it out in Listing 6.1.

LISTING 6.1 Calling the Built in `abs()` Function

```
 1: <html>
 2: <head>
 3: <title>Listing 6.1</title>
 4: </head>
 5: <body>
 6: <?php
 7: $num = -321;
 8: $newnum = abs( $num );
 9: print $newnum;
10: // prints "321"
11: ?>
12: </body>
13: </html>
```

In this example, we assign the value `-321` to a variable `$num`. We then pass that variable to the `abs()` function, which made the necessary calculation and returned a new value. We assign this to the variable `$newnum` and print the result. In fact, we could have dispensed with temporary variables altogether, passing our number straight to `abs()`, and directly printing the result:

```
print( abs( -321 ) );
```

The rules for calling user-defined functions are almost exactly the same.

NEW TERM An *argument* is a value passed to a function. Arguments are included within the parentheses of a function call. User-defined functions include comma-separated argument names within the parentheses of the function definition. These arguments then become available to the function as local variables.

Defining a Function

You can define a function using the `function` statement:

```
function some_function( $argument1, $argument2 )
     {
     // function code here
     }
```

The name of the function follows the `function` statement and precedes a set of parentheses. If your function is to require arguments, you must place comma-separated variable names within the parentheses. These variables will be filled by the values passed to your function. If your function requires no arguments, you must nevertheless supply the parentheses.

Listing 6.2 declares a function.

LISTING 6.2 Declaring a Function

```
 1: <html>
 2: <head>
 3: <title>Listing 6.2</title>
 4: </head>
 5: <body>
 6: <?php
 7: function bighello()
 8:      {
 9:      print "<h1>HELLO!</h1>";
10:      }
11: bighello();
12: ?>
13: </body>
14: </html>
```

The script in Listing 6.2 will simply output the string `"HELLO"` wrapped in an HTML `<H1>` element. We declare a function `bighello()` that requires no arguments. Because of this, we leave the parentheses empty. `bighello()` is a working function but not terribly useful. Listing 6.3 creates a function that requires an argument and actually does something helpful with it.

LISTING 6.3 Declaring a Function That Requires Arguments

```
 1: <html>
 2: <head>
 3: <title>Listing 6.3</title>
 4: </head>
 5: <body>
 6: <?php
 7: function printBR( $txt )
 8:      {
 9:      print ("$txt<br>\n");
10:      }
11: printBR("This is a line");
12: printBR("This is a new line");
13: printBR("This is yet another line");
14: ?>
15: </body>
16: </html>
```

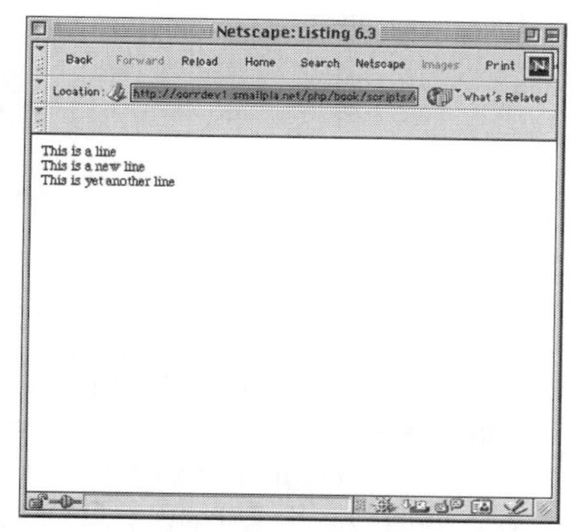

FIGURE 6.1
A function that prints a string with an appended
 tag.

You can see the output from the script in Listing 6.3 in Figure 6.1. The `printBR()` function expects a string, so we place the variable name `$txt` between the parentheses when we declare the function. Whatever is passed to `printBR()` is stored in `$txt`. Within the body of the function, we print the `$txt` variable, appending a `<br>` element and a newline character to it.

Now when we want to write a line to the browser, we can call `printBR()` instead of the built-in `print()`, saving us the bother of typing the `<br>` element.

Returning Values from User-Defined Functions

A function can return a value using the `return` statement in conjunction with a value or object. `return` stops the execution of the function and sends the value back to the calling code.

Listing 6.4 creates a function that returns the sum of two numbers.

LISTING 6.4 A Function That Returns a Value

```
1: <html>
2: <head>
3: <title>Listing 6.4</title>
4: </head>
5: <body>
6: <?php
7: function addNums( $firstnum, $secondnum )
8:      {
9:      $result = $firstnum + $secondnum;
10:     return $result;11:     }
12: print addNums(3,5);
13: // will print "8"
14: ?>
15: </body>
16: </html>
```

The script in Listing 6.4 will print the number '8'. `addNums()` should be called with two numeric arguments (3 and 5 in this case). These are stored in the variables `$firstnum` and `$secondnum`. Predictably, `addNums()` adds the numbers contained in these variables together and stores the result in a variable called `$result`. Once again, we can dispense with a stage in this code, doing away with the temporary `$result` variable altogether:

```
function addNums( $firstnum, $secondnum )
     {
     return ( $firstnum + $secondnum );
     }
```

The `return` statement can return a value, an object, or even nothing at all. How a value passed by `return` is arrived at can vary. The value could be hard-coded:

```
return 4;
```

It could be the result of an expression:

```
return ( $a/$b );
```

It could be the value returned by yet another function call:

```
return ( another_function( $an_argument ) );
```

Dynamic Function Calls

It is possible to assign function names as strings to variables and then treat these variables exactly as you would the function name itself. Listing 6.5 creates a simple example of this.

LISTING 6.5 Calling a Function Dynamically

```
 1: <html>
 2: <head>
 3: <title>Listing 6.5</title>
 4: </head>
 5: <body>
 6: <?php
 7: function sayHello()
 8:     {
 9:     print "hello<br>";
10:     }
11: $function_holder = "sayHello";
12: $function_holder();
13: ?>
14: </body>
15: </html>
```

A string identical to the name of the `sayHello()` function is assigned to the `$function_holder` variable. Once this is done, we can use this variable in conjunction with parentheses to call the `sayHello()` function.

Why would we want to do this? In the example, we simply made more work for ourselves by assigning the string `"sayHello"` to `$function_holder`. Dynamic function calls are useful when you want to alter program flow according to changing circumstances. We might want our script to behave differently according to a parameter set in a URL's query string, for example. We could extract the value of this parameter and use it to call one of a number of functions.

PHP's built-in functions also make use of this feature. The `array_walk()` function, for example uses a string to call a function for every element in an array. You can see an example of `array walk()` in action in Hour 16.

Variable Scope

A variable declared within a function remains local to that function. In other words, it will not be available outside the function or within other functions. In larger projects, this can save you from accidentally overwriting the contents of a variable when you declare two variables of the same name in separate functions.

Listing 6.6 creates a variable within a function and then attempts to print it outside the function.

LISTING 6.6 Variable Scope: A Variable Declared Within a Function Is Unavailable Outside the Function

```
 1: <html>
 2: <head>
 3: <title>Listing 6.6</title>
 4: </head>
 5: <body>
 6: <?php
 7: function test()
 8:      {
 9:      $testvariable = "this is a test variable";
10:      }
11: print "test variable: $testvariable<br>";
12: ?>
13: </body>
14: </html>
```

FIGURE 6.2
Attempting to reference a variable defined within a function.

You can see the output of the script in Listing 6.6 in Figure 6.2. The value of the variable `$testvariable` is not printed. This is because no such variable exists outside the `test()` function. Note that attempting to access a nonexistent variable does not cause an error.

Similarly, a variable declared outside a function will not automatically be available within it.

Accessing Variables with the `global` Statement

From within a function, it is not possible by default to access a variable that has been defined elsewhere. If you attempt to use a variable of the same name, you will set or access a local variable only. Let's put this to the test in Listing 6.7.

LISTING 6.7 Variables Defined Outside Functions Are Inaccessible from Within a Function by Default

```
 1: <html>
 2: <head>
 3: <title>Listing 6.7</title>
 4: </head>
 5: <body>
 6: <?php
 7: $life = 42;
 8: function meaningOfLife()
 9:      {
10:      print "The meaning of life is $life<br>";
11:      }
12: meaningOfLife();
13: ?>
14: </body>
15: </html>
```

You can see the output from the script in Listing 6.7 in Figure 6.3. As you might expect, the `meaningOfLife()` function has no access to the `$life` variable; `$life` is empty when the function attempts to print it. On the whole, this is a good thing. We're saved from potential clashes between identically named variables, and a function can always demand an argument if it needs information about the outside world. Occasionally, however, you may want to access an important global variable from within a function without passing it in as an argument. This is where the `global` statement comes into its own. Listing 6.8 uses `global` to restore order to the universe.

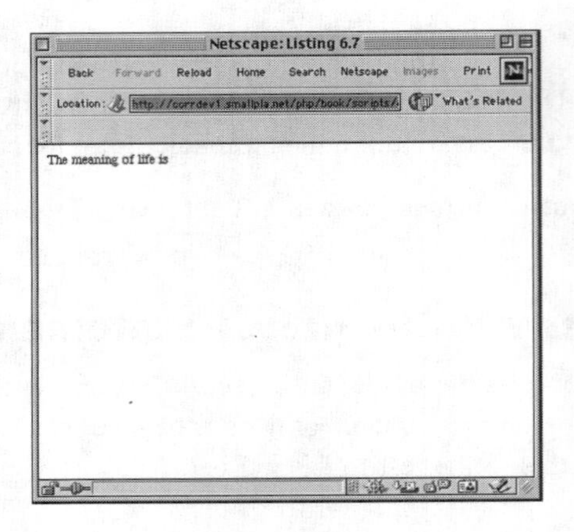

FIGURE 6.3
Attempting to print a global variable from within a function.

LISTING 6.8 Accessing Global Variables with the `global` Statement

```
 1: <html>
 2: <head>
 3: <title>Listing 6.8</title>
 4: </head>
 5: <body>
 6: <?php
 7: $life=42;
 8: function meaningOfLife()
 9:      {
10:      global $life;
11:      print "The meaning of life is $life<br>";
12:      }
13: meaningOfLife();
14: ?>
15: </body>
16: </html>
```

You can see the output from the script in Listing 6.8 in Figure 6.4. By placing `global` in front of the `$life` variable when we declare it in the `meaning_of_life()` function, we make it refer to the `global $life` variable declared outside the function.

You will need to use the global statement for every function that wishes to access a particular global variable.

Be careful, though. If we manipulate the contents of the variable within the function, `$life` will be changed for the script as a whole. Usually, an argument is a copy of whatever value is passed by the calling code; changing it in a function has no effect beyond the function block. Changing a global variable within a function on the other hand changes the original and not a copy. Use the `global` statement sparingly.

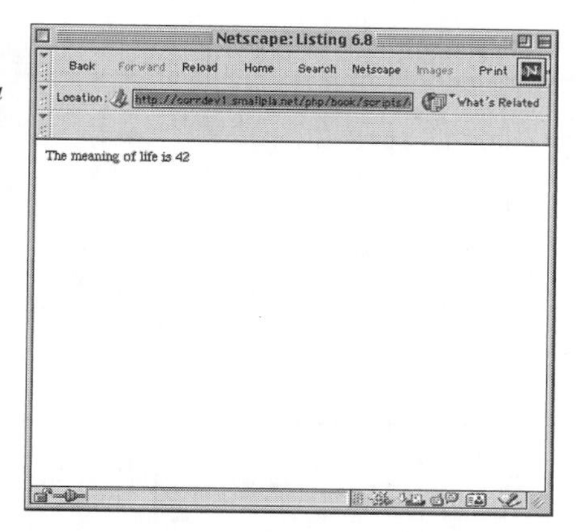

FIGURE 6.4
Successfully accessing a global variable from within a function using the `global` keyword.

Saving State Between Function Calls with the `static` Statement

Variables within functions have a short but happy life on the whole. They come into being when the `andAnotherThing()` function is called and die when execution is finished. Once again, this is as it should be. It is usually best to build a script as a series of self-contained blocks, each with as little knowledge of others as possible. Occasionally, however, you may want to give a function a rudimentary memory.

Let's assume that we want a function to keep track of the number of times it has been called. Why? In our examples, the function is designed to create numbered headings in a script that dynamically builds online documentation.

We could, of course use our newfound knowledge of the `global` statement to do this. We have a crack at this in Listing 6.9.

LISTING 6.9 Using the `global` Statement to Remember the Value of a Variable Between Function Calls

```
 1: <html>
 2: <head>
 3: <title>Listing 6.9</title>
 4: </head>
 5: <body>
 6: <?php
 7: $num_of_calls = 0;
 8: function andAnotherThing( $txt )
 9:     {
10:     global $num_of_calls;
```

LISTING 6.9 continued

```
11:     $num_of_calls++;
12:     print "<h1>$num_of_calls. $txt</h1>";
13:     }
14: andAnotherThing("Widgets");
15: print("We build a fine range of widgets<p>");
16: andAnotherThing("Doodads");
17: print("Finest in the world<p>");
18: ?>
19: </body>
20: </html>
```

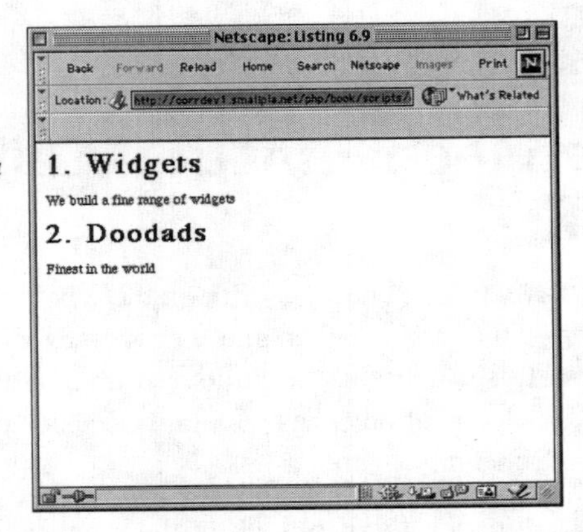

FIGURE 6.5
Using the `global` *statement to keep track of the number of times a function has been called.*

This does the job. We declare a variable, `$num_of_calls`, outside the function `andAnotherThing()`. We make this variable available to the function with the `global` statement. You can see the output of Listing 6.9 in Figure 6.5.

Every time `andAnotherThing()` is called, `$num_of_calls` is incremented. We can then print out a heading complete with a heading number.

This is not the most elegant solution, however. Functions that use the `global` statement cannot be read as standalone blocks of code. In reading or reusing them, we need to look out for the global variables that they manipulate.

This is where the `static` statement can be useful. If you declare a variable within a function in conjunction with the `static` statement, the variable remains local to the function. On the other hand, the function "remembers" the value of the variable from execution to execution. Listing 6.10 adapts the code from Listing 6.9 to use the `static` statement.

LISTING 6.10 Using the `static` Statement to Remember the Value of a Variable Between Function Calls

```
 1: <html>
 2: <head>
 3: <title>Listing 6.10</title>
 4: </head>
 5: <body>
 6: <?php
 7: function andAnotherThing( $txt )
 8:      {
 9:      static $num_of_calls = 0;
10:      $num_of_calls++;
11:      print "<h1>$num_of_calls. $txt</h1>";
12:     }
13: andAnotherThing("Widgets");
14: print("We build a fine range of widgets<p>");
15: andAnotherThing("Doodads");
16: print("Finest in the world<p>");
17: ?>
18: </body>
19: </html>
```

`andAnotherThing()` has become entirely self-contained. When we declare the `$num_of_calls` variable, we assign an initial value to it. This initial assignment is ignored when the function is called a second time. Instead, the previous value of `$num_of_calls` is remembered. We can now paste the `andAnotherThing()` function into other scripts without worrying about global variables. Although the output of Listing 6.10 is exactly the same as that for Listing 6.9, we have made the code more elegant.

More About Arguments

You've already seen how to pass arguments to functions, but there's more to cover yet. In this section, you'll look at a technique for giving your arguments default values and explore a method of passing references to variables rather than copies of their values to your functions.

Setting Default Values for Arguments

PHP gives you a nifty feature to help build flexible functions. Until now, we've said that some functions "demand" one or more arguments. By making some arguments optional, you can render your functions a little less autocratic.

Listing 6.11 creates a useful little function that wraps a string in an HTML `font` element. We want to give the user of the function the chance to change the `font` element's `size` attribute, so we demand a `$size` argument in addition to the string.

LISTING 6.11 A Function Requiring Two Arguments

```
 1: <html>
 2: <head>
 3: <title>Listing 6.11</title>
 4: </head>
 5: <body>
 6: <?php
 7: function fontWrap( $txt, $size )
 8:     {
 9: print "<font size=\"$size\" face=\"Helvetica,Arial,Sans-Serif\">$txt</
➥font>";10:  }
11: fontWrap("A heading<br>",5);
12: fontWrap("some body text<br>",3);
13: fontWrap("some more body text<BR>",3);
14: fontWrap("yet more body text<BR>",3);
15: ?>
16: </body>
17: </html>
```

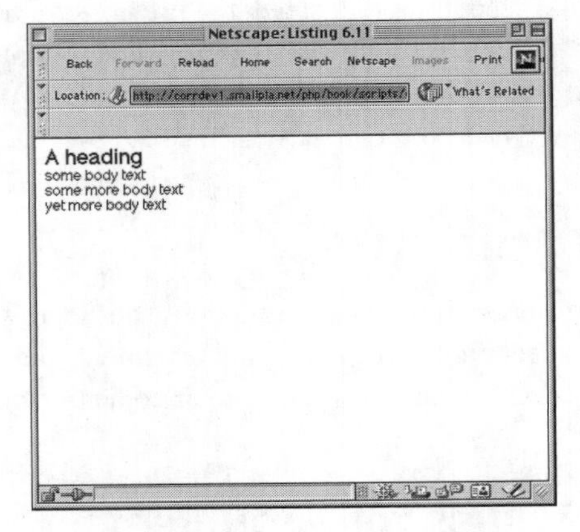

FIGURE 6.6
A function that formats and outputs strings.

You can see the output from the script in Listing 6.11 in Figure 6.6. Useful though this function is, we really only need to change the font size occasionally. Most of the time we default to 3. By assigning a value to an argument variable within the function definition's parentheses, we can make the `$size` argument optional. If the function call doesn't define an argument for this, the value we have assigned to the argument is used instead. Listing 6.12 uses this technique to make the `$size` argument optional.

LISTING 6.12 A Function with an Optional Argument

```
 1: <html>
 2: <head>
 3: <title>Listing 6.12</title>
 4: </head>
 5: <body>
 6: <?php
 7: function fontWrap( $txt, $size=3 )
 8:     {
 9: print "<font size=\"$size\"face=\"Helvetica,Arial,Sans-Serif\">$txt</font>";
10:     }
11: fontWrap("A heading<br>",5);
12: fontWrap("some body text<br>");
13: fontWrap("some more body text<br>");
14: fontWrap("yet more body text<br>");
15: ?>
16: </body>
17: </html>
```

When the `fontWrap()` function is called with a second argument, this value is used to set the size attribute of the font element. When we omit this argument, the default value of 3 is used instead. You can create as many optional arguments as you want, but when you've given an argument a default value, all subsequent arguments should also be given defaults.

Passing References to Variables to Functions

When you pass arguments to functions they are stored as copies in parameter variables. Any changes made to these variables in the body of the function are local to that function and are not reflected beyond it. This is illustrated in Listing 6.13.

LISTING 6.13 Passing an Argument to a Function by Value

```
 1: <html>
 2: <head>
 3: <title>Listing 6.13</title>
 4: </head>
 5: <body>
 6: <?php
 7: function addFive( $num )
 8:      {
 9:      $num += 5;
10:      }
```

LISTING 6.13 continued

```
11: $orignum = 10;
12: addFive( $orignum );
13: print( $orignum );
14: ?>
15: </body>
16: </html>
```

The `addFive()` function accepts a single numeric value and adds 5 to it. It returns nothing. We assign a value to a variable `$orignum` and then pass this variable to `addFive()`. A copy of the contents of `$orignum` is stored in the variable `$num`. Although we increment `$num` by 5, this has no effect on the value of `$orignum`. When we print `$orignum`, we find that its value is still 10. By default, variables passed to functions are passed by value. In other words, local copies of the values of the variables are made.

It is possible to pass arguments to functions by reference. This means that a reference to the variable is manipulated by the function rather than a copy of the variable's value. Any changes made to an argument in these cases will change the value of the original variable. You can pass an argument by reference by adding an ampersand to the variable name in either the function call or the function definition. Listings 6.14 and 6.15 show each technique in turn.

LISTING 6.14 Using a Function Call to Pass an Argument to a Function by Reference

```
 1: <html>
 2: <head>
 3: <title>Listing 6.14</title>
 4: </head>
 5: <body>
 6: <?php
 7: function addFive( $num )
 8:      {
 9:      $num += 5;
10:      }
11: $orignum = 10;
12: addFive( &$orignum );
13: print( $orignum );
14: ?>
15: </body>
16: </html>
```

LISTING 6.15 Using a Function Definition to Pass an Argument to a Function by Reference

```
 1: <html>
 2: <head>
 3: <title>Listing 6.15</title>
 4: </head>
 5: <body>
 6: <?php
 7: function addFive( &$num )
 8:      {
 9:      $num += 5;
10:      }
11: $orignum = 10;
12: addFive( $orignum );
13: print( $orignum );
14: ?>
15: </body>
16: </html>
```

On the whole, it makes more sense to add the ampersand to the function definition. In this way, you can be sure that the function behaves consistently from call to call.

Summary

In this hour, you learned about functions and how to deploy them. You learned how to define and pass arguments to a function. You learned how to use the `global` and `static` statements. You learned how to pass references to functions and how to create default values for function arguments.

Q&A

Q Apart from the global keyword, is there any way that a function can access and change global variables?

A You can also access global variables anywhere in your scripts with a built-in associative array called `$GLOBALS`. To access a global variable called `$test` within a function, you could reference it as `$GLOBALS[test]`. You can learn more about associative arrays in the next hour.

You can also change global variables from within a function if it has been passed in by reference.

Q Can you include a function call within a string, as you can with a variable?

A No. You must call functions outside quotation marks.

Workshop

The Workshop provides quiz questions to help you solidify your understanding of the material covered. Try to understand the quiz answers before continuing to the next hour's lesson. Quiz answers are provided in Appendix A.

Quiz

1. True or False: If a function doesn't require an argument, you can omit the parentheses in the function call.
2. How do you return a value from a function?
3. What would the following code fragment print to the browser?

```
$number = 50;

function tenTimes()
        {
        $number = $number * 10;
        }

tenTimes();
print $number;
```

4. What would the following code fragment print to the browser?

```
$number = 50;

function tenTimes()
        {
        global $number;
        $number = $number * 10;
        }

tenTimes();
print $number;
```

5. What would the following code fragment print to the browser?

```
$number = 50;

function tenTimes( $n )
        {
        $n = $n * 10;
        }
```

```
tenTimes( $number );
print $number;
```

6. What would the following code fragment print to the browser?

```
$number = 50;

function tenTimes( &$n )
          {
          $n = $n * 10;
          }

tenTimes( $number );
print $number;
```

Activity

1. Create a function that accepts four string variables and returns a string that contains an HTML table element, enclosing each of the variables in its own cell.

Hour 7

Arrays

Arrays, and the tools to manipulate them, greatly enhance the scope and flexibility of PHP4 scripts. After you've mastered arrays, you will be able to store and organize complex data structures.

This hour introduces arrays and some of the functions that help you work with them. In this hour, you will learn

- What arrays are and how to create them
- How to access data from and about arrays
- How to access and sort the data contained in arrays

What Is an Array?

You already know that a variable is a "bucket" in which you can temporarily store a value. By using variables, you can create a script that stores, processes, and outputs different information every time it is run. Unfortunately, you can only store one value at a time in a variable. Arrays are special variables that allow you to overcome this limitation. An array allows you to store as many values as you want in the same variable. Each value is indexed within the array by a number or a string. If a variable is a bucket, you can think of an array as a filing cabinet—a single container that can store many discrete items.

NEW TERM An *array* is a list variable. That is, a variable that contains multiple elements indexed by numbers or strings. It enables you to store, order, and access many values under one name.

Of course, if you have five values to store, you could always define five variables. So, why use an array rather than a variable? First, an array is flexible. It can store two values or two hundred values without the need to define further variables. Second, an array allows you to work easily with all its items. You can loop through each item or pull one out at random. You can sort items numerically, alphabetically, or even according to a system of your own.

Each item in an array is commonly referred to as an element. Each element can be accessed directly via its index. An index to an array element can be either a number or a string.

By default, array elements are indexed by number starting at zero. It's important to remember, therefore, that the index of the last element of a numerically indexed array is always one less than the number of elements the array contains.

For example, Table 7.1 shows the elements in an array called `users`. Notice that the third element has an index of 2.

TABLE 7.1 The Elements in the `users` Array

Index Number	*Value*	*Which Element?*
0	Bert	First
1	Sharon	Second
2	Betty	Third
3	Harry	Fourth

Indexing arrays by string can be useful in cases where you need to store both names and values.

PHP4 provides tools to access and manipulate arrays indexed by both name and number. Some of these are covered in this hour, and others will be covered in Hour 16, "Working with Data."

Creating Arrays

By default, arrays are lists of values indexed by number. Values can be assigned to an array in two ways: with the `array()` function or directly using the array identifier [ ]. You'll meet both of these in the next two sections.

Defining Arrays with the `array()` Function

The `array()` function is useful when you want to assign multiple values to an array at one time. Let's define an array called `$users` and assign four strings to it:

```
$users = array ("Bert", "Sharon", "Betty", "Harry" );
```

You can now access the third element in the `$user` array by using the index "2":

```
print "$users[2]";
```

This would return the string "Sharon". The index of an array element is placed between square brackets directly after the array name. You can use this notation either to set or retrieve a value.

Remember that arrays are indexed from zero by default, so the index of any element always is one less than the element's place in the list.

Defining or Adding to Arrays with the Array Identifier

You can create a new array (or add to an existing one) by using the array identifier in conjunction with the array name. The array identifier is a set of square brackets with no index number or name inside it.

Let's re-create our `$users` array in this way:

```
$users[] = " Bert";
$users[] = " Sharon";
$users[] = " Betty";
$users[] = " Harry";
```

Notice that we didn't need to place any numbers between the square brackets. PHP4 automatically takes care of the index number, which saves you from having to work out which is the next available slot.

We could have added numbers if we wanted, and the result would have been exactly the same. It's not advisable to do this, though. Take a look at the following code:

```
$users[0] = " Bert";
$users[200] = "Sharon";
```

The array has only two elements, but the index of the final element is 200. PHP4 will not initialize the intervening elements. This could lead to confusion when attempting to access elements in the array.

In addition to creating arrays, you can use the array identifier to add new values onto the end of an existing array. In the following code, we define an array with the `array()` function and use the array identifier to add a new element:

```
$users = array ("Bert", " Sharon", "Betty", "Harry" );
$users[] = "sally";
```

Associative Arrays

Numerically indexed arrays are useful for storing values in the order in which they were added or according to a sort pattern. Sometimes, though, you need to access elements in an array by name. An associative array is indexed with strings between the square brackets rather than numbers. Imagine an address book. Which would be easier, indexing the "name" field as 4 or as "name"?

Arrays indexed by strings are known as *associative arrays*. You may also see them referred to as hashes.

Once again, you can define an associative array using either `array()` or the array identifier [].

The division between an associative array and a numerically indexed array is not absolute in PHP. They are not separate types as arrays and hashes are in Perl. It is a good idea, nevertheless, to treat them separately. Each demands different strategies for access and manipulation.

Defining Associative Arrays with the `array()` Function

To define an associative array with the `array()` function, you must define both the key and value for each element. The following code creates an associative array called `$character` with four elements:

```
$character = array (
            name=>"bob",
            occupation=>"superhero",
            age=>30,
            "special power"=>"x-ray vision"
                    );
```

We can now access any of the fields of `$character`:

```
print $character[age];
```

The keys in an associative array are strings, but it isn't necessary to surround them with quotation marks unless the key contains more than one word.

Directly Defining or Adding to an Associative Array

You can create or add a name/value pair to an associative array simply by assigning a value to a named element. In the following, we re-create our `$character` array by directly assigning a value to each key:

```
$character[name] = "bob";
$character[occupation] = "superhero";
$character[age] = 30;
$character["special power"] = "x-ray vision";
```

Multidimensional Arrays

Until now, we've simply said that elements of arrays are values. In our `$character` array, three of the elements held strings, and one held an integer. The reality is a little more complex, however. In fact, an element of an array could be a value, an object, or even another array. A multidimensional array is an array of arrays. Imagine an array that stores an array in each of its elements. To access the third element of the second element, you would have to use two indices:

```
$array[1][2]
```

Arrays that contain arrays as their elements are known as *multidimensional arrays*.

The fact that an array element can itself be an array enables you to create sophisticated data structures relatively easily. Listing 7.1 defines an array that has an associative array as each of its elements.

LISTING 7.1 Defining a Multidimensional Array

```
 1: <html>
 2: <head>
 3: <title>Listing 7.1</title>
 4: </head>
 5: <body>
 6: <?php
 7: $characters = array (
 8:             array ( name=>"bob",
 9:                 occupation=>"superhero",
10:                 age=>30,
11:                 specialty=>"x-ray vision" ),
12:             array ( name=>"sally",
13:                 occupation=>"superhero",
14:                 age=>24,
15:                 specialty=>"superhuman strength" ),
16:             array ( name=>"mary",
17:                 occupation=>"arch villain",
18:                 age=>63,
19:                 specialty=>"nanotechnology" )
20:                 );
21:
22: print $characters[0][occupation];
23: // prints "superhero"
24: ?>
25: </body>
26: </html>
```

Notice that we have nested array function calls within an array function call. At the first level, we define an array. For each of its elements, we define an associative array.

Accessing `$user[2]`, therefore, gives us access to the third associative array in the top-level array. We can then go ahead and access any of the associative array's fields. `$user[2][name]` will be "mary", and `$user[2][age]` will be 63.

When this concept is clear, it will be easy to create complex combinations of associative and numerically indexed arrays.

Accessing Arrays

So far, you've seen the ways in which you can create and add to arrays. In this section, you will examine some of the tools that PHP4 provides to allow you to acquire information about arrays and access their elements.

Getting the Size of an Array

You can access an element of an array by using its index:

```
print $user[4]
```

Because of the flexibility of arrays, however, you won't always know how many elements a particular array contains. That's where the `count()` function comes into play. `count()` returns the number of elements in an array. In the following code, we define a numerically indexed array and use `count()` to access its last element:

```
 $users = array ("Bert", "Sharon", "Betty", "Harry" );
print $users[count($users)-1];
```

Notice that we subtract 1 from the value returned by `count()`. This is because `count()` returns the number of elements in an array, not the index of the last element.

Although arrays are indexed from zero by default, it is possible to change this. For the sake of clarity and consistency, however, this is not usually advisable.

Looping Through an Array

There are many ways of looping through each element of an array. For these examples, you'll use PHP4's powerful `foreach` statement. You will examine some other methods in Hour 16.

The `foreach` statement was introduced with PHP4.

In the context of numerically indexed arrays, you would use a `foreach` statement like this:

```
foreach( $array as $temp )
     {
     //...
     }
```

where `$array` is the array you want to loop through, and `$temp` is a variable in which you will temporarily store each element.

In the following code, we define a numerically indexed array and use `foreach` to access each of its elements in turn:

```
$users = array ("Bert", "Sharon", "Betty", "Harry" );
foreach ( $users as $val )
    {
    print "$val<br>";
    }
```

You can see the output from this code fragment in Figure 7.1.

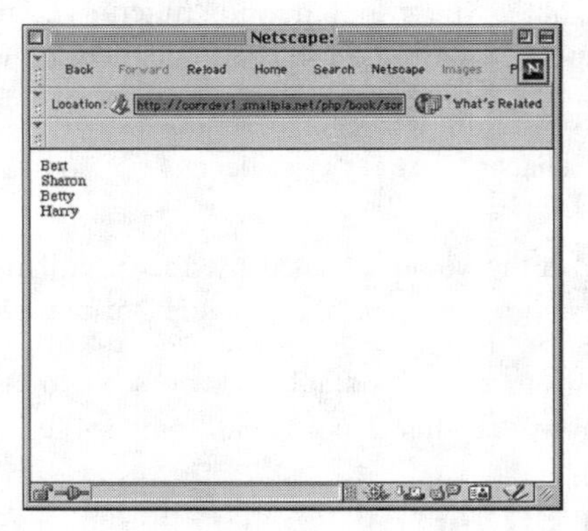

FIGURE 7.1
Looping through an array.

The value of each element is temporarily placed in the variable `$val`, which we then print to the browser. If you are moving to PHP4 from Perl, be aware of a significant difference in the behavior of `foreach`. Changing the value of the temporary variable in a Perl `foreach` loop changes the corresponding element in the array. Changing the temporary variable in the preceding example would have no effect on the `$users` array. You will look at a way of using `foreach` to change the values of a numerically indexed array in Hour 16.

Looping Through an Associative Array

To access both the keys and values of an associative array, you need to alter the use of `foreach` slightly.

In the context of associative arrays, you would use a `foreach` statement like this:

```
foreach( $array as $key=>$value )
     {
     //...
     }
```

where `$array` is the array we are looping through, `$key` is a variable that temporarily holds each key, and `$value` is a variable that temporarily holds each value.

Listing 7.2 creates an associative array and accesses each key and value in turn.

LISTING 7.2 Looping Through an Associative Array with `foreach`

```
 1: <html>
 2: <head>
 3: <title>Listing 7.2</title>
 4: </head>
 5: <body>
 6: <?php
 7: $character = array (
 8:             name=>"bob",
 9:             occupation=>"superhero",
10:             age=>30,
11:             "special power"=>"x-ray vision"
12:                             );
13: foreach ( $character as $key=>$val )
14:     {
15:     print "$key = $val<br>";
16:     }
17:
18: ?>
19: </body>
20: </html>
```

You can see the output from Listing 7.2 in Figure 7.2.

Outputting a Multidimensional Array

You can now combine these techniques to output the multidimensional array created in Listing 7.1. Listing 7.3 defines a similar array and uses `foreach` to loop through each of its elements.

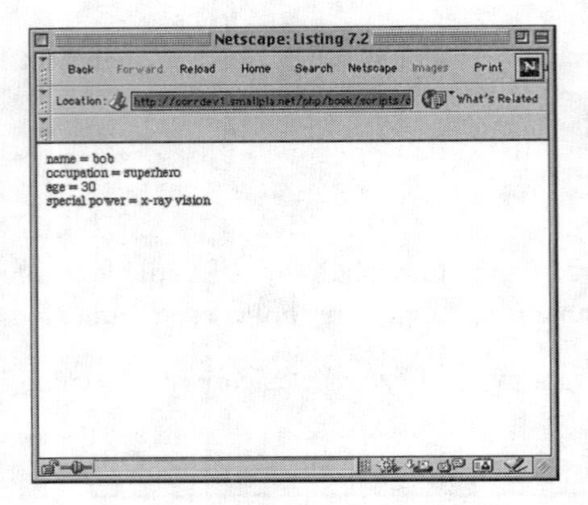

FIGURE 7.2
Looping through an associative array.

LISTING 7.3 Looping Through a Multidimensional Array

```
 1: <html>
 2: <head>
 3: <title>Listing 7.3</title>
 4: </head>
 5: <body>
 6: <?php
 7: $characters = array (
 8:             array ( name=>"bob",
 9:                 occupation=>"superhero",
10:                 age=>30,
11:                 specialty=>"x-ray vision" ),
12:             array ( name=>"sally",
13:                  occupation=>"superhero",
14:                  age=>24,
15:                  specialty=>"superhuman strength" ),
16:             array ( name=>"mary",
17:                  occupation=>"arch villain",
18:                  age=>63,
19:                  specialty=>"nanotechnology" )
20:                 );
21:
22: foreach ( $characters as $val )
23:     {
24:     foreach ( $val as $key=>$final_val )
25:         {
26:         print "$key: $final_val<br>";
27:         }
28:     print "<br>";
29:     }
30: ?>
31: </body>
32: </html>
```

You can see the output from Listing 7.3 in Figure 7.3. We create two `foreach` loops. The outer loop accesses each element in the numerically indexed array `$users`, placing each one in `$val`. Because `$val` itself then contains an associative array, we can loop through this, outputting each of its elements (temporarily stored in `$key` and `$final_val`) to the browser.

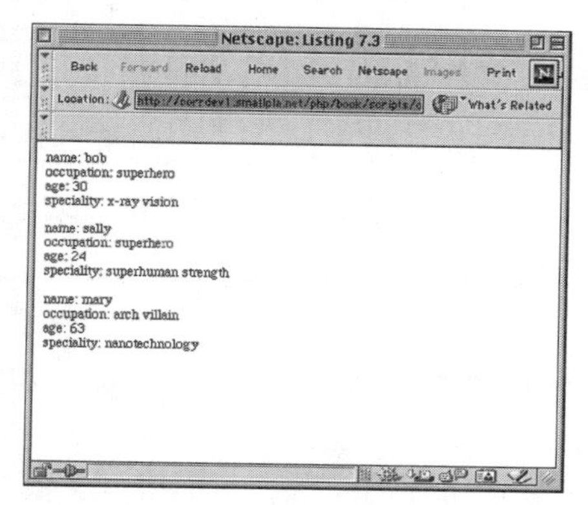

FIGURE 7.3
Looping through a multidimensional array.

For this technique to work as expected, we need to make sure in advance that `$val` will always contain an array. To make this code a little more robust, we could use the function `is_array()` to test `$val`. `is_array()` accepts a variable, returning `true` if the variable is an array, or `false` otherwise.

Manipulating Arrays

You can now populate arrays and access their elements, but PHP4 has functions to help you do much more than that with arrays. If you're used to Perl, you'll find some of these eerily familiar!

Joining Two Arrays with `array_merge()`

`array_merge()` accepts two or more arrays and returns a merged array combining all their elements. In the following example, we create two arrays, joining the second to the first, and loop through the resultant third array:

```
$first = array("a", "b", "c");
$second = array(1,2,3);
$third = array_merge( $first,  $second  );
```

```
foreach ( $third as $val )
    {
    print "$val<BR>";
    }
```

The `$third` array contains copies of all the elements of both the `$first` and `$second` arrays. The `foreach` statement prints this combined array ('a', 'b', 'c', 1, 2, 3) to the browser with a <BR> tag between each element. Remember that the arrays passed to `array_merge()` are not themselves transformed.

The `array_merge()` function was introduced with PHP4.

Adding Multiple Variables to an Array with `array_push()`

`array_push()` accepts an array and any number of further parameters, each of which is added to the array. Note that the `array_push()` function is unlike `array_merge()` in that the array passed in as the first argument is transformed. `array_push()` returns the total number of elements in the array. Let's create an array and add some more values to it:

```
$first = array("a", "b", "c");
$total = array_push( $first, 1, 2, 3  );

print "There are $total elements in \$first<P>";
foreach ( $first as $val )
    {
    print "$val<BR>";
    }
```

Because `array_push()` returns the total number of elements in the array it transforms, we are able to store this value (6) in a variable and print it to the browser. The `$first` array now contains its original elements as well the three integers we passed to the `array_push()` function, all of these are printed to the browser within the `foreach` statement.

Notice that we used a backslash character when we printed the string "\$first". If you use a dollar sign followed by numbers and letters within a string, PHP will attempt to insert the value of a variable by that name. In the example above we wished to print the string `'$first'` rather than the value of the $first variable. To print the special character '$', therefore, we must precede it with a backslash. PHP will now print the character instead of interpreting it. This process is often referred to as "escaping" a character.

> Perl users beware! If you're used to working with Perl's `push()`, you should note that if you pass a second array variable to `array_push()` it will be added as a single element, creating a multidimensional array. If you want to combine two arrays, use `array_merge()`.

Removing the First Element of an Array with `array_shift()`

`array_shift()` removes and returns the first element of an array passed to it as an argument. In the following example, we use `array_shift()` in conjunction with a `while` loop. We test the value returned from `count()` to check whether the array still contains elements:

```
<?php
$an_array = array("a", "b", "c");

while ( count( $an_array) )
    {
    $val = array_shift( $an_array);
    print "$val<BR>";
    print "there are ".count($an_array)." elements in \$an_array <br>";
    }
?>
```

You can see the output from this fragment of code in Figure 7.4.

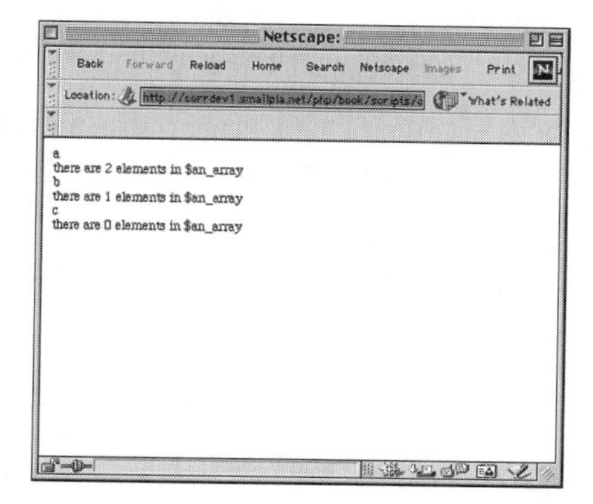

FIGURE 7.4
Using `array_shift()` *to remove and print every element in an array.*

7

`array_shift()` is useful when you need to create a queue and act on it until the queue is empty.

The `array_shift()` function was added to the language with the advent of PHP4.

Slicing Arrays with `array_slice()`

`array_slice()` allows you to extract a chunk of an array. It accepts an array as an argument, a starting position (offset), and an (optional) length. If the length is omitted, `array_slice()` generously assumes that you want all elements from the starting position onward returned. `array_slice()` does not alter the array you pass to it. It returns a new array containing the elements you have requested.

In the following example, we create an array and extract a new three-element array from it:

```
$first = array("a", "b", "c", "d", "e", "f");
$second = array_slice($first, 2, 3);

foreach ( $second as $var )
    {
    print "$var<br>";
    }
```

This will print the elements 'c', 'd', and 'e', separating each by a `<BR>` tag. Notice that the offset is inclusive if we think of it as the index number of the first element we are requesting. In other words, the first element of the `$second` array is equivalent to `$first[2]`.

If we pass `array_slice()` an offset argument that is less than zero, the returned slice will begin that number of elements from the end of the given array.

If we pass `array_slice()` a length argument that is less than zero, the returned slice will contain all elements from the offset position to that number of elements from the end of the given array.

Once again, `array_slice()` was added to PHP with PHP4.

Sorting Arrays

Sorting is perhaps the greatest magic you can perform on an array. Thanks to the functions that PHP4 offers to achieve just this, you can truly bring order from chaos. This section introduces some functions that allow you to sort both numerically indexed and associative arrays.

Sorting Numerically Indexed Arrays with `sort()`

`sort()` accepts an array as its argument and sorts it either alphabetically if any strings are present or numerically if all elements are numbers. The function doesn't return any data, transforming the array you pass it. Note that it differs from Perl's `sort()` function in this respect. The following fragment of code initializes an array of single character strings, sorts it, and outputs the transformed array:

```
$an_array = array("x","a","f","c");
sort( $an_array);

foreach ( $an_array as $var )
    {
    print "$var<BR>";
    }
```

Don't pass an associative array to `sort()`. You will find that the values are sorted as expected but that your keys have been lost—replaced by numerical indices that follow the sort order.

You can reverse sort a numerically indexed array by using `rsort()` in exactly the same way as `sort()`.

Sorting an Associative Array by Value with `asort()`

`asort()` accepts an associative array and sorts its values just as `sort()` does. However, it preserves the array's keys:

```
$first = array("first"=>5,"second"=>2,"third"=>1);

asort( $first );
```

```
foreach ( $first as $key => $val )
    {
    print "$key = $val<BR>";
    }
```

You can see the output from this fragment of code in Figure 7.5.

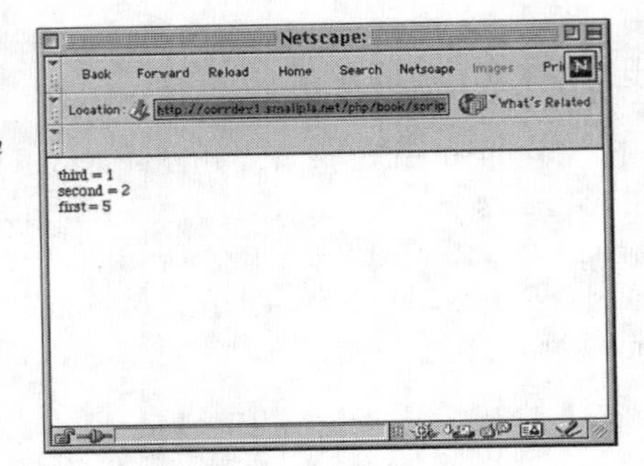

FIGURE 7.5
Sorting an associative array by its values with `asort()`.

You can reverse sort an associative array by value with `arsort()`.

Sorting an Associative Array by Key with `ksort()`

`ksort()` accepts an associative array and sorts its keys. Once again, the array you pass it will be transformed and nothing will be returned:

```
$first = array("x"=>5,"a"=>2,"f"=>1);

ksort( $first );

foreach ( $first as $key => $val )
    {
    print "$key = $val<BR>";
    }
```

You can see the output from this fragment of code in Figure 7.6.

You can reverse sort an associative array by key with `krsort()`.

FIGURE 7.6
Sorting an associative array by its keys with `ksort()`.

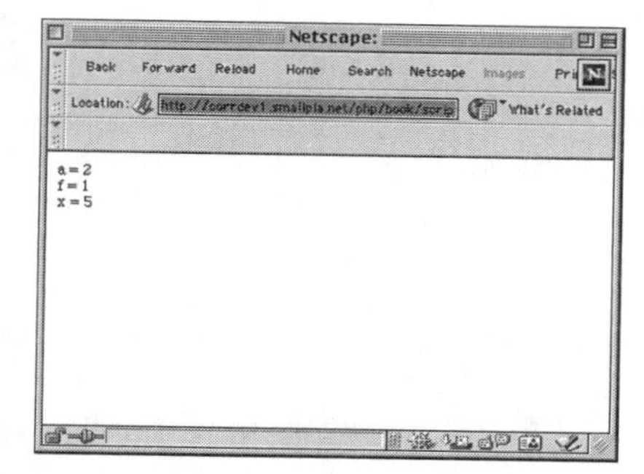

Summary

In this hour, you learned about arrays and some of the many tools that PHP4 provides to work with them. You should now be able to create both numerically indexed and associative arrays, and output data from them using a `foreach` loop.

You should be able to combine arrays to create multidimensional arrays and loop through the information they contain. You learned how to manipulate arrays by adding or removing multiple elements. Finally, you learned some of the techniques that PHP4 makes available to sort arrays.

Q&A

Q If the `foreach` statement was introduced with PHP4, how did programmers using PHP3 iterate through arrays?

A The PHP3 technique for looping through an array involved a function called `each()`, which was used in conjunction with a `while` statement. You can read about this technique in Hour 16.

Q Are there any functions for manipulating arrays that we have not covered here?

A PHP4 supports many array functions. You can read about some more of these in Hour 16 and find them all in the official PHP manual at `http://www.php.net/manual/ref.array.php`.

Q I can discover the number of elements in an array, so should I use a `for` statement to loop through an array?

A You should be cautious of this technique. You cannot be absolutely sure that the array you are reading is indexed by consecutively numbered keys.

Workshop

The Workshop provides quiz questions to help you solidify your understanding of the material covered. Try to understand the quiz answers before continuing to the next hour's lesson. Quiz answers are provided in Appendix A.

Quiz

1. What function can you use to define an array?
2. What is the index number of the last element of the array defined below?

   ```
   $users = array("Harry", "Bob", "Sandy");
   ```

3. Without using a function, what would be the easiest way of adding the element "Susan" to the `$users` array defined previously?
4. Which function could you use to add the string "Susan" to the `$users` array?
5. How would you find out the number of elements in an array?
6. In PHP4, what is the simplest way of looping through an array?
7. What function would you use to join two arrays?
8. How would you sort an associative array by its keys?

Activities

1. Create a multidimensional array of movies organized by genre. This should take the form of an associative array with genres as keys (`"SF"`, `"Action"`, `"Romance"`, and so on). Each of this associative array's elements should be an array containing movie names (`"2001"`, `"Alien"`, `"Terminator"`, and so on).
2. Loop through the array you created in Activity 1, outputting each genre and its associated movies to the browser.

HOUR 8

Objects

Object-oriented programming is dangerous. It changes the way you think about coding, and once the concepts have a hold on you, they don't let go. PHP, like Perl before it, has progressively incorporated more object-oriented aspects into its syntax and structure. With the advent of PHP4, it becomes possible to use object-oriented code at the heart of your projects.

Throughout this hour, you'll take a tour of PHP4's object-oriented features and apply them to some real-world code. In this hour, you will learn

- What objects and classes are
- How to create classes and instantiate objects
- How to create and access properties and methods
- How to create classes that inherit functionality from others
- Some of the reasons why object-oriented programming can help you to organize your projects

What Is an Object?

An object is an enclosed bundle of variables and functions forged from a special template called a class. Objects hide a lot of their inner workings away from the code that uses them, providing instead easy interfaces through which you can send them orders and they can return information. These interfaces are special functions called methods. All the methods of an object have access to special variables called properties.

By defining a class, you lay down a set of characteristics. By creating objects of that type, you create entities that share these characteristics but might initialize them as different values. You might create an `automobile` class, for example. This class would have a `color` characteristic. All automobile objects would share the characteristic of `color`, but some would initialize it to "blue," others to "green," and so on.

A *class* is a collection of special functions called methods and special variables called properties. You can declare a class with the `class` keyword. Classes are the templates from which objects are created.

NEW TERM Existing in memory rather than as code, an *object* is an instance of a class. That is, an object is the working embodiment of the functionality laid down in a class. An object is instantiated with the `new` statement in conjunction with the name of the class of which it is to be a member. When an object is instantiated, you can access all its properties and all its methods.

Perhaps the greatest benefit of object-oriented code is its reusability. Because the classes used to create objects are self-enclosed, they can be easily pulled from one project and used in another. Additionally, it is possible to create child classes that inherit and override the characteristics of their parents. This technique can allow you to create progressively more complex and specialized objects that can draw on base functionality while adding more of their own.

Perhaps the best way to explain object-oriented programming is to do it.

Creating an Object

To create an object, you must first design the template from which it can be instantiated. This template is known as a class, and in PHP4 it must be declared with the `class` keyword:

```
class first_class
    {
```

```
    // a very minimal class
    }
```

The `first_class` class is the basis from which you can instantiate any number of `first_class` objects. To create an instance of an object, you must use the `new` statement:

```
$obj1 = new first_class();
$obj2 = new first_class();
print "\$obj1 is a ".gettype($obj1)."<br>";
print "\$obj2 is a ".gettype($obj2)."<br>";
```

You can test that `$obj1` and `$obj2` contain objects with PHP's `gettype()` function. `gettype()` accepts any variable and returns a string that should tell you what you are dealing with. In a loosely typed language like PHP, `gettype()` is useful when checking arguments sent to functions. In the previous code fragment, `gettype()` returns the string `"object"`, which is then written to the browser.

So, you have confirmed that you have created two objects. Of course they're not very useful yet, but they help to make an important point. You can think of a class as a mold with which you can press as many objects as you want. Let's add some more features to the class to make your objects a little more interesting.

Object Properties

Objects have access to special variables called properties. These can be declared anywhere within the body of your class, but for the sake of clarity should be defined at the top. A property can be a value, an array, or even another object:

```
class first_class
    {
    var $name = "harry";
    }
```

Notice that we declared our variable with the `var` keyword. This is essential in the context of a class, and you will be rewarded with a parse error if you forget it. Now any `first_class` object that is created will contain a property called name with the value of `"harry"`. You can access this property from outside the object and even change it:

```
class first_class
    {
     var $name = "harry";
    }

$obj1 = new first_class();
$obj2 = new first_class();
```

```
$obj1->name = "bob";
print "$obj1->name<BR>";
print "$obj2->name<BR>";
```

The `->` operator allows you to access or change the properties of an object. Although `$obj1` and `$obj2` were born with the name of `"harry"`, we have helped `$obj2` to change its mind by assigning the string `"bob"` to its `name` property, before using the `->` operator once again to print each object's `name` property to the screen.

> Object-oriented languages, such as Java, demand that the programmer set a level of privacy for all properties and methods. This means that access can be limited to only those features needed to use the object effectively, and properties meant only for internal use can be safely tucked away. PHP has no such protection. You can access all the fields of an object, which can cause problems if a property isn't meant to be changed.

You can use objects to store information, but that makes them little more interesting than associative arrays. In the next section, you will look at object methods, and your objects can get a little more active.

Object Methods

A method is a function defined within a class. Every object instantiated from the class will have the method's functionality. Listing 8.1 adds a method to the `first_class` class.

LISTING 8.1 A Class with a Method

```
 1: <html>
 2: <head>
 3: <title>Listing 8.1</title>
 4: <body>
 5: <?php
 6: class first_class
 7:     {
 8:     var $name;
 9:     function sayHello()
10:         {
11:         print "hello";
12:         }
13:     }
14:
15: $obj1 = new first_class();
```

LISTING 8.1 continued

```
16: $obj1->sayHello();
17: // outputs "hello"
18: ?>
19: </body>
20: </html>
```

As you can see, a method looks and behaves much like a normal function. A method is always defined within a class, however. You can call an object method using the `->` operator. Importantly, methods have access to the class's member variables. You've already seen how to access a property from outside an object, but how does an object refer to itself? Find out in Listing 8.2.

LISTING 8.2 Accessing a Property from Within a Method

```
 1: <html>
 2: <head>
 3: <title>Listing 8.2</title>
 4: <body>
 5: <?php
 6: class first_class
 7:     {
 8:     var $name="harry";
 9:     function sayHello()
10:         {
11:         print "hello my name is $this->name<BR>";
12:         }
13:     }
14:
15: $obj1 = new first_class();
16: $obj1->sayHello();
17: // outputs "hello my name is harry"
18: ?>
19: </body>
20: </html>
```

A class uses the special variable `$this` to refer to the currently instantiated object. You can think of it as a personal pronoun. Although you refer to an object by the handle you have assigned it to (`$obj1`, for example), an object must refer to itself by means of the `$this` variable. Combining the `$this` variable and the `->` operator, you can access any property or method in a class from within the class itself.

Imagine that you want to assign a different value to the name property to every object of type first_class you create. You could do this by manually resetting the name property as you did earlier, or you could create a method to do it for you, as shown in Listing 8.3.

LISTING 8.3 Changing the Value of a Property from Within a Method

```
1: <html>
2: <head>
3: <title>Listing 8.3</title>
4: </head>
5: <body>
6: <?php
7: class first_class
8:      {
9:      var $name="harry";
10:     function setName( $n )
11:         {
12:         $this->name = $n;
13:         }
14:     function sayHello()
15:         {
16:         print "hello my name is $this->name<BR>";
17:         }
18:     }
19:
20:
21: $obj1 = new first_class();
22: $obj1->setName("william");
23: $obj1->sayHello();
24: // outputs "hello my name is william"
25: ?>
26: </body>
27: </html>
```

The name property of the object begins as "harry", but after the object's setName() method is called, it is changed to "william". Notice how the object is capable of adjusting its own property. Notice also that you can pass arguments to the method in exactly the same way as you would to a function.

We're still missing a trick here, however. If you create a method with exactly the same name as the first_class class, it will automatically be called when a new object is instantiated. In this way, you can give your objects arguments to process at the moment you instantiate them. Objects can run code to initialize themselves based on these arguments or other factors. These special methods are called constructors. Listing 8.4 adds a constructor to the first_class class.

LISTING 8.4 A Class with a Constructor

```
 1: <html>
 2: <head>
 3: <title>Listing 8.4</title>
 4: </head>
 5: <body>
 6: <?php
 7: class first_class
 8:     {
 9:     var $name;
10:     function first_class( $n="anon" )
11:         {
12:         $this->name = $n;
13:         }
14:     function sayHello()
15:         {
16:         print "hello my name is $this->name<BR>";
17:         }
18:     }
19: $obj1 = new first_class("bob");
20: $obj2 = new first_class("harry");
21: $obj1->sayHello();
22: // outputs "hello my name is bob"
23: $obj2->sayHello();
24: // outputs "hello my name is harry"
25: ?>
26: </body>
27: </html>
```

The `first_class()` constructor method is automatically called when we instantiate a `first_class` object. We set up a default so that the string `"anon"` is assigned to the parameter if we don't include an argument when we create our object.

An Example

Let's bring these techniques together to create an example that might be a little more useful. We will create a class that can maintain a table of fields, organized in named columns. This data should be built up on a row-by-row basis, and crude a method should be included so that the data can be written to the browser. Neatly formatting the data is not necessary at this stage.

Defining the Class's Properties

First, we must decide what properties we need to store the data in. We will keep the column names in an array and the rows in a multidimensional array. We'll also store an integer so that we can easily keep track of the number of columns we're dealing with:

```
class Table
    {
    var $table_array = array();
    var $headers = array();
    var $cols;
    }
```

Creating a Constructor

We need to get the names of the columns that we'll be working with straight away. We can do this in the constructor by asking for an array of strings as a parameter. Armed with this information, we can calculate the number of columns and assign the result to the `cols` property:

```
function Table( $headers )
    {
    $this->headers = $headers;
    $this->cols = count ( $headers );
    }
```

Assuming that the correct information is provided when the new `Table` object is created, we will know right away the number of columns we'll be storing and the name of each column. Because this information has been stored in properties, it will be available to all the object's methods.

The `addRow()` Method

The `Table` object accepts each row of data in the form of an array, assuming, of course, that this information is provided in the same order as that of the column names:

```
function addRow( $row )
    {
    if ( count ($row) != $this->cols )
        return false;
    array_push($this->table_array, $row);
    return true;
    }
```

The `addRow()` method expects an array, which is stored in a parameter variable called `$row`. We have stored the number of columns that the object expects to handle in the `$cols` property. We can check that the `$row` array parameter contains the right number of elements using the `count()` function. If it doesn't, a `boolean bfalse` is returned.

We then use PHP4's `array_push()` function to add the row array to the `table_array` property. `array_push()` accepts two arguments—an array to add to and the value to push onto it. If the second argument is itself an array, it will be added as a single element of the first array, creating a multidimensional array. In this way, we can build up an array of arrays.

The `addRowAssocArray()` Method

The `addRow()` method is fine as long as the elements of the array passed to it are ordered correctly. The `addRowAssocArray()` method allows for a little more flexibility. It expects an associative array. The keys for each value should match one of the header names we are storing in our headers property, or they'll be ignored:

```
function addRowAssocArray( $row_assoc )
    {
    $row = array();
    foreach ( $this->headers as $header )
        {
        if ( ! isset( $row_assoc[$header] ))
            $row_assoc[$header] =  "";
        $row[] = $row_assoc[$header];
        }
    array_push($this->table_array, $row);
    return true;
    }
```

The associative array passed to `addRowAssocArray()` is stored in the parameter variable `$row_assoc`. We create an empty array called `$row` to store the values that we will eventually add to the `table_array` property. We loop through the headers array to check that a value corresponding to each string exists in the `$row_assoc` array. To do this, we use the PHP4 function `isset()`, which expects any variable as its argument. It returns `true` if the variable passed to it has been set and `false` otherwise. We pass `isset()` the element in the `$row_assoc` array whose key is the current value in the headers property we are looping through. If no element indexed by that string exists in `$row_assoc`, we go ahead and create one with the value of an empty string. We can then continue to build up our `$row` array, adding to it the element in `$row_assoc` indexed by the current string in the headers array. By the time we have finished looping through the `headers` array property, `$row` contains an ordered copy of the values passed to us in `$row_assoc`, with empty strings in place of any omissions.

We now have two simple methods to allow the addition of rows of data to a `Table` object's `table_array` property. All we need now is a way of outputting the data.

The `output()` Method

The `output()` method writes both the headers and the `table_array` array properties to the browser. This method is provided mainly for the purpose of debugging. You'll see a more satisfactory solution later in the hour.

```
function output()
    {
    print "<pre>";
    foreach ( $this->headers as $header )
        print "<B>$header</B>  ";
    print "\n";
    foreach ( $this->table_array as $y )
        {
        foreach ( $y as $xcell )
            print "$xcell  ";
        print "\n";
        }
    print "</pre>";
    }
```

This code fragment should be fairly self-explanatory. We loop first through the headers array property, writing each element to the screen. We then do the same for the `table_array` property. Because the `table_array` property is a two-dimensional array, each of its elements is itself an array that must be looped through within the main loop.

Bringing It All Together

Listing 8.5 includes the entire `Table` class, as well the code that instantiates a `Table` object and calls each of its methods.

LISTING 8.5 The `Table` Class

```
 1: <html>
 2: <head>
 3: <title>Listing 8.5</title>
 4: </head>
 5: <body>
 6: <?php
 7: class Table
 8:     {
 9:     var $table_array = array();
10:     var $headers = array();
11:     var $cols;
```

LISTING 8.5 continued

```
12:     function Table( $headers )
13:         {
14:         $this->headers = $headers;
15:         $this->cols = count ( $headers );
16:         }
17:
18:     function addRow( $row )
19:         {
20:         if ( count ($row) != $this->cols )
21:             return false;
22:         array_push($this->table_array, $row);
23:         return true;
24:         }
25:
26: function addRowAssocArray( $row_assoc )
27:         {
28:         $row = array();
29:         foreach ( $this->headers as $header )
30:             {
31:             if ( ! isset( $row_assoc[$header] ))
32:                 $row_assoc[$header] = "";
33:             $row[] = $row_assoc[$header];
34:             }
35:         array_push($this->table_array, $row);
36:         return true;
37:         }
38:
39:     function output()
40:         {
41:         print "<pre>";
42:         foreach ( $this->headers as $header )
43:             print "<B>$header</B>  ";
44:         print "\n";
45:         foreach ( $this->table_array as $y )
46:             {
47:             foreach ( $y as $xcell )
48:                 print "$xcell  ";
49:             print "\n";
50:             }
51:         print "</pre>";
52:         }
53:     }
54:
55: $test = new table( array("a","b","c") );
56: $test->addRow( array(1,2,3) );
57: $test->addRow( array(4,5,6) );
58: $test->addRowAssocArray( array ( b=>0, a=>6, c=>3 ) );
59: $test->output();
60: ?>
```

LISTING 8.5 continued

```
61: </body>
62: </html>
```

You can see the output of Listing 8.5 in Figure 8.1.

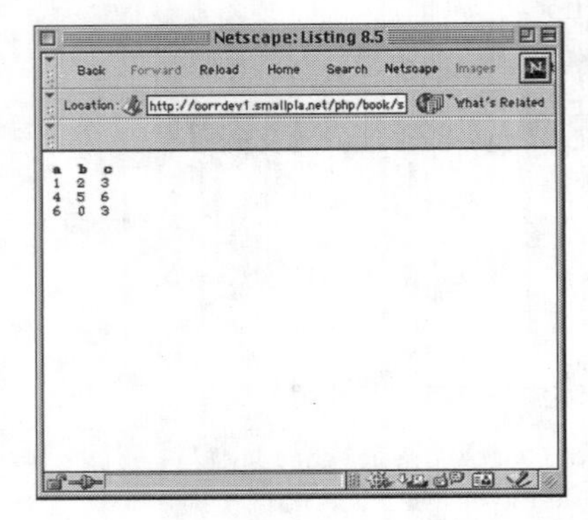

FIGURE 8.1
The `Table` object in action.

The output looks neat as long as the individual strings are the same length. This will change if we vary the length of any of the elements.

What's Missing?

Although this class will do a job effectively for us, with more time and space, we might have added some features and safeguards.

Because PHP is loosely typed, it is our responsibility to make sure that parameters passed to our methods are the type we are expecting. For this purpose, we can use the data functions covered in Hour 16, "Working with Data." We might also want to make the `Table` object a little more flexible, adding methods to sort the rows according to the values in any column before we output, for example.

Why a Class?

So, what's better about using an object to achieve this task than simply manipulating arrays ourselves as and when we need to? It certainly isn't efficiency. We've added overheads to the process of storing and retrieving information.

First, this code is reusable. It has a clear purpose—to represent data in a certain way, and we can now slot it into any project that needs data stored and output in this way.

Second, a `Table` object is active. We can ask it to output its data without bothering to write code to loop through its `table_array` property.

Third, we've built an interface to the object's functionality. If we decide later to optimize the code in the class, we can do so without disturbing the rest of the project, as long as the same methods remain, expecting the same arguments and returning the same data types.

Finally, we can build classes that inherit, extend, and override its functionality. This makes object-oriented code truly cool.

Inheritance

To create a class that inherits functionality from a parent class, we need to alter our class declaration slightly. Listing 8.6 returns to our simple example.

LISTING 8.6 Creating a Class That Inherits from Another

```
 1: <html>
 2: <head>
 3: <title>Listing 8.6</title>
 4: </head>
 5: <body>
 6: <?php
 7: class first_class
 8:     {
 9:     var $name = "harry";
10:     function first_class( $n )
11:         {
12:         $this->name = $n;
13:         }
14:     function sayHello()
15:         {
16:         print "Hello my name is $this->name<br>";
17:         }
18:     }
19:
20: class second_class extends first_class
21:     {
22:
23:     }
24:
25: $test = new second_class("son of harry");
26: $test->sayHello();
```

LISTING 8.6 continued

```
27: // outputs "Hello my name is son of harry"
28: ?>
29: </body>
30: </html>
```

In addition to the simple `first_class` class, we have created an even more basic `second_class` class. Notice the `extends` clause in the class declaration. This means that a `second_class` object inherits all the functionality laid down in the `first_class` class. Any `second_class` object will have a `sayHello()` method and a `name` property just as any `first_class` object would.

If that's not enough, there's even more magic to be found in Listing 8.6. Notice that we didn't define a constructor method for the `second_class` class. So, how was the name property changed from the default, `"harry"` to the value passed to the `second_class` class, `"son of harry"`? Because we didn't provide a constructor, the `first_class` class's constructor was automatically called.

If a class extending another doesn't contain a constructor method, the parent class's constructor method will be called automatically when a child object is created. This feature is new in PHP4.

Overriding the Method of a Parent Class

The `second_class` class currently creates objects that behave in exactly the same way as `first_class` objects. In object-oriented code, child classes can override the methods of their parents, allowing objects instantiated from them to behave differently, while otherwise retaining much of the same functionality. Listing 8.7 gives the `second_class` class its own `sayHello()` method.

LISTING 8.7 The Method of a Child Class Overriding That of Its Parent

```
1: <html>
2: <head>
3: <title>Listing 8.7</title>
4: </head>
5: <body>
6: <?php
7: class first_class
```

LISTING 8.7 continued

```
 8:      {
 9:      var $name = "harry";
10:      function first_class( $n )
11:          {
12:          $this->name = $n;
13:          }
14:      function sayHello()
15:          {
16:          print "Hello my name is $this->name<br>";
17:          }
18:      }
19:
20: class second_class extends first_class
21:      {
22:      function sayHello()
23:          {
24:          print "I'm not going to tell you my name<br>";
25:          }
26:      }
27:
28: $test = new second_class("son of harry");
29: $test->sayHello();
30: // outputs "I'm not going to tell you my name"
31: ?>
32: </body>
33: </html>
```

The `sayHello()` method in the `second_class` class is called in preference to that in the parent class.

Calling an Overridden Method

Occasionally, you will want the functionality of a parent class's method, as well as the benefit of your own additions. Object-oriented programming allows you to have your cake and eat it too. In Listing 8.8, the `second_class`'s `sayHello()` method calls the method in the `first_class` class that it has overridden.

LISTING 8.8 Calling an Overridden Method

```
1: <html>
2: <head>
3: <title>Listing 8.8</title>
4: </head>
5: <body>
6: <?php
7: class first_class
```

LISTING 8.8 continued

```
 8:     {
 9:     var $name = "harry";
10:     function first_class( $n )
11:         {
12:         $this->name = $n;
13:         }
14:     function sayHello()
15:         {
16:         print "Hello my name is $this->name<br>";
17:         }
18:     }
19:
20: class second_class extends first_class
21:     {
22:     function sayHello()
23:         {
24:         print "I'm not going to tell you my name -- ";
25:         first_class::sayHello();
26:         }
27:     }
28:
29: $test = new second_class("son of harry");
30: $test->sayHello();
31: // outputs "I'm not going to tell you my name -- Hello my name is son of harry"
32: ?>
33: </body>
34: </html>
```

By using the syntax

```
parentclassname::methodname()
```

we can call any method that we have overridden. This syntax is new to PHP4—the same code will result in a parse error with PHP3.

Inheritance: An Example

You've seen how one class can inherit, override, and extend the functionality of another. Now we can use some of these techniques to create a class that inherits from the `Table` class created in Listing 8.5. The new class will be called `HTMLTable` and will be designed to overcome the deficiencies of `Table`'s `output()` method.

8

Defining HTMLTable's Properties

HTMLTable will format the data that it stores courtesy of Table's functionality using a standard HTML table. For this example, we will allow an HTMLTable's user to change the CELLPADDING argument of the TABLE element and the BGCOLOR argument of the TD element. A real-world example should allow for many more changes than this.

```
class HTMLTable extends Table
    {
    var $bgcolor;
    var $cellpadding = "2";
    }
```

We have defined a new class and established that it will inherit from Table by using the extends clause. We create two properties, bgcolor and cellpadding, giving cellpadding a default value of 2.

Creating the Constructor

You have already seen that a parent class's constructor is called automatically if you don't define a constructor for a child class. In this case, however, we want to do more work with our constructor than has already been written for the Table class:

```
function HTMLTable( $headers, $bg="#ffffff" )
    {
    Table::Table($headers);
    $this->bgcolor=$bg;
    }
```

The HTMLTable constructor accepts an array of column names and a string. The string becomes our bgcolor property, and we give it a default value, making it an optional argument. We call the Table class's constructor, passing the $header array to it. Laziness is a virtue in programming, so we let the Table class's constructor do its thing and worry no more about it. We initialize the HTMLObject's bgcolor property.

If a child class is given a constructor method, the parent's constructor is no longer called implicitly. The child class's constructor must explicitly call that of its parent.

The `setCellpadding()` Method

A child class can of course create its own entirely new methods. `setCellpadding()` allows a user to change the `cellpadding` property from the default. Of course, it would be perfectly possible to set the `cellpadding` property directly from outside the object, but this is not good practice on the whole. As a rule of thumb, it is best to create methods that will change properties on behalf of an object's user. In a more complex version of this class, the `setCellpadding()` method might need to change other properties to reflect the change made to the `cellpadding` property. Unfortunately, there is no neat way of enforcing privacy in PHP4.

```
function setCellpadding( $padding )
    {
    $this->cellpadding = $padding;
    }
```

The `Output()` Method

The `Output()` method completely overrides the equivalent method in the `Table` class. It outputs data according to exactly the same logic as its parent, adding HTML table formatting:

```
function output()
    {
    print "<table cellpadding=\"$this->cellpadding\" border=1>";
    foreach ( $this->headers as $header )
        print "<td bgcolor=\"$this->bgcolor\"><b>$header</b></td>";
    foreach ( $this->table_array as $row=>$cells )
        {
        print "<tr>";
        foreach ( $cells as $cell )
            print "<td bgcolor=\"$this->bgcolor\">$cell</td>";
        print "</tr>";
        }
    print "</table>";
    }
```

The `output()` method should be fairly clear if you understood the `Table` class's version. We loop through both the `header` and `table_array` arrays, outputting each to the browser. Crucially, though, we format the data into a table, using the `cellpadding` and `bgcolor` properties to change the spacing and color of the table that the end user sees.

The `Table` and `HTMLTable` Classes in Their Entirety

Listing 8.9 brings the entire `Table` and `HTMLTable` examples together. We also instantiate an `HTMLTable` object, change its `cellpadding` property, add some data, and call its ouptut() method. In a real-world example, we would probably get our row data directly from a database.

LISTING 8.9 The Table and HTMLTable Classes

```
 1: <html>
 2: <head>
 3: <title>testing objects</title>
 4: </head>
 5: <body>
 6: <?php
 7: class Table
 8:     {
 9:     var $table_array = array();
10:     var $headers = array();
11:     var $cols;
12:     function Table( $headers )
13:         {
14:         $this->headers = $headers;
15:         $this->cols = count ( $headers );
16:         }
17:
18:     function addRow( $row )
19:         {
20:         if ( count ($row) != $this->cols )
21:             return false;
22:         array_push($this->table_array, $row);
23:         return true;
24:         }
25:
26:     function addRowAssocArray( $row_assoc )
27:         {
28:         if ( count ($row_assoc) != $this->cols )
29:             return false;
30:         $row = array();
31:         foreach ( $this->headers as $header )
32:             {
33:             if ( ! isset( $row_assoc[$header] ))
34:                 $row_assoc[$header] = " ";
35:             $row[] = $row_assoc[$header];
36:             }
37:         array_push($this->table_array, $row);
38:         }
39:
40:     function output()
41:         {
42:         print "<pre>";
43:         foreach ( $this->headers as $header )
44:             print "<B>$header</B>  ";
```

LISTING 8.9 continued

```
45:         print "\n";
46:         foreach ( $this->table_array as $y )
47:             {
48:             foreach ( $y as $xcell )
49:                 print "$xcell  ";
50:             print "\n";
51:             }
52:         print "</pre>";
53:         }
54:     }
55:
56: class HTMLTable extends Table
57:     {
58:     var $bgcolor;
59:     var $cellpadding = "2";
60:     function HTMLTable( $headers, $bg="#ffffff" )
61:         {
62:         Table::Table($headers);
63:         $this->bgcolor=$bg;
64:         }
65:     function setCellpadding( $padding )
66:         {
67:         $this->cellpadding = $padding;
68:         }
69:     function output()
70:         {
71:         print "<table cellpadding=\"$this->cellpadding\" border=1>";
72:         foreach ( $this->headers as $header )
73:             print "<td bgcolor=\"$this->bgcolor\"><b>$header</b></td>";
74:         foreach ( $this->table_array as $row=>$cells )
75:             {
76:             print "<tr>";
77:             foreach ( $cells as $cell )
78:                 print "<td bgcolor=\"$this->bgcolor\">$cell</td>";
79:             print "</tr>";
80:             }
81:         print "</table>";
82:         }
83:     }
84: $test = new HTMLTable( array("a","b","c"), "#00FF00");
85: $test->setCellpadding( 7 );
86: $test->addRow( array(1,2,3));
87: $test->addRow( array(4,5,6));
88: $test->addRowAssocArray( array ( b=>0, a=>6, c=>3 ));
89: $test->output();
90: ?>
91: </body>
92: </html>
```

You can see the output from Listing 8.9 in Figure 8.2.

FIGURE 8.2

The `HTMLTable` *object in action.*

Why Use Inheritance?

So, why did we split `Table` from `HTMLTable`? Surely we could have saved ourselves time and space by building HTML table capabilities into the `Table` class? The answer lies in flexibility.

Imagine that a client gave you the brief to create a class that can maintain a table of fields, organized in named columns. If you had built a monolithic class that collected and stored the data, customized HTML, and output the result to the browser, all would seem to be well.

If the same client came back to you and asked whether the code could be adapted additionally to write neatly formatted data to a text file, you could probably add some more methods and properties to make it do this too.

A week or so later, the client realizes that she would like the code to be able to send data out as an email, and while you're at it, the company intranet uses a subset of XML; could this be accommodated too? At this stage, including all the functionality in a single class is beginning to look a little unwieldy, and you would already be considering a complete rewrite of the code.

Let's try this scenario out with our `Table` and `HTMLTable` examples. We have already substantially separated formatting the data from acquiring and preparing it. When our client asks that the code should be capable of outputting to a file, we only need to create a new class that inherits from `Table`. Let's call it `FileTable`. We need make no changes at all to our existing code. The same would be true for `MailTable` and `XMLTable`. Figure 8.3 illustrates the relationship between these classes.

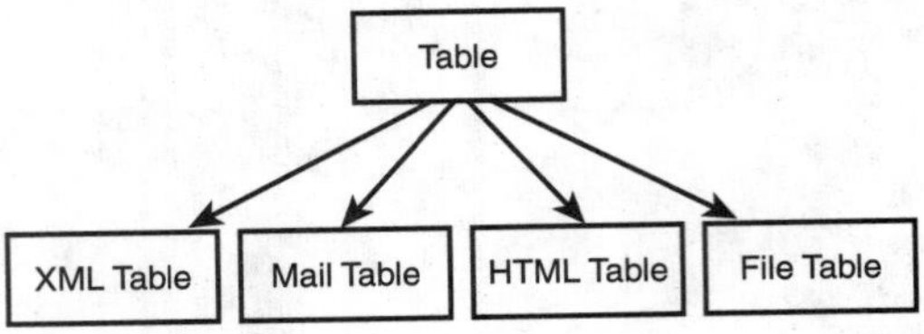

FIGURE 8.3
The relationship between the `Table` *class and multiple child classes.*

What's more, we know that *any* object that inherits from `Table` will have an `output()` method, so we can group a bunch of them into an array. When we're ready, we can loop through the lot, calling `output()` without worrying about the mechanics. From a single array of `Table`-derived objects, we can write emails, HTML, XML, or plain text, simply by repeatedly calling `output()`!

Summary

It is not possible to introduce you to all the aspects of object-oriented programming in one short hour, but I hope I have introduced you to some of the possibilities.

The extent to which you use objects and classes in your projects is a matter of choice. It is likely that heavily object-oriented projects will be somewhat more resource-intensive at runtime than more traditional code. However, effective deployment of object-oriented techniques can significantly improve the flexibility and organization of your code.

Throughout this hour, you learned how to create classes and instantiate objects from them. You learned how to create and access properties and methods. Finally, you learned how to build new classes that inherit and override the features of other classes.

Q&A

Q This hour introduced some unfamiliar concepts. Do I really need to understand object-oriented programming to become a good PHP programmer?

A The short answer is no. Most PHP scripts use little or no object-oriented code at all. The object-oriented approach won't help you do things that you couldn't otherwise achieve. The benefits of object-oriented programming lie in the organization of your scripts, their reusability, and their extensibility.

Even if you decide not to produce object-oriented code, however, you may need to decipher third-party programs that contain classes. This hour should help you understand such code.

Q I'm confused by the special variable `$this`.

A Within a class, you sometimes need to call the class's methods or access its properties. By combining the `$this` variable and the `->` operator, you can do both. The `$this` variable is the handle a class is automatically given to refer to itself and to its components.

Workshop

The Workshop provides quiz questions to help you solidify your understanding of the material covered. Try to understand the quiz answers before continuing to the next hour's lesson. Quiz answers are provided in Appendix A.

Quiz

1. How would you declare a class called `emptyClass()` that has no methods or properties?
2. Given a class called `emptyClass()`, how would you create an object that is an instance of it?
3. How can you declare a property within a class?
4. How would you choose a name for a constructor method?
5. How would you create a constructor method in a class?
6. How would you create a regular method within a class?
7. How can you access and set properties or methods from within a class?
8. How would you access an object's properties and methods from outside the object's class?
9. What should you add to a class definition if you want to make it inherit functionality from another class?

Activities

1. Create a class called `baseCalc()` that stores two numbers as properties. Give it a `calculate()` method that prints the numbers to the browser.

2. Create a class called `addCalc()` that inherits its functionality from `baseCalc()`. Override the `calculate()` method so that the sum of the properties is printed to the browser.
3. Repeat activity 2, for a class called `minusCalc()`. Give `minusCalc()` a calculate method that subtracts the first property from the second, outputting the result to the browser.

PART III

Working with PHP

Hour

HOUR 9

Working with Forms

Until now, all examples in this book have been missing a crucial dimension. You can set variables and arrays, create and call functions, and work with objects. All this is meaningless if users can't reach into a language's environment to offer it information. In this hour, you will look at strategies for acquiring and working with user input.

On the World Wide Web, HTML forms are the principal means by which substantial amounts of information can pass from the user to the server. PHP is designed to acquire and work with information submitted via HTML forms.

In this hour, you will learn

- How to get and use environment variables
- How to access information from form fields
- How to work with form elements that allow multiple selections
- How to create a single document that contains both an HTML form and the PHP code that handles its submission
- How to save state with hidden fields

- How to redirect the user to a new page
- How to build HTML forms that upload files and how to write the PHP code to handle them

Global and Environment Variables

Before you actually build a form and use it to acquire data, you need to make a small detour and look again at global variables. You first met these in Hour 6, "Functions." A global variable is any variable declared at the "top level" of a script—that is, declared outside a function. All functions are made available in a built-in associative array called `$GLOBALS`. This is useful in Listing 9.1 because we can take a peek at all our script's global variables with a single loop.

LISTING 9.1 Looping Through the `$GLOBALS` Array

```
 1: <html>
 2: <head>
 3: <title>Listing 9.1 Looping through the $GLOBALS array</title>
 4: </head>
 5: <body>
 6: <?php
 7: $user1 = "Bob";
 8: $user2 = "Harry";
 9: $user3 = "Mary";
10: foreach ( $GLOBALS as $key=>$value )
11:     {
12:     print "\$GLOBALS[\"$key\"] == $value<br>";
13:     }
14: ?>
15: </body>
16: </html>
```

We declare three variables and then loop through the built-in `$GLOBALS` associative array, writing both array keys and values to the browser. In the output, we were able to locate the variables we defined, but we saw an awful lot more besides these. PHP automatically defines global variables that describe both the server and client environments. These are known, therefore, as environment variables. According to your system, server, and configuration, the availability of these variables will vary, but they can be immensely useful. Table 9.1 lays out some common environment variables. These can be accessed as part of the `$GLOBALS` array, or directly.

9

TABLE 9.1 Environment Variables

Variable	*Contains*	*Example*
`$HTTP_USER_AGENT`	The name and version of the client	Mozilla/4.6 (X11;I; Linux2.2.6-15apmac ppc)
`$REMOTE_ADDR`	The IP address of the client	158.152.55.35
`$REQUEST_METHOD`	Whether the request was `GET` or `POST`	`POST`
`$QUERY_STRING`	For `GET` requests, the encoded data send appended to the URL	`name=matt&address=unknown`
`$REQUEST_URI`	The full address of the request including query string	`/matt/php-book/forms/eg9.14.html?name=matt`
`$HTTP_REFERER`	The address of the page from which the request was made	`http://www.test.com/a_page.html`

In addition to environment variables, PHP makes some other global variables available to you. The variable `$GLOBALS["PHP_SELF"]`, for example, gives you the path to the script currently running. On my system this was as follows:

```
/matt/php-book/forms/eg9.1.php
```

This variable can also be directly accessed as the global variable `$PHP_SELF`. This will be useful in many of the examples in this hour. We will often include the HTML forms we use in the same page as the PHP code that analyzes the content they submit. We can use `$PHP_SELF` as the string assigned to the HTML `FORM` element's `ACTION` argument, saving us the trouble of hard-coding the name of the page.

PHP's `$GLOBALS` array will become useful in other ways as well.

A Script to Acquire User Input

For now, we'll keep our HTML separate from our PHP code. Listing 9.2 builds a simple HTML form.

LISTING 9.2 A Simple HTML Form

```
 1: <html>
 2: <head>
 3: <title>Listing 9.2 A simple HTML form</title>
 4: </head>
 5: <body>
 6: <form action="eg9.3.php" method="GET">
 7: <input type="text" name="user">
 8: <br>
 9: <textarea name="address" rows="5" cols="40">
10: </textarea>
11: <br>
12: <input type="submit" value="hit it!">
13: </form>
14: </body>
15: </html>
```

We define a form that contains a text field with the name `"user"`, a text area with the name `"address"`, and a submit button. It is beyond the remit of this book to cover HTML in detail. If you find the HTML in these examples hard going, take a look at *Sams Teach Yourself HTML in 24 Hours* or one of the numerous online HTML tutorials. The `FORM` element's `ACTION` argument points to a file called `eg9.3.php`, which processes the form information. Because we haven't added anything more than a filename to the `ACTION` argument, the file `eg9.3.php` should be in the same directory on the server as the document that contains our HTML.

Listing 9.3 creates the code that receives our users' input.

LISTING 9.3 Reading Input from the Form in Listing 9.2

```
 1: <html>
 2: <head>
 3: <title>Listing 9.3 Reading input from the form in Listing 9.2</title>
 4: </head>
 5: <body>
 6: <?php
 7: print "Welcome <b>$user</b><P>\n\n";
 8: print "Your address is:<P>\n\n<b>$address</b>";
 9: ?>
10: </body>
11: </html>
```

This is the first script in this book that is not designed to be called by hitting a link or typing directly into the browser's location field. We include the code from Listing 9.3 in a file called `eg9.3.php`. This file is called when a user submits the form defined in Listing 9.2.

In the code, we have accessed two variables, `$user` and `$address`. It should come as no surprise that these variables contain the values that the user added to the text field named `"user"` and the text area named `"address"`. Forms in PHP4 really are as simple as that. Any information submitted by a user will be available to you in global variables that will have the same names as those of the form elements on an HTML page.

9

Accessing Input from Multiple SELECT Elements

The examples so far enable us to gather information from HTML elements that submit a single value per element name. This leaves us with a problem when working with SELECT elements. These elements make it possible for the user to choose multiple items. If we name the SELECT element with plain name

```
<select name="products" multiple>
```

the script that receives this data will only have access to a single value corresponding to this name. We can change this behavior by renaming any elements of this kind so that its name ends with an empty set of square brackets. We do this in Listing 9.4.

Listing 9.4 An HTML Form Including a SELECT Element

```
 1: <html>
 2: <head>
 3: <title>Listing 9.4 An HTML form including a SELECT element</title>
 4: </head>
 5: <body>
 6: <form action="eg9.5.php" method="POST">
 7: <input type="text" name="user">
 8: <br>
 9: <textarea name="address" rows="5" cols="40">
10: </textarea>
11: <br>
12: <select name="products[]" multiple>
13: <option>Sonic Screwdriver
14: <option>Tricorder
15: <option>ORAC AI
16: <option>HAL 2000
17: </select>
18: <br>
19: <input type="submit" value="hit it!">
20: </form>
21: </body>
22: </html>
```

In the script that processes the form input, we now find that input from the `"products[]"` element will be available in an array called `$products`. We demonstrate this in Listing 9.5.

LISTING 9.5 Reading Input from the Form in Listing 9.4

```
 1: <html>
 2: <head>
 3: <title>Listing 9.5 Reading input from the form in Listing 9.4</title>
 4: </head>
 5: <body>
 6: <?php
 7: print "Welcome <b>$user</b><p>\n\n";
 8: print "Your address is:<p>\n\n<b>$address</b><p>\n\n";
 9: print "Your product choices are:<p>\n\n";
10: print "<ul>\n\n";
11: foreach ( $products as $value )
12:     {
13:     print "<li>$value<br>\n";
14:     }
15: print "</ul>";
16: ?>
17: </body>
18: </html>
```

The `SELECT` element is not the only one that allows for multiple values. By giving a number of check boxes the same name, you can allow a user to choose many values within a single field name. As long as the name you choose ends with empty square brackets, PHP compiles the user input for this field into an array. We can replace the `SELECT` element in Listing 9.4 with a series of check boxes to achieve exactly the same effect:

```
<input type="checkbox" name="products[]" value="Sonic Screwdriver">
➥Sonic Screwdriver<br>
<input type="checkbox" name="products[]" value="Tricorder">Tricorder<br>
<input type="checkbox" name="products[]" value="ORAC AI">ORAC AI<br>
<input type="checkbox" name="products[]" value="HAL 2000">HAL 2000<br>
```

Accessing All the Fields from a Form in an Associative Array

The techniques you have looked at so far work well, as long as your script knows in advance what fields to expect. You may often want to write code that can adapt to changes in a form or even service more than one form, without worrying itself about the names of specific form fields. The global variables that PHP4 makes available provide the solution to this problem. According to whether or not a submitting form used the `GET` or `POST` method, you will have access to one or both of $HTTP_GET_VARS or $HTTP_POST_VARS. These are associative arrays that contain the name/value pairs submitted. Listing 9.6 takes advantage of this to list all the fields submitted from a form via a GET request.

LISTING 9.6 Reading Input from Any Form Using the $HTTP_GET_VARS Array

```
 1: <html>
 2: <head>
 3: <title>Listing 9.6 Reading input from any form using the $HTTP_GET_VARS
➥array</title>
 4: </head>
 5: <body>
 6: <?php
 7: foreach ( $HTTP_GET_VARS as $key=>$value )
 8:     {
 9:     print "$key == $value<BR>\n";
10:     }
11: ?>
12: </body>
13: </html>
```

This code lists the names and values of all parameters passed to it via a GET transaction. Of course, it's not yet smart enough to deal with parameters that have been set up to resolve to arrays. If we were to amend the HTML form in Listing 9.4 that includes a multiple SELECT element to point to the script in Listing 9.6, we would typically get the following output when the form was submitted:

```
user == Matt Zandstra
address == London, England
products == Array
```

The products array exists in the $HTTP_GET_VARS[products] array item, but we haven't yet written code to take account of this eventuality. Listing 9.7 tests the data type of each of the elements in $HTTP_GET_VARS and amends the output accordingly.

LISTING 9.7 Reading Input from Any Form Using the $HTTP_GET_VARS array

```
 1: <html>
 2: <head>
 3: <title>Listing 9.7 Reading input from any form using the $HTTP_GET_VARS
➥array</title>
 4: </head>
 5: <body>
 6: <?php
 7: foreach ( $HTTP_GET_VARS as $key=>$value )
 8:     {
```

LISTING 9.7 continued

```
 9:     if ( gettype( $value ) == "array" )
10:         {
11:         print "$key == <br>\n";
12:         foreach ( $value as $two_dim_value )
13:             print ".........$two_dim_value<br>";
14:         }
15:     else
16:         {
17:         print "$key == $value<br>\n";
18:         }
19:     }
20: ?>
21: </body>
22: </html>
```

As before, we use `foreach` to loop through the `$HTTP_GET_VARS` array. We use the `gettype()` function to ascertain whether each of its values is an array. If the value is itself an array, we create a second `foreach` statement to loop through it, outputting each value to the browser.

Distinguishing Between GET and POST Transactions

To work flexibly, a script that can accept data from any source must be able to decide whether to read the `$HTTP_GET_VARS` or `$HTTP_POST_VARS` arrays. On most systems, you can discover whether you are dealing with a `GET` or `POST` transaction in the environment variable `$REQUEST_METHOD`, which should contain the string `"post"` or `"get"`. To be absolutely sure that your scripts are entirely portable, however, you can take advantage of the fact that the `$HTTP_POST_VARS` array will only be present if a `POST` request has been made.

Listing 9.8 amends our form parser script to work with the correct array every time.

LISTING 9.8 Extracting Parameters from Either a GET or POST Request

```
1: <html>
2: <head>
3: <title>Listing 9.8 Extracting parameters from
4:         either a GET or POST request</title>
5: </head>
6: <body>
7: <?php
```

LISTING 9.8 continued

```
 8: $PARAMS = ( isset( $HTTP_POST_VARS ) )
 9:   ? $HTTP_POST_VARS : $HTTP_GET_VARS;
10: foreach ( $PARAMS as $key=>$value )
11:    {
12:   if ( gettype( $value ) == "array" )
13:      {
14:      print "$key == <br>\n";
15:      foreach ( $value as $two_dim_value )
16:         print "........$two_dim_value<br>";
17:      }
18:   else
19:      {
20:       print "$key == $value<br>\n";
21:       }
22:    }
23: ?>
24: </body>
25: </html>
```

We use the ternary operator to set a variable called `$PARAMS`. Using the built-in `isset()` function, we first check whether the `$HTTP_POST_VARS` array has been set. `isset()` returns true if the variable it is passed has been defined. If the `$HTTP_POST_VARS` array has been defined, the ternary expression resolves to this; otherwise, it resolves to `$HTTP_GET_VARS`. We can now use the `$PARAMS` array throughout the rest of the script without worrying about whether it has been populated as the result of a `GET` or a `POST` request.

Combining HTML and PHP Code on a Single Page

In some circumstances, you may want to include form-parsing code on the same page as a hard-coded HTML form. Such a combination can be useful if you need to present the same form to the user more than once. You would have more flexibility if you were to write the entire page dynamically, of course, but you would miss out on one of the great strengths of PHP. The more standard HTML you can leave in your pages, the easier they will be for designers and page builders to amend without reference to you. You should avoid scattering substantial chunks of PHP code throughout your documents, however. This will make them hard to read and maintain. Where possible you should create functions that can be called from within your HTML code, and can be reused in other projects.

For the following examples, imagine that we are creating a site that teaches basic math to preschool children and have been asked to create a script that takes a number from form input and tells the user whether it is larger or smaller than a predefined integer.

Listing 9.9 creates the HTML. For this example, we need only a single text field, but even so, we'll include a little PHP.

LISTING 9.9 An HTML Form That Calls Itself

```
 1: <html>
 2: <head>
 3: <title>Listing 9.9 An HTML form that calls itself</title>
 4: </head>
 5: <body>
 6: <form action="<?php print $PHP_SELF?>" method="POST">
 7: Type your guess here: <input type="text" name="guess">
 8: </form>
 9: </body>
10: </html>
```

Whatever we name the page that contains this form, the form always calls it because we have assigned the value of `$PHP_SELF` to the `FORM` element's `ACTION` argument. Note that we have not created a submit button. Most recent browsers will submit a form consisting of a single text field when the user hits the return key, but you should be aware that some older browsers cannot do this.

The script in Listing 9.9 will not produce any output. In Listing 9.10, we begin to build up the PHP element of the page. First, we need to define the number that the user will guess. In a fully working version, we would probably randomly generate this, but for now we will keep it simple. Next, we need to decide whether the form has been submitted; otherwise, we will attempt to assess variables that have not yet been made available. We can test for submission by testing for the existence of the variable `$guess`. `$guess` will have been made available as a global variable if your script has been sent a `"guess"` parameter. If this isn't present, we can safely assume that the user has arrived at the page without submitting a form. If the value *is* present, we can go ahead and test the value it contains.

LISTING 9.10 A PHP Number Guessing Script

```
1: <?php
2: $num_to_guess = 42;
3: $message = "";
4: if ( ! isset( $guess ) )
5:     {
6:     $message = "Welcome to the guessing machine!";
```

LISTING 9.10 continued

```
 7:     }
 8: elseif    ( $guess > $num_to_guess )
 9:     {
10:     $message = "$guess is too big! Try a smaller number";
11:     }
12: elseif    ( $guess < $num_to_guess )
13:     {
14:     $message = "$guess is too small! Try a larger number";
15:     }
16: else // must be equivalent
17:     {
18:     $message = "Well done!";
19:     }
20: ?>
21: <html>
22: <head>
23: <title>Listing 9.10 A PHP number guessing script</title>
24: </head>
25: <body>
26: <h1>
27: <?php print $message ?>
28: </h1>
29: <form action="<?php print $PHP_SELF?>" method="POST">
30: Type your guess here: <input type="text" name="guess">
31: </form>
32: </body>
33: </html>
```


The bulk of this script consists of an `if` statement that determines which string to assign to the variable `$message`. If the `$guess` variable has not been defined, we assume that the user has arrived for the first time and assign a welcome string the variable. Otherwise, we test the `$guess` variable against the number we have stored in `$num_to_guess`, and assign advice to `$message` accordingly. If `$guess` is neither larger nor smaller than `$num_to_guess`, we can assume that it is equivalent and assign a congratulations message to the variable. Now all we need to do is print the `$message` variable within the body of the HTML.

There are a few more additions yet, but you can probably see how easy it would be to hand this page over to a designer. He can make it beautiful without having to disturb the programming in any way.

Using Hidden Fields to Save State

The script in Listing 9.10 has no way of knowing how many guesses a user has made. We can use a hidden field to keep track of this. A hidden field behaves exactly the same as a text field, except that the user cannot see it, unless he views the HTML source of the document that contains it. Listing 9.11 adds a hidden field to the number guessing script and some PHP to work with it.

LISTING 9.11 Saving State with a Hidden Field

```
 1: <?php
 2: $num_to_guess = 42;
 3: $message = "";
 4: $num_tries = ( isset( $num_tries ) ) ? ++$num_tries : 0;
 5: if ( ! isset( $guess ) )
 6:     {
 7:     $message = "Welcome to the guessing machine!";
 8:     }
 9: elseif   ( $guess > $num_to_guess )
10:     {
11:     $message = "$guess is too big! Try a smaller number";
12:     }
13: elseif   ( $guess < $num_to_guess )
14:     {
15:     $message = "$guess is too small! Try a larger number";
16:     }
17: else // must be equivalent
18:     {
19:     $message = "Well done!";
20:     }
21: $guess = (int) $guess;
22: ?>
23: <html>
24: <head>
25: <title>Listing 9.11 Saving state with a hidden field</title>
26: </head>
27: <body>
28: <h1>
29: <?php print $message ?>
30: </h1>
31: Guess number: <?php print $num_tries?>
32: <form action="<?php print $PHP_SELF?>" method="POST">
33: Type your guess here:
34: <input type="text" name="guess" value="<?php print $guess?>">
35: <input type="hidden" name="num_tries" value="<?php print $num_tries?>">
36: </form>
37: </body>
38: </html>
```

The hidden field is given the name `"num_tries"`. We also use PHP to write its value. While we're at it, we do the same for the `"guess"` field, so that the user can always see his last guess. This technique is useful for scripts that parse user input. If we were to reject a form submission for some reason we can at least allow our user to edit his previous query.

When you need to output the value of an expression to the browser, you can of course use print() or echo(). When you are entering PHP mode explicitly to output such a value you can also take advantage of a special extension to PHP's short opening tags. If you add an equals (=) sign to the short PHP opening tag, the value contained will be printed to the browser. So

```
<? print $test;?>
```

is equivalent to

```
<?=$test?>
```

Within the main PHP code, we use a ternary operator to increment the `$num_tries` variable. If the `$num_tries` variable is set, we add one to it and reassign this incremented value; otherwise, we initialize `$num_tries` to 0. Within the body of the HTML, we can now report to the user how many guesses he has made.

Don't entirely trust hidden fields. You don't know where their values have been! This isn't to say that you shouldn't use them, just be aware that your users are capable of viewing and amending source code should they want to cheat your scripts.

Use hidden fields for aesthetic reasons. They have no value as security features.

Redirecting the User

Our simple script still has one major drawback. The form is rewritten whether or not the user guesses correctly. The fact that the HTML is hard-coded makes it difficult to avoid writing the entire page. We can, however, redirect the user to a congratulations page, thereby sidestepping the issue altogether.

When a server script communicates with a client, it must first send some headers that provide information about the document to follow. PHP usually handles this for you automatically, but you can choose to send your own header lines with PHP's `header()` function. To call the `header()` function, you must be sure that no output has been sent to the browser. The first time that content is sent to the browser, PHP will send out headers and it will be too late for you to send your own. Any output from your document, even a line break or a space outside of your script tags will cause headers to be sent. If you intend to use the `header()` function in a script you must make certain that nothing precedes the PHP code that contains the function call. You should also check any libraries that you might be using. Listing 9.12 shows typical headers sent to the browser by PHP.

LISTING 9.12 Typical Server Headers Sent from a PHP Script

```
1: HEAD /matt/php-book/forms/eg9.1.php HTTP/1.0
2: HTTP/1.1 200 OK
3: Date: Sun, 09 Jan 2000 18:37:45 GMT
4: Server: Apache/1.3.9 (UNIX) PHP/4.0
5: Connection: close
6: Content-Type: text/html
```

You can see headers sent in response to a request by using a telnet client. Connect to a Web host at port 80 and then type

`HEAD /path/to/file.html HTTP/1.0`

followed by two returns. The headers should be displayed on your client.

By sending a `"Location"` header instead of PHP's default, you can cause the browser to be redirected to a new page:

```
header( "Location: http://www.corrosive.co.uk" );
```

Assuming that we have created a suitably upbeat page called `"congrats.html"`, we can amend our number guessing script to redirect the user if she guesses correctly, as shown in Listing 9.13.

LISTING 9.13 Using `header()` to Send Raw Headers

```
1: <?php
2: $num_to_guess = 42;
3: $message = "";
```

9

LISTING 9.13 continued

```
 4: $num_tries = ( isset( $num_tries ) ) ? ++$num_tries : 0;
 5: if ( ! isset( $guess ) )
 6:     {
 7:     $message = "Welcome to the guessing machine!";
 8:     }
 9: elseif   ( $guess > $num_to_guess )
10:     {
11:     $message = "$num is too big! Try a smaller number";
12:     }
13: elseif   ( $guess < $num_to_guess )
14:     {
15:     $message = "$num is too small! Try a larger number";
16:     }
17: else // must be equivalent
18:     {
19:     header( "Location: congrats.html" );
20:     exit;
21:     }
22: $guess = (int) $guess;
23: ?>
24: <html>
25: <head>
26: <title>Listing 9.13 Using header() to send raw headers</title>
27: </head>
28: <body>
29: <h1>
30: <?php print $message ?>
31: </h1>
32: Guess number: <?php print $num_tries?>
33: <form action="<?php print $PHP_SELF?>" method="POST">
34: Type your guess here:
35: <input type="text" name="guess" value="<?php print $guess?>">
36: <input type="hidden" name="num_tries"
37:     value="<?php print $num_tries ?>">
38: </form>
39: </body>
40: </html>
```

The `else` clause of our `if` statement now causes the browser to download `"congrats.html"`. We ensure that all output from the current page is aborted with the `exit` statement, which abruptly ends parsing and output, whether HTML or PHP.

File Upload Forms and Scripts

So far we've looked at simple form input. Browsers Netscape 2 or better and Internet Explorer 4 or better all support file uploads, and so, of course, does PHP4. In this section, you will examine the features that PHP makes available to deal with this kind of input.

First, we need to create the HTML. HTML forms that include file upload fields must include an `ENCTYPE` argument:

```
ENCTYPE="multipart/form-data"
```

PHP also requires that a hidden field be included before the file upload field. This should be called `MAX_FILE_SIZE` and should have a value representing the maximum size in bytes of the file that you are willing to accept. This size cannot override the maximum size set in the `upload_max_filesize` field in your `php.ini` file that defaults to 2 megabytes. After the `MAX_FILE_SIZE` field has been entered, you are ready to add the upload field itself. This is simply an `INPUT` element with a `TYPE` argument of `"file"`. You can give it any name you want. Listing 9.14 brings all this together into an HTML upload form.

LISTING 9.14 A Simple File Upload Form

```
 1: <html>
 2: <head>
 3: <title>Listing 9.14 A simple file upload form</title>
 4: </head>
 5: <body>
 6: <form enctype="multipart/form-data" action="<?print $PHP_SELF?>" method="
    POST">
 7: <input type="hidden" name="MAX_FILE_SIZE" value="51200">
 8: <input type="file" name="fupload"><br>
 9: <input type="submit" value="upload!">
10: </form>
11: </body>
12: </html>
```

Notice that once again this form calls the page that contains it. This is because we are going to add some PHP code to handle the uploaded file. We limited file uploads to 50KB and named our upload field `"fupload"`. As you might expect, this name will soon become important.

When a file is successfully uploaded, it is given a unique name and stored in a temporary directory (/tmp on UNIX systems). The full path to this file becomes available to you in a global variable with the same name as the file upload form field (`$fupload` in this case). PHP stores more information about the file for you in a series of global variables. These consist of the variable name (as derived from the form file upload field) followed by an underscore character and `"name"`, `"size"`, and `"type"`. Table 9.2 shows the meaning of these variables.

TABLE 9.2 File Upload Global Variables

Variable Name	*Contains*	*Example*
`$fupload`	Path to temporary variable	`/tmp/php5Pq3fU`
`$fuploadname`	Name of uploaded file	`test.gif`
`$fuploadsize`	Size (in bytes) of uploaded file	6835
`$fupload type`	MIME type of uploaded file (where given by client)	image/gif

PHP4 also provides a new built-in variable that contains file upload information in array format. If one or more files has been uploaded via a form, the `$HTTP_POST_FILES` array will be indexed by the names of each upload field in the form. The corresponding value for each of these keys will itself be an associative array. These fields are described in Table 9.3.

TABLE 9.3 File Upload Global Variables

Element	*Contains*	*Example*
`$HTTP_POST_FILES[fupload][name]`	Name of uploaded file	`test.gif`
`$HTTP_POST_FILES[fupload][size]`	Size (in bytes) of uploaded file	6835
`$HTTP_POST_FILES[fupload][type]`	MIME type of uploaded file (where given by client)	image/gif

Armed with this information, we can write a quick and dirty script that displays information about uploaded files (see Listing 9.15). If the uploaded file is in GIF format, the script will even attempt to display it.

LISTING 9.15 A File Upload Script

```
 1: <html>
 2: <head>
 3: <title>Listing 9.15 A file upload script</title>
 4: </head>
 5: <?php
 6: $file_dir = "/home/matt/htdocs/uploads";
 7: $file_url = "http://www.corrosive.co.uk/matt/uploads";
 8: if ( isset( $fupload ) )
 9:     {
10:     print "path: $fupload<br>\n";
11:     print "name: $fupload_name<br>\n";
```

LISTING 9.15 continued

```
12:     print "size: $fupload_size bytes<br>\n";
13:     print "type: $fupload_type<p>\n\n";
14:     if ( $fupload_type == "image/gif" )
15:         {
16: copy ( $fupload, "$file_dir/$fupload_name") or die ("Couldn't copy");
17:
18:         print "<img src=\"$file_url/$fupload_name\"><p>\n\n";
19:         }
20:     }
21: ?>
22: <body>
23: <form enctype="multipart/form-data" action="<?php print $PHP_SELF?>"
    method="POST">
24: <input type="hidden" name="MAX_FILE_SIZE" value="51200">
25: <input type="file" name="fupload"><br>
26: <input type="submit" value="Send file!">
27: </form>
28: </body>
29: </html>
```

In Listing 9.15, we first check to see whether the `$fupload` global variable exists. If it does, we can assume that a file upload exists (at least for the purposes of this exercise).

Never assume that data sent to your scripts originates from a particular source or that a request contains the type and range of data that your script was designed to accept. In Listing 9.15, we make the assumption that a particular variable derives its name from a form upload field. In fact, there is nothing to stop a mischievous user from creating her own form that sends data to our script. She could easily send our script a parameter with the same name as our form upload file but with plain text content.

If this sounds paranoid, it is meant to. Paranoia is a good thing in server-side Web programming. Never trust data that comes from an external source, even if that source seems to be a form that you have created.

If a file has been uploaded, the path to the uploaded file on the server is contained in the variable `$fupload`, and we print this to the browser. We also print the filename, which is stored in `$fupload_name`, the file's size, which is stored in `$fupload_size`, and the file's MIME type, which is stored in `$fupload_type`.

We then test the value contained by `$fupload_type`. If this is `"image/gif"`, we assume that we are dealing with a GIF. In fact, it would be a good idea to test this ignoring case, and you will see how to do this in Hour 17, "Working with Strings." Our assumption here also glosses over the possibility that another kind of file altogether was named with a `".gif"` extension, but let's ease off on the caution for now.

If we are dealing with a GIF image, we use the `copy()` function to copy the uploaded file from its default location to a directory in our server space. The `copy()` function requires two string arguments; the original and new paths to a file. It returns true if the copy is successful. The original path to our file is stored in `$fupload`. We have created a variable `$file_dir` that contains the full path to the directory we want to use to store uploaded images. This, combined with the file's name as stored in `$fupload_name`, forms the second argument passed to `copy()`. As a result of this function call, the uploaded file should be copied to our upload directory with its original name restored. Note that on UNIX systems server scripts run as a special user, often 'nobody'. Before you copy a file to a directory you should make sure that your process is allowed to do so. We are using the `or` operator and the `die()` function to abort the script if copying fails. We will cover this technique in more detail in Hour 10, "Working with Files."

Having copied the file, we do not need to delete the original. PHP will handle this for us.

When we created the `$file_dir` variable to store the file path to our upload directory, we also created a variable called `$file_url` to store the URL of the same directory. We wrap up the script by writing an HTML image element that references our newly written image.

Summary

If you've kept up so far, things should be getting exciting now. You have the tools to create truly sophisticated and interactive environments. There are still a few things missing, of course. Now that you can get information from the user, it would be nice to be able to do something with it. Write it to a file, perhaps. That is the subject of the next hour.

Throughout this hour, you have learned how to work with the `$GLOBALS` associative array and acquire environment variables, form input, and uploaded files using global variables. You have also learned how to send raw headers to the client to redirect a browser. You have learned how to acquire list information from form submissions and how to pass information from script call to script call using hidden fields.

Q&A

Q Can I create arrays for values entered into elements other than select and check box fields?

A Yes, in fact any element name ending with empty square brackets in a form will resolve to an array element when the form is submitted. You can use this fact to group values submitted from multiple fields of any type into an array.

Q The `header()` function seems powerful. Will we look at HTTP headers in more detail?

A We cover HTTP (Hypertext Transfer Protocol) in more detail in Hour 13, "Beyond the Box."

Q Automatically converting form element names into variables seems a little risky. Can I disable this feature?

A Yes, you can ensure that submitted form element names are not converted into global variables by setting the `gpc_globals` directive to `"off"` in the `php.ini` file.

Workshop

The Workshop provides quiz questions to help you solidify your understanding of the material covered. Try to understand the quiz answers before continuing to the next hour's lesson. Quiz answers are provided in Appendix A.

Quiz

1. Which environment variable could you use to determine the IP address of a user?
2. Which environment variable could you use to find out about the browser that called your script?
3. What should you name your form fields to access their submitted values from an array variable called `$form_array`?
4. Which built-in associative array contains all values submitted as part of a `GET` request?
5. Which built-in associative array contains all values submitted as part of a `POST` request?
6. What function would you use to redirect the browser to a new page? What string would you pass it?

7. How must you limit the size of a file that a user can submit via a particular upload form?
8. How can you set a limit to the size of upload files for all forms and scripts?

Activities

1. Create a calculator script that allows the user to submit two numbers and choose an operation to perform on them (addition, multiplication, division, subtraction).
2. Use hidden fields with the script you created in activity 1 to store and display the number of requests that the user has submitted.

HOUR 10

Working with Files

Testing, reading, and writing to files are staple activities for any full-featured programming language. PHP is no exception, providing you with functions that make the process straightforward. In this hour, you will learn

- How to include files in your documents
- How to test files and directories
- How to open a file before working with it
- How to read data from files
- How to write or append to a file
- How to lock a file
- How to work with directories

Including Files with `include()`

The `include()` function enables you to incorporate files into your PHP documents. PHP code in these files can be executed as if it were part of the main document. This can be useful for including library code in multiple pages.

Having created a killer function, your only option until now would have been to paste it into every document that needs to use it. Of course, if you discover a bug, or want to add a feature, you will have to find every page that uses the function to make the change. The `include()` statement can save you from this chore. You can add the function to a single document and, at runtime, read this into any page that needs it. The `include()` function requires a single argument, a relative path to the file to be included. Listing 10.1 creates a simple PHP script that uses `include()` to incorporate and output the contents of a file.

LISTING 10.1 Using `include()`

```
 1: <html>
 2: <head>
 3: <title>Listing 10.1 Using include()</title>
 4: </head>
 5: <body>
 6: <?php
 7: include("eg10.2.php");
 8: ?>
 9: </body>
10: </html>
```

The `include()` statement in Listing 10.1 incorporates the document `eg10.2.php`, the contents of which you can see in Listing 10.2. When run, Listing 10.1 outputs the string `"I have been included!!"`, which may seem strange, given that we have included plain text within a block of PHP code. Shouldn't this cause an error? In fact, the contents of an included file are displayed as HTML by default. If you want to execute PHP code in an included file, you must enclose it in PHP start and end tags. In Listings 10.3 and 10.4, we amend the previous example so that code is executed in the included file.

LISTING 10.2 The File Included in Listing 10.1

```
1: I have been included!!
```

LISTING 10.3 Using the `include()` Function to Execute PHP in Another File

```
 1: <html>
 2: <head>
 3: <title>Listing 10.3 Using include to execute PHP in another file</title>
 4: </head>
 5: <body>
 6: <?php
 7: include("eg10.4.php");
 8: ?>
 9: </body>
10: </html>
```

LISTING 10.4 An Include File Containing PHP Code

```
1: <?php
2: print "I have been included!!<BR>";
3: print "But now I can add up...  4 + 4 = ".(4 + 4);
4: ?>
```


Included files in PHP4 can return a value in the same way as functions do. As in a function, using the `return` statement ends the execution of code within the included file. Additionally, no further HTML will be included. In Listings 10.5 and 10.6, we include a file, assigning its return value to a variable.

LISTING 10.5 Using `include()` to Execute PHP and Assign the Return Value

```
 1: <html>
 2: <head>
 3: <title>Listing 10.5 Using include() to execute PHP and assign the return
    Avalue</title>
 4: </head>
 5: <body>
 6: <?php
 7: $addResult = include("eg10.6.php");
 8: print "The include file returned $addResult";
 9: ?>
10: </body>
11: </html>
```

LISTING 10.6 An Include File That Returns a Value

```
1: <?php
2: $retval = ( 4 + 4 );
3: return $retval;
```

LISTING 10.6 continued

```
4: ?>
5: This HTML should never be displayed because it comes after a return statement!
```

Returning values from included files would only work in PHP3 if the `return` statement was contained in a function. The code in Listing 10.6 would cause an error.

You can use an `include()` statement in a conditional statement, and the referenced file will only be read if the condition is met. The `include()` statement in the following fragment will never be called, for example

```
$test = false;
if ( $test )
  {
  include( "a_file.txt" ); // won't be included
  }
```

If you use an `include()` statement within a loop, it will be replaced with the contents of the referenced file each time the `include()` statement is called. This content will be executed for every call. Listing 10.7 illustrates this by using an `include()` statement in a `for` loop. The `include()` statement references a different file for each iteration.

LISTING 10.7 Using `include()` Within a Loop

```
 1: <html>
 2: <head>
 3: <title>Listing 10.7 Using include() within a loop</title>
 4: </head>
 5: <body>
 6: <?php
 7: for ( $x = 1; $x<=3; $x++ )
 8:    {
 9:    $incfile = "incfile$x".".txt";
10:    print "Attempting include $incfile<br>";
11:    include( "$incfile" );
12:    print "<p>";
13:    }
14: ?>
15: </body>
16: </html>
```

When Listing 10.7 is run, it includes the content of three different files, `"incfile1.txt"`, `"incfile2.txt"`, and `"incfile3.txt"`. Assuming that each of these files simply contains a confirmation of its own name, the output should look something like this:

```
This is incfile1.txt
Attempting to include incfile2.txt
This is incfile2.txt
Attempting to include incfile3.txt
```

PHP also has a `require()` statement, which performs a similar function. As of PHP4, you can include a `require()` statement in a loop as you can with `include()`. A file included as a result of a `require()` statement cannot return a value, however.

Testing Files

Before you work with a file or directory, it is often a good idea to learn more about it. PHP4 provides many functions that help you to discover information about files on your system. This section briefly covers some of the most useful.

Checking for Existence with `file_exists()`

You can test for the existence of a file with the `file_exists()` function. This requires a string representing an absolute or relative path to a file that may or may not be there. If the file is found, it returns `true`; otherwise, it returns `false`.

```
if ( file_exists("test.txt") )
   print "The file exists!";
```

A File or a Directory?

You can confirm that the entity you are testing is a file, as opposed to a directory, with the `is_file()` function. `is_file()` requires the file path and returns a Boolean value:

```
if ( is_file( "test.txt" ) )
   print "test.txt is a file!";
```

Conversely, you might want to check that the entity you are testing is a directory. You can do this with the `is_dir()` function. `is_dir()` requires the path to the directory and returns a Boolean value:

```
if ( is_dir( "/tmp" ) )
   print "/tmp is a directory";
```

Checking the Status of a File

When you know that a file exists, and it is what you expect it to be, you can then find out some things that you can do with it. Typically, you might want to read, write to, or execute a file. PHP can help you with all of these.

`is_readable()` tells you whether you can read a file. On UNIX systems, you may be able to see a file but still be barred from reading its contents. `is_readable()` accepts the file path as a string and returns a Boolean value:

```
if ( is_readable( "test.txt" ) )
   print "test.txt is readable";
```

`is_writable()` tells you whether you can write to a file. Once again it requires the file path and returns a Boolean value:

```
if ( is_writable( "test.txt" ) )
   print "test.txt is writable";
```

`is_executable()` tells you whether you can run a file, relying on either the file's permissions or its extension depending on your platform. It accepts the file path and returns a Boolean value:

```
if ( is_executable( "test.txt" )
   print "test.txt is executable";
```

Determining File Size with `filesize()`

Given the path to a file, `filesize()` attempts to determine and return its size in bytes. It returns `false` if it encounters problems.

```
print "The size of test.txt is.. ";
print filesize( "test.txt" );
```

Getting Date Information About a File

Sometimes you will need to know when a file was last written to or accessed. PHP provides several functions that can provide this information.

You can find out when a file was last accessed with `fileatime()`. This function requires the file path and returns the date that the file was last accessed. To access a file means either to read or write to it. Dates are returned from all these functions in UNIX epoch format. That is, the number of seconds since 1 January 1970. In our examples, we use the `date()` function to translate this into human readable form. You learn more about date functions in Hour 15, "Working with Dates."

```
$atime = fileatime( "test.txt" );
print "test.txt was last accessed on ";
print date("D d M Y g:i A", $atime);
// Sample output: Thu 13 Jan 2000 2:26 PM
```

You can discover the modification date of a file with the function `filemtime()`, which requires the file path and returns the date in UNIX epoch format. To modify a file means to change its contents in some way.


```
$mtime = filemtime( "test.txt" );
print "test.txt was last modified on ";
print date("D d M Y g:i A", $mtime);
// Sample output: Thu 13 Jan 2000 2:26 PM]
```

PHP also allows you to test the change time of a document with the `filectime()` function. On UNIX systems, the change time is set when a file's contents are modified or changes are made to its permissions or ownership. On other platforms, the `filectime()` returns the creation date.

```
$ctime = filectime( "test.txt" );
print "test.txt was last changed on ";
print date("D d M Y g:i A", $ctime);
// Sample output: Thu 13 Jan 2000 2:26 PM]
```

Creating a Function That Performs Multiple File Tests

Listing 10.8 creates a function that brings the file test functions we have looked at together into one script.

LISTING 10.8 A Function to Output the Results of Multiple File Tests

```
1: <html>
2: <head>
3: <title>Listing 10.8 A function to output the results of multiple file tests</
   title>
4: </head>
5: <body>
6: <?php
7: $file = "test.txt";
8: outputFileTestInfo( $file );
```

LISTING 10.8 continued

```
 9: function outputFileTestInfo( $f )
10:     {
11:     if ( ! file_exists( $f ) )
12:         {
13:         print "$f does not exist<BR>";
14:         return;
15:         }
16:     print "$f is ".(is_file( $f )?"":"not ")."a file<br>";
17:     print "$f is ".(is_dir( $f )?"":"not ")."a directory<br>";
18:     print "$f is ".(is_readable( $f )?"":"not ")."readable<br>";
19:     print "$f is ".(is_writable( $f )?"":"not ")."writable<br>";
20:     print "$f is ".(is_executable( $f )?"":"not ")."executable<br>";
21:     print "$f is ".(filesize($f))." bytes<br>";
22:     print "$f was accessed on ".date( "D d M Y g:i A", fileatime( $f ) )."<br>";
23:     print "$f was modified on ".date( "D d M Y g:i A", filemtime( $f ) )."<br>";
24:     print "$f was changed on ".date( "D d M Y g:i A", filectime( $f ) )."<br>";
25:     }
26:
27: ?>
28: </body>
29: </html>
```

Notice that we have used the ternary operator as a compact way of working with some of these tests. Let's look at one of these in more detail:

```
print "$f is ".(is_file( $f )?"":"not ")."a file<br>";
```

We use the `is_file()` function as the right-hand expression of the ternary operator. If this returns `true`, an empty string is returned. Otherwise, the string `"not "` is returned. The return value of the ternary expression is added to the string to be printed with concatenation operators. This statement could be made clearer but less compact, as follows:

```
$is_it = is_file( $f )?"":"not ";
print "$f is $isit"."a file";
```

We could, of course, be even clearer with an `if` statement, but imagine how large the function would become if we had used the following:

```
if ( is_file( $f ) )
    print "$fi is a file<br>";
else
    print "$f is not a file<br>";
```

Because the result of these three approaches is the same, the approach you take becomes broadly a matter of preference.

Creating and Deleting Files

If a file does not yet exist, you can create one with the `touch()` function. Given a string representing a file path, `touch()` attempts to create an empty file of that name. If the file already exists, the contents are not disturbed, but the modification date is updated to the time at which the function executed.

```
touch("myfile.txt");
```

You can remove an existing file with the `unlink()` function. Once again, `unlink()` accepts a file path:

```
unlink("myfile.txt");
```

All functions that create, delete, read, write, or modify files on UNIX systems require that the correct file or directory permissions are set.

Opening a File for Writing, Reading, or Appending

Before you can work with a file, you must first open it for reading, writing, or both. PHP provides the `fopen()` function for this. `fopen()` requires a string containing the file path, followed by a string containing the mode in which the file is to be opened. The most common modes are read (`'r'`), write (`'w'`), and append (`'a'`). `fopen()` returns an integer you will later use to work with the open file. This integer is known as a file pointer and should be assigned to a variable. To open a file for reading, you would use the following:

```
$fp = fopen( "test.txt", 'r' );
```

You would use the following to open a file for writing:

```
$fp = fopen( "test.txt", 'w' );
```

To open a file for appending (that is, to add data to the end of a file), you would use this:

```
$fp = fopen( "test.txt", 'a' );
```

`fopen()` returns `false` if the file cannot be opened for any reason. It is a good idea, therefore, to test the function's return value before proceeding to work with it. You can do this with an `if` statement:

```
if ( $fp = fopen( "test.txt", "w" ) )
   {
   // do something with $fp
   }
```

Or you can use a logical operator to end execution if an essential file can't be opened:

```
( $fp = fopen( "test.txt", "w" ) ) or die ("Couldn't open file, sorry");
```

If the `fopen()` function returns `true`, the rest of the expression won't be parsed, and the `die()` function (which writes a message to the browser and ends the script) will never be reached. Otherwise, the right-hand side of the `or` operator will be parsed, and the `die()` function will be called.

Assuming that all is well and you go on to work with your open file, you should remember to close it when you have finished. You can do this by calling `fclose()`, which requires the file pointer returned from a successful `fopen()` call as its argument:

```
fclose( $fp );
```

Reading from Files

PHP provides a number of functions for reading data from files. These enable you to read by the byte, the line, or even the character.

Reading Lines from a File with `fgets()` and `feof()`

After you have opened a file for reading, you will often need to access it line by line. To read a line from an open file, you can use `fgets()`, which requires the file pointer returned from `fopen()` as an argument. You must also pass it an integer as a second argument. This specifies the number of bytes the function should read if it doesn't first encounter a line end or the end of the file. The `fgets()` function reads the file until it reaches a newline character (`"\n"`), the number of bytes specified in the length argument, or the end of the file.

```
$line = fgets( $fp, 1024 ); // where $fp is the file pointer returned by fopen()
```

Although you can read lines with `fgets()`, you need some way of telling when you have reached the end of the file. The `feof()` function does this, returning `true` when the end of the file has been reached and `false` otherwise. Once again this function requires a file pointer as its argument:

```
feof( $fp ); // where $fp is the file pointer returned by fopen()
```

You now have enough information to read a file line by line, as shown in Listing 10.9.

Listing 10.9 Opening and Reading a File Line by Line

```
 1: <html>
 2: <head>
 3: <title>Listing 10.9 Opening and reading a file line by line</title>
 4: </head>
 5: <body>
 6: <?php
 7: $filename = "test.txt";
 8: $fp = fopen( $filename, "r" ) or die("Couldn't open $filename");
 9: while ( ! feof( $fp ) )
10:     {
11:     $line = fgets( $fp, 1024 );
12:     print "$line<br>";
13:     }
14: ?>
15: </body>
16: </html>
```


We call `fopen()` with the name of the file that we want to read, using the `or` operator to ensure that script execution ends if the file cannot be read. This usually occurs if the file does not exist, or (on a UNIX system) if the file's permissions won't allow the script read access to the file. The actual reading takes place in the `while` statement. The `while` statement's test expression calls `feof()` for each iteration, ending the loop when it returns `true`. In other words, the loop continues until the end of the file is reached. Within the code block, we use `fgets()` to extract a line (or 1024 bytes) of the file. We assign the result to `$line` and then print it to the browser, appending a `<BR>` tag for the sake of readability.

Reading Arbitrary Amounts of Data from a File with `fread()`

Rather than reading text by the line, you can choose to read a file in arbitrarily defined chunks. The `fread()` function accepts a file pointer as an argument, as well as the number of bytes you want to read. It returns the amount of data you have requested unless the end of the file is reached first.

```
$chunk = fread( $fp, 16 );
```

Listing 10.10 amends our previous example so that it reads data in chunks of 16 bytes rather than by the line.

LISTING 10.10 Reading a File with `fread()`

```
 1: <html>
 2: <head>
 3: <title>Listing 10.10 Reading a file with fread()</title>
 4: </head>
 5: <body>
 6: <?php
 7: $filename = "test.txt";
 8: $fp = fopen( $filename, "r" ) or die("Couldn't open $filename");
 9: while ( ! feof( $fp ) )
10:     {
11:     $chunk = fread( $fp, 16 );
12:     print "$chunk<br>";
13:     }
14: ?>
15: </body>
16: </html>
```

Although `fread()` allows you to define the amount of data acquired from a file, it won't let you decide the position from which the acquisition begins. You can set this manually with the `fseek()` function. `fseek()` enables you to change your current position within a file. It requires a file pointer and an integer representing the offset from the start of the file (in bytes) to which you want to jump:

```
fseek( $fp, 64 );
```

Listing 10.11 uses `fseek()` and `fread()` to output the second half of a file to the browser.

LISTING 10.11 Moving Around a File with `fseek()`

```
 1: <html>
 2: <head>
 3: <title>Listing 10.11 Moving around a file with fseek()</title>
 4: </head>
 5: <body>
 6: <?php
 7: $filename = "test.txt";
 8: $fp = fopen( $filename, "r" ) or die("Couldn't open $filename");
 9: $fsize = filesize($filename);
10: $halfway = (int)( $fsize / 2 );
11: print "Halfway point: $halfway <BR>\n";
12: fseek( $fp, $halfway );
13: $chunk = fread( $fp, ($fsize - $halfway) );
14: print $chunk;
15: ?>
16: </body>
17: </html>
```

We calculate the halfway point of our file by dividing the return value of `filesize()` by 2. We can then use this as the second argument to `fseek()`, jumping to the halfway point. Finally, we call `fread()` to extract the second half of the file, printing the result to the browser.

Reading Characters from a File with `fgetc()`

`fgetc()` is similar to `fgets()` except that it returns only a single character from a file every time it is called. Because a character is always 1 byte in size, `fgetc()` doesn't require a length argument. You simply need to pass it a file pointer:

```
$char = fgetc( $fp );
```

Listing 10.12 creates a loop that reads the file `"test.txt"` a character at a time, outputting each character to the browser on its own line.

LISTING 10.12 Moving Around a File with `fseek()`

```
 1: <html>
 2: <head>
 3: <title>Listing 10.12 Moving around a file with fseek()</title>
 4: </head>
 5: <body>
 6: <?php
 7: $filename = "test.txt";
 8: $fp = fopen( $filename, "r" ) or die("Couldn't open $filename");
 9: while ( ! feof( $fp ) )
10:     {
11:     $char = fgetc( $fp );
12:     print "$char<BR>";
13:     }
14: ?>
15: </body>
16: </html>
```

Writing or Appending to a File

The processes for writing to or appending to a file are the same. The difference lies in the `fopen()` call. When you write to a file, you should use the mode argument `"w"` when you call `fopen()`:

```
$fp = fopen( "test.txt", "w" );
```

All subsequent writing will occur from the start of the file. If the file doesn't already exist, it will be created. If the file already exists, any prior content will be destroyed and replaced by the data you write.

When you append to a file, you should use mode `"a"` in your `fopen()` call:

```
$fp = fopen( "test.txt", "a" );
```

Any subsequent writes to your file are added to the existing content.

Writing to a File with `fwrite()` or `fputs()`

`fwrite()` accepts a file pointer and a string. It then writes the string to the file. `fputs()` works in exactly the same way.

```
fwrite( $fp, "hello world" );
fputs( $fp, "hello world" );
```

Writing to files is as straightforward as that. Listing 10.13 uses `fwrite()` to print to a file. We then append a further string to the same file using `fputs()`.

LISTING 10.13 Writing and Appending to a File

```
 1: <html>
 2: <head>
 3: <title>Listing 10.13 Writing and appending to a file</title>
 4: </head>
 5: <body>
 6: <?php
 7: $filename = "test.txt";
 8: print "Writing to $filename<br>";
 9: $fp = fopen( $filename, "w" ) or die("Couldn't open $filename");
10: fwrite( $fp, "Hello world\n" );
11: fclose( $fp );
12: print "Appending to $filename<br>";
13: $fp = fopen( $filename, "a" ) or die("Couldn't open $filename");
14: fputs( $fp, "And another thing\n" );
15: fclose( $fp );
16: ?>
17: </body>
18: </html>
```

Locking Files with `flock()`

The techniques you have learned for reading and amending files will work fine if you are only presenting your script to a single user. In the real world, however, you would expect many users to access your projects more or less at the same time. Imagine what would happen if two users were to execute a script that writes to one file at the same moment. The file will quickly become corrupt.

PHP4 provides the `flock()` function to forestall this eventuality. `flock()` will lock a file to warn other process against writing to or reading from a file while the current process is working with it. `flock()` requires a valid file pointer, and an integer representing the kind of lock you would like to set. In Table 10.1 we list three kinds of locks you can apply to a file.

TABLE 10.1 Integer Arguments to the `flock()` Function

Integer	*Lock Type*	*Description*
1	Shared	Allows other processes to read the file but prevents writing (used when reading a file)
2	Exclusive	Prevents other processes from either reading from or writing to a file (used when writing to a file)
3	Release	Releases a shared or exclusive lock

You should call `flock()` directly after calling `fopen()` and then call it again to release the lock before closing the file.

```
$fp = fopen( "test.txt", "a" );
flock( $fp, 2 ); // exclusive lock
// write to the file
flock( $fp, 1 ); // release the lock
fclose( $fp );
```

Locking with `flock()` is advisory. Only other scripts that use `flock()` will respect a lock that you set.

Working with Directories

Now that you can test, read, and write to files, turn your attention to directories. PHP provides many functions to work with directories. You will look at how to create, remove, and read them.

Creating Directories with `mkdir()`

`mkdir()` enables you to create a directory. `mkdir()` requires a string representing the path to the directory you want to create and an integer that should be an octal number representing the mode you want to set for the directory. You specify an octal (base 8) number with a leading 0. The mode argument will only have an effect on UNIX systems. The mode should consist of three numbers between 0 and 7, representing permissions for the directory owner, group, and everyone, respectively. This function returns `true` if it successfully creates a directory, or `false` if it doesn't. If `mkdir()` fails, this will usually be because the containing directory has permissions that preclude processes with the script's user ID from writing.

```
mkdir( "testdir", 0777 ); // global read/write/execute permissions
```

Removing a Directory with `rmdir()`

`rmdir()` enables you to remove a directory from the file system, if the process running your script has the right to do so, and if the directory is empty. `rmdir()` requires only a string representing the path to the directory you want to create.

```
rmdir( "testdir" );
```

Opening a Directory for Reading with `opendir()`

Before you can read the contents of a directory, you must first obtain a directory pointer. You can do this with the `opendir()` function. `opendir()` requires a string representing the path to the directory you want to open. `opendir()` returns a directory handle unless the directory is not present or readable, in which case it returns `false`.

```
$dh = opendir( "testdir" );
```

Reading the Contents of a Directory with `readdir()`

Just as you use `gets()` to read a line from a file, you can use `readdir()` to read a file or directory name from a directory. `readdir()` requires a directory handle and returns a string containing the item name. If the end of the directory has been reached, `readdir()` returns `false`. Note that `readdir()` returns only the names of its items, rather than full paths. Listing 10.14 shows the contents of a directory.

LISTING 10.14 Listing the Contents of a Directory with `readdir()`

```
 1: <html>
 2: <head>
 3: <title>Listing 10.14 Listing the contents
 4: of a directory with readdir()</title>
 5: </head>
 6: <body>
 7: <?php
 8: $dirname = "testdir";
 9: $dh = opendir( $dirname );
10: while ( gettype( $file = readdir( $dh )) != boolean )
11:     {
12:     if ( is_dir( "$dirname/$file" ) )
13:         print "(D)";
14:     print "$file<br>";
15:     }
16: closedir( $dh );
17: ?>
18: </body>
19: </html>
```


We open our directory for reading with the `opendir()` function and use a `while` statement to loop through each of its elements. We call `readdir()` as part of the `while` statement's test expression, assigning its result to the `$file` variable. Within the body of the `while` statement, we use the `$dirname` variable in conjunction with the `$file` variable to create a full file path, which we can then test. If the path leads to a directory, we print `"(D)"` to the browser. Finally, we print the filename.

We have used a cautious construction in the test of the `while` statement. Most PHP programmers (myself included) would use something like the following:

```
while ( $file = readdir( $dh ) )
      {
      print "$file<BR>\n";
      }
```

The value returned by `readdir()` will be tested. Because any string other than "0" will resolve to `true`, there should be no problem. Imagine, however, a directory that contains four files, `"0"`, `"1"`, `"2"`, and `"3"`. The output from the preceding code on my system is as follows:

```
.
..
```

When the loop reaches the file named `"0"`, the string returned by `readdir()` resolves to `false`, causing the loop to end. The approach in Listing 10.14 tests the type of the value returned by the `readdir()` function, thus circumventing the problem.

Summary

In this hour, you learned how to use `include()` to incorporate files into your documents and to execute any PHP code contained in include files. You learned how to use some of PHP's file test functions. You explored functions for reading files by the line, by the character, or in arbitrary chunks. You learned how to write to files, either replacing or appending to existing content. Finally, you learned how to create, remove, and read directories.

Q&A

Q Will the `include()` function slow down my scripts?

A Because an included file must be opened and parsed by the interpreter, it will add some overhead. The effect should be negligible, however.

Q Should I always end script execution if a file cannot be opened for writing or reading?

A You should always allow for this possibility. If your script absolutely depends on the file you want to work with, you might want to use the `die()` function, writing an informative error message to the browser. In less critical situations, you will still need to allow for the failure, perhaps adding it to a log file. You can read more about logging in Hour 22, "Debugging."

Workshop

The Workshop provides quiz questions to help you solidify your understanding of the material covered. Try to understand the quiz answers before continuing to the next hour's lesson. Quiz answers are provided in Appendix A.

Quiz

1. What functions could you use to add library code to the currently running script?
2. What function would you use to find out whether a file is present on your file system?
3. How would you determine the size of a file?

4. What function would you use to open a file for reading or writing?
5. What function would you use to read a line of data from a file?
6. How can you tell when you have reached the end of a file?
7. What function would you use to write a line of data to a file?
8. How would you open a directory for reading?
9. What function would you use to read the name of a directory item after you have opened a directory for reading?

Activities

1. Create a form that accepts a user's first and second name. Create a script that saves this data to a file.
2. Create a script that reads the data file you created in activity 1. As well as writing its contents to the browser (adding a `<BR>` tag to each line), print a summary that includes the number of lines in the file and the file's size.

HOUR 11

Working with the DBM Functions

If you don't have access to a SQL database such as MySQL or Oracle, you will almost certainly have a DBM-style database system available to you. Even if you don't have such a library on your system, PHP can emulate the functionality for you. Essentially, the DBM functions allow you to store and manipulate name/value pairs on your system.

Although these functions do not offer you the power of a SQL database, they are flexible and easy to use. Because the format is so common, code written to take advantage of these functions is likely to be portable, although the DBM files themselves might not be.

In this hour, you will learn

- How to open a DBM database
- How to add data to the database
- How to extract data from the database

- How to change and delete items
- How to store more complex kinds of data in DBM databases

Opening a DBM Database

You can open a DBM database with the function `dbmopen()`. This function requires two arguments: the path to a DBM file and a string containing the flags with which you want to open the database. `dbmopen()` returns a special DBM identifier that you can then pass to other DBM functions to access or manipulate your database. Because `dbmopen()` involves reading from and writing to files, PHP must have permission to write to the directory that will contain your database.

The flags that you pass to `dbmopen()` determine the way in which you can work with your database. They are listed in Table 11.1

TABLE 11.1 Flags for Use with `dbmopen()`

Flag	*Description*
`r`	Open database reading only
`w`	Open database for writing and reading
`c`	Create database (or open for read/write access if it exists)
`n`	Create new database (truncate old version if it exists)

The following code fragment opens a database, creating a new one if it does not already exist:

```
$dbh = dbmopen( "./data/products", "c" ) or die( "Couldn't open DBM" );
```

Notice that we use a `die()` statement to end script execution if our attempt to open the database fails.

When you finish working with a database, close it using the function `dbmclose()`. This is because PHP locks a database that you are working with so that other processes cannot attempt to modify the data you are reading or writing. If you don't close the database, then other processes are going to have to wait longer before getting their bite of the cherry. `dbmclose()` requires a valid DBM identifier:

```
dbmclose ( $dbh );
```

Adding Data to the Database

You can add name/value pairs to your open database with the function `dbminsert()`, which requires a valid DBM identifier (as returned by `dbmopen()`), the name of a key, and the value that you want to store. This function returns 0 if all is well, 1 if the element already exists in the database, and -1 if an error occurs (such as an attempt to write to a database opened in read-only mode). If the element you are attempting to insert already exists, then the data is not overwritten.

Listing 11.1 creates or opens a database called `products` and adds some data to it.

LISTING 11.1 Adding Items to a DBM Database

```
 1: <html>
 2: <head>
 3: <title>Listing 11.1 Adding items to a DBM database</title>
 4: </head>
 5: <body>
 6: Adding products now...
 7:
 8: <?php
 9: $dbh = dbmopen( "./data/products", "c" ) or die( "Couldn't open DBM" );
10:
11: dbminsert( $dbh, "Sonic Screwdriver", "23.20" );
12: dbminsert( $dbh, "Tricorder", "55.50" );
13: dbminsert( $dbh, "ORAC AI", "2200.50" );
14: dbminsert( $dbh, "HAL 2000", "4500.50" );
15:
16: dbmclose( $dbh );
17: ?>
18: </body>
19: </html>
```

All values are converted to strings when added to the database, so we add quotes to the product prices to maintain their format. We can treat these strings as doubles when we extract them from the database if we need to. Notice also that we can use keys that have more than one word.

If we now attempt to call `dbminsert()` with the same key argument as one of the keys we have already used, `dbminsert()` returns 1 and makes no change to the database. In some circumstances, this might be what you want; but in others, you will want to amend existing data, as well as create new elements.

Amending Elements in a Database

You can amend an entry in a DBM database with the `dbmreplace()` function. `dbmreplace()` requires a valid DBM identifier, the name of a key, and the new value to add. It returns 0 if all goes well and -1 if an error occurs. Listing 11.2 amends the code in Listing 11.1 so that keys are added regardless of existence.

LISTING 11.2 Adding or Changing Items to a DBM Database

```
 1: <html>
 2: <head>
 3: <title>Listing 11.2 Adding or changing items to a DBM database</title>
 4: </head>
 5: <body>
 6: Adding products now...
 7: <?php
 8: $dbh = dbmopen( "./data/products", "c" )
 9:          or die( "Couldn't open DBM" );
10: dbmreplace( $dbh, "Sonic Screwdriver", "25.20" );
11: dbmreplace( $dbh, "Tricorder", "56.50" );
12: dbmreplace( $dbh, "ORAC AI", "2209.50" );
13: dbmreplace( $dbh, "HAL 2000", "4535.50" );
14: dbmclose( $dbh );
15: ?>
16: </body>
17: </html>
```

We have only had to change the function calls from `dbminsert()` to `dbmreplace()` to change the functionality of the script.

Reading from a DBM Database

Now that we can add data to our database, we need to find a way to fetch it. We can extract an individual element from the database with the `dbmfetch()` function. `dbmfetch()` requires a valid DBM identifier and the name of the element you want to access. The function returns the value you are accessing as a string. So to access the price of the `"Tricorder"` item, we would use the following code:

```
$price = dbmfetch( $dbh, "Tricorde" );
```

If the `"Tricorder"` element does not exist in the database, then `dbmfetch()` returns an empty string.

You won't always know the names of all the keys in the database, however. What would you do if you needed to output every product and price to the browser without hard-coding the product names into your script? PHP provides a mechanism by which you can loop through every element in a database.

You can get the first key in a database with the `dbmfirstkey()` function. This requires a DBM identifier and returns the first key. Note that this won't necessarily be the first element that you added because DBM databases often maintain their own ordering systems. After you've retrieved the first key, you can access each subsequent key with the `dbmnextkey()` function. Once again `dbmnextkey()` requires a DBM identifier and returns an element's key. By combining these functions with `dbmfetch()`, you can now list an entire database.

Listing 11.3 outputs the products database to the browser.

LISTING 11.3 Reading All Records from a DBM Database

```
 1: <html>
 2: <head>
 3: <title>Listing 11.3 Reading all
 4: records from a DBM Database </title>
 5: </head>
 6: <body>
 7: Here at the Impossible Gadget Shop
 8:    we're offering the following exciting
 9:    products:
10: <p>
11: <table border=1 cellpadding ="5">
12: <tr>
13: <td align="center"> <b>product</b></td>
14: <td align="center"> <b>price</b> </td>
15: </tr>
16: <?php
17: $dbh = dbmopen( "./data/products", "c" )
18:        or die( "Couldn't open DBM" );
19: $key = dbmfirstkey( $dbh );
20: while ( $key != "" )
21:     {
22:     $value = dbmfetch( $dbh, $key );
23:     print "<tr><td align = \"left\"> $key </td>";
24:     print "<td align = \"right\"> \$$value </td></tr>";
25:     $key = dbmnextkey( $dbh, $key );
26:     }
27: dbmclose( $dbh );
28: ?>
29: </table>
```

11

LISTING 11.3 continued

```
30: </body>
31: </html>
```

Figure 11.1 shows the output from Listing 11.3.

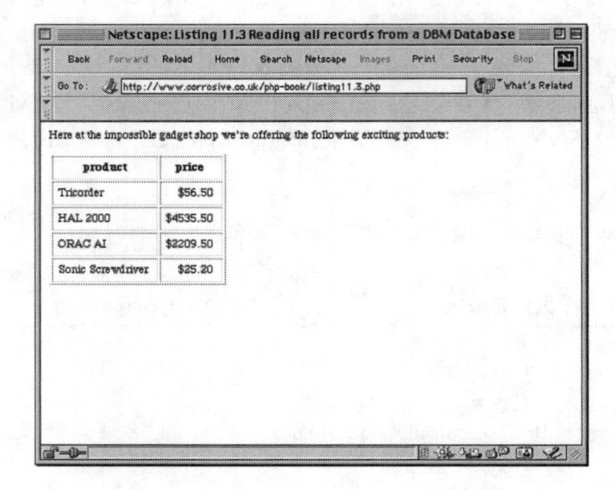

FIGURE 11.1
Reading all records from a DBM database.

Determining Whether an Item Exists in a Database

Before reading or setting an element in a DBM database, it is sometimes useful to know whether the element exists. You can do this with the `dbmexists()` function. `dbmexists()` requires a valid DBM identifier and the name of the element for which you are testing. It returns `true` if the element exists.

```
if ( dbmexists( $dbh, "Tricorder" ) )
   print dbmfetch( $dbh, "Tricorder" );
```

Deleting an Item from a Database

You can delete an item from a database using the `dbmdelete()` function. `dbmdelete()` requires a valid DBM identifier and the name of the element you want to remove from the database. It returns `true` if the item was successfully deleted, and `false` if the element did not exist to be deleted.

```
dbmdelete( $dbh, "Tricorder" );
```

Adding Complex Data Structures to a DBM Database

All data in a DBM database is extracted in string format, so you are limited to storing integers, strings, and doubles. Any other data type will be lost. Let's try to store an array, for example:

```
$array = array( 1, 2, 3, 4 );
$dbh = dbmopen( "./data/test", "c" ) or die("Couldn't open test DBM");
dbminsert( $dbh, "arraytest", $array );
print gettype( dbmfetch( $dbh, "arraytest" ) );
// prints "string"
```

We create an array and store it in the variable `$array`. We then open a database and attempt to insert an element called `"arraytest"`, passing it the `$array` variable as the value. We then test the return type from `dbmfetch()` when attempting to access `"arraytest"` and ascertain that a string has been returned. In fact, if we printed the value stored in the `"arraytest"` record, we would get the string `"Array"`. That would seem to wrap up any hopes for storing arrays and objects.

Fortunately, PHP provides a feature that allows you to "freeze-dry" values of any data type in string format. The data can then be stored in a database or file until it is needed. You can use this technique to store arrays and even objects in a DBM database.

To convert the array in the previous example to a string, we must use the `serialize()` function. `serialize()` requires a value of any type and returns a string:

```
$array = array( 1, 2, 3, 4 );
print serialize( $array );
// prints a:4:{i:0;i:1;i:1;i:2;i:2;i:3;i:3;i:4;}
```

We can now store this string in the DBM database. When we want to resurrect it, we can use the `unserialize()` function. `unserialize()` requires a serialized string and returns a value of the appropriate data type.

This allows you to store complex data structures within the relatively simple format allowed by DBM databases. Listing 11.4 serializes an associative array for each of the items in our list of products and adds the result to our database.

LISTING 11.4 Adding Complex Data to a DBM Database

```
 1: <html>
 2: <head>
 3: <title>Listing 11.4 Adding complex data to a DBM database</title>
 4: </head>
 5: <body>
 6: Adding complex data to database
 7: <?php
 8: $products = array(
 9:          "Sonic Screwdriver" => array( price=>"22.50",
10:                                         shipping=>"12.50",
11:                                         color=>"green" ),
12:          "Tricorder"         => array( price=>"55.50",
13:                                         shipping=>"7.50",
14:                                         color=>"red" ),
15:          "ORAC AI"           => array( price=>"2200.50",
16:                                         shipping=>"34.50",
17:                                         color=>"blue" ),
18:          "HAL 2000"          => array( price=>"4500.50",
19:                                         shipping=>"18.50",
20:                                         color=>"pink" )
21:          );
22: $dbh = dbmopen( "./data/newproducts", "c" )
23:          or die("Couldn't open products DBM");
24: while ( list ( $key, $value ) = each ( $products ) )
25:      dbmreplace( $dbh, $key,  serialize( $value ) );
26: dbmclose( $dbh );
27: ?>
28: </table>
29: </body>
30: </html>
```

We build a multidimensional array, containing the product names as keys and four arrays of product information as values. We then open the database and loop through the array. For each element, we pass the product name and a serialized version of the product array to `dbmreplace()`. We then close the database.

Listing 11.5 writes the code that extracts this data.

LISTING 11.5 Retrieving Serialized Data from a DBM Database

```
1: <html>
2: <head>
3: <title>Listing 11.5 Retrieving serialized
4:           data from a DBM database</title>
5: </head>
6: <body>
```

LISTING 11.5 continued

```
 7:  Here at the Impossible Gadget Shop
 8:     we're offering the following exciting
 9:     products:
10: <p>
11: <table border=1 cellpadding ="5">
12: <tr>
13: <td align="center"> <b>product</b></td>
14: <td align="center"> <b>color</b> </td>
15: <td align="center"> <b>shipping</b> </td>
16: <td align="center"> <b>price</b> </td>
17: </tr>
18: <?php
19: $dbh = dbmopen( "./data/newproducts", "c" )
20:           or die("Couldn't open test DBM");
21: $key = dbmfirstkey( $dbh );
22: while ( $key != "" )
23:     {
24:     $prodarray = unserialize( dbmfetch( $dbh, $key ) );
25:     print "<tr><td align=\"left\"> $key </td>";
26:     print "<td align=\"left\">$prodarray[color] </td>\n";
27:     print "<td align=\"right\">\$$prodarray[shipping] </td>\n";
28:     print "<td align=\"right\">\$$prodarray[price] </td></tr>\n";
29:     $key = dbmnextkey( $dbh, $key );
30:     }
31: dbmclose( $dbh );
32: ?>
33: </table>
34: </body>
35: </html>
```

Listing 11.5 is similar to the example in Listing 11.3. In this case though, we are displaying more fields. We open the database and then use `dbmfirstkey()` and `dbmnextkey()` to loop through each item in the database. We extract the value and use `unserialize()` to reconstruct the product array. It is then simple to print each element of the product array to the browser. Figure 11.2 shows the output from Listing 11.5.

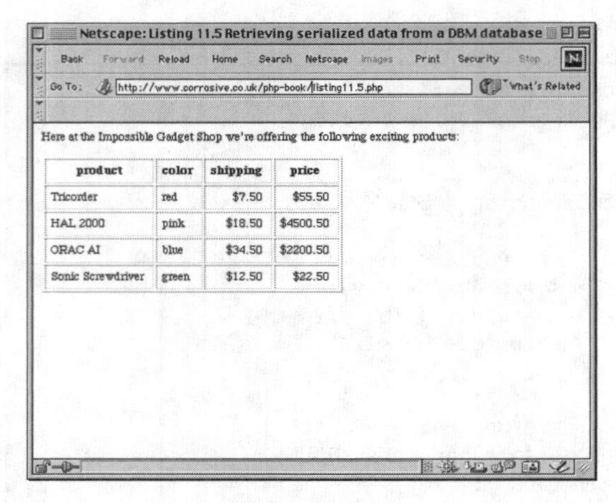

FIGURE 11.2
Retrieving serialized data from a DBM database.

An Example

We now have enough information to build an example using some of the techniques discussed in this hour. Our brief is to build an administration page to enable a site editor to change the prices in the products database created in Listing 11.2. The administrator should also be able to remove elements from the database and add new ones. The page will not be hosted on a publicly available server, so security is not a problem for this project.

First, we must build a form that incorporates all the elements in the database. The user will be able to change any price using a text field and choose which items to delete using a check box. She will also have two text fields for adding a new item to the database. Listing 11.6 shows the code to create the form.

LISTING 11.6 Building an HTML Form Based on Content from a DBM Database

```
 1: <?
 2: $dbh = dbmopen( "./data/products", "c" )
 3:         or die("Couldn't open test DBM");
 4: ?>
 5: <html>
 6: <head>
 7: <title>Listing 11.6 Building an html form based
 8:         on content from a DBM database</title>
 9: </head>
10: <body>
11: <form action="POST">
12: <table border="1">
13: <tr>
14: <td>delete</td>
```

LISTING 11.6 continued

```
15: <td>product</td>
16: <td>price</td>
17: </tr>
18: <?php
19: $key = dbmfirstkey( $dbh );
20: while ( $key != "" )
21:     {
22:     $price = dbmfetch( $dbh, $key );
23:     print "<tr><td><input type='checkbox' name=\"delete[]\" ";
24:     print "value=\"$key\"></td>";
25:     print "<td>$key</td>";
26:     print "<td> <input type=\"text\" name=\"prices[$key]\" ";
27:     print "value=\"$price\"> </td></tr>";
28:     $key = dbmnextkey( $dbh, $key );
29:     }
30: dbmclose( $dbh );
31: ?>
32: <tr>
33: <td> </td>
34: <td><input type="text" name="name_add"></td>
35: <td><input type="text" name="price_add"></td>
36: </tr>
37: <tr>
38: <td colspan=3 align="right">
39: <input type="submit" value="amend">
40: </td>
41: </tr>
42: </table>
43: </form>
44: </body>
45: </html>
```

We start by opening the database as usual. We then begin an HTML form that points back to the current page using PHP's `$PHP_SELF` variable.

Having written some table headers to the screen, we loop through the contents of our database using `dbmfirstkey()` and `dbmnextkey()` to get each key in turn, and `dbmfetch()` to extract the value.

In the first table cell of each row, we create a check box. Notice that we give all these the name `"delete[]"`. This instructs PHP to construct an array called `$delete` of all submitted values that share this name. We use the database element name (stored in `$key`) as the value for each check box. When the form is submitted, therefore, we should have a `$delete` array with the names of all the database elements that we want to delete.

11

We then print the element name to the browser and create another text field. This field presents the product price to the user, ready for amendment. We name the field using a similar technique as we did for the previous field. This time, however, we include the name of the database element in the square brackets of the field name. PHP constructs an associative array called `$prices` from these submitted fields with the DBM element names as keys.

We close the database and revert to HTML mode to write the final fields. These allow the user to add new product and price combinations. Only two fields are required, and we give them the names `name_add` and `price_add`.

Figure 11.3 shows the output from Listing 11.6.

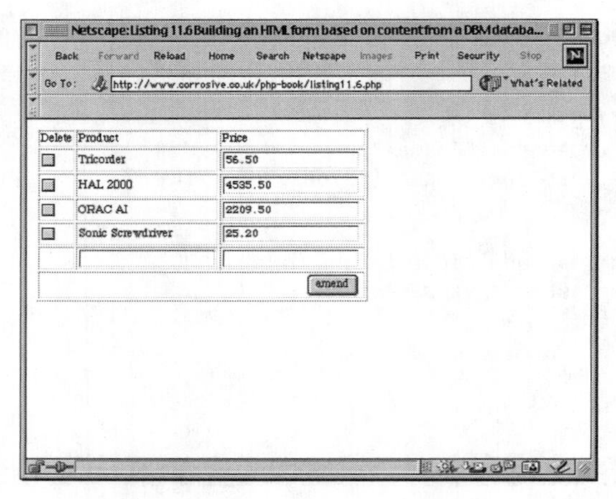

FIGURE 11.3
Building an HTML form based on content from a DBM database.

Now that we have created the form, we need to write code to deal with the user input. This is not as difficult as it sounds. There are three possible actions we can take. First, we can delete items from the database; second, we can amend prices in the database; and third, we can add new elements to the database.

If the form has been submitted, we know which items we need to delete because a `$delete` array variable will have been made available. We need to loop through this array and delete the elements whose names it contains.

```
if ( isset ( $delete ) )
    {
    while ( list ( $key, $val ) = each ( $delete ) )
```

```
        {
        unset( $prices[$val]);
        dbmdelete( $dbh, $val );
        }
    }
```

First we test that the `$delete` variable is set. If the user has only just arrived at the page, or if she has not chosen to delete any items, the variable will not exist. If the variable exists, we can go ahead and loop through it. For each string held in the `$delete` array, we call `dbmdelete()` removing the element by that name from the database. We also interfere with another array variable. The `$prices` array contains all the key value pairs in the database, although some of the values might have been changed by the user. If we do not remove the elements, we delete from the database the `$price` array as well. The next block of code adds them to the database once again.

To update the database according to the user amendments, we have a choice. We could only update those elements that the user has elected to change. We would choose this option if we expected many users to be using the script at the same time. As it is, this script will be run by a single administrator, so we opt to update every element in the database:

```
if ( isset ( $prices ) )
    {
    while ( list ( $key, $val ) = each ( $prices ) )
        dbmreplace( $dbh, $key, $val );
    }
```

We test for the existence of the `$prices` array. This should contain a new version of the entire database. We loop through the array, calling `dbmreplace()` for each of its elements.

Finally, we need to check whether the user has submitted a new product for inclusion in the database:

```
if ( ! empty( $name_add ) && ! empty( $price_add ) )
    dbmreplace( $dbh, "$name_add", "$price_add" );
```

Instead of testing whether the `$name_add` and `$price_add` variables are set, we test whether they are empty. This is a subtle but important difference. When the user submits the form we have built, these variables will always be set. They may, however, contain empty strings. We do not want to add empty strings to our database, so we only execute the code to insert new values if neither variable is empty:

```
if ( ! empty( $name_add ) && ! empty( $price_add ) )
    dbmreplace( $dbh, "$name_add", "$price_add" );
```

We use `dbminsert()` rather than `dbmreplace()` to guard against the user inadvertently overwriting an element that has already been defined.

You can see the complete code in Listing 11.7.

Listing 11.7 The Complete Product Maintenance Code

```
 1: <?php
 2: $dbh = dbmopen( "./data/products", "c" )
 3:         or die("Couldn't open test DBM");
 4:
 5: if ( isset ( $delete ) )
 6:     {
 7:     while ( list ( $key, $val ) = each ( $delete ) )
 8:         {
 9:         unset( $prices[$val]);
10:         dbmdelete( $dbh, $val );
11:         }
12:     }
13:
14: if ( isset ( $prices ) )
15:     {
16:     while ( list ( $key, $val ) = each ( $prices ) )
17:         dbmreplace( $dbh, $key, $val );
18:     }
19:
20: if ( ! empty( $name_add ) && ! empty( $price_add ) )
21:     dbminsert( $dbh, "$name_add", "$price_add" );
22: ?>
23:
24: <html>
25: <head>
26: <title>Listing 11.7 The complete product maintenance code</title>
27: </head>
28: <body>
29:
30: <form action="<? print $PHP_SELF; ?>" action="POST">
31:
32: <table border="1">
33: <tr>
34: <td>delete</td>
35: <td>product</td>
36: <td>price</td>
37: </tr>
38:
39: <?php
40: $key = dbmfirstkey( $dbh );
41: while ( $key != "" )
42:     {
43:     $price = dbmfetch( $dbh, $key );
44:     print "<tr><td><input type='checkbox' name=\"delete[]\" ";
45:     print "value=\"$key\"></td>";
46:     print "<td>$key</td>";
```

LISTING 11.7 continued

```
47:     print "<td> <input type=\"text\" name=\"prices[$key]\" ";
48:     print "value=\"$price\"> </td></tr>";
49:     $key = dbmnextkey( $dbh, $key );
50:     }
51:
52: dbmclose( $dbh );
53: ?>
54:
55: <tr>
56: <td> </td>
57: <td><input type="text" name="name_add"></td>
58: <td><input type="text" name="price_add"></td>
59: </tr>
60:
61: <tr>
62: <td colspan=3 align="right">
63: <input type="submit" value="amend">
64: </td>
65: </tr>
66:
67: </table>
68: </form>
69:
70: </body>
71: </html>
```


Summary

In this hour, you learned how to use PHP's powerful DBM functions to store and retrieve data. You learned how to use `dbmopen()` to acquire a DBM identifier, which you can use with other DBM functions. You learned how to add data to a database with `dbminsert()`, alter it with `dbmreplace()`, and delete data with `dbmdelete()`. You learned how to use `dbmfetch()` to retrieve data. You learned how to use `serialize()` and `unserialize()` to save complex data structures to a DBM database. Finally, you worked through an example that uses many of the techniques we have examined.

Q&A

Q When should I use a DBM database as opposed to a SQL database?

A A DBM database is a good option when you want to store small amounts of relatively simple data (typically name/value pairs). Scripts built to use a DBM database have the virtue of portability. If you intend to store large amounts of data or many fields, consider using a SQL database, such as MySQL.

Workshop

The Workshop provides quiz questions to help you solidify your understanding of the material covered. Try to understand the quiz answers before continuing to the next hour's lesson. Quiz answers are provided in Appendix A.

Quiz

1. What function would you use to open a DBM database?
2. What function would you use to insert a record into a DBM database?
3. What function would you use to replace a record in a DBM database?
4. How would you access a record from a DBM database by name?
5. How would you get the name (as opposed to the value) of the first element in a DBM database?
6. How would you get subsequent element names?
7. How would you delete a named element from a DBM database?

Activities

1. Create a DBM database to keep track of user names and passwords. Create a script that allows users to register their combinations. Don't forget to check for duplications.
2. Create an authentication script that checks a user name and password. If the user input matches an entry in the database, present the user with a special message. Otherwise, represent the login form to the user.

HOUR 12

Database Integration—MySQL

One of the defining features of PHP is the ease with which you can connect to and manipulate databases. In this hour, we will concentrate on MySQL, but you will find similar functions for many of the databases that PHP supports. Why MySQL? It fits well with the spirit of PHP in that it is free to the individual user, yet remains a powerful tool that can be used as the basis of demanding real-world projects. Furthermore, versions of MySQL are available for multiple platforms. You can download MySQL from `http://www.mysql.org`. In this hour, you will learn

- A few SQL samples
- How to connect to the MySQL database server
- How to select a database
- About error handling
- How to add data to a table

- How to retrieve data from a table
- How to alter data in a table
- About the structure of databases

A (Very) Brief Introduction to SQL

NEW TERM *SQL* stands for *Structured Query Language*. It provides a standardized syntax by which different types of database can be queried. Most SQL database products provide their own extensions to the language, just as many browsers provide their own extensions to HTML. Nonetheless, an understanding of SQL enables you to work with a wide range of database products across multiple platforms.

This book cannot even begin to describe the intricacies of SQL. Nonetheless, we can fill in some background about MySQL and SQL in general.

MySQL runs as a server daemon to which users on the same or even remote machines can connect. Once connected to the server, you can select a database if you have the privileges to do so.

Within a database, there will be a varying number of tables of data. Each table is arranged in rows and columns. The intersection between a row and a column is the point at which each item of data you want to store and access sits. Each column only accepts a predefined type of data, `INT` for integer, for example, or `VARCHAR` for a variable number of characters up to a defined limit.

To create a new table within a database we have selected, we might use a SQL query like the following:

```
CREATE TABLE mytable (  first_name VARCHAR(30), second_name VARCHAR(30), age INT);
```

Our new table has three columns. `first_name` and `second_name` can contain strings of up to 30 characters. `age` can contain any integer.

To add data to this table, we could use an `INSERT` statement:

```
INSERT INTO mytable ( first_name, second_name, age ) VALUES ( 'John', 'Smith', 36
➥);
```

The field names to which we want to add data are defined in the first set of parentheses. The values we want to insert are defined in the second.

To acquire all the data in a table, we would use a `SELECT` statement:

```
SELECT * FROM mytable;
```

The "*" symbol represents a wildcard which means "all fields." To acquire the information from a single field, you can use the column name in place of the wildcard:

```
SELECT age FROM mytable;
```

To change the values already stored in a table, you can use an `UPDATE` statement:

```
UPDATE mytable SET first_name = 'Bert';
```

This changes the `first_name` field in every row to "Bert". We can narrow the focus of `SELECT` and `UPDATE` statements with a `WHERE` clause. For example,

```
SELECT * FROM mytable WHERE first_name = 'Bert';
```

returns only those rows whose `first_name` fields contain the string "Bert". This next example

```
UPDATE mytable SET first_name = "Bert" WHERE second_name = "Baker";
```

changes the `first_name` fields of all rows whose `second_name` fields contain "Baker".

For more information on SQL, see *Sams Teach Yourself SQL in 21 Days* by Ryan K. Stephens et. al.

Connecting to the Database Server

Before you can begin working with your database, you must first connect to the server. PHP provides the `mysql_connect()` function to do just this. `mysql_connect()` does not require any arguments but accepts up to three strings: the hostname, a username, and a password. If you omit any or all of these arguments, the function assumes `localhost` as the host and that no password or username has been set up in the `mysqluser` table, unless defaults have been set up in the `php.ini` file. Naturally, this is unwise for anything but a test database, so we will always include a username and password in our examples. `mysql_connect()` returns a link identifier if the connection is successful. You can store this return value in a variable so that you can continue to work with the database server.

12

The following code fragment uses `mysql_connect()` to connect to the MySQL database server:

```
$link =  mysql_connect( "localhost", "root", "n1ckel"  );
if ( ! $link )
   die( "Couldn't connect to MySQL" );
```

If you are using PHP in conjunction with Apache, you could also connect to the database server with `mysql_pconnect()`. From the coder's perspective, this function works in exactly the same way as `mysql_connect()`. In fact, there is an important difference. If you use this function, the connection does not die when your script stops executing or if you call `mysql_close()` (which ends a standard connection to the MySQL server). Instead, the connection is left active, waiting for another process to call `mysql_pconnect()`. In other words, the overhead of opening a new connection to the server can be saved if you use `mysql_pconnect()` and a previous call to the script has left the connection open.

Selecting a Database

Now that we have established a connection to the MySQL daemon, we must choose which database we want to work with. You can select a database with the `mysql_select_db()` function. `mysql_select_db()` requires a database name and optionally accepts a link identifier. If you omit this, the identifier returned from the last connection to the server will be assumed. `mysql_select_db()` returns `true` if the database exists and you are able to access it. In the following fragment, we select a database called `sample`.

```
$database = "sample";
mysql_select_db( $sample ) or die ( "Couldn't open $sample );
```

Finding Out About Errors

So far we have tested the return values of the MySQL functions that we have used and called `die()` to end script execution if a problem occurs. You might, however, want to print more informative error messages to the browser to aid debugging. MySQL sets an error number and an error string whenever an operation fails. You can access the error number with `mysql_errno()`, and the error string with `mysql_error()`. Listing 12.1 brings our previous examples together into a simple script that connects to the server and selects a database. We use `mysql_error()` to make our error messages more useful.

LISTING 12.1 Opening a Connection and Selecting a Database

```
 1: <html>
 2: <head>
 3: <title>Listing 12.1 Opening a connection and
 4: selecting a database</title>
 5: </head>
 6: <body>
 7: <?php
 8: $user = "harry";
 9: $pass = "elbomonkey";
10: $db = "sample";
11: $link = mysql_connect( "localhost", $user, $pass  );
12: if ( ! $link )
13:     die( "Couldn't connect to MySQL" );
```

LISTING 12.1 continued

```
14: print "Successfully connected to server<P>";
15: mysql_select_db( $db )
16:     or die ( "Couldn't open $db: ".mysql_error() );
17: print "Successfully selected database \"$db\"<P>";
18: mysql_close( $link );
19: ?>
20: </body>
21: </html>
```

If we change the value of the `$db` variable to `"notthere"`, we will be attempting to open a nonexistent database. The output of our `die()` function call will look something like the following:

```
Couldn't open sample2: Access denied for user: 'harry@localhost' to database
'sample2'
```

Adding Data to a Table

Now that we have access to our database, we can add information to one of its tables. For the following examples, imagine that we are building a site that allows people to buy domain names.

We have created a table within the `sample` database called `domains`. The table was created with five columns: a primary key field called `id` that will automatically increment an integer as data is added, a `domain` field that will contain a variable number of characters (`VARCHAR`), a `sex` field that will contain a single character, and a `mail` field that will contain a user's email address. The following SQL statement was used in the MySQL client to create the table:

```
create table domains ( id INT NOT NULL AUTO_INCREMENT,
                PRIMARY KEY( id ),
                domain VARCHAR( 20 ),
                sex CHAR(1),
                mail VARCHAR( 20 ) );
```

To add data to this table, we will need to construct and execute a SQL query. PHP provides the `mysql_query()` function for this purpose. `mysql_query()` requires a string containing a SQL query and, optionally, a link identifier. If the identifier is omitted, the query is sent to the database server to which you last connected. `Mysql_query()` returns a positive value if the query is successful. If your query contains a syntax error, or if you don't have permission to access the database in question, then `query()` returns `false`. Note that a successful query does not necessarily result in any altered rows. Listing 12.2 extends our previous examples and uses `mysql_query()` to send an `INSERT` statement to the `domains` table in the `sample` database.

LISTING 12.2 Adding a Row to a Table

```
 1: <html>
 2: <head>
 3: <title>Listing 12.2 Adding a row to a table</title>
 4: </head>
 5: <body>
 6: <?php
 7: $user = "harry";
 8: $pass = "elbomonkey";
 9: $db = "sample";
10: $link =  mysql_connect( "localhost", $user, $pass  );
11: if ( ! $link )
12:     die( "Couldn't connect to MySQL" );
13: mysql_select_db( $db, $link )
14:         or die ( "Couldn't open $db: ".mysql_error() );
15: $query = "INSERT INTO domains ( domain, sex, mail )
16:         values( '123xyz.com', 'F', 'sharp@adomain.com' )";
17: mysql_query( $query, $link )
18: or die ( "Couldn't add data to \"domains\" table: "
19: .mysql_error() );
20: mysql_close( $link );
21: ?>
22: </body>
23: </html>
```

Notice that we did not insert a value for the `id` column. This field will auto-increment.

Of course, every time we reload the script in Listing 12.2, the same data is added to a new row. Listing 12.3 creates a script that will enter user input into our database.

LISTING 12.3 Adding User Input to a Database

```
 1: <html>
 2: <head>
 3: <title>Listing 12.3 Adding user input to a database</title>
 4: </head>
 5: <body>
 6: <?php
 7: if ( isset( $domain ) && isset( $sex ) && isset( $domain ) )
 8:     {
 9:     // check user input here!
10:     $dberror = "";
11:     $ret = add_to_database( $domain, $sex, $mail, $dberror );
12:     if ( ! $ret )
```

LISTING 12.3 continued

```
13:         print "Error: $dberror<BR>";
14:     else
15:         print "Thank you very much";
16:     }
17: else    {
18:     write_form();
19:     }
20:
21: function add_to_database( $domain, $sex, $mail, &$dberror )
22:     {
23:     $user = "harry";
24:     $pass = "elbomonkey";
25:     $db = "sample";
26:     $link =  mysql_pconnect( "localhost", $user, $pass  );
27:     if ( ! $link )
28:         {
29:         $dberror = "Couldn't connect to MySQL server";
30:         return false;
31:         }
32:     if ( ! mysql_select_db( $db, $link ) )
33:         {
34:         $dberror = mysql_error();
35:         return false;
36:         }
37: $query = "INSERT INTO domains ( domain, sex, mail )
38:     values( '$domain', '$sex', '$mail' )";
39:     if ( ! mysql_query( $query, $link ) )
40:         {
41:         $dberror = mysql_error();
42:         return false;
43:         }
44:     return true;
45:     }
46:
47: function write_form()
48:     {
49:     global $PHP_SELF;
50:     print "<form action=\"$PHP_SELF\" method=\"POST\">\n";
51:     print "<input type=\"text\" name=\"domain\"> ";
52:     print "The domain you would like<p>\n";
53:     print "<input TYPE=\"text\" name=\"mail\"> ";
54:     print "Your mail address<p>\n";
55:     print "<select name=\"sex\">\n";
56:     print "\t<option value=\"F\"> Female\n";
57:     print "\t<option value=\"M\"> Male\n";
58:     print "</select>\n";
59:     print "<input type=\"submit\" value=\"submit!\">\n</form>\n";
60:     }
61: ?>
```

LISTING 12.3 continued

```
62: </body>
63: </html>
```

To keep the example brief, we have left out one important process in Listing 12.3. We are trusting our users. We should in fact check any kind of user input. We deal with the string functions that help you test user input in Hour 17, "Working with Strings."

We check for the variables `$domain`, `$sex`, and `$mail`. If they exist, we can be fairly certain that the user has submitted data, and we call the `add_to_database()` function.

The `add_to_database()` function requires four arguments: the `$domain`, `$sex`, and `$mail` variables submitted by the user, and a string variable called `$dberror`. We populate this last argument with any error strings we encounter. For this reason, we accept `$dberror` as a reference to a variable. Any changes made to this string within the function will change the original argument rather than a copy.

We attempt to open a connection to the MySQL server. If this fails, we assign an error string to `$dberror` and end the execution of the function by returning `false`. We select the database that contains the `domains` table and build a SQL query to insert the user-submitted values. We pass this to `mysql_query()`, which makes the query for us. If either `mysql_select_db()` or `mysql_query()` fail, we assign the value returned by `mysql_error()` to `$dberror` and return `false`. Assuming that all went well, the function returns `true`.

Back in the calling code, we can test the return value from `add_to_database()`. If the function returns `true`, we can be sure that we have added to the database and thank the user. Otherwise, we write an error message to the browser. We know that the `$dberror` variable that we passed to `add_to_database()` will now contain useful information, so we include it in our error message.

If our initial `if` statement fails to find `$domain`, `$sex`, or `$mail` variables, we can assume that no data has been submitted and call another user-defined function, `write_form()`, which outputs an HTML form to the browser.

Acquiring the Value of an Automatically Incremented Field

In our previous examples, we have added data to our database without worrying about the `id` column, which automatically increments as data is inserted. If we need the value of this field for a record at a later date, we can always extract it with a SQL query. What if we need the value straight away, though? It would be wasteful to look it up. Luckily, PHP provides `mysql_insert_id()`, a function that returns the value of an auto-incremented key field after a SQL `INSERT` statement has been performed. `mysql_insert_id()` optionally accepts a link identifier as an argument. With no arguments, it works with the most recent link established.

So, if we want to tell a user the number we have allocated to her order, we could call `mysql_insert_id()` directly after adding the user's data to our database.

```
$query = "INSERT INTO domains ( domain, sex, mail ) values( '$domain', '$sex',
➥ '$mail' )";
mysql_query( $query, $link );
$id =  mysql_insert_id();
print "Thank you. Your transaction number is $id. Please quote it in any
➥queries.";
```

Accessing Information

Now that we can add information to a database, we need to look at strategies for retrieving the information that it contains. As you might guess, you can use `mysql_query()` to make a `SELECT` query. How do you use this to look at the returned rows, though? When you perform a successful `SELECT` query, `mysql_query()` returns a result identifier. You can pass this identifier to other functions to access and gain information about a resultset.

Finding the Number of Rows Found by a Query

You can find the number of rows returned as a result of a `SELECT` query using the `mysql_num_rows()` function. `mysql_num_rows()` requires a result identifier and returns a count of the rows in the set. Listing 12.4 uses a SQL `SELECT` statement to request all rows in the `domains` table and then uses `mysql_num_rows()` to determine the table's size.

LISTING 12.4 Finding the Number of Rows Returned by a `SELECT` Statement with `mysql_num_rows()`

```
1: <html>
2: <head>
3: <title>Listing 12.4 Using mysql_num_rows()</title>
4: </head>
5: <body>
6: <?php
7: $user = "harry";
8: $pass = "elbomonkey";
9: $db = "sample";
```

LISTING 12.4 continued

```
10: $link =  mysql_connect( "localhost", $user, $pass  );
11: if ( ! $link )
12:     die( "Couldn't connect to MySQL" );
13: mysql_select_db( $db, $link )
14:     or die ( "Couldn't open $db: ".mysql_error() );
15: $result = mysql_query( "SELECT * FROM domains" );
16: $num_rows = mysql_num_rows( $result );
17: print "There are currently $num_rows rows in the table<P>";
18: mysql_close( $link );
19: ?>
20: </body>
21: </html>
```

The `mysql_query()` function returns a result identifier. We then pass this to `mysql_num_rows()`, which returns the total number of rows found.

Accessing a Resultset

After you have performed a `SELECT` query and gained a result identifier, you can use a loop to access each found row in turn. PHP maintains an internal pointer that keeps a record of your position within a found set. This moves on to the next row as each one is accessed.

You can easily get an array of the fields in each found row with `mysql_fetch_row()`. This function requires a result identifier, returning an array containing each field in the row. When the end of the found set is reached, `mysql_fetch_row()` returns `false`. Listing 12.5 outputs the entire `domains` table to the browser.

LISTING 12.5 Listing All Rows and Fields in a Table

```
 1: <html>
 2: <head>
 3: <title>Listing 12.5 Listing all rows and fields in a table</title>
 4: </head>
 5: <body>
 6: <?php
 7: $user = "harry";
 8: $pass = "elbomonkey";
 9: $db = "sample";
10: $link =  mysql_connect( "localhost", $user, $pass  );
11: if ( ! $link )
12:     die( "Couldn't connect to MySQL" );
13: mysql_select_db( $db, $link )
14:     or die ( "Couldn't open $db: ".mysql_error() );
15: $result = mysql_query( "SELECT * FROM domains" );
16: $num_rows = mysql_num_rows( $result );
```

LISTING 12.5 continued

```
17: print "There are currently $num_rows rows in the table<P>";
18: print "<table border=1>\n";
19: while ( $a_row = mysql_fetch_row( $result ) )
20:     {
21:     print "<tr>\n";
22:     foreach ( $a_row as $field )
23:         print "\t<td>$field</td>\n";
24:     print "</tr>\n";
25:     }
26: print "</table>\n";
27: mysql_close( $link );
28: ?>
29: </body>
30: </html>
```

After we have connected to the server and selected the database, we use `mysql_query()` to send a `SELECT` statement to the database server. We store the returned result pointer in a variable called `$result`. We use this to acquire the number of found rows as before.

In the test expression of our `while` statement, we assign the result of `mysql_fetch_row()` to the variable `$a_row`. Remember that an assignment operator returns the value of its right-hand operand, so the assignment resolves to `true` as long as `mysql_fetch_row()` returns a positive value. Within the body of the `while` statement, we loop through the row array contained in `$a_row`, outputting each element to the browser embedded in a table cell.

You can also access fields by name in one of two ways. `mysql_fetch_array()` returns a numeric array, as does `mysql_fetch_row()`. It also returns an associative array, with the names of the fields as the keys. The following fragment rewrites the `while` statement from Listing 12.5, incorporating `mysql_fetch_array()`:

```
print "<TABLE BORDER=1>\n";
while ( $a_row = mysql_fetch_array( $result ) )
    {
    print "<TR>\n";
    print "<TD>$a_row[mail]</TD><TD>$a_row[domain]</TD>\n";
    print "</TR>\n";
    }
print "</TABLE>\n";
```

You can also extract the fields from a row as properties of an object with `mysql_fetch_object()`. The field names become the names of the properties. The following fragment once again rewrites the `while` statement from Listing 12.5, this time incorporating `mysql_fetch_object()`:

```
print "<table border=1>\n";
while ( $a_row = mysql_fetch_object( $result ) )
    {
    print "<tr>\n";
    print "<td>$a_row->mail</td><td>$a_row->domain</td>\n";
    print "</tr>\n";
    }
print "</table>\n";
```

Both `mysql_fetch_array()` and `mysql_fetch_object()` make it easier for you to selectively extract information from a row. Neither of these functions takes much longer than `mysql_fetch_row()` to execute.

Changing Data

You can change data using the `mysql_query()` function in conjunction with an `UPDATE` statement. Once again, a successful `UPDATE` statement does not necessarily change any rows. You need to use a function to call `mysql_affected_rows()` to discover whether you have changed data in your table. `mysql_affected_rows()` optionally accepts a link identifier. If this is missing, the most recent connection is assumed. This function can be used with any SQL query that can alter data in a table row.

Listing 12.6 builds a script that allows an administrator to change any of the values in the `domain` column of our example table.

LISTING 12.6 Using `mysql_query()` to Alter Rows in a Database

```
 1: <html>
 2: <head>
 3: <title>Listing 12.6 Using mysql_query()
 4: to alter rows in a database</title>
 5: </head>
 6: <body>
 7: <?php
 8: $user = "harry";
 9: $pass = "elbomonkey";
10: $db = "sample";
11: $link =  mysql_connect( "localhost", $user, $pass  );
12: if ( ! $link )
13:     die( "Couldn't connect to MySQL" );
14: mysql_select_db( $db, $link )
15:     or die ( "Couldn't open $db: ".mysql_error() );
16: if ( isset( $domain ) && isset( $id ) )
17:     {
18:     $query = "UPDATE domains SET domain = '$domain' where id=$id";
```

LISTING 12.6 continued

```
19:     $result = mysql_query( $query );
20:     if ( ! $result )
21:         die ("Couldn't update: ".mysql_error());
22: print "<h1>Table updated ". mysql_affected_rows() .
23:     " row(s) changed</h1><p>";
24:     }
25: ?>
26: <form action="<? print $PHP_SELF ?>" method="POST">
27: <select name="id">
28: <?
29: $result = mysql_query( "SELECT domain, id  FROM domains" );
30: while( $a_row = mysql_fetch_object( $result ) )
31:     {
32:     print "<OPTION VALUE=\"$a_row->id\"";
33:     if ( isset($id) && $id == $a_row->id )
34:         print " SELECTED";
35:     print "> $a_row->domain\n";
36:     }
37: mysql_close( $link );
38: ?>
39: </select>
40: <input type="text" name="domain">
41: </form>
42: </body>
43: </html>
```

We open a connection to the database server and select a database as normal. We then test for the presence of the variables `$domain` and `$id`. If these are present, we build a SQL `UPDATE` query that changes the value of the `domain` field where the `id` field contains the same value as our `$id` variable. We do not get an error if a nonexistent id is used or if the `$domain` variable is the same as the current value for `domain` in the relevant row. Instead, the `mysql_affected_rows()` simply returns 0. We print this return value (usually 1 in this example) to the browser.

We print an HTML form to allow the administrator to make her changes. Note that we use `mysql_query()` once again to extract the values of the `id` and `domain` column and incorporate them in an HTML `SELECT` element. The administrator will use this pop-up menu to choose which domain to change. If the administrator has already submitted the form and the id value she chose matches the value of the `id` field we are currently outputting, we add the string `SELECTED` to the `OPTION` element. This ensures that her changed value will be instantly visible to her in the menu.

Getting Information About Databases

Until now, we have primarily looked at adding information to and extracting information from a database. PHP provides a range of functions that allow you to find out about the number and structure of databases available from the current connection.

Listing Databases

You can get a list of all databases available from the current connection with the function `mysql_list_dbs()`. This function optionally accepts a link identifier and returns a result identifier that can be used to output all the databases available. To do this, you can call the function `mysql_tablename()` for each of the databases found. `mysql_tablename()` accepts two arguments: a result pointer and the index of a database. It returns the name of the database referenced. Databases are indexed from 0. You can find the total number of databases found by your call to `mysql_list_dbs()` by calling `mysql_num_rows()` with the result identifier returned by `mysql_list_dbs()`.

Listing 12.7 connects to the MySQL daemon and prints a list of databases to the browser.

LISTING 12.7 Listing the Databases Available in a Connection

```
 1: <html>
 2: <head>
 3: <title>Listing 12.7 Listing the databases
 4: available in a connection</title>
 5: </head>
 6: <body>
 7: <?php
 8: $user = "harry";
 9: $pass = "elbomonkey";
10: $link =  mysql_connect( "localhost", $user, $pass  );
11: if ( ! $link )
12:     die( "Couldn't connect to MySQL" );
13: $db_res = mysql_list_dbs( $link );
14: $num = mysql_num_rows( $db_res );
15: for( $x = 0; $x < $num; $x++ )
16:     print mysql_tablename( $db_res, $x )."<br>";
17: mysql_close( $link );
18: ?>
19: </body>
20: </html>
```

Our call to `mysql_list_dbs()` gives us a result pointer. We can use the result pointer to get the total number of items found by passing it to `mysql_num_rows()` as an argument. We assign this total to a variable (`$num`), which we then use in a `for` statement.

For each iteration, we pass `mysql_tablename()` our result pointer and an index number, `$x`, which is incremented from 0 to one less than the total number of databases found. Figure 12.1 shows the output from Listing 12.7.

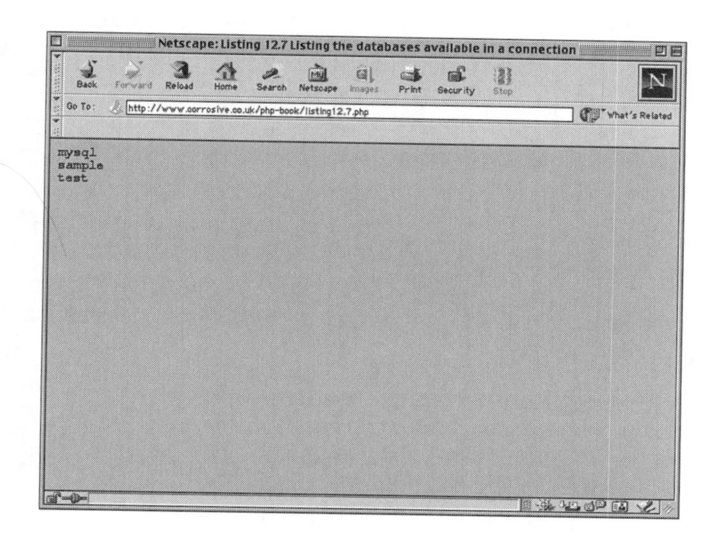

FIGURE 12.1
Listing available databases.

You could also use the result identifier returned by `mysql_list_dbs()` in the same way as that returned by `mysql_query()` for a `SELECT` query. In other words, you can pass the identifier to `mysql_fetchrow()`. `mysql_fetchrow()` returns an array with the database name in the first element of the array.

Listing the Tables Within a Database

Given a database name and (optionally) a link identifier, you can list all the tables in a database using the `mysql_list_tables()` function. If the database can be found and you have the right privileges, `mysql_list_tables()` returns a result identifier that you can use with `fetch` functions such as `mysql_fetch_row()`. Alternatively, you can use the `mysql_tablename()` function as we did with `mysql_list_dbs()`.

The following fragment uses mysql_list_tables() to list all the tables in a database:

```
$result = mysql_list_tables( "sample", $link );
while ( $tab_rows =  mysql_fetch_row( $result ) )
        print "$tab_rows[0]<BR>\n";
```

Listing and Exploring Fields

When you acquire a result identifier from mysql_query() using a SELECT query, you can calculate the number of columns returned using mysql_num_fields(). mysql_num_fields() requires a result identifier and returns an integer representing the number of fields found:

```
$result = mysql_query( "SELECT * from domains" );
$num_fields = mysql_num_fields( $result );
```

Each field in a found set has an index (beginning at zero). Using a result identifier and a field's index number, you can discover many of the field's attributes, including its name, type, maximum length, and flags.

To get the name of a field, pass a result identifier and an index number to mysql_field_name():

```
$result = mysql_query( "SELECT * from domains" );
$num_fields = mysql_num_fields( $result );
for ( $x=0; $x<$num_fields; $x++ )
     mysql_field_name( $result, $x ) . "<BR>\n";
```

To get the maximum length of a field, pass the same arguments to mysql_field_len():

```
$result = mysql_query( "SELECT * from domains" );
$num_fields = mysql_num_fields( $result );
for ( $x=0; $x<$num_fields; $x++ )
     mysql_field_len( $result, $x ) . "<BR>\n";
```

To get the flags associated with a field, pass a result identifier and an index number to mysql_field_flags():

```
$result = mysql_query( "SELECT * from domains" );
$num_fields = mysql_num_fields( $result );
for ( $x=0; $x<$num_fields; $x++ )
     mysql_field_flags( $result, $x ) . "<BR>\n";
```

You can also get the type of a field with the mysql_field_type() function. It requires the same arguments:

```
$result = mysql_query( "SELECT * from domains" );
$num_fields = mysql_num_fields( $result );
```

```
for ( $x=0; $x<$num_fields; $x++ )
     mysql_field_flags( $result, $x ) . "<BR>\n";
```

Database Structure—Bringing It All Together

Listing 12.8 combines all these techniques to list every database, table, and field available to us from a connection.

LISTING 12.8 Listing Every Database, Table, and Field

```
 1: <html>
 2: <head>
 3: <title>Listing 12.8 Listing every database, table, and field</title>
 4: </head>
 5: <body>
 6: <?php
 7: $user = "root";
 8: $pass = "n1ckel";
 9: $db = "sample";
10: $link =  mysql_connect( "localhost", $user, $pass  );
11: if ( ! $link )
12:     die( "Couldn't connect to MySQL" );
13: $db_res = mysql_list_dbs( $link );
14: while ( $db_rows = mysql_fetch_row( $db_res ) )
15:     {
16:     print "<b>$db_rows[0]</b>\n";
17:     if ( !@mysql_select_db( $db_rows[0], $link ) )
18:         {
19:         print "<dl><dd>couldn't connect -- " .  mysql_error() ." </dl>";
20:         continue;
21:         }
22:     $tab_res = mysql_list_tables( $db_rows[0], $link );
23:     print "\t<dl><dd>\n";
24:     while ( $tab_rows =  mysql_fetch_row( $tab_res ) )
25:         {
26:         print "\t<b>$tab_rows[0]</b>\n";
27:         $query_res = mysql_query( "SELECT * from $tab_rows[0]" );
28:         $num_fields = mysql_num_fields( $query_res );
29:         print "\t\t<dl><dd>\n";
30:         for ( $x=0; $x<$num_fields; $x++ )
31:             {
32:             print "\t\t<i>";
33:             print mysql_field_type( $query_res, $x );
34:             print "</i> <i>";
35:             print mysql_field_len( $query_res, $x );
36:             print "</i> <b>";
37:             print mysql_field_name( $query_res, $x );
38:             print "</b> <i>";
39:             print mysql_field_flags( $query_res, $x );
```

12

LISTING 12.8 continued

```
40:             print "</i><br>\n";
41:             }
42:         print "\t\t</dl>\n";
43:         }
44:     print "\t</dl>\n";
45:     }
46: mysql_close( $link );
47: ?>
48: </body>
49: </html>
```

We connect to the MySQL server in the usual way and call `mysql_list_dbs()` to acquire a result identifier. We pass this to `mysql_fetch_row()`, which returns the name of every database available in turn (stored in the first element of the `$db_rows` array).

We pass each database name to `mysql_select_db()`. If we don't have permission to access the database, we print a message to the browser and use the `continue` statement to begin the next iteration. If we are able to select the database, we can go ahead and print its table names.

We pass the database name to `mysql_list_tables()` and acquire a new result identifier. Once again, we can pass this to `mysql_fetch_row()`, beginning a new loop to list each table name. We print the table name and then use it to construct a SQL `SELECT` query, requesting all fields and rows from the table. We pass the query to `mysql_query()` and acquire yet another result identifier.

The result identifier acquired from `mysql_query()` is passed to `mysql_num_fields()` to get the number of fields in the found set.

We use a `for` statement to loop from zero to one less than the total number of columns in the resultset. The counter variable (`$x`) represents the index number of each field in the table that we want to test. We call each of the field test functions we covered in the last section in turn, outputting their return values to the browser.

When this script is run, we should get a reasonably neat listing of every database, table, and field available from a connection. Figure 12.2 shows part of the output from this script.

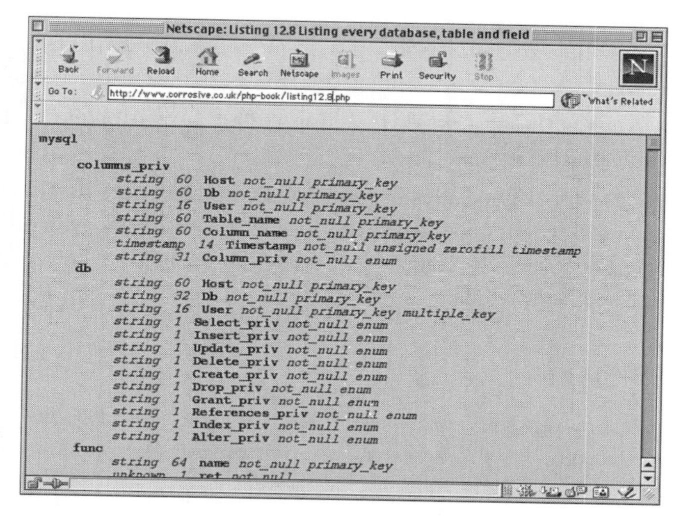

FIGURE 12.2
Listing every database, table, and field.

Summary

In this hour, we covered some of the basics of storing and retrieving information from a MySQL database.

You should now be able to establish a connection to the MySQL server using `mysql_connect()` or `mysql_pconnect()`.

You should be able to select a database with `mysql_select_db()`. If the selection fails, you should be able to discover more about the error with `mysql_error()`.

You should be able to make SQL queries using `mysql_query()`. With the result identifier this function returns, you should be able to access data, or discover the number of rows you have transformed.

You should be able to use PHP's MySQL functions to list the number of databases, tables, and fields accessible to you and to find out more about the attributes of individual fields.

Q&A

Q This hour is specific to MySQL. How transferable are these examples to other SQL databases?

A There are functions for mSQL that mirror those for MySQL almost exactly. Other database servers have corresponding PHP functions that support their features and capabilities. The common feature of many suites of database function is the capability to send SQL queries. If you work with ANSI (standard) SQL, you should have little problem adapting scripts across database servers.

Q What is the best way of writing code that can be easily adapted to work with different database servers?

A It is often a good idea to group code that queries a database into a single class or library. If you need to rewrite your project to work with a different database, you will only need to change a discrete portion of your code without disturbing the project as a whole.

Workshop

The Workshop provides quiz questions to help you solidify your understanding of the material covered. Try to understand the quiz answers before continuing to the next hour's lesson. Quiz answers are provided in Appendix A.

Quiz

1. How would you open a connection to a MySQL database server?
2. What function would you use to select a database?
3. What function would you use to send a SQL query to a database?
4. What does the `mysql_insert_id()` function do?
5. Assuming that you have sent a successful `SELECT` query to MySQL, name three functions that you might use to access each row returned.
6. Assuming that you have sent a successful `UPDATE` query to MySQL, what function might you use to determine how many rows have been updated?
7. What function would you call if you want to list all databases available from a MySQL server?
8. What function would you use to list all tables within a database?

Activities

1. Create a database with three fields: email (up to 70 characters), message (up to 250 characters), and date (an integer that will contain a UNIX time stamp). Build a script to allow users to populate the database.
2. Create a script that displays the information from the database you created in activity 1.

HOUR 13

Beyond the Box

In this hour, we will look at some of the functions that allow you to gain information from or interact with the outside world. In this hour, you will learn

- More about environmental variables
- The anatomy of an HTTP connection
- How to acquire a document from a remote server
- How to create your own HTTP connection
- How to connect to other network services
- How to send email from your scripts

Environmental Variables

You have already encountered some of the environmental variables that PHP, in conjunction with your server, makes available for you. Some of these variables are useful in discovering more information about your visitors. You should be aware, though, that these variables might not be available on your system or with your server software, so it is a good idea to check before using them in scripts. Table 13.1 lists some of the variables that you might be able to use to find out more about your visitors.

TABLE 13.1 Some Useful Environmental Variables

Variable	*Description*
`$HTTP_REFERER`	The URL from which the current script was called (the misspelling is deliberate).
`$HTTP_USER_AGENT`	Information about the browser and platform that the visitor is using.
`$REMOTE_ADDR`	The visitor's IP address.
`$REMOTE_HOST`	The visitor's hostname.
`$QUERY_STRING`	The (encoded) string that may be appended to the URL (in the format `?akey=avalue&anotherkey=anothervalue`). These keys and values should become available to your scripts in global variables.
`$PATH_INFO`	Additional information that may be appended to the URL.

Listing 13.1 builds a script that outputs the contents of these variables to the browser.

LISTING 13.1 Listing Some Environmental Variables

```
 1: <html>
 2: <head>
 3: <title>Listing 13.1 Listing some environmental variables</title>
 4: </head>
 5: <body>
 6: <?php
 7: $envs = array( "HTTP_REFERER", "HTTP_USER_AGENT", "REMOTE_ADDR", "REMOTE_
    HOST", "QUERY_STRING", "PATH_INFO" );
 8: foreach ( $envs as $env )
 9:     {
10:     if ( isset( $$env ) )
11:         print "$env: ${$env}<br>";
12:     }
13: ?>
14: </body>
15: </html>
```

Notice our use of dynamic variables to convert strings into variables of the same name. We covered this technique in Hour 4, "The Building Blocks."

Figure 13.1 shows the output from Listing 13.1. The data in Figure 13.1 was generated as a result of calling the script from a link in another page. The link that called the script looked like this:

```
<A HREF='eg13.1.php/my_path_info?query_key=query_value'>go</A>
```

As you can see, the link uses a relative path to call `listing13.1.php`.

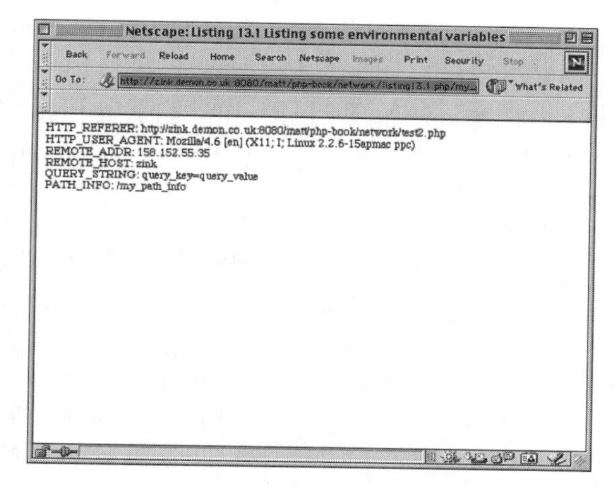

FIGURE 13.1
Printing some environmental variables to the browser.

Additional path information (`my_path_info`) is included after the document name, which becomes available in `$PATH_INFO`.

We have hard-coded a query string (`query_key=query_value`) into the link, which becomes available in `$QUERY_STRING`. You will most often encounter a query string when using a form with a `GET` method argument, but you can also build your own query strings to pass information from page to page. The query string consists of name value pairs separated by ampersand (&) symbols. These pairs are URL encoded, which means that any characters that are illegal or have other meanings in URLs will be converted to their hexadecimal equivalents. Although you have access to the entire query string in the `$QUERY_STRING` environmental variable, you will rarely need to use this fact. Each key name will be available to you as a global variable (`$query_value` in our example) that will hold a corresponding decoded value (`"query_value"`).

13

The $HTTP_REFERER variable can be useful to you if you want to track which hits on your script originate from which links. Beware, though; this and other environmental variables can be easily faked. You will see how later in this hour. Because correcting it would cause compatibility problems, we are stuck with the incorrect spelling of 'referrer'. Not all browser will supply this header, so you should avoid relying upon it.

You can parse the $HTTP_USER_AGENT variable to work out the platform and browser that the visitor is using. Once again, this can be faked. This variable can be useful if you need to present different HTML code or JavaScript according to the browser type and version the visitor is using. Hour 17, "Working with Strings," and Hour 18, "Working with Regular Expressions," will give you the tools you need to extract any information you want from this string.

The $REMOTE_ADDR variable contains the user's IP address and can be used to track unique visitors to your site. Be aware, though, that many Web users do not have a fixed IP address. Instead, their Internet service providers dynamically allocate them an address when they dial up. This means that a single IP address might be used by different visitors to your site, and that a single visitor might enter using different IP addresses from the same account.

The $REMOTE_HOST variable might not be available to you, depending on the configuration of your server. If available, it will hold the hostname of the user. The presence of this variable requires that the server look up the hostname for every request, so it is often disabled for the sake of efficiency. If you don't have access to this variable, you can acquire it yourself using the value of the $REMOTE_ADDR variable. You will see how to do this later in the hour.

A Brief Summary of an HTTP Client/Server Negotiation

It is beyond the scope of this book to explore all the information exchanged between server and client when a request is made, not least because PHP handles most of these details for you. It is a good idea to gain a basic understanding of this process, however, especially if you intend to write scripts that fetch Web pages or check the status of Web addresses.

NEW TERM *HTTP* stands for *hypertext transfer protocol*. It is essentially a set of rules that define the process by which a client sends a request and a server returns a response. Both client and server provide information about themselves and the data to be transferred. Much of this information becomes available to you in environmental variables.

The Request

A client requests data from the server according to a strict set of rules. The request consists of up to three components:

- A request line
- A header section
- An entity body

The request line is mandatory. It consists of a request method, typically `GET`, `HEAD`, or `POST`; the address of the document to required; and the HTTP version to be used (HTTP/1.0 or HTTP/1.1). A typical request for a document called `mydoc.html` might look like this:

```
GET /mydoc.html HTTP/1.0
```

The client is making a `GET` request. In other words, it is requesting an entire document but sending no data itself (in fact you *can* send small amounts of data as part of a GET request by adding a query string to the URL. The `HEAD` method would be used if you only wanted information about a document. The `POST` method is used to transfer data from a client to the server, usually from an HTML form.

The request line is enough in itself to make a valid `GET` request. To inform the server that a request is complete, an empty line must be sent.

Most clients will follow the request line with a header section in which name/value pairs can be sent to the server. Some of these will become available to you as environmental variables. Each client header consists of a key and value on one line separated by a colon. Table 13.2 lists a few of these.

TABLE 13.2 Some Client Headers

Name	*Description*
Accept	The media types that the client can work with.
Accept-Encoding	The types of data compression that the client can handle.
Accept-Charset	The character sets that the client prefers.
Accept-Language	The language that the client prefers ('en' for English).
Host	The host to which a request is being made. Some servers that maintain multiple virtual servers rely heavily on this header.
Referer	The document from which a request is being made.
User-Agent	Information about the client type and version.

For `GET` and `HEAD` methods, the header section ends the request, and an empty line is sent to the server. For requests made using the `POST` method, an empty line is followed by the entity body. An entity body consists of any data to be sent to the server. This is usually a set of URL-encoded name/value pairs similar to those found in a query string.

Listing 13.2 shows a request sent to a server by Netscape 4.6.

LISTING 13.2 Typical Client Headers Sent by a Netscape Browser

```
GET / HTTP/1.0
Referer: http://zink.demon.co.uk:8080/matt/php-book/network/test2.php
Connection: Keep-Alive
User-Agent: Mozilla/4.6  (X11; I; Linux 2.2.6-15apmac ppc)
Host: www.corrosive.co.uk
Accept: image/gif, image/x-xbitmap, image/jpeg, image/pjpeg, image/png, */*
Accept-Encoding: gzip
Accept-Language: en
Accept-Charset: iso-8859-1,*,utf-8
```

The Response

After a server has received a client's request, it sends a response back to the client. The response usually consists of three parts:

- A status line
- A header section
- An entity body

As you can see, there's a lot of symmetry between a request and a response. In fact, certain headers can be sent by either client or server, especially those that provide information about an entity body.

The status line consists of the HTTP version that the server is using (HTTP/1.0 or HTTP/1.1), a response code, and a text message that clarifies the meaning of the response code.

There are many response codes that a server can send to a browser. Each code provides some information about the success or otherwise of the request. Table 13.3 lists some of the more common response codes.

TABLE 13.3 Some Response Codes

Code	*Text*	*Description*
200	OK	The request was successful, and the requested data will follow.
301	Moved Permanently	The requested data no longer exists on the server. A location header will contain a new address.
302	Moved Temporarily	The requested data has been moved. A location header will contain a new address.
404	Not Found	The data could not be found at the supplied address.
500	Internal Server Error	The server or a CGI script has encountered a severe problem in attempting to serve the data.

A typical response line, therefore might look something like the following:

```
HTTP/1.1 200 OK
```

The header section includes a series of response headers, formatted in the same way as request headers. Table 13.4 lists some headers commonly sent by servers.

TABLE 13.4 Some Common Server Headers

Name	*Description*
Date	The current date
Server	The server name and version
Content-Type	The MIME type of content in the entity body
Content-Length	The size of the entity in bytes
Location	The full address of an alternative document

After the headers have been sent, the server sends an empty line to the client followed by the entity body (the document originally requested). Listing 13.3 shows a typical server response.

LISTING 13.3 A Server Response

```
1: HTTP/1.1 200 OK
2: Date: Sun, 30 Jan 2000 18:02:20 GMT
3: Server: Apache/1.3.9 (UNIX)
4: Connection: close
5: Content-Type: text/html
```

LISTING 13.3 continued

```
 6:
 7: <html>
 8: <head>
 9: <title>Listing 13.3 A server response</title>
10: </head>
11: <body>
12: Hello
13: </body>
14: </html>
```

Getting a Document from a Remote Address

Although PHP is a server-side language, it can act as a client, requesting data from remote servers and making the output available to your scripts. If you are already comfortable reading files from the server, you will have no problem using PHP to acquire information from the Web. In fact, the syntax is exactly the same. You can use `fopen()` to connect to a Web address in the same way as you would with a file. Listing 13.4 opens a connection to a remote server and requests a page, printing the result to the browser.

LISTING 13.4 Getting and Printing a Web Page with `fopen()`

```
 1: <html>
 2: <head>
 3: <title>Listing 13.4 Getting and printing a web page with fopen()</title>
 4: </head>
 5: <body>
 6: <?php
 7: $webpage = "http://www.corrosive.co.uk/php/hello.html";
 8: $fp = fopen( $webpage, "r" ) or die("couldn't open $webpage");
 9: while ( ! feof( $fp ))
10:     print fgets( $fp, 1024 );
11: ?>
12: </body>
13: </html>
```

When this script is run, you should see the PHP homepage. Notice that the images on the page we include are "broken." This is because paths to images in IMG elements are often relative. When our script outputs the data it has downloaded, the user's browser will look on our server for the images referenced. We could work around this problem to some extent by adding the following tag to the HEAD element of our script:

```
<base href="http://www.php.net">
```

It is unlikely that you will want to output an entire page to the browser. More commonly, you would parse the document you download.

`fopen()` returns a file pointer if the connection is successful and `false` if the connection cannot be established or the page doesn't exist. After you have a file pointer, you can use it as normal to read the file. PHP introduces itself to the remote server as a client. On my system, it sends the following request:

```
GET /  HTTP/1.0
Host: www.php.net
User-Agent: PHP/4.0b3
```

This process is simple and is the approach you will use to access a Web page in most instances. You might want to connect to other network services, however, or learn more about a Web document by parsing the server headers. You will look at how to do this later in the hour.

Converting IP Addresses and Hostnames

Even if your server does not provide you with a `$REMOTE_HOST` variable, you will probably know the IP address of a visitor from the `$REMOTE_ADDR` environmental variable. You can use this in conjunction with the function `gethostbyaddr()` to get the user's hostname. `gethostbyaddr()` requires a string representing an IP address. It returns the equivalent hostname. If an error occurs, it returns the IP address it was given. Listing 13.5 creates a script that uses `gethostbyaddr()` to acquire the user's hostname if the `$REMOTE_HOST` variable is not available.

LISTING 13.5 Using `gethostbyaddr()` to Get a Hostname

```
 1: <html>
 2: <head>
 3: <title>Listing 13.5 Using gethostbyaddr() to get a host name</title>
 4: </head>
 5: <body>
 6: <?php
 7: if ( isset( $REMOTE_HOST ) )
 8:     print "Hello visitor at $REMOTE_HOST<br>";
 9: elseif ( isset ( $REMOTE_ADDR ) )
10:     print "Hello visitor at ".gethostbyaddr( $REMOTE_ADDR )."<br>";
11: else
12:     print "Hello you, wherever you are<br>";
13: ?>
14: </body>
15: </html>
```

If we have access to the `$REMOTE_HOST` variable, we simply print this to the browser. Otherwise, if we have access to the `$REMOTE_ADDR` variable, we attempt to acquire the user's hostname using `gethostbyaddr()`. If all else fails, we print a generic welcome message.

To attempt to convert a hostname to an IP address, you can use `gethostbyname()`. This function requires a hostname as its argument. It returns an IP address or, if an error occurs, the hostname you provided.

Making a Network Connection

So far we have had it easy. This is because PHP makes working with a Web page on a remote server as simple as opening a file on your own system. Sometimes, though, you need to exercise a little more control over a network connection or acquire more information about it.

You can make a connection to an Internet server with `fsockopen()`, which requires a hostname or IP address, a port number, and two reference variables. Remember that you can pass a reference to a variable by prepending an ampersand (&) symbol. The reference variables you passed to `fsockopen()` are populated to provide more information about the connection attempt should it fail. You can also pass `fsockopen()` an optional timeout integer, which determines how long `fsockopen()` will wait (in seconds) before giving up on a connection. If the connection is successful, a file pointer is returned. Otherwise, it returns `false`.

The following fragment initiates a connection to a Web server:

```
$fp = fsockopen( "www.corrosive.co.uk", 80, &$errno, &errdesc, 30 );
```

80 is the usual port number that a Web server listens on.

The first reference variable, `$errno`, contains an error number if the connection is unsuccessful, and `$errdesc` might contain more information about the failure.

After you have the file pointer, you can both write to the connection with `fputs()` and read from it with `fgets()` as you might with a file. When you have finished working with your connection, you should close it with `fclose()`.

We now have enough information to initiate our own connection to a Web server. Listing 13.6 makes an HTTP connection, retrieving a page and storing it in a variable.

LISTING 13.6 Retrieving a Web Page Using `fsockopen()`

```
 1: <html>
 2: <head>
 3: <title>Listing 13.6 Retrieving a Web page using fsockopen()</title>
 4: </head>
 5: <body>
 6: <?php
 7: $host = "www.corrosive.co.uk";
 8: $page = "/index.html";
 9: $fp = fsockopen( "$host", 80, &$errno, &$errdesc);
10: if ( ! $fp )
11: die ( "Couldn't connect to $host:\nError: $errno\nDesc: $errdesc\n" );
12:
13: $request = "GET $page HTTP/1.0\r\n";
14: $request .= "Host: $host\r\n";
15: $request .= "Referer: http://www.corrosive.co.uk/refpage.html\r\n";
16: $request .= "User-Agent: PHP test client\r\n\r\n";
17: $page = array();
18: fputs ( $fp, $request );
19: while ( ! feof( $fp ) )
20:      $page[] = fgets( $fp, 1024 );
21: fclose( $fp );print "the server returned ".(count($page))." lines!";
22: ?>
23: </body>
24: </html>
```

Notice the request headers that we send to the server. The Webmaster at the remote host will see the value you sent in the User-Agent header in her log file. She may also assume that a visitor to our page connected from a link at `http://www.corrosive.co.uk/refpage.html`. For this reason, you should be cautious of some of the environmental variables available to your scripts. Treat them as an invaluable guide, rather than a set of facts.

There are some legitimate reasons why you might want to fake some headers. You might need to parse some data that will only be sent to Netscape compatible browsers. The only way you can do this is to include the word "Mozilla" in the User-Agent header. Nevertheless, pity the poor Webmaster. Operational decisions are made as a result of server statistics, so try not to distort the information you provide.

The example in Listing 13.6 adds little to PHP's built-in method of acquiring Web pages. Listing 13.7 uses `fsockopen()` to check the status codes returned by servers when we request a series of pages.

LISTING 13.7 Outputting the Status Lines Returned by Web Servers

```
 1: <html>
 2: <head>
 3: <title>Listing 13.7 Outputting the status lines returned by web servers</
    title>
 4: </head>
 5: <body>
 6: <?php
 7: $to_check = array (     "www.corrosive.co.uk"  =>  "/index.html",
 8:                     "www.virgin.com"       =>  "/notthere.html",
 9:                     "www.4332blah.com"     =>  "/nohost.html"
10:                     );
11: foreach ( $to_check as $host => $page )
12:     {
13:     $fp = fsockopen( "$host", 80, &$errno, &$errdesc, 10);
14:     print "Trying $host<BR>\n";
15:     if ( ! $fp )
16:         {
17:         print "Couldn't connect to $host:\n<br>Error: $errno\n<br>Desc:
            $errdesc\n";
18:         print "<br><hr><br>\n";
19:         continue;
20:         }
21:     print "Trying to get $page<br>\n";
22:     fputs( $fp, "HEAD $page HTTP/1.0\r\n\r\n" );
23:     print fgets( $fp, 1024 );
24:     print "<br><br><br>\n";
25:     fclose( $fp );
26:     }
27: ?>
28: </body>
29: </html>
```

We create an associative array of the server names and page addresses we want to check. We loop through this using a `foreach` statement. For every element, we initiate a connection using `fsockopen()`, setting a timeout of 10 seconds. If the connection fails, we print a message to the browser and use `continue` to move on to the next pair. If the connection is successful, we send a request to the server. We use the `HEAD` method because we are not interested in parsing an entity body. We use `fgets()` to get the status line from the server. We are not going to work with server headers for this example, so we close the connection with `fclose()` and move on to the next element in the list.

Figure 13.2 shows the output from Listing 13.7.

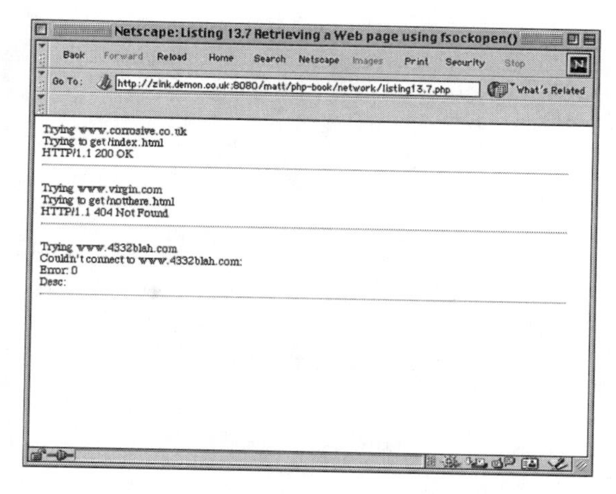

FIGURE 13.2

A script to print server response headers.

Making an NNTP Connection Using `fsockopen()`

`fsockopen()` can be used to make a connection to any Internet server. In Listing 13.8, we connect to an NNTP (Usenet) server, select a newsgroup, and list the headers of the first message.

LISTING 13.8 A Basic NNTP Connection Using `fsockopen()`

```
 1: <html>
 2: <head>
 3: <title>Listing 13.8 A basic NNTP connection using fsockopen()</title>
 4: </head>
 5: <body>
 6: <?php
 7: $server = "news"; // change this to your news server
 8: $group  = "alt.test";
 9: $line = "";
10: print "<pre>\n";
11: print "-- Trying to connect to $server\n\n";
12: $fp = fsockopen( "$server", 119, &$error, &$description, 10 );
13: if ( ! $fp )
14:     die("Couldn't connect to $server\n$errno\n$errdesc\n\n");
15: print "-- Connected to $server\n\n";
16: $line = fgets( $fp, 1024 );
17: $status = explode( " ", $line );
18: if ( $status[0] != 200 )
19:     {
20:     fputs( $fp, "close" );
21:     die("Error: $line\n\n");
22:     }
23: print "$line\n";
```

LISTING 13.8 continued

```
24: print "-- Selecting $group\n\n";
25: fputs( $fp, "group alt.test\n" );
26: $line = fgets( $fp, 1024 );
27: $status = explode( " ", $line );
28: if ( $status[0] != 211 )
29:     {
30:     fputs( $fp, "close" );
31:     die("Error: $line\n\n");
32:     }
33: print "$line\n";
34: print "-- Getting headers for first message\n\n";
35: fputs( $fp, "head\n" );
36: $line = fgets( $fp, 1024 );
37: $status = explode( " ", $line );
38: print "$line\n";
39: if ( $status[0] != 221 )
40:     {
41:     fputs( $fp, "close" );
42:     die("Error: $line\n\n");
43:     }
44: while ( ! ( strpos($line, ".")  === 0 ) )
45:     {
46:     $line = fgets( $fp, 1024 );
47:     print $line;
48:     }
49: fputs( $fp, "close\n" );
50: print "</pre>";
51: ?>
52: </body>
53: </html>
```

The code in Listing 13.8 does little more than demonstrate that an NNTP connection is possible with `fsockopen()`. In a real-world example, you would want to handle the line parsing in a function to save repetition and to extract more information from the server's output. Rather than reinvent the wheel in this way, you might want to investigate PHP's IMAP functions, which will automate much of this work for you.

We store the hostname of our server in a variable, `$server`, and the group we want to select in `$group`. If you wish to run this script, you should assign the hostname of your Internet Service Provider's news server to the `$server` variable. We use `fsockopen()` to connect to the host on port 119, which is the usual port for NNTP connections. If a valid file pointer is not returned, we use `die()` to print the error number and description to the browser and end script execution. On connection, the server should have sent us a confirmation message, so we attempt to acquire this with `fgets()`. If all is well, this string begins with the status code

200. To test this, we use `explode()` to split the `$line` string into an array using the space character as the delimiter. You can learn more about the `explode` function in Hour 17. If the first element of this array is 200, we can continue; otherwise, we end the script.

If all is proceeding as expected, we send the news server the "group" command that should select a newsgroup. If this is successful, the server should return a string beginning with the status code 211. We test this once again, and end execution if we don't get what we are expecting.

Now that we have selected our newsgroup, we send the "head" command to the server, which requests the headers for the first message in the group. Again, we test the server response, looking for the status code 221. Finally, we acquire the header itself. The server's listing of a header will end with a single dot (.) on its own line, so we test for this in a `while` statement. As long as the server's output line does not begin with a dot, we request and print the next line.

Finally, we close the connection. Figure 13.3 shows a typical output from Listing 13.8.

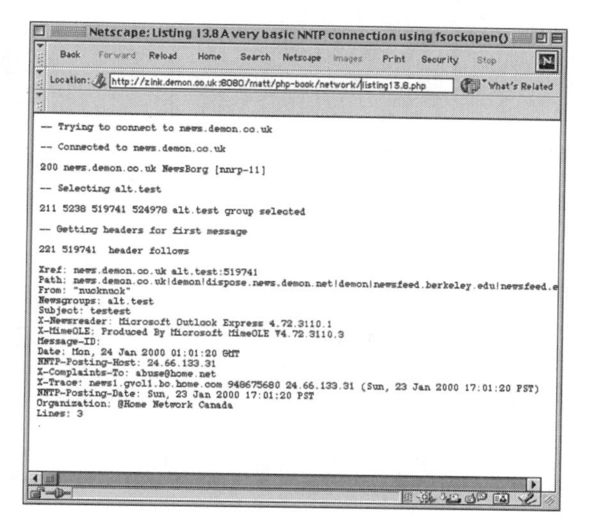

FIGURE 13.3

Making an NNTP connection.

Sending Mail with the `mail()` Function

PHP can automate the sending of Internet mail for you. The `mail()` function requires three strings representing the recipient of the mail, the mail subject, and the message. `mail()` returns `false` if it encounters an error. In the following fragment, we send an email:

```
$to = "someone@adomain.com";
$subject = "hi";
$message = "just a test message! ";
mail( $to, $subject, $message ) or print "Could not send mail";
```

If you are running PHP on a UNIX system, `mail()` will use Sendmail. On other systems, the function will connect to a local or remote SMTP mail server. You should set this using the `SMTP` directive in the php.ini file.

You are not limited to the mail headers implied by the `mail()` function's required arguments. You can include as many mail headers as you want in an optional fourth string argument. These should be separated by CRLF characters ('\r\n'). In the following example, we include a From field in our mail message, as well as an X-Priority header that some clients will recognize:

```
$to = "someone@adomain.com";
$from = "book@corrosive.co.uk";
$subject = "hi";
$message = "just a test message! ";
mail( $to, $subject, $message, "$from\r\nX-Priority: 1 (Highest)" )
or print "Could not send mail";
```

Summary

In this hour, you learned how to use environmental variables to learn more about your visitors. If you don't have access to a user's hostname, you should now be able to use `gethostbyaddr()` to acquire it.

You learned some of the basics about the negotiation that takes place between client and server when an HTTP connection is made.

You learned how to use `fopen()` to get a document from the Web, and how to use `fsockopen()` to make your own HTTP connection. You should also be able to use `fsockopen()` to make connections to other network services. Finally, you learned how to use `mail()` to send email from your scripts.

Q&A

Q HTTP seems a little esoteric. Do I really need to know about it to write good PHP code?

A No. You can write excellent code with knowing the intricacies of client/server interaction. On the other hand, a basic understanding of the process is useful if you want to do more than just download pages from remote servers.

Q If I can send fake headers to a remote server, how suspicious should I be of environmental variables myself?

A You should not trust environmental variables such as `$HTTP_REFERRER` and `$HTTP_USER_AGENT` if their accuracy is essential to the operation of your script. Remember, though, that the vast majority of clients that you deal with will tell you the truth. If you are merely ensuring a productive user experience by detecting browser type or gathering overall statistical information, there is no need to distrust this data.

Workshop

The Workshop provides quiz questions to help you solidify your understanding of the material covered. Try to understand the quiz answers before continuing to the next hour's lesson. Quiz answers are provided in Appendix A.

Quiz

1. What environmental variable might give you the URL of the referring page?
2. Why can you not rely on the `$REMOTE_ADDR` variable to track an individual user across multiple visits to your script?
3. What does HTTP stand for?
4. What client header line tells the server about the browser that is making the request?
5. What does the server response code 404 mean?
6. Without making your own network connection, what function might you use to access a Web page on a remote server?
7. Given an IP address, what function could you use to get a hostname?
8. What function would you use to make a network connection?
9. What PHP function would you use to send an email?

Activities

1. Create a script that accepts a Web hostname (such as `http://www.microsoft.com`) from user input. Send the host a `HEAD` request using `fsockopen()` to create the connection. Print the response to the browser. Remember to handle the possibility that no connection can be established.
2. Create a script that accepts a message from the user and mails it to you. Add environmental variables to the user's message to tell you about his or her browser and IP address.

Hour 14

Working with Dynamic Images

The functions included in this hour rely on an open source library called GD.

The GD library is a set of tools that enable programmers to create and work with images on-the-fly. You can find out more about GD at `http://www.boutell.com/gd/`. If you have the GD library installed on your system and PHP was compiled to use it, you will be able to use PHP's image functions to create dynamic images. Many systems will still run the older version of the library, which allows the creation of images in GIF format. Later versions of the library do not support GIFs for licensing reasons. If your system is using a later library, it is possible to compile PHP so that the image functions output images in PNG format, which is supported by the more popular browsers.

If you have the GD library, you will be able to use PHP's image functions to create sophisticated graphics on-the-fly. In this hour, you will learn

- How to create and output an image
- How to work with colors
- How to draw shapes, including arcs, rectangles, and polygons
- How to fill areas with color
- How to work with TrueType fonts

Creating and Outputting Images

Before you can begin to work with an image, you must acquire an image identifier. You can do this using the `imagecreate()` function. `imagecreate()` requires two arguments, one for the image's height and another for its width. It returns an image identifier, which you will use with most of the functions that we will cover in this hour.

After you have an image identifier, you are nearly ready to output your first image to the browser. To do this, you need the `imagegif()` function, which requires the image identifier as an argument. Listing 14.1 uses these functions to create and output an image.

LISTING 14.1 A Dynamically Created Image

```
1: <?php
2: header("Content-type: image/gif");
3: $image = imagecreate( 200, 200 );
4: imagegif($image);
5: ?>
```

Notice that we sent a `Content-type` header to the browser before doing anything else. We need to tell the browser to expect image information; otherwise, it treats the script's output as HTML. This script can now be called directly by the browser, or as part of an IMG element.

```
<img src="eg14.1.php" alt="a PHP generated image">
```

Figure 14.1 shows the output of Listing 14.1.

We have created a square, but we have no way as yet of controlling its color.

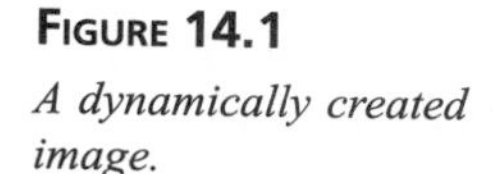

FIGURE 14.1
A dynamically created image.

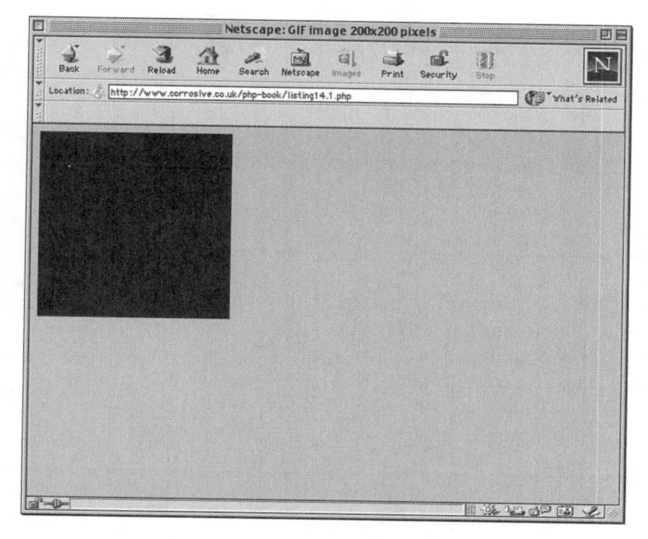

Acquiring Color

To work with color, you need to acquire a color identifier. You can do this with the `imagecolorallocate()` function, which requires an image identifier and three integers between 0 and 255 representing red, green, and blue. The function returns an image identifier that you can use to define the color of shapes, fills, and text.

```
$red = imagecolorallocate($image, 255,0,0);
```

Coincidentally, the first time you call `imagecolorallocate()`, you also set the default color for your image; so by adding the previous code fragment to Listing 14.1, we would create a red square.

Drawing Lines

Before you draw a line on an image, you need to determine the points from and to which you want to draw.

You can think of an image as a block of pixels indexed from 0 on both the horizontal and vertical axes. Their origin is the top left-hand corner of the image.

In other words, the pixel with the coordinates 5, 8 is the sixth pixel along and the ninth pixel down, looking from left to right, top to bottom.

The `imageline()` function draws a line between one pixel coordinate and another. It requires an image identifier, four integers representing the start and end coordinates of the line, and a color identifier.

Listing 14.2 adds to the image created in Listing 14.1, drawing a line from corner to corner.

LISTING 14.2 Drawing a Line with `imageline()`

```
1: <?php
2: header("Content-type: image/gif");
3: $image = imagecreate( 200, 200 );
4: $red = imagecolorallocate($image, 255,0,0);
5: $blue = imagecolorallocate($image, 0,0,255 );
6: imageline( $image, 0, 0, 199, 199, $blue );
7: imagegif($image);
8: ?>
```

We acquire two color identifiers, one for red and one for blue. We then use the identifier stored in the variable `$blue` for the line's color. Notice that our line ends at the coordinates 199, 199 and not 200, 200. Remember that pixels are indexed from 0. Figure 14.2 shows the output from Listing 14.2.

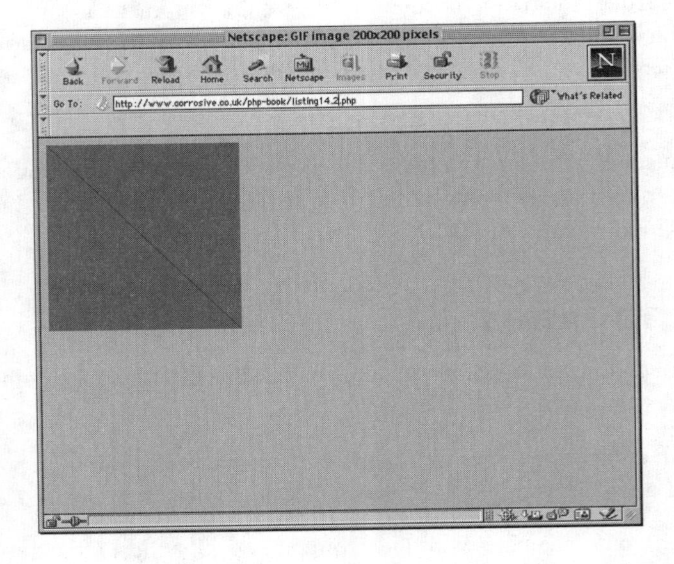

FIGURE 14.2
Drawing a line with `imageline()`.

Applying Color Fills

You can fill an area with color using PHP just as you can with your favorite graphics application. The function `imagefill()` requires an image identifier, starting coordinates for the fill it is to perform, and a color identifier. It then transforms the starting pixel and all adjacent pixels of the same color. Listing 14.3 adds a call to `imagefill()` to our script, making the image a little more interesting.

LISTING 14.3 Using `imagefill()`

```
1: <?php
2: header("Content-type: image/gif");
3: $image = imagecreate( 200, 200 );
4: $red = imagecolorallocate($image, 255,0,0);
5: $blue = imagecolorallocate($image, 0,0,255 );
6: imageline( $image, 0, 0, 199, 199, $blue );
7: imagefill( $image, 0, 199, $blue );
8: imagegif($image);
9: ?>
```

Figure 14.3 shows the output from Listing 14.3.

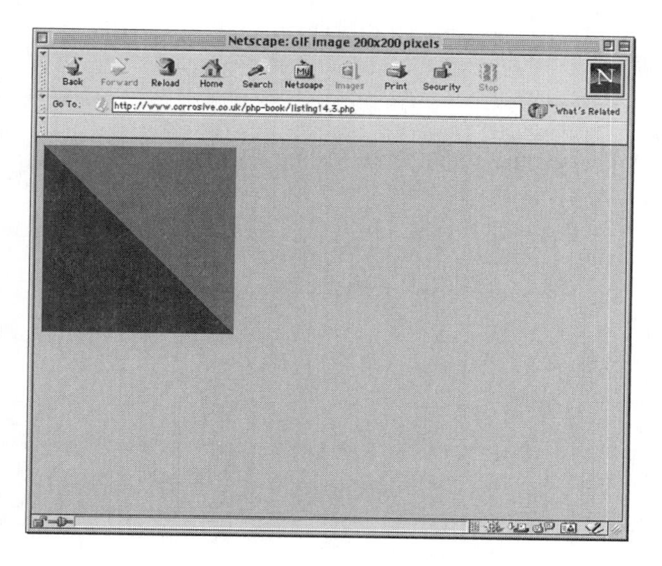

FIGURE 14.3
Using `imagefill()`.

Drawing an Arc

You can add partial or complete arcs to your images with the `imagearc()` function. `imagearc()` requires an image object, coordinates for the center point, an integer for width, an integer for height, a start point and an end point (in degrees), and a color identifier. Arcs are drawn clockwise starting from 3 o'clock. The following fragment draws a quarter circle:

```
imagearc( $image, 99, 99, 200, 200, 0, 90, $blue );
```

This draws a partial arc, with its center at the coordinates 99, 99. The total height and width will both be 200 pixels. Drawing starts at 3 o'clock and continues for 90 degrees (to 6 o'clock).

Listing 14.4 draws a complete circle and fills it with blue.

LISTING 14.4 Drawing a Circle with `imagearc()`

```
1: <?php
2: header("Content-type: image/gif");
3: $image = imagecreate( 200, 200 );
4: $red = imagecolorallocate($image, 255,0,0);
5: $blue = imagecolorallocate($image, 0,0,255 );
6: imagearc( $image, 99, 99, 180, 180, 0, 360, $blue );
7: imagefill( $image, 99, 99, $blue );
8: imagegif($image);
9: ?>
```

Figure 14.4 shows the output from Listing 14.4.

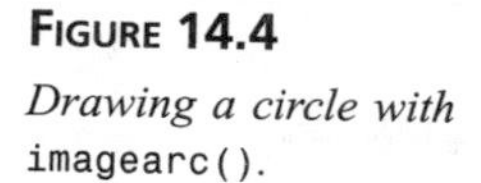

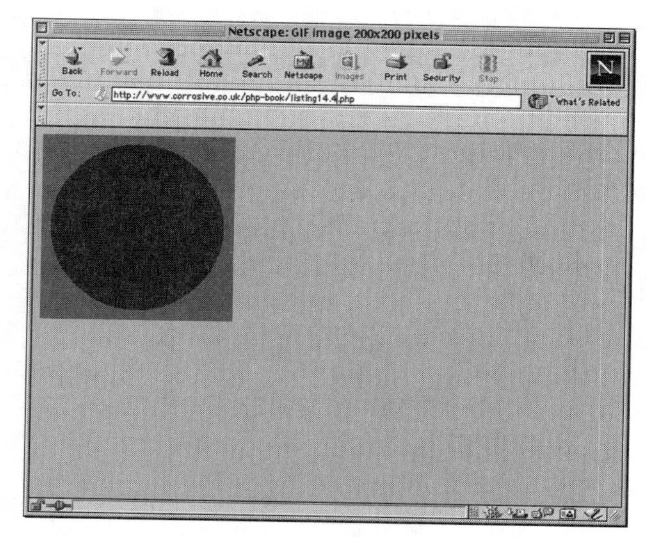

FIGURE 14.4
Drawing a circle with `imagearc()`.

Drawing a Rectangle

You can draw a rectangle in PHP using the `imagerectangle()` function. `imagerectangle()` requires an image identifier, the coordinates for your rectangle's top-left corner, the coordinates for its bottom-right corner, and a color identifier. The following fragment draws a rectangle whose top-left coordinates are 19, 19 and bottom-right coordinates are 179, 179:

```
imagerectangle( $image, 19, 19, 179, 179,  $blue );
```

You could then fill this with `imagefill()`. Because this is such a common operation, however, PHP provides the`imagefilledrectangle()` function, which expects exactly the same arguments as `imagerectangle()` but produces a rectangle filled with the color you specify. Listing 14.5 creates a filled rectangle and outputs the image to the browser.

LISTING 14.5 Drawing a Filled Rectangle with `imagefilledrectangle()`

```
1: <?php
2: header("Content-type: image/gif");
3: $image = imagecreate( 200, 200 );
4: $red = imagecolorallocate($image, 255,0,0);
5: $blue = imagecolorallocate($image, 0,0,255 );
6: imagefilledrectangle( $image, 19, 19, 179, 179,  $blue );
```

LISTING 14.5 continued

```
7: imagegif( $image );
8: ?>
```

Figure 14.5 shows the output from Listing 14.5.

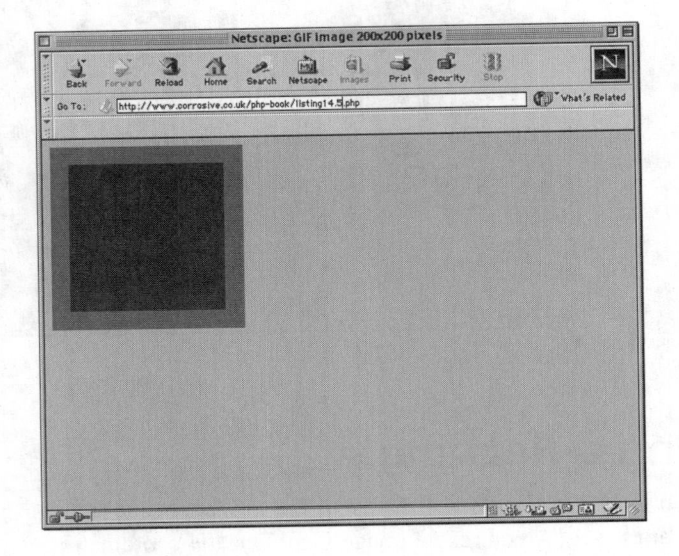

FIGURE 14.5
Drawing a filled rectangle with `imagefilledrectangle()`.

Drawing a Polygon

You can draw more sophisticated shapes using `imagepolygon()`. This function requires an image identifier, an array of point coordinates, an integer representing the number of points in the shape, and a color identifier. The array passed to `imagepolygon()` should be numerically indexed. The first two elements give the coordinates of the first point, the second two give the coordinates of the second point, and so on. `imagepolygon()` fills in the lines between the points, automatically closing your shape by joining the final point to the first. You can create a filled polygon with the `imagefilledpolygon()` function.

Listing 14.6 draws a filled polygon, outputting the result to the browser.

LISTING 14.6 Drawing a Polygon with `imagefilledpolygon()`

```
 1: <?php
 2: header("Content-type: image/gif");
 3: $image = imagecreate( 200, 200 );
 4: $red = imagecolorallocate($image, 255,0,0);
 5: $blue = imagecolorallocate($image, 0,0,255 );
 6: $points = array (     10, 10,
 7:             190, 190,
 8:             190, 10,
 9:             10, 190
10:             );
11: imagefilledpolygon( $image, $points, count( $points )/2 , $blue );
12: imagegif($image);
13: ?>
```

Notice that to tell `imagefilledpolygon()` how many points we want to connect, we count the number of elements in the `$points` array and divide the result by 2. Figure 14.6 shows the output from Listing 14.6.

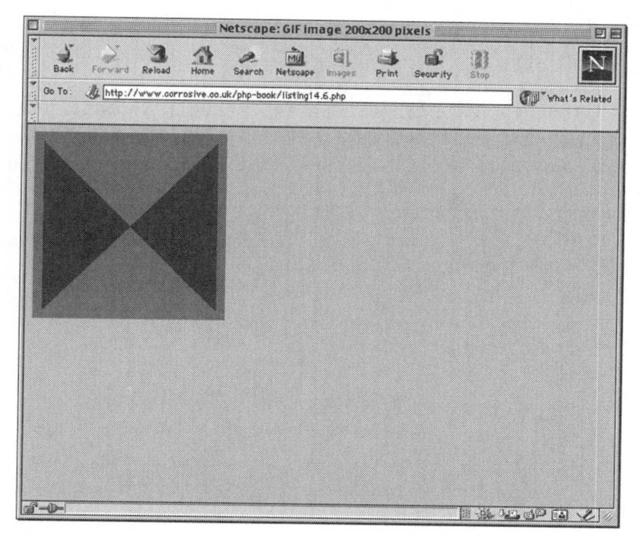

FIGURE 14.6
Drawing a polygon with `imagefilledpolygon()`.

Making a Color Transparent

PHP allows you to make selected colors within your image transparent with `imagecolortransparent()`. This function requires an image identifier and a color identifier. When you output your image to the browser, the color you pass to `imagecolortransparent()` will be transparent. Listing 14.7 changes our polygon code so that the shape "floats" on the browser instead of sitting against a background color.

LISTING 14.7 Making Colors Transparent with `imagecolortransparent()`

```
 1: <?php
 2: header("Content-type: image/gif");
 3:
 4: $image = imagecreate( 200, 200 );
 5: $red = imagecolorallocate($image, 255,0,0);
 6: $blue = imagecolorallocate($image, 0,0,255 );
 7:
 8: $points = array (     10, 10,
 9:             190, 190,
10:             190, 10,
11:             10, 190
12:             );
13:
14: imagefilledpolygon( $image, $points, count( $points )/2 , $blue );
15: imagecolortransparent( $image, $red );
16: imagegif($image);
17: ?>
```

Figure 14.7 shows the output from Listing 14.7.

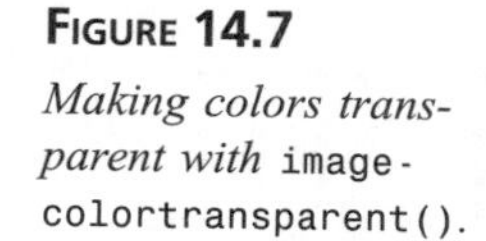

FIGURE 14.7

Making colors transparent with `imagecolortransparent()`.

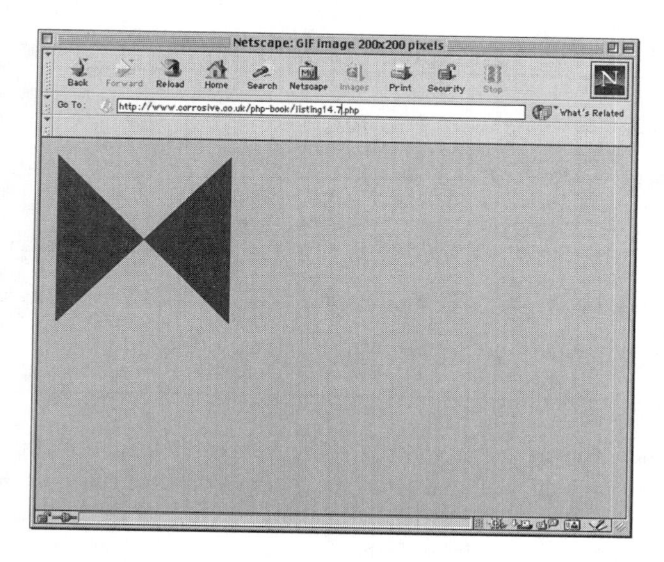

Working with Text

If you have TrueType fonts on your system, you can use these to write text into your images. In addition to the GD library, you need to have the FreeType library installed on your system. If you have this combination, you can create image-based charts or navigation elements. PHP even gives you the tool you need to check that any text that you write will fit within the space available.

Writing a String with `imageTTFtext()`

You can write text to your image with the `imageTTFtext()` function. This requires eight arguments: an image identifier, a size argument representing the height of the characters to be written, an angle, the starting coordinates (one argument for the x axis and another for the y axis), a color identifier, the path to a TrueType font, and the text you want to write.

The start point for any text you write determines where the baseline of the first character in the string will be.

Listing 14.8 writes a string to an image and outputs the result to the browser.

LISTING 14.8 Writing a String with `imageTTFtext()`

```
 1: <?php
 2: header("Content-type: image/gif");
 3:
 4: $image = imagecreate( 400, 200 );
 5: $red = imagecolorallocate($image, 255,0,0);
 6: $blue = imagecolorallocate($image, 0,0,255 );
 7: $font = "/usr/local/jdk121_pre-v1/jre/lib/fonts/LucidaSansRegular.ttf";
 8:
 9: imageTTFtext( $image, 50, 0, 20, 100, $blue, $font, "Welcome!" );
10:
11: imagegif($image);
12: ?>
```

We create a canvas with a width of 400 pixels and a height of 200 pixels. We define two colors and store the path to a TrueType font in a variable called `$font`. Note that font files are likely to be stored in a different directory on your server. If you are not sure where, you could try searching for files with the `.ttf` extension. We then write the text "Welcome!" to the image.

For the call to `imageTTFtext()`, we define a size of 50, an angle of 0, a starting position of 20 on the x axis and 100 on the y axis. We also pass the function the color identifier stored in the `$blue` variable, the font path stored in `$font`, and, finally, the text we want to output. You can see the result in Figure 14.8.

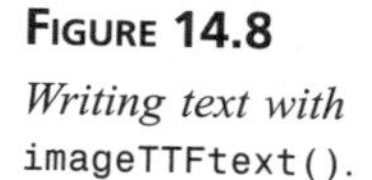

FIGURE 14.8
Writing text with `imageTTFtext()`.

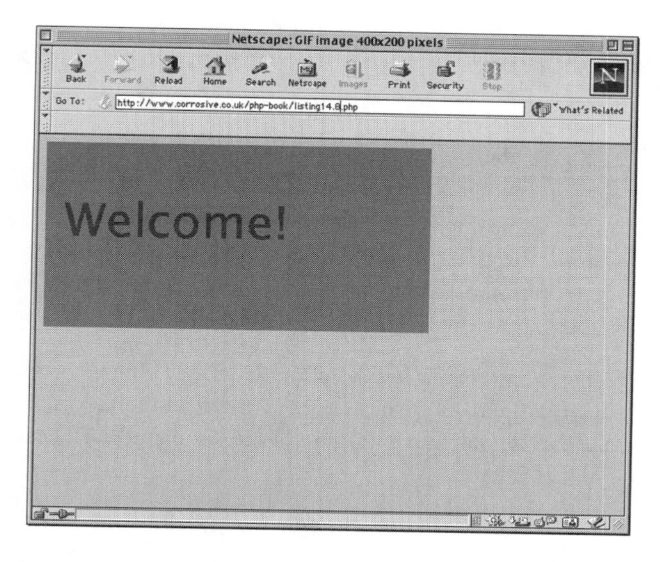

Of course, we have to guess where to put the text at the moment. The size argument does not give us an accurate idea of the text's height, and the width is a mystery. In fact, `imageTTFtext()` will return dimension information, but by then the deed is done. Luckily, PHP provides a function that allows you to try before you buy.

Testing Text Dimensions with `imageTTFbox()`

You can get information about the dimensions of text using the `imageTTFbox()` function, which is so called because it tells you about the text's bounding box. `imageTTFbox()` requires the font size, the angle, a path to a font file, and the text to be written. It is one of the few image functions that do not require an image identifier. It returns an eight-element array, which is explained in Table 14.1.

TABLE 14.1 The Array Returned by `imageTTFbox()`

Index	*Description*
0	bottom left (horizontal axis)
1	bottom left (vertical axis)
2	bottom right (horizontal axis)
3	bottom right (vertical axis)
4	top right (horizontal axis)
5	top right (vertical axis)

TABLE 14.1 continued

Index	*Description*
6	top left (horizontal axis)
7	top left (vertical axis)

All figures on the vertical axis are relative to the text's baseline, which is 0. Figures for the vertical axis at the top of the text count down from this figure, and so usually are minus numbers. Figures for the vertical axis at the bottom of the text count up from 0, giving the number of pixels the text drops from the baseline.

So, if you test a string containing a "y" with `imageTTFbbox()`, for example, the return array might have a figure of 3 for element 1 because the tail of the "y" drops 3 pixels below the baseline. It could have a figure of -10 for element 7 because the text is raised 10 pixels above the baseline.

To complicate matters, there seems to be a 2-pixel difference between the baseline as returned by `imageTTFbbox()` and the visible baseline when drawing text. You may need to adjust for this, by thinking of the height of the baseline as 2 pixels greater than that returned by the `imageTTFbbox()`.

On the horizontal axis, figures for left-hand side `imageTTFbbox()` will take account of text that begins before the given start point by returning the offset as a minus number in elements 6 and 0. This usually will be a small number so whether you adjust alignment to take account of this depends on the level of accuracy you require.

You can use the information returned by `imageTTFbbox()` to align text within an image. Listing 14.9 creates a script that dynamically outputs text, centering it within our image on both the vertical and horizontal planes.

LISTING 14.9 Aligning Text Within a Fixed Space Using `imageTTFbbox()`

```
 1: <?php
 2: header("Content-type: image/gif");
 3: $height = 100;
 4: $width = 200;
 5: $fontsize = 50;
 6: if ( ! isset ( $text ) )
 7:     $text = "Change me!";
 8: $image = imagecreate( $width, $height );
 9: $red = imagecolorallocate($image, 255,0,0);
10: $blue = imagecolorallocate($image, 0,0,255 );
11: $font = "/usr/local/jdk121_pre-v1/jre/lib/fonts/LucidaSansRegular.ttf";
12: $textwidth = $width;
13: $textheight;
```

LISTING 14.9 continued

```
14: while ( 1 )
15:     {
16:     $box = imageTTFbbox( $fontsize, 0, $font, $text );
17:     $textwidth =  abs( $box[2] );
18:     $textbodyheight = ( abs($box[7]) )-2;
19:     if ( $textwidth < $width - 20 )
20:         break;
21:     $fontsize--;
22:     }
23: $gifXcenter = (int) ( $width/2 );
24: $gifYcenter = (int) ( $height/2 );
25: imageTTFtext(    $image, $fontsize, 0,
26:         (int) ($gifXcenter-($textwidth/2)),
27:         (int) ($gifYcenter+(($textbodyheight)/2) ),
28:         $blue, $font, $text );
29: imagegif($image);
30: ?>
```

We store the height and width of the image in the variables `$height` and `$width`, and set a default font size of 50. We test for the presence of a variable called `$text`, setting a default if it isn't present. In this way, the image can accept data from a Web page, either in the query string of an image URL or from form submission. We use `imagecreate()` to acquire an image identifier. We acquire color identifiers in the usual way and store the path to a TrueType font file in a variable called `$font`.

We want to fit the string stored in `$text` into the available space, but we have no way of knowing yet whether it will. Within a `while` statement, we pass the font path and string to `imageTTFbbox()`, storing the resultant array in a variable called `$box`. The element `$box[2]` contains the position of the lower-right corner on the horizontal axis. We take this to be the width of the string and store it in `$textwidth`.

We want to vertically center the text, but only accounting for the area above the text's baseline. We can use the absolute value of `$box[7]` to find the height of the text above the baseline, although we need to adjust this by 2 pixels. We store this value in `$textbodyheight`.

Now that we have a working figure for the text's width, we can test it against the width of the image (less 10 pixels border). If the text is smaller than the width of the canvas we are using, then we end the loop. Otherwise, we reduce the font size, ready to try again.

Dividing the `$height` and `$width` values by 2, we can find the approximate center point of the image. We write the text to the image, using the figures we have calculated for the image's center point in conjunction with the text's height and width to calculate the offset.

Finally, we write the image to the browser. Figure 14.9 shows the output from Listing 14.9.

This code can now be called from another page as part of an IMG element. The following fragment writes some simple code that would allow a user to add her own string to be included in the image:

```
1: <?php
2: if ( ! isset( $text ) )
3:     $text = "Dynamic text!";
4: ?>
5: <form action="<? print $PHP_SELF ?>" method="POST">
6: <input type="text" name="text">
7: </form>
8: <p>
9: <img src="eg14.9.php?<? print "text=".urlencode($text) ?>">
```

When we call the script in Listing 14.9, we append a query string that includes the text to be added to the image. You can learn more about this technique for passing information from script to script in Hour 19, "Saving State with Cookies and Query Strings."

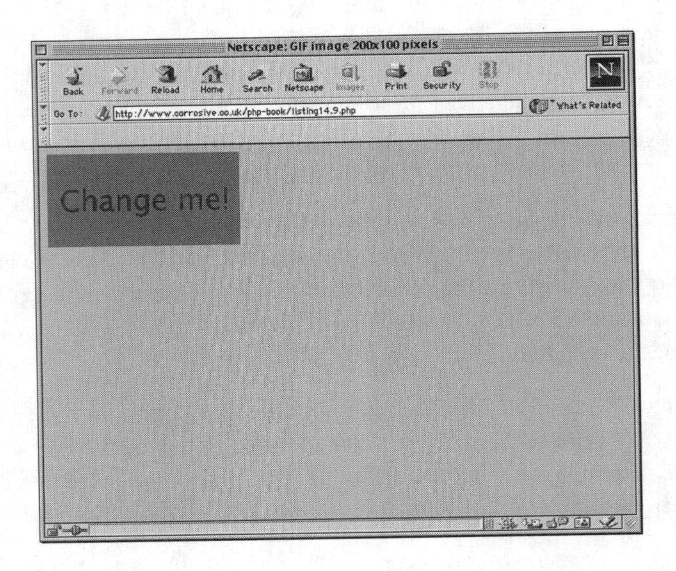

FIGURE 14.9
Aligning text within a fixed space using `imageTTFbbox()`.

Bringing It Together

Let's build an example that uses some of the functions that we have looked at in this hour. Suppose that we have been asked to produce a dynamic bar chart that compares a range of labeled numbers. The bar chart must include the relevant label below each bar. Our client must be able to change the number of bars on the chart, the height and width of the image, and the size of the border around the chart. The bar chart will be used for consumer votes, and all that is needed is an "at a glance" representation of the data. A more detailed breakdown will be included in the HTML portion of the containing page.

The easiest way of storing labels and values is in an associative array. After we have this array, we need to calculate the number of bars we will be dealing with and the greatest value in the array:

```
$cells = array ( liked=>200, hated=>400, indifferent=>900 );
$max = max( $cells );
$total = count ( $cells );
```

We must set up some variables to allow the client to customize the image:

```
$totalwidth = 400;
$totalheight = 200;
$xgutter = 20; // left/right margin
$ygutter = 20; // top/bottom margin
$internalgap = 5; // space between cells
$bottomspace = 40; // gap at the bottom (in addition to margin)
$font = "/usr/local/jdk121_pre-v1/jre/lib/fonts/LucidaSansRegular.ttf";
```

The client can change the variables to define the image height and width. The `$xgutter` and `$ygutter` variables determine the margin around the chart horizontally and vertically. `$internalgap` determines the space between the bars. The `$bottomspace` variable contains the space available to label the bars at the bottom of the screen.

Now that we have these values, we can do some calculations to arrive at some useful variables:

```
$graphCanX = ( $totalwidth - $xgutter*2 );
$graphCanY = ( $totalheight - $ygutter*2 - $bottomspace );
$posX = $xgutter; // starting draw position x - axis
$posY = $totalheight - $ygutter - $bottomspace; // starting draw pos - y - axis
$cellwidth = (int) (( $graphCanX - ( $internalgap * ( $total-1 ) )) / $total) ;
$textsize = (int)($bottomspace);
```


We calculate the graph canvas (the space in which the bars are to be written). On the x axis, this will be the total width minus twice the size of the margin. On the y axis, we need also to take account of the `$bottomspace` variable to leave room for the labels.

`$posX` stores the point on the x axis at which we will start drawing the bars, so we set this to the same value as `$xgutter`, which contains the value for the margin on the `$x` axis. `$posY` stores the bottom point of our bars; it is equivalent to the total height of the image less the margin and the space for the labels stored in `$bottomheight`.

`$cellwidth` contains the width of each bar. To arrive at this value, we must calculate the total amount of space between bars and take this from the chart width, dividing this result by the total number of bars.

We initially set the size of the text to be the same as the height left free for label text (as stored in `$bottomspace`).

Before we can create and work with our image, we need to determine the text size. Our problem is that we don't know how long the labels will be, and we want to make sure that each of the labels will fit within the width of the bar above it. We loop through the `$cells` array to calculate the maximum text size we can use:

```
while ( list( $key, $val ) = each ( $cells ) )
    {
    while ( 1 )
        {
        $box = ImageTTFbBox( $textsize, 0, $font, $key );
        $textWidth = $box[2];
        if ( $textWidth < $cellwidth )
            break;
        $textsize--;
        }
    }
```

For each of the elements, we begin a loop, acquiring dimension information for the label using `imageTTFbbox()`. We take the text width to be `$box[2]` and test it against the `$cellwidth` variable, which contains the width of a single bar in the chart. We break the loop if the text is smaller than the bar width; otherwise, we decrement `$textsize` and try again. `$textsize` continues to shrink until every label in the array fits within the bar width.

Now, at last we can create an image identifier and begin to work with it:

```
$image = imagecreate( $totalwidth, $totalheight );
$red = ImageColorAllocate($image, 255, 0, 0);
$blue = ImageColorAllocate($image, 0, 0, 255 );
$black = ImageColorAllocate($image, 0, 0, 0 );
reset ($cells);
while ( list( $key, $val ) = each ( $cells ) )
    {
    $cellheight = (int) (($val/$max) * $graphCanY);
    $center = (int)($posX+($cellwidth/2));
    imagefilledrectangle( $image, $posX, ($posY-$cellheight),
```

```
        ($posX+$cellwidth), $posY, $blue );
    $box = ImageTTFbBox( $textsize, 0, $font, $key );
    $tw = $box[2];
    ImageTTFText(     $image, $textsize, 0, ($center-($tw/2)),
            ($totalheight-$ygutter), $black, $font, $key );
    $posX += ( $cellwidth + $internalgap);
    }
imagegif( $image );
```

We begin by creating an image identifier with `imagecreate()` and allocate some colors. Once again, we loop through our `$cells` array. We calculate the height of the bar, storing the result in `$cellheight`. We calculate the center point (on the x axis) of the bar, which is `$posX` plus half the width of the bar.

We draw the bar, using `imagefilledrectangle()` and the variables `$posX`, `$posY`, `$cellheight`, and `$cellwidth`.

To align our text, we need `imageTTFbbox()` once again, storing its return array in `$box`. We use `$box[2]` as our working width and assign this to a temporary variable, `$tw`. We now have enough information to write the label. We derive our x position from the `$center` variable minus half the width of the text, and our y position from the image's height minus the margin.

We increment `$posX` ready to start working with the next bar.

Finally, we output the image.

You can see the complete script in Listing 14.10 and sample output in Figure 14.10.

LISTING 14.10 A Dynamic Bar Chart

```
 1: <?php
 2: header("Content-type: image/gif");
 3: $cells = array ( liked=>200, hated=>400, indifferent=>900 );
 4: $max = max( $cells );
 5: $total = count ( $cells );
 6: $totalwidth = 300;
 7: $totalheight = 200;
 8: $xgutter = 20; // left/right margin
 9: $ygutter = 20; // top/bottom margin
10: $internalgap = 10; // space between cells
11: $bottomspace = 30; // gap at the bottom (in addition to margin)
12: $font = "/usr/local/jdk121_pre-v1/jre/lib/fonts/LucidaSansRegular.ttf";
13: $graphCanX = ( $totalwidth - $xgutter*2 );
14: $graphCanY = ( $totalheight - $ygutter*2 - $bottomspace );// starting draw
    position x - axis
```

Listing 14.10 continued

```
15: $posX = $xgutter; // starting draw pos - y - axis
16: $posY = $totalheight - $ygutter - $bottomspace;
17: $cellwidth = (int) (( $graphCanX -            ( $internalgap * ( $total-1 ) ))
    / $total) ;
18: $textsize = (int)($bottomspace);
19: // adjust font size
20: while ( list( $key, $val ) = each ( $cells ) )
21:     {
22:     while ( 1 )
23:         {
24:         $box = ImageTTFbBox( $textsize, 0, $font, $key );
25:         $textWidth = abs( $box[2] );
26:         if ( $textWidth < $cellwidth )
27:             break;
28:         $textsize--;
29:         }
30:     }
31: $image = imagecreate( $totalwidth, $totalheight );
32: $red = ImageColorAllocate($image, 255, 0, 0);
33: $blue = ImageColorAllocate($image, 0, 0, 255 );
34: $black = ImageColorAllocate($image, 0, 0, 0 );
35: $grey = ImageColorAllocate($image, 100, 100, 100 );
36: reset ($cells);
37: while ( list( $key, $val ) = each ( $cells ) )
38:     {
39:     $cellheight = (int) (($val/$max) * $graphCanY);
40:     $center = (int)($posX+($cellwidth/2));
41:     imagefilledrectangle( $image, $posX, ($posY-$cellheight), ($posX+$cell
        width), $posY, $blue );
42:     $box = ImageTTFbBox( $textsize, 0, $font, $key );
43:     $tw = $box[2];
44:     ImageTTFText(     $image, $textsize, 0, ($center-($tw/2)),
45:             ($totalheight-$ygutter), $black, $font, $key );
46:     $posX += ( $cellwidth + $internalgap);
47:     }
48: imagegif( $image );
49: ?>
```

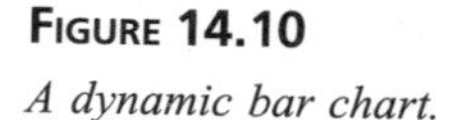

FIGURE 14.10
A dynamic bar chart.

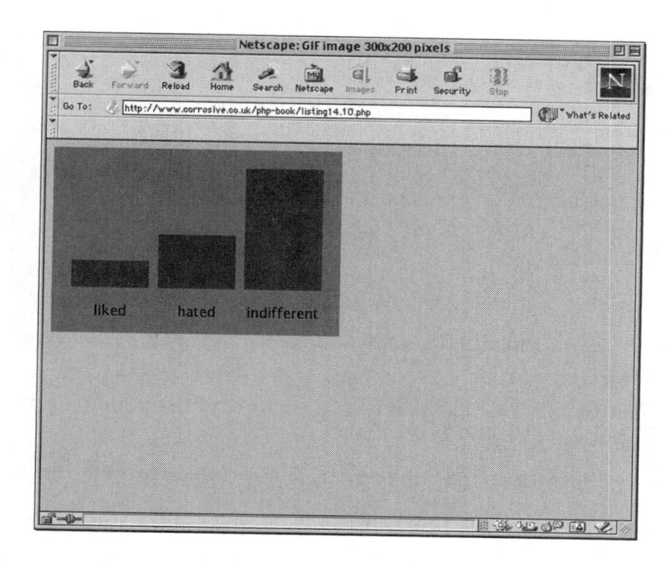

Summary

PHP's support for the GD library enables you to produce dynamic charts and navigation elements with relative ease.

In this hour, you learned how to use `imagecreate()` and `imagegif()` to create and output an image. You learned how to acquire color identifiers with `imagecolorallocate()` and to use color identifiers with `imagefill()` to fill areas with color. You learned how to use line and shape functions to create outline and filled shapes. You learned how to use PHP's support for the FreeType library to work with TrueType fonts, and worked through an example that wrote text to an image. Finally, you worked through a bar chart example that brought some of these techniques together into a single script.

Q&A

Q Are there any performance issues with regard to dynamic images?

A A dynamically created image will be slower to arrive at the browser than an image that already exists. Depending on the efficiency of your script, the impact is not likely to be noticeable to the user if you use dynamic images sparingly.

Workshop

The Workshop provides quiz questions to help you solidify your understanding of the material covered. Try to understand the quiz answers before continuing to the next hour's lesson. Quiz answers are provided in Appendix A.

Quiz

1. What header should you send to the browser before building and outputting a GIF image?
2. What function would you use to acquire an image identifier that you can use with other image functions?
3. What function would you use to output your GIF after building it?
4. What function could you use to acquire a color identifier?
5. With which function would you draw a line on a dynamic image?
6. What function would you use to fill an area in a dynamic image?
7. What function might you use to draw an arc?
8. How might you draw a rectangle?
9. How would you draw a polygon?
10. What function would you use to write a string to a dynamic image (utilizing the FreeType library)?

Activities

1. Write a script that creates a "progress bar" such as might be used on a fund-raising site to indicate how much money has been raised in relation to the target.
2. Write a script that writes a headline image based on input from a form or query string. Allow user input to determine the canvas size, background and foreground colors, and the presence and offset of a drop shadow.

HOUR 15

Working with Dates

Dates are so much part of everyday life that it becomes easy to work with them without thinking. The quirks of our calendar can be difficult to work with in programs, though. Fortunately, PHP provides powerful tools for date arithmetic that make manipulating dates easy.

In this chapter, you will learn

- How to acquire the current date and time
- How to get information about a date
- How to format date information
- How to test dates for validity
- How to set dates
- How to build a simple calendar script

Getting the Date with `time()`

PHP's `time()` function gives you all the information that you need about the current date and time. It requires no arguments but returns an integer. This number is a little hard on the eyes, for us humans, but extremely useful nonetheless.

```
print time();
// sample output: 948316201
```

The integer returned by `time()` represents the number of seconds elapsed since midnight GMT on January 1, 1970. This moment is known as the UNIX epoch, and the number of seconds that have elapsed since then is referred to as a time stamp. PHP offers excellent tools to convert a time stamp into a form that humans are comfortable with. Even so, isn't a time stamp a needlessly convoluted way of storing a date? In fact, the opposite is true. From just one number, you can extract enormous amounts of information. Even better, a time stamp can make date arithmetic much easier than you might imagine.

Think of a homegrown date system in which you record days of the month, as well as months and years. Now imagine a script that needs to add one day to a given date. If this date happened to be 31 December 1999, rather than add 1 to the date, you would have to write code to set the day of the month to 1, the month to January, and the year to 2000. Using a time stamp, you need only add a day's worth of seconds to your current figure, and you are done. You can convert this new figure into something more friendly at your leisure.

Converting a Time Stamp with `getdate()`

Now that you have a time stamp to work with, you must convert it before you present it to the user. `getdate()` optionally accepts a time stamp and returns an associative array containing information about the date. If you omit the time stamp, it works with the current time stamp as returned by `time()`. Table 15.1 lists the elements contained in the array returned by `getdate()`.

TABLE 15.1 The Associative Array Returned by `getdate()`

Key	*Description*	*Example*
seconds	Seconds past the minute (0-59)	28
minutes	Minutes past the hour (0-59)	7
hours	Hours of the day (0-23)	12
mday	Day of the month (1-31)	20
wday	Day of the week (0-6)	4

TABLE 15.1 continued

Key	*Description*	*Example*
mon	Month of the year (1-12)	1
year	Year (4 digits)	2000
yday	Day of year (0-365)	19
weekday	Day of the week (name)	Thursday
month	Month of the year (name)	January
0	Timestamp	948370048

Listing 15.1 uses `getdate()` to extract information from a time stamp, using a `foreach` statement to print each element. You can see a typical output in Figure 15.1. `getdate()` returns the date according to the local time zone.

LISTING 15.1 Acquiring Date Information with `getdate()`

```
 1: <html>
 2: <head>
 3: <title>Listing 15.1 Acquiring date information with getdate()</title>
 4: </head>
 5: <body>
 6: <?php
 7: $date_array = getdate(); // no argument passed so today's date will be used
 8: foreach ( $date_array as $key => $val )
 9:     {
10:     print "$key = $val<br>";
11:     }
12: ?>
13: <hr>
14: <?
15: print "Today's date: $date_array[mday]/$date_array[mon]/
    $date_array[year]<p>";
16: ?>
17: </body>
18: </html>
```

Converting a Time Stamp with `date()`

You can use `getdate()` when you want to work with the elements that it outputs. Sometimes, though, you only want to display the date as a string. The `date()` function returns a formatted string representing a date. You can exercise an enormous amount of control over the format that `date()` returns with a string argument that you must pass to it.

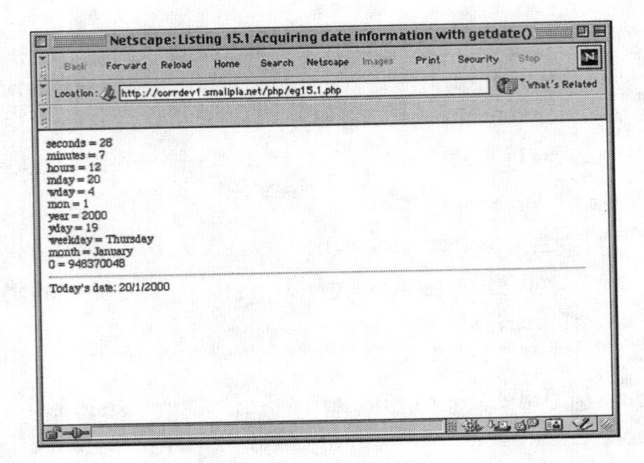

FIGURE 15.1
Using `getdate()`.

In addition to the format string, `date()` optionally accepts a time stamp. Table 15.2 lists the codes that a format string can contain. Any other data you include in the format string passed to `date()` will be included in the return value.

TABLE 15.2 Format Codes for Use with `date()`

Format	*Description*	*Example*
a	'am' or 'pm' lowercase	pm
A	'AM' or 'PM' uppercase	PM
d	Day of month (number with leading zeroes)	20
D	Day of week (three letters)	Thu
F	Month name	January
h	Hour (12-hour format—leading zeroes)	12
H	Hour (24-hour format—leading zeroes)	12
g	Hour (12-hour format—no leading zeroes)	12
G	Hour (24-hour format—no leading zeroes)	12
i	Minutes	47
j	Day of the month (no leading zeroes)	20
l	Day of the week (name)	Thursday
L	Leap year ('1' for yes, '0' for no)	1
m	Month of year (number—leading zeroes)	01
M	Month of year (three letters)	Jan
n	Month of year (number—no leading zeroes)	1
s	Seconds of hour	24
U	Time stamp	948372444

TABLE 15.2 continued

Format	*Description*	*Example*
y	Year (two digits)	00
Y	Year (four digits)	2000
z	Day of year (0-365)	19
Z	Offset in seconds from GMT	0

Listing 15.2 puts a few format codes to the test.

LISTING 15.2 Formatting a Date with `date()`

```
 1: <html>
 2: <head>
 3: <title>Listing 15.2 Formatting a date with date()</title>
 4: </head>
 5: <body>
 6: <?php
 7: print date("m/d/y G.i:s<br>", time());
 8: // 01/20/00 13.27:55
 9: print "Today is ";
10: print date("j of F Y, \a\\t g.i a", time());
11: // Today is 20 of January 2000, at 1.27 pm
12: ?>
13: </body>
14: </html>
```

Although the format string looks arcane, it is easy to build. If you want to add a string to the format that contains letters that are format codes, you can escape them by placing a backslash (\) in front of them. For characters that become control characters when escaped, you must escape the backslash that precedes them. "\n" should become "\\n", for example, if you want to include an "n" in the format string. `date()` returns information according to your local time zone. If you want to format a date in GMT, you should use the `gmdate()` function, which works in exactly the same way.

Creating Time Stamps with `mktime()`

You can already get information about the current time, but you cannot yet work with arbitrary dates. `mktime()` returns a time stamp that you can then use with `date()` or `getdate()`. `mktime()` accepts up to six integer arguments in the following order:

hour

minute

second

month

day of month

year

Listing 15.3 uses `mktime()` to get a time stamp that we then use with the `date()` function.

LISTING 15.3 Creating a Time Stamp with `mktime()`

```
1: <html>
2: <head>
3: <title>Listing 15.3 Creating a timestamp with mktime()</title>
4: </head>
5: <body>
6: <?php
7: // make a timestamp for 1/5/99 at 2.30 am
8: $ts = mktime( 2, 30, 0, 5, 1, 1999 );
9: print date("m/d/y G.i:s<br>", $ts);
10: // 05/01/99 2.30:00
11: print "The date is ";
12: print date("j of F Y, \a\\t g.i a", $ts );
13: // The date is 1 of May 1999, at 2.30 am
14: ?>
15: </body>
16: </html>
```

You can choose to omit some or all of the arguments to `mktime()`, and the value appropriate to the current time will be used instead. `mktime()` will also adjust for values that go beyond the relevant range, so an hour argument of 25 will translate to 1.00am on the day after that specified in the month, day, and year arguments.

Testing a Date with `checkdate()`

You may need to accept date information from user input. Before you work with this date, or store it in a database, you should check that the date is valid. `checkdate()` accepts three integers: month, day, and year. `checkdate()` returns `true` if the month is between 1 and 12, the day is acceptable for the given month and year (accounting for leap years, and the year is between 0 and 32767. Be careful, though, a date may well be valid but not acceptable to other date functions. For example, the following line returns true:

```
checkdate( 4, 4, 1066 )
```

If you were to attempt to build a date with `mktime()` using these values, you would end up with a time stamp of -1. As a rule of thumb, do not use `mktime()` with years below 1902 and be cautious of using date functions with any date before 1970.

An Example

Let's bring most of these functions together into an example. We are going to build a calendar that can display the dates for any month between 1980 and 2010. The user will be able to select both month and year with pull-down menus, and the dates for that month will be organized according to the days of the week. We will use two global variables `$month` and `$year`, which should be filled by data by the user. We will use these to build a time stamp based on the first day of the month defined. If the input is invalid or absent, we will default to the first day of the current month.

Checking User Input

When the user comes to our page for the first time, he or she will not be submitting any information. We must therefore make sure that our script can handle the fact that the `$month` and `$year` variables may not be defined. We could use the `isset()` function for this. `isset()` returns `false` if the variable it has been passed has not been defined. However, we choose instead to use `checkdate()`. Listing 15.4 shows the fragment of code that checks the `$month` and `$year` variables and builds a time stamp based on them.

LISTING 15.4 Checking User Input for the Calendar Script

```
 1: <?php
 2: if ( ! checkdate( $month, 1, $year ) )
 3:     {
 4:     $nowArray = getdate();
 5:     $month = $nowArray[mon];
 6:     $year = $nowArray[year];
 7:     }
 8: $start = mktime ( 0, 0, 0, $month,     1, $year );
 9: $firstDayArray = getdate($start);
10: ?>
```

Listing 15.4 is a fragment of a larger script so it does not produce any output itself. In our `if` statement, we use `checkdate()` to test the `$month` and `$year` variables. If they have not been defined, `checkdate()` returns `false` because you cannot make a valid date from undefined month and year arguments. This approach has the added bonus of ensuring that data that has been submitted by the user will make a valid date.

If the date is not valid, we use `getdate()` to create an associative array based on the current time. We then set values for `$month` and `$year` ourselves, using the array's `mon` and `year` elements.

Now that we are sure that we have valid data in `$month` and `$year`, we can use `mktime()` to create a time stamp for the first day of the month. We will need information about this time stamp later on, so we create a variable called `$firstDayArray` that will store an associative array returned by `getdate()` and based on this time stamp.

Building the HTML Form

We need to create an interface by which users can ask to see data for a month and year. For this, we will use `SELECT` elements. Although we could hard-code these in HTML, we must also ensure that the pull-downs default to the currently chosen month, so we will dynamically create these pull-downs, adding a `SELECT` attribute to the `OPTION` element where appropriate. The form is generated in Listing 15.5.

LISTING 15.5 Building the HTML Form for the Calendar Script

```
 1: <?php
 2: if ( ! checkdate( $month, 1, $year ) )
 3:     {
 4:     $nowArray = getdate();
 5:     $month = $nowArray[mon];
 6:     $year = $nowArray[year];
 7:     }
 8: $start = mktime ( 0, 0, 0, $month, 1, $year );
 9: $firstDayArray = getdate($start);
10: ?>
11: <html>
12: <head>
13: <title><?php print "Calendar: $firstDayArray[month]
14:           $firstDayArray[year]" ?></title>
15: <head>
16: <body>
17: <form method="post">
18: <select name="month">
19: <?php
20: $months = Array("January", "February", "March", "April",
21:                 "May", "June", "July", "August", "September",
22:                 "October", "November", "December");
23: for ( $x=1; $x <= count( $months ); $x++ )
24:     {
25:     print "\t<option value=\"$x\"";
26:     print ($x == $month)?" SELECTED":"";
27:     print ">".$months[$x-1]."\n";
28:     }
```

LISTING 15.5 continued

```
29: ?>
30: </select>
31: <select name="year">
32: <?php
33: for ( $x=1980; $x<2010; $x++ )
34:     {
35:     print "\t<option";
36:     print ($x == $year)?" SELECTED":"";
37:     print ">$x\n";
38:     }
39: ?>
40: </select>
41: <input type="submit" value="Go!">
42: </form>
43: </body>
44: </html>
```

Having created the `$start` time stamp and the `$firstDayArray` date array, we go on to write the HTML for the page. Notice that we use `$firstDayArray` to add the month and year to the `TITLE` element. In previous examples we have used the global variable `$PHP_SELF` within the `FORM` element to ensure that the form will call itself when submitted. In our script we have taken advantage of the fact that leaving the `ACTION` argument out of a `FORM` tag will cause the form to submit to its containing page by default. To create the `SELECT` element for the month pull-down, we drop back into PHP mode to write the individual `OPTION` tags. First we create an array called `$months` that contains the 12 month names. We then loop through this, creating an `OPTION` tag for each one. This would probably be an overcomplicated way of writing a simple `SELECT` element were it not for the fact that we are testing `$x` (the counter variable in the `for` statement) against the `$month` variable. If `$x` and `$month` are equivalent, we add the string `SELECTED` to the `OPTION` tag, ensuring that the correct month will be selected automatically when the page loads. We use a similar technique to write the year pull-down. Finally, back in HTML mode, we create a submit button.

We should now have a form that can send the month and year parameters to itself, and will default either to the current month and year, or the month and year previously chosen. You can see this in Figure 15.2.

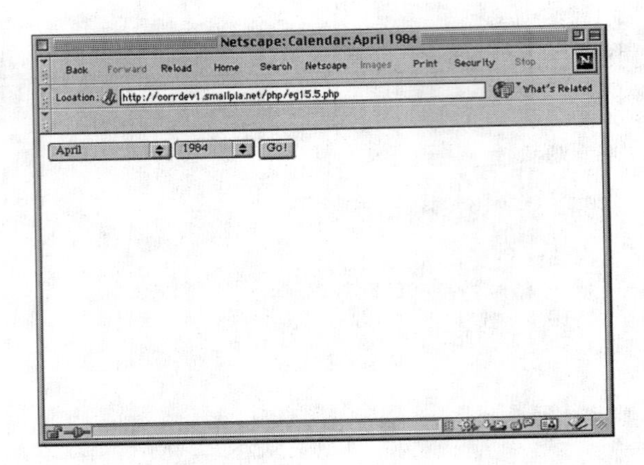

FIGURE 15.2
The calendar form.

Creating the Calendar Table

We now need to create a table and populate it with dates for the chosen month. We do this in Listing 15.6, which represents the complete calendar script.

LISTING 15.6 The Complete Calendar Script

```
 1: <?php
 2: define("ADAY", (60*60*24) );
 3: if ( ! checkdate( $month, 1, $year ) )
 4:     {
 5:      $nowArray = getdate();
 6:     $month = $nowArray[mon];
 7:     $year = $nowArray[year];
 8:     }
 9: $start = mktime ( 0, 0, 0, $month,    1, $year );
10: $firstDayArray = getdate($start);
11: ?>
12: <html>
13: <head>
14: <title><?php print "Calendar: $firstDayArray[month]
15:         $firstDayArray[year]" ?></title>
16: <head>
17: <body>
18: <form action="<? print $PHP_SELF ?>" method="post">
19: <select name="month">
20: <?php
21: $months = Array("January", "February", "March", "April",
22:                 "May", "June", "July", "August", "September",
23:                 "October", "November", "December");
24: for ( $x=1; $x <= count( $months ); $x++ )
25:     {
26:     print "\t<option value=\"$x\"";
```

LISTING 15.6 continued

```
27:      print ($x == $month)?" SELECTED":"";
28:      print ">".$months[$x-1]."\n";
29:      }
30: ?>
31: </select>
32: <select name="year">
33: <?php
34: for ( $x=1980; $x<2010; $x++ )
35:      {
36:      print "\t<option";
37:      print ($x == $year)?" SELECTED":"";
38:      print ">$x\n";
39:      }
40: ?>
41: </select>
42: <input type="submit" value="Go!">
43: </form>
44: <p>
45: <?php
46: $days = Array("Sunday", "Monday", "Tuesday", "Wednesday",
47:                "Thursday", "Friday", "Saturday");
48: print "<TABLE BORDER = 1 CELLPADDING=5>\n";
49: foreach ( $days as $day )
50:      print "\t<td><b>$day</b></td>\n";
51: for ( $count=0; $count < (6*7); $count++ )
52:      {
53:      $dayArray = getdate( $start );
54:      if ( (($count) % 7) == 0 )
55:          {
56:          if ( $dayArray[mon] != $month )
57:              break;
58:          print "</tr><tr>\n";
59:          }
60:      if ( $count < $firstDayArray[wday] || $dayArray[mon] != $month )
61:          {
62:          print "\t<td><br></td>\n";
63:          }
64:      else
65:          {
66:          print "\t<td>$dayArray[mday] $dayArray[month]</td>\n";
67:          $start += ADAY;
68:          }
69:      }
70: print "</tr></table>";
71: ?>
72: </body>
73: </html>
74:
```

Because the table will be indexed by days of the week, we loop through an array of day names, printing each to its own cell. All the real magic of the script happens in the final `for` statement.

We initialize a variable called `$count` and ensure that the loop will end after 42 iterations. This is to make sure that we will create enough cells to populate with date information. Within the loop, we transform the `$start` variable into a date array with `getdate()`, assigning the result to `$dayArray`. Although `$start` is the first day of the month during the loop's initial execution, we will increment this time stamp by 24 hours for every iteration.

We test the `$count` variable against 7 using the modulus operator. The block of code belonging to this `if` statement will therefore only be run when `$count` is either 0 or a multiple of 7. This is our way of knowing whether we should end the loop altogether or start a new row.

After we have established that we are in the first iteration or at the end of a row, we can go on to make another test. If the `mon` (month number) element of the `$dayArray` is no longer equivalent to the `$month` variable, we must have finished. Remember that `$dayArray` contains information about the `$start` time stamp, which is in turn our current place in the month that we are displaying. When `$start` goes beyond the current month, `$dayArray[mon]` will hold a different figure than the `$month` number provided by user input. Our modulus test demonstrated that we are at the end of a row, and the fact that we are in a new month means that we can leave the loop altogether.

Assuming, however, that we are still in the month that we are displaying, we end the row and start a new one.

In the next `if` statement, we determine whether to write date information to a cell. Not every month begins on a Sunday, so it's likely that we will start with an empty cell or two. Few months will finish at the end of one of our rows, so it's also likely that we will need to write a few empty cells before we close the table. We have stored information about the first day of the month in `$firstDayArray`; in particular, we can access the number of the day of the week in `$firstDayArray[wday]`. If `$count` is smaller than this number, then we know that we haven't yet reached the correct cell for writing. By the same token, if the `$month` variable is no longer equal to `$dayArray[mon]`, we know that we have reached the end of the month (but not the end of the row, as we determined in our earlier modulus test). In either case, we write an empty `cell` to the browser.

In the final `else` clause, we can do the fun stuff. We have already ascertained that we are within the month that we want to list and that the current day column matches the day number stored in `$firstDayArray[wday]`. Now we must use the `$dayArray` associative array that we established early in the loop to write the day of the month and the month name to a cell.

Finally, we need to increment the `$start` variable, which contains our date stamp. We simply add the number of seconds in a day to it (we have defined this value at the top of the script), and we're ready to begin the loop again with a new value in `$start` to be tested. You can see the output from a call to this script in Figure 15.3.

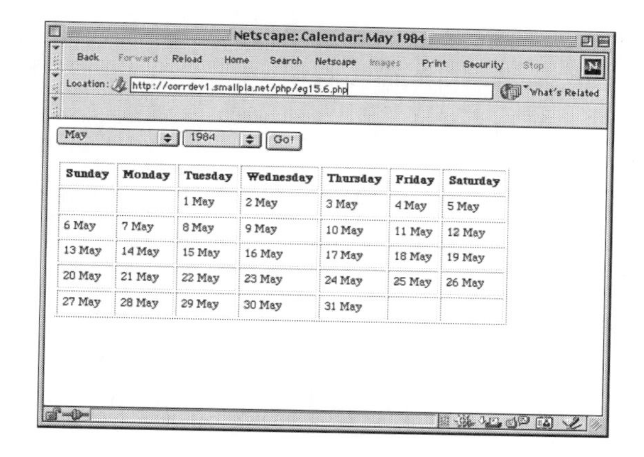

FIGURE 15.3
The calendar script.

Summary

In this hour, you learned how to use `time()` to get a date stamp for the current date and time. You learned how to use `getdate()` to extract date information from a time stamp and `date()` to convert a time stamp into a formatted string. You learned how to create a time stamp using `mktime()`. You learned how to test a date for validity with `checkdate()`. Finally, you worked through an example script, which applies some of the tools you have looked at.

Q&A

The Workshop provides quiz questions to help you solidify your understanding of the material covered. Try to understand the quiz answers before continuing to the next hour's lesson. Quiz answers are provided in Appendix A.

Q Are there any functions for converting between different calendars?

A Yes. PHP provides an entire suite of functions that cover alternative calendars. You can read about these in the official PHP manual at `http://www.php.net/manual/ref.calendar.php`.

Workshop

The Workshop provides quiz questions to help you solidify your understanding of the material covered. Try to understand the quiz answers before continuing to the next hour's lesson. Quiz answers are provided in Appendix A.

Quiz

1. How would you acquire a UNIX time stamp representing the current date and time?
2. What function accepts a time stamp and returns an associative array representing the given date?
3. What function would you use to format date information?
4. How would you acquire a time stamp for an arbitrary date?
5. What function could you use to check the validity of a date?

Activity

1. Create a birthday countdown script. Given form input of month, day, and year, output a message that tells the user how many days, hours, minutes, and seconds until the big day.

HOUR 16

Working with Data

In this hour, we are going to delve a little deeper into data testing and manipulation. We will look again at data types. PHP handles data types for you automatically, but an understanding of how data is handled in your scripts is essential if you are to build robust online applications. We will also return to arrays and discover some of the more advanced features that PHP provides to manipulate and sort these data types.

In this hour, you will learn

- How to convert data from one type to another
- How PHP automatically converts data for you in expressions
- More ways of testing data types
- Why an understanding of data types can be useful
- How to test whether a variable has been set
- Another method of traversing an array
- How to check that an element exists in an array

- How to transform every element in an array
- How to custom sort arrays

Data Types Revisited

You learned about PHP's data types in some detail in Hour 4, "The Building Blocks." There is a little more ground to cover, however. This section examines a few more functions for checking the data type of a variable and looks at the conditions under which PHP automatically converts data types for you.

A Recap

You already know that PHP variables can contain values that are integers, doubles, strings, booleans, objects, or arrays. You can test the type of any variable with the `gettype()` function. `gettype()` requires a value of any type, and returns a string describing the value's data type:

```
$data = 454;
print gettype( $data );
// prints "integer"
```

You can change variables from one type to another, either by casting or with the `settype()` function. To cast a function, place the name of a data type in brackets before the variable or value you want to convert. By casting a variable, you do not change the contents of a variable in any way. Instead, a converted copy is returned to you. The following code fragment casts a double to an integer:

```
$data = 4.333;
print ( integer ) $data;
// prints 4
```

The `$data` variable still contains the double that we assigned to it. We have merely printed the return value of the cast.

To transform the type of a variable, you can use the `settype()` function. `settype()` requires the name of a data type and a variable to convert:

```
$data = 4.333;
settype( $data, integer );
print $data;
// prints 4
```

The `$data` variable now contains an integer. `settype()` is a rare function in PHP in that it transforms one of the arguments you pass it in your scope as well as its own.

Converting Complex Types

You have already looked in some detail at the process of converting between simple data types (scalars and strings). What happens when you convert between simple data types such as doubles or integers and more complex types such as objects and arrays?

When you cast a simple data type to an array, an array is created, with the original value in the first element:


```
$str = "this is my string";
$arr_str = (array) $str;
print $arr_str[0];
// prints "this is my string"
```

When you cast a scalar or string variable to an object, an object is created with a single property called *scalar*. This contains the original value:

```
$str = "this is my string";
$arr_str = (object) $str;
print $arr_str->scalar;
// prints "this is my string"
```

Things get a little more interesting when you convert between arrays and objects. When you convert an array to an object, a new object is created with a property for each key in the array:

```
$addresses = array ( street => "Williams Street", town => "Stockton" );
$obj_addresses = ( object ) $addresses;
print $obj_addresses->street;
// prints "Williams Street"
```

Conversely, converting an object to an array creates an array with an element for each object property. Methods are discarded.

```
class Point
    {
    var $x;
    var $y;
    function Point( $x, $y )
        {
        $this->x = $x;
        $this->y = $y;
        }
    }
$point = new Point( 5, 7 );
$array_point = (array) $point;
print $array_point[x];
// prints 5
```

Automatic Conversion of Data Types

If you build an expression that has values of two different data types as operands, PHP automatically converts one to the type of the other to arrive at a result. You have probably taken advantage of this already without thinking about it. Variables compiled from form input will always be strings, but you might have used them in a test expression or a calculation as if they were numbers.

Suppose that you have asked a user to tell the number of hours they spend online a week, storing the input in a variable called `$hours`. This initially will be stored as a string.

```
$hours = "15";
if ( $hours == 15 )
    print "As a frequent user you may qualify for a discount";
```

In the test for equivalence, the string `"15"` is cast to an integer, and the test expression resolves to `true`.

The rules for automatic conversion are relatively simple. In the context of integers or doubles, strings will be converted according to their contents. If a string begins with an integer, it will be converted to that number. So the following line will give `80`:

```
4 * "20mb";
```

If a string does not begin with a number, it will be converted to 0. So this line will give `0`:

```
4 * "about 20mb";
```

If a string contains a number followed by a dot, it will be converted into a double. So the following example will give `4.8`:

```
4 * "1.2";
```

The autoincrement and autodecrement operators are a special case when applied to strings. Incrementing a string adds 1 to the converted value of the string as you would expect, but only if the string contains nothing but numbers. The new value will itself be a string:

```
$str = "4";
$str++;
print $str;  // prints 5
print gettype( $str ); // prints "string"
```

If you attempt to autoincrement a string that contains letters, the final character alone will be incremented:

```
$str = "hello";
$str++;
print $str;  // prints "hellp"
```

Compare this with another approach to incrementing a string:

```
$str = "hello";
$str += 1;
print $str; // prints 1;
print gettype( $str ); // prints "integer"
```

In the previous example, `$str` is converted to the integer 0 when we add 1 to it. The result of this operation, `1`, is stored back in `$str`. `$str` will now hold an integer.

Automatic conversions between integers and doubles are more straightforward. If either operand in an expression is a double, then the other operand will be converted to a double, and the result will be a double:

```
$result = ( 1 + 20.0 );
print gettype ( $result );
// prints "double"
```

It is important to note that when automatic conversions occur for the purposes of evaluating an expression, neither operand in the expression is itself changed. If an operand needs to be converted, it is a transformed copy that will be used as part of the expression.

Testing Data Types

You've already seen that you can test any data type with the `gettype()` function. This is useful for debugging because it tells you exactly what type any variable is. Often, though, you will only want to check whether a variable contains a specific type. PHP provides a special function corresponding to each data type. These functions accept a variable or value and return a boolean. Table 16.1 lists these functions.

TABLE 16.1 Functions to Test Data Types

Function	*Description*
`is_array()`	Returns `true` if the argument is an array
`is_bool()`	Returns `true` if the argument is boolean
`is_double()`	Returns `true` if the argument is a double
`is_int()`	Returns `true` if the argument is an integer
`is_object()`	Returns `true` if the argument is an object
`is_string()`	Returns `true` if the argument is a string

These functions make testing data types a little easier.

```
if ( gettype( $var ) == "array" )
    print "it's an array";
```

is equivalent to

```
if ( is_array( $var ) )
    print "it's an array";
```

The second way of testing the `$var` variable is a little more compact and is nicely intuitive.

More Ways of Changing Type

You have already seen two ways of converting data types. You can either cast a value or use the `settype()` function. In addition to these techniques, PHP provides functions to convert values into integers, doubles, and strings. These functions accept values of any type apart from array or object and return a converted value. Table 16.2 lists these functions.

TABLE 16.2 Functions to Convert Data Types

Function	*Description*
`doubleval()`	Accepts a value and returns double equivalent
`intval()`	Accepts a value and returns integer equivalent
`strval()`	Accepts a value and returns string equivalent

Why Are Data Types Important?

PHP does not demand that you declare a data type when you create a variable. It implicitly converts types for you when you use variables of different data types in expressions. If PHP makes things so easy, why is it important to be able to keep track of the types of data you are storing?

It is often a good idea to keep track of the data that your variables store to prevent errors. Imagine that you are writing a function that prints the keys and values of an array to the browser. PHP is relaxed about arguments to functions, so you can't demand that the calling code pass you an array when you declare your function.

```
function printArray( $array )
    {
    foreach ( $array as $key => $val )
        print "$key: $val<P>";
        }
```

The preceding function will work nicely if the function is called with an array argument.

```
printArray( array(4, 4, 55) );
```

If you carelessly pass a scalar, you will get an error, as in the following example:

```
printArray( 4 );
// Warning: Non array argument supplied for foreach() in
// /home/matt/htdocs/php-book/data/test2.php on line 5
```

By testing the data type of the supplied argument, you can make the function more accommodating. You could make the function quietly return if it receives a scalar value:

```
function printArray( $array )
     {
     if ( ! is_array( $array ) )
        return false;
     foreach ( $array as $key => $val )
         print "$key: $val<P>";
     return true;
         }
```

The calling code can now test the return value of the function to ascertain whether it was able to complete its task.

You could even use a cast to convert scalar data into an array:

```
function printArray( $array )
     {
     if ( ! is_array( $array ) )
        $array = (array) $array;
     foreach ( $array as $key => $val )
         print "$key: $val<P>";
     return true;
         }
```

The `printArray()` function has become vastly more flexible. It will now output any data type in an array context, even an object.

Checking data types can also be useful when testing the return value of some functions. Some languages, such as Java, always return a predetermined data type from any method. PHP has no such restriction. This flexibility can occasionally lead to ambiguities.

You saw an example of this in Hour 10, "Working with Files." The `readdir()` function returns `false` when it has reached the end of the directory that you are reading, and a string containing the name of an item in the directory at all other times. Traditionally, you would use a construction similar to

```
$dh = opendir( "mydir" );
while ( $name = readdir( $dh ) )
        print "$name<br>";
closedir( $dh );
```

to read the items in a directory. If a directory is named 0, however, the `while` statement's test expression will evaluate this string to `false`, ending the listing. By testing the data type of the return value of `readdir()`, you can circumvent this problem:

```
$dh = opendir( "mydir" );
while ( is_string( $name = readdir( $dh ) ) )
        print "$name<br>";
closedir( $dh );
```

Testing for Absence and Emptiness

Testing the data type of variables can be useful, but you must first be sure that a variable exists and, if it does exist, that a value has been assigned to it. You can do this with the `isset()` function. `isset()` requires a variable and returns `true` if the variable contains a value:

```
$notset;
if ( isset( $notset ) )
    print "\$notset is set";
else
    print "\$notset is not set";
// prints "$notset is not set"
```

A variable that is declared but has not yet been assigned a value will not be recognized as set.

You should be aware of one danger, however. If you assign 0 or an empty string to a variable, it will be recognized as having been set:

```
$notset = "";
if ( isset( $notset ) )
    print "\$notset is set";
else
    print "\$notset is not set";
// prints "$notset is set"
```

Variables that have been initialized as a result of form submissions will always be set, even if the user did not add any data to a field. To deal with situations like this, you must test whether a variable is empty. `empty()` accepts a variable and returns `true` if the variable is not set, or if it contains data other than 0 or an empty string. It also returns `true` if the variable contains an empty array:

```
$notset = "";
if ( empty( $notset ) )
    print "\$notset is empty";
else
```

```
    print "\$notset contains data";
// prints "$notset is empty"
```

More About Arrays

In Hour 7, "Arrays," we introduced arrays and some of the functions that you can use to work with them. This section introduces some more functions and techniques.

An Alternative Approach to Traversing Arrays

PHP4 introduced the `foreach` statement, a powerful tool for reading array elements. We use this in most of the examples in this book. For scripts written in PHP3, it was necessary to use a different technique to traverse arrays. If you intend to distribute scripts that should be compatible with PHP3 or are interested in learning from source code that was written before the release of PHP4, it is essential that you know about this.

When you create an array, PHP maintains an internal pointer that initially points at the first element in the array. You can access this element's key and value with a function called `each()`. `each()` requires an array variable and returns a four-element array. Two of these elements will be numerically indexed, and two will be labeled with the names "key" and "value," respectively. After `each()` has been called, the internal pointer moves on to the next element in the array that you are examining, unless the end of the array has been reached, in which case the function returns `false`. Let's create an array and try out the `each()` function:

```
$details = array( school => "Slickly High", course => "Selective Indifference" );
$element = each( $details );
print "$element[0]<BR>";     // prints "school"
print "$element[1]<P>";         // prints "Slickly High"
print "$element[key]<BR>";    // prints "school"
print "$element[value]<BR>";    // prints "Slickly High"
```

We initialize an array called `$details` with two elements. We then pass `$details` to the `each()` function, storing the return value in a new array called `$element`. The `$element` array holds the key and value of the first element of the `$details`.

Assigning the array returned by `each()` to an array variable is cumbersome. Fortunately, PHP provides the `list()` function. `list()` accepts any number of variables and populates each of them with the corresponding values from an array value:

```
$array = array( 44, 55, 66, 77 );
list( $first, $second ) = $array;
print "$first";           // prints 44
print "<BR>";
print "$second";    // prints 55
```

Notice how we were able to copy the first two elements of the array in the previous example into named variables using the `list()` function.

We can use the `list()` function to assign values to two variables every time `each()` is called. We can then work with these, just as we would in a `foreach` statement.

```
$details = array( school => "Slickly High",
                  course => "Selective Indifference" );
while ( list ( $key, $value ) = each( $details ) )
    print "$key: $value<BR>";
```

Although this code will work, a line still is missing. If your array has been traversed before, the internal pointer will still be set beyond the last element. You can set the internal pointer back to the beginning of an array with the `reset()` function. `reset()` requires an array variable as its argument.

So, the more familiar construction

```
foreach( $details as $key => $value )
     print "$key: $value<BR>";
```

is equivalent to

```
reset( $details );
while ( list ( $key, $value ) = each( $details ) )
    print "$key: $value<BR>";
```

Checking That a Value Exists in an Array

Prior to PHP4, if you needed to check whether a value existed in an array, you had to traverse the array until you had either found a match or reached the last element. PHP4 provides the `in_array()` function. `in_array()` requires two arguments, the value for which you are searching and the array you want to search. The function returns `true` if the value is found with the given array and `false` otherwise.

```
$details = array( school => "Slickly High",
                  course => "Selective Indifference" );
if ( in_array( "Selective Indifference", $details ) )
    print "This course has been suspending pending investigation<P>\n";
```

Removing an Element from an Array

You can remove any element from an array with the `unset()` function. `unset()` requires a variable or an array element as an argument and will unceremoniously destroy it. If the argument is an array element, the array will be automatically shortened.

```
unset( $test[address] );
unset( $numbers[1] );
```

One potential pitfall with `unset()` is the fact that array indices are not subsequently changed to reflect the new size of the array. So, having removed `$numbers[1]` in the previous example, the `$numbers` array might now look something like this:

```
$numbers[0]
$numbers[2]
$numbers[3]
```

You can still loop through this with a `foreach` statement without problems, however.

Applying a Function to Every Element in an Array

You can change a scalar variable easily in an expression. Applying a change to every element of an array is a little more difficult. If you want to add a number to the value of every array element, for example, one solution would be to loop through the array updating each element. PHP provides a neater answer, however.

The `array_walk()` function passes the key and value of every element in an array to a user-defined function. `array_walk()` requires an array variable, a string representing the name of a function, and an optional additional argument that will be passed to the function you have chosen.

Let's create an example. We have an array of prices acquired from a database, but before working with it we need to add sales tax to each price. First, we should create the function to add the tax:

```
function add_tax( &$val, $key, $tax_pc )
    {
    $val += ( ($tax_pc/100) * $val );
    }
```

Any function to be used with `array_walk()` should expect arguments representing a key, a value, and, optionally, a further argument.

If you want to change the value that is passed to your function, you need to append an ampersand to the argument in the function declaration. This ensures that the value will be passed by reference and any changes you make to the value within the function will be reflected in the array. That is why our `add_tax()` function does not return a value.

Now that we have created the function, we can call it via `array_walk()`:

```
function add_tax( &$val, $key, $tax_pc )
    {
    $val += ( ($tax_pc/100) * $val );
    }
$prices = array( 10, 17.25, 14.30 );
```

```
array_walk( $prices, "add_tax", 10 );
foreach ( $prices as $val )
    print "$val<BR>";
// Output:
// 11
// 18.975
// 15.73
```

We pass the `$prices` array variable to `array_walk()` along with the name of the `add_tax()` function. `add_tax()` needs to know the current sales tax rate. The optional third argument to `array_walk()` will be passed to the nominated function, so this is where we set the tax rate.

Custom Sorting Arrays

You have already seen how to sort arrays by key or value. You do not always want to sort an array in such a straightforward way, however. You may want to sort it according to the values of an element buried in a multidimensional array, for example, or to use a criterion completely different to the standard alphanumeric comparison.

PHP enables you to define your own comparison functions to sort arrays. To do this for a numerically indexed array, you would call the `usort()` function, which requires the array you want to sort and the name of the function you want to make the necessary comparisons.

The function you define should accept two arguments, which will hold the array values to be compared. If they are equivalent according to your criterion, the function should return `0`; if the first argument should come before the second in the subject array, the function should return `-1`. If the first argument should come after the second, the function should return `1`.

Listing 16.1 uses `usort()` to sort a multidimensional array.

LISTING 16.1 Using `usort()` to Sort a Multidimensional Array by One of Its Fields

```
 1: <?php
 2: $products = array(
 3:         array( name=>"HAL 2000",          price=>4500.5  ),
 4:         array( name=>"Tricorder",         price=>55.5  ),
 5:         array( name=>"ORAC AI",           price=>2200.5  ),
 6:         array( name=>"Sonic Screwdriver", price=>22.5   )
 7:         );
 8: function priceCmp( $a, $b )
 9:     {
10:     if ( $a[price] == $b[price] )
11:         return 0;
```

LISTING 16.1 continued

```
12:     if ( $a[price] < $b[price] )
13:         return -1;
14:     return 1;
15:     }
16: usort( $products, priceCmp );
17: foreach ( $products as $val )
18:     print "$val[name]: $val[price]<BR>\n";
19: ?>
```

We define an array called `$products`, which we want to sort by the `price` field of each of its values.

We then create the custom sort function, `priceCmp()`. This function accepts two arguments, `$a` and `$b`. These arguments will hold two the arrays that make up the second level of the `$products` array. We compare their price elements, returning `0` if the prices are the same, `-1` if the first is less than the second, and `1` otherwise.

Having defined both function and array, we call the `usort()` function, passing it the `$products` array and the name of our comparison function. `usort()` calls our function repeatedly, passing it elements from the `$products` array and switching the order of the elements according to the return value it receives.

Finally, we loop through the array, to demonstrate our new ordering.

Use `usort()` for sorting numerically indexed arrays. If you want to apply a similar custom sort to an associative array, use `uasort()`. `uasort()` will sort maintaining the association between keys and values. Listing 16.2 sorts an associative array using `uasort()`.

LISTING 16.2 Using `uasort()` to Sort a Multdimensional Associative Array by One of Its Fields

```
 1: <?php
 2: $products = array(
 3:         "HAL 2000" => array( color =>"red",   price=>4500.5  ),
 4:         "Tricorder" => array( color =>"blue",  price=>55.5    ),
 5:         "ORAC AI" => array( color =>"green", price=>2200.5  ),
 6:         "Sonic Screwdriver" => array( color =>"red",   price=>22.5    )
 7:         );
 8: function priceCmp( $a, $b )
 9:     {
10:     if ( $a[price] == $b[price] )
11:         return 0;
12:     if ( $a[price] < $b[price] )
13:         return -1;
```

LISTING 16.2 continued

```
14:     return 1;
15:     }
16: uasort( $products, priceCmp );
17: foreach ( $products as $key => $val )
18:     print "$key: $val[price]<BR>\n";
19: ?>
```

You can custom sort an associative array by its keys using the function `uksort()`. `uksort()` is exactly the same in principle as `usort()` and `uasort()`, except that `uksort()` compares the keys of the array.

Listing 16.3 uses `uksort()` to sort an array by the number of characters in each key. Looking ahead to the next hour, we use the function `strlen()` to ascertain the length in characters of each key. `strlen()` requires a single string argument and returns an integer representing the number of characters in the string.

LISTING 16.3 Using `uksort()` to Sort an Associative Array by the Length of Its Keys

```
 1: <?php
 2: $exes = array(
 3:         xxxx => 4,
 4:         xxx => 5,
 5:         xx => 7,
 6:         xxxxx => 2,
 7:         x => 8
 8:         );
 9: function priceCmp( $a, $b )
10:     {
11:     if ( strlen( $a ) == strlen( $b ) )
12:         return 0;
13:     if ( strlen( $a ) < strlen( $b ) )
14:         return -1;
15:     return 1;
16:     }
17: uksort( $exes, priceCmp );
18: foreach ( $exes as $key => $val )
19:     print "$key: $val<BR>\n";
20:
21: // output:
22: // x: 8
23: // xx: 7
24: // xxx: 5
25: // xxxx: 4
26: // xxxxx: 2
27:
28: ?>
```

Summary

In this hour, you got your hands dirty with some of the more advanced aspects of working with arrays and data types. You learned what happens when you cast complex data types to scalars and vice versa. You learned how PHP deals with different data types in an expression, automatically casting one of them for you. You learned about functions, such as `is_array()`, that test for specific data types, and functions, such as `intval()`, that convert data to a specific type. You learned about the traditional way of traversing an array in PHP using `each()` and `list()`. You learned how to check that a value exists in an array with `in_array()` and how to remove an element from an array with `unset()`. You learned how to transform an array with `array_walk()`. Finally, you learned about the custom sort functions with `usort()`, `uasort()`, and `uksort()`.

Q&A

Q Have we now covered every array function that PHP4 provides?

A No, there are even more array functions than we have space to cover in this book! You can see them all listed and described at `http://www.php.net/manual/ref.array.php`.

Workshop

The Workshop provides quiz questions to help you solidify your understanding of the material covered. Try to understand the quiz answers before continuing to the next hour's lesson. Quiz answers are provided in Appendix A.

Quiz

1. What single function could you use to convert any data type to any other data type?
2. Could you achieve the same thing without a function?
3. What will the following code print?

```
print "four" * 200;
```

4. How would you determine whether a variable contains an array?
5. Which function is designed to return the integer value of its argument?
6. How would you test whether a variable has been set?
7. How would you test whether a variable contains an empty value, such as 0 or an empty string?

8. What function would you use to delete an array element?
9. What function could you use to custom sort a numerically indexed array?

Activities

1. Look back through some of the scripts you have created whilst working with this book. Convert any that use the `foreach` statement so that they are compatible with PHP3.
2. Create an array of mixed data types. Custom sort the array by data type.

HOUR 17

Working with Strings

The World Wide Web is very much a plain text environment. No matter how rich Web content becomes, HTML lies behind it all. It is no accident, then, that PHP4 provides many functions with which you can format, investigate, and manipulate strings.

In this hour, you will learn

- How to format strings
- How to determine the length of a string
- How to find a substring within a string
- How to break a string down into component parts
- How to remove white space from the beginning or end of a string
- How to replace substrings
- How to change the case of a string

Formatting Strings

Until now, we have simply printed any strings that we want to display directly to the browser. PHP provides two functions that allow you first to apply formatting, whether to round doubles to a given number of decimal places, define alignment within a field, or display data according to different number systems. In this section, you will look at a few of the formatting options provided by `printf()` and `sprintf()`.

Working with `printf()`

If you have any experience with C, you will be familiar with the `printf()` function. The PHP version is similar but not identical. `printf()` requires a string argument, known as a format control string. It also accepts additional arguments of different types. The format control string contains instructions as to how to display these additional arguments. The following fragment, for example, uses `printf()` to output an integer as a decimal:

```
printf("This is my number: %d", 55 );
// prints "This is my number: 55"
```

Within the format control string (the first argument), we have included a special code, known as a *conversion specification*.

NEW TERM A conversion specification begins with a percent (%) symbol and defines how to treat the corresponding argument to `printf()`. You can include as many conversion specifications as you want within the format control string, as long as you send an equivalent number of arguments to `printf()`.

The following fragment outputs two numbers using `printf()`:

```
printf("First number: %d<br>\nSecond number: %d<br>\n", 55, 66 );
// Output:
// First number: 55
// Second number: 66
```

The first conversion specification corresponds to the first of the additional arguments to `printf()`, which is 55. The second conversion specification corresponds to 66. The `d` following the percent symbol requires that the data be treated as a decimal integer. This part of a conversion specification is a type specifier.

`printf()` and Type Specifiers

You have already come across one type specifier `d`, which displays data in decimal format. Table 17.1 lists the other type specifiers that are available.

TABLE 17.1 Type Specifiers

Specifier	*Description*
d	Display argument as a decimal number
b	Display an integer as a binary number
c	Display an integer as ASCII equivalent
f	Display an integer as a floating-point number (double)
o	Display an integer as an octal number (base 8)
s	Display argument as a string
x	Display an integer as a lowercase hexadecimal number (base 16)
X	Display an integer as an uppercase hexadecimal number (base 16)

Listing 17.1 uses `printf()` to display a single number according to some of the type specifiers listed in Table 17.1.

Notice that we do not only add conversion specifications to the format control string. Any additional text we include will be printed.

LISTING 17.1 Demonstrating Some Type Specifiers

```
 1: <html>
 2: <head>
 3: <title>Demonstrating some type specifiers</title>
 4: </head>
 5: <body>
 6: <?php
 7: $number = 543;
 8: printf("Decimal: %d<br>", $number );
 9: printf("Binary: %b<br>", $number );
10: printf("Double: %f<br>", $number );
11: printf("Octal: %o<br>", $number );
12: printf("String: %s<br>", $number );
13: printf("Hex (lower): %x<br>", $number );
14: printf("Hex (upper): %X<br>", $number );
15: ?>
16: </body>
17: </html>
```

Figure 17.1 shows the output for Listing 17.1. As you can see, `printf()` is a quick way of converting data from one number system to another and outputting the result.

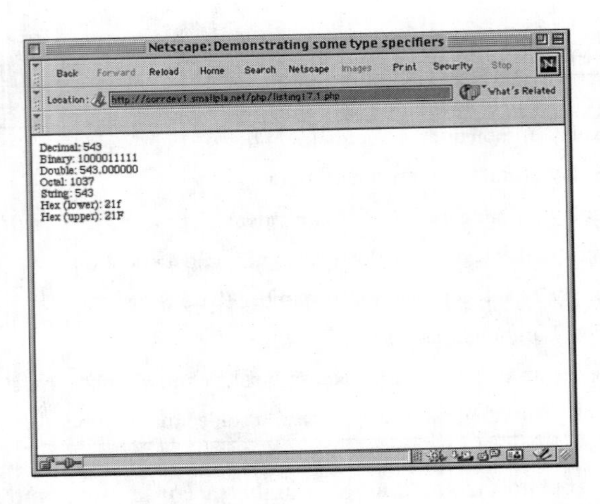

FIGURE 17.1
Demonstrating conversion specifiers.

When you specify a color in HTML, you combine three hexadecimal numbers between 00 and FF, representing the values for red, green, and blue. You can use `printf()` to convert three decimal numbers between 0 and 255 to their hexadecimal equivalents:

```
$red = 204;
$green = 204;
$blue = 204;
printf( "#%X%X%X", $red, $green, $blue );
// prints "#CCCCCC"
```

Although you can use the type specifier to convert from decimal to hexadecimal numbers, you can't use it to determine how many characters the output for each argument should occupy. Within an HTML color code, each hexadecimal number should be padded to two characters, which would become a problem if we changed our `$red`, `$green`, and `$blue` variables in the previous fragment to contain 1, for example. We would end up with the output `"#111"`. You can force the output of leading zeroes by using a padding specifier.

Padding Output with the Padding Specifier

You can require that output be padded by leading characters. The padding specifier should directly follow the percent sign that begins a conversion specification. To pad output with leading zeroes, the padding specifier should consist of a zero followed by the number of characters you want the output to take up. If the output occupies fewer characters than this total, the difference will be filled with zeroes:

```
printf( "%04d", 36 );
// prints "0036"
```

To pad output with leading spaces, the padding specifier should consist of a space character followed by the number of characters that the output should occupy:

```
printf( "% 4d", 36 )
// prints "  36"
```

A browser will not display multiple spaces in an HTML document. You can force the display of spaces and newlines by placing <PRE> tags around your output.

```
<pre>
<?php
print "The     spaces     will be visible";
?>
</pre>
```

If you wish to format an entire document as text, you can use the `header()` function to change the Content-Type header.

```
header("Content-Type: Text/Plain");
```

Remember that your script must not have sent any output to the browser for the `header()` function to work as desired.

You can specify any character other than a space or a zero in your padding specifier with a single quotation mark followed by the character you want to use:

```
printf ( "%'x4d", 36 );
// prints "xx36"
```

We now have the tools we need to complete our HTML code example. Until now, we could convert three numbers, but we could not pad them with leading zeroes:

```
$red = 1;
$green = 1;
$blue = 1;
printf( "#%02X%02X%02X", $red, $green, $blue );
// prints "#010101"
```

Each variable is output as a hexadecimal number. If the output occupies fewer than two spaces, leading zeroes will be added.

Specifying a Field Width

You can specify the number of spaces within which your output should sit. The field width specifier is an integer that should be placed after the percent sign that begins a conversion specification (assuming that no padding specifier is defined). The following fragment outputs a list of four items, all of which sit within a field of 20 spaces. To make the spaces visible on the browser, we place all our output within a PRE element.

```
print "<pre>";
printf("%20s\n", "Books");
printf("%20s\n", "CDs");
printf("%20s\n", "Games");
printf("%20s\n", "Magazines");
print "</pre>";
```

Figure 17.2 shows the output of this fragment.

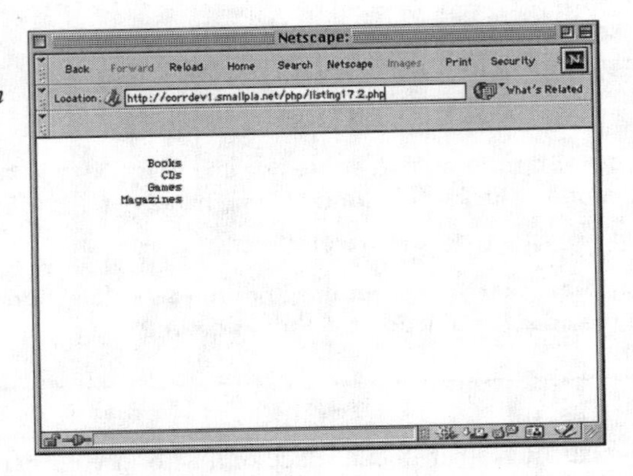

FIGURE 17.2
Aligning with field width specifiers.

By default, output is right-aligned within the field you specify. You can make it left-aligned by prepending a minus (-) symbol to the field width specifier:

```
printf("%-20s\n", "Left aligned");
```

Note that alignment applies to the decimal portion of any number that you output. In other words, only the portion before the decimal point of a double will sit flush to the end of the field width when right aligned.

Specifying Precision

If you want to output data in floating-point format, you can specify the precision to which you want to round your data. This is particularly useful when dealing with currency. The precision identifier should be placed directly before the type specifier. It consists of a dot followed by the number of decimal places to which you want to round. This specifier only has an effect on data that is output with the `f` type specifier:

```
printf( "%.2f", 5.333333 );
// prints "5.33"
```

In the C language, it is possible to use a precision specifier with `printf()` to specify padding for decimal output. The precision specifier will have no effect on decimal output in PHP4. Use the padding specifier to add leading zeroes to integers.

Conversion Specifications: A Recap

Table 17.2 lists the specifiers that can make up a conversion specification in the order that they would be included. Note that it is difficult to use both a padding specifier and a field width specifier. You should choose to use one or the other, but not both.

TABLE 17.2 Components of Conversion Specification

Name	*Description*	*Example*
Padding specifier	Determines the number of characters that output should occupy, and the characters to add otherwise	`' 4'`
Field width specifier	Determines the space within which output should be formatted	`'20'`
Precision specifier	Determines the number of decimal places to which a double should be rounded	`'.4'`
Type specifier	Determines the data type that should be output	`'d'`

Listing 17.2 uses `printf()` to output a list of products and prices.

LISTING 17.2 Using `printf()` to Format a List of Product Prices

```
 1: <html>
 2: <head>
 3: <title>Using printf() to format a list of product prices</title>
 4: </head>
 5: <body>
 6: <?php
 7: $products = Array(    "Green armchair"=>"222.4",
 8:                 "Candlestick"=>"4",
 9:                 "Coffee table"=>80.6
10:                 );
11: print "<pre>";
```

LISTING 17.2 continued

```
12: printf("%-20s%23s\n", "Name", "Price");
13: printf("%'-43s\n", "");
14: foreach ( $products as $key=>$val )
15:     printf( "%-20s%20.2f\n", $key, $val );
16: printf("</pre>");
17: ?>
18: </body>
19: </html>
```

We first define an associative array containing product names and prices. We print a `PRE` element, so that the browser will recognize our spaces and newlines. Our first `printf()` call defines the following format control string:

```
"%-20s%23s\n"
```

The first conversion specification (`"%-20s"`) uses a field width specifier of 20 characters, with the output left-justified. We use a string type specifier. The second conversion specification (`"%23s"`) sets up a right-aligned field width. This `printf()` call will output our field headers.

Our second `printf()` function call draws a line of `-` characters across a field of 43 characters. We achieve this with a padding specifier, which adds padding to an empty string.

The final `printf()` call is part of a `foreach` statement that loops through our product array. We use two conversion specifications. The first (`"%-20s"`) prints the product name as a string left-justified within a 20-character field. The second conversion specification (`"%20.2f"`) uses a field width specifier to ensure that output will be right-aligned within a 20-character field, and a precision specifier to ensure that the double we output is rounded to two decimal places.

Figure 17.3 shows the output of Listing 17.2.

Storing a Formatted String

`printf()` outputs data to the browser, which means that the results are not available to your scripts. You can, however, use the function`sprintf()`, which works in exactly the same way as `printf()` except that it returns a string that you can then store in a variable for later use. The following fragment uses `sprintf()` to round a double to two decimal places, storing the result in `$dosh`:

```
$dosh = sprintf("%.2f", 2.334454);
print "You have $dosh dollars to spend";
```

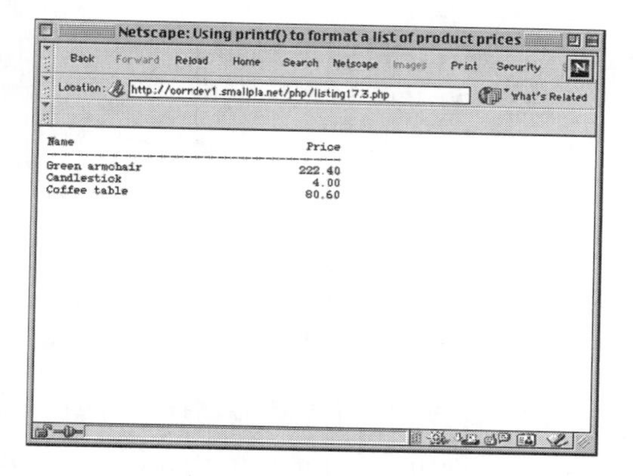

FIGURE 17.3
Products and prices formatted with `printf()`.

A particular use of `sprintf()` is to write formatted data to a file. You can call `sprintf()` and assign its return value to a variable that can then be printed to a file with `fputs()`.

Investigating Strings

You do not always know everything about the data that you are working with. Strings can arrive from many sources, including user input, databases, files, and Web pages. Before you begin to work with data from an external source, you often will need to find out more about it. PHP4 provides many functions that enable you to acquire information about strings.

A Note About Indexing Strings

We will frequently use the word *index* in relation to strings. You will have come across the word more frequently in the context of arrays. In fact, strings and arrays are not as different as you might imagine. You can think of a string as an array of characters. So you can access individual characters of a string as if they were elements of an array:

```
$test = "scallywag";
print $test[0]; // prints "s"
print $test[2]; // prints "a"
```

It is important to remember, therefore, that when we talk about the position or index of a character within a string, characters, like array elements, are indexed from 0.

Finding the Length of a String with `strlen()`

You can use `strlen()` to determine the length of a string. `strlen()` requires a string and returns an integer representing the number of characters in the variable you have passed it.

`strlen()` might typically be used to check the length of user input. The following fragment tests a membership code to ensure that it is four digits long:

```
if ( strlen( $membership ) == 4 )
   print "Thank you!";
else
   print "Your membership number must have 4 digits<P>";
```

The user is thanked for his input only if the global variable `$membership` contains four characters; otherwise, an error message is generated.

Finding a Substring Within a String with `strstr()`

You can use `strstr()` to test whether a string exists embedded within another string. `strstr()` requires two arguments: a source string and the substring you want to find within it. The function returns `false` if the substring is absent. Otherwise, it returns the portion of the source string beginning with the substring. For the following example, imagine that we want to treat membership codes that contain the string `AB` differently from those that do not:

```
$membership = "pAB7";
if ( strstr( $membership, "AB" ) )
   print "Thank you. Don't forget that your membership expires soon!";
else
   print "Thank you!";
```

Because our test variable `$membership` does contain the string `AB`, `strstr()` returns the string `AB7`. This resolves to `true` when tested, so we print a special message. What happens if our user enters `"pab7"`? `strstr()` is case sensitive, so `AB` will not be found. The `if` statement's test will fail, and the default message will be printed to the browser. If we want search for either `AB` or `ab` within the string, we must use `stristr()`, which works in exactly the same way but is not case sensitive.

Finding the Position of a Substring with `strpos()`

`strpos()` tells you both whether a string exists within a larger string and where it is to be found. `strpos()` requires two arguments: the source string and the substring you are seeking. The function also accepts an optional third argument, an integer representing the index from which you want to start searching. If the substring does not exist, `strpos()` returns `false`; otherwise, it returns the index at which the substring begins. The following fragment uses `strpos()` to ensure that a string begins with the string `mz`:

```
$membership = "mz00xyz";
if ( strpos($membership, "mz") === 0 )
   print "hello mz";
```

Notice the trick we had to play to get expected results. `strpos()` finds `mz` in our string, but it finds it at the first element of the string. This means that it will return zero, which will resolve to `false` in our test. To work around this, we use PHP4's new equivalence operator ===, which returns `true` if the left- and right-hand operands are equivalent and of the same type.

Extracting Part of a String with `substr()`

`substr()` returns a portion of a string based on the start index and length of the portion you are looking for. `strstr()` demands two arguments, a source string, and the starting index. It returns all characters from the starting index to the end of the string you are searching. `substr()` optionally accepts a third argument, which should be an integer representing the length of the string you want returned. If this argument is present, `substr()` returns only the number of characters specified from the start index onwards.

```
$test = "scallywag";
print substr($test,6);  // prints "wag"
print substr($test,6,2) // prints "wa"
```

If you pass `substr()` a minus number as its second (starting index) argument, it will count from the end rather than the beginning of the string. The following fragment writes a specific message to people who have submitted an email address ending in `.uk`.

```
$test = "matt@corrosive.co.uk";
if ( $test = substr( $test, -3 ) == ".uk" )
   print "Don't forget our special offers for British customers";
else
   print "Welcome to our shop!";
```

Tokenizing a String with `strtok()`

You can parse a string word by word using `strtok()`. `strtok()` initially requires two arguments, the string to be tokenized and the delimiters by which to split the string. The delimiter string can include as many characters as you want. `strtok()` will return the first token found. After `strtok()` has been called for the first time, the source string will be cached. For subsequent calls, you should only pass `strtok()` the delimiter string. The function will return the next found token every time it is called, returning `false` when the end of the string is reached. `strtok()` will usually be called repeatedly within a loop. Listing 17.3 uses `strtok()` to tokenize a URL, splitting the host and path from the query string, and further dividing the name/value pairs of the query string. Figure 17.3 shows the output from Listing 17.3.

Listing 17.3 Dividing a String into Tokens with `strtok()`

```
 1: <html>
 2: <head>
 3: <title>Listing 17.3 Dividing a string into
 4:          tokens with strtok()</title>
 5: </head>
 6: <body>
 7: <?php
 8: $test = "http://www.deja.com/qs.xp?
 9: OP=dnquery.xp&ST=MS&DBS=2&QRY=developer+php";
10: $delims = "?&";
11: $word = strtok( $test, $delims );
12: while ( is_string( $word ) )
13:     {
14:     if ( $word )
15:         print "$word<br>";
16:     $word = strtok( $delims);
17:     }
18: ?>
19: </body>
20: </html>
```

`strtok()` is something of a blunt instrument, and a few tricks are required to work with it. We first store the delimiters that we want to work with in a variable, `$delims`. We call `strtok()`, passing it the URL we want to tokenize and the `$delims` string. We store the first result in `$word`. Within the conditional expression of the `while` loop, we test that `$word` is a string. If it isn't, we know that end of the string has been reached and no further action is required.

We are testing the return type because a string containing two delimiters in a row would cause `strtok()` to return an empty string when it reaches the first of these delimiters. So a more conventional test such as

```
while ( $word )
    {
    $word = strtok( $delims );
    }
```

would fail if `$word` is an empty string, even if the end of the source string has not yet been reached.

Having established that `$word` contains a string, we can go on to work with it. If `$word` does not contain an empty string, we print it to the browser. We must then call `strtok()` again to repopulate the `$word` variable for the next test. Notice that we don't pass the source string to `strtok()` a second time. If we were to do this, the first word of the source string would be returned once again, and we would find ourselves in an infinite loop.

Manipulating Strings

PHP4 provides many functions that will transform a string argument, subtly or radically.

Cleaning Up a String with `trim()` and `ltrim()`

When you acquire text from the user or a file, you can't always be sure that you haven't also picked up white space at the beginning and end of your data. `trim()` shaves any white space characters, including newlines, tabs, and spaces, from both the start and end of a string. It accepts the string to be modified, returning the cleaned-up version.


```
$text = "\t\t\tlots of room to breath      ";
$text = trim( $text );
print $text;
// prints "lots of room to breath";
```

Of course this might be more work than you require. You might want to keep white space at the beginning of a string but remove it from the end. You can use PHP's `chop()` function exactly the same as you would `trim()`. Only white space at the end of the string argument will be removed, however:

```
$text = "\t\t\tlots of room to breath      ";
$text = chop( $text );
print $test;
// prints "                 lots of room to breath";
```

PHP provides the `ltrim()` function to strip white space only from the beginning of a string. Once again, this is called with the string you want to transform and returns a new string, shorn of tabs, newlines, and spaces:

```
$text = "\t\t\tlots of room to breath      ";
$text = ltrim( $text );
print $test;
// prints "lots of room to breath      ";
```

Replacing a Portion of a String using `substr_replace()`

`substr_replace()` works similarly to `substr()` except that it allows you replace the portion of a string that you extract. The function requires three arguments: the string you are transforming, the text you want to add to it, and the starting index. It also accepts an optional length argument. `substr_replace()` finds the portion of a string specified by the starting index and length arguments, replacing this portion with the string provided in the replace string argument and returning the entire transformed string.

In the following code fragment, to renew a user's membership code, we must change its second two characters:

```
<?
$membership = "mz99xyz";
$membership = substr_replace( $membership, "00", 2, 2 );
print "New membership number: $membership<p>";
// prints "New membership number: mz00xyz"
?>
```

Replacing Substrings Using `str_replace`

`str_replace()` replaces all instances of a string within another string. It requires three arguments: a search string, the replacement string, and the string on which this transformation is to be effected. The function returns the transformed string. The following example uses `str_replace()` to change all references to 1999 to 2000 within a string:

```
$string = "Site contents copyright 1999. ";
$string .= "The 1999 Guide to All Things Good in Europe";
print str_replace("1999","2000",$string);
```

Converting Case

PHP provides several functions that allow you to convert the case of a string. When you write user-submitted data to a file or database, you may want to convert it all to upper- or lowercase text first, to make it easy to compare later on. To get an uppercase version of a string, use the function `strtoupper()`. This function requires only the string that you want to convert and returns the converted string:

```
$membership = "mz00xyz";
$membership = strtoupper( $membership );
print "$membership<P>"; // prints "MZ00XYZ"
```

To convert a string to lowercase characters, use the function `strtolower()`. Once again, this requires the string you want to convert and returns a converted version:

```
$home_url = "WWW.CORROSIVE.CO.UK";
$home_url = strtolower( $home_url );
if ( ! ( strpos ( $home_url, "http://" ) === 0 ) )
   $home_url = "http://$home_url";
print $home_url; // prints "http://www.corrosive.co.uk"
```

PHP also provides a case function that has a useful cosmetic purpose. ucwords() makes the first letter of every word in a string uppercase. In the following fragment, we make the first letter of every word in a user-submitted string uppercase:

```
$full_name = "violet elizabeth bott";
$full_name = ucwords( $full_name );
print $full_name; // prints "Violet Elizabeth Bott"
```

Although this function makes the first letter of each word uppercase, it does not touch any other letters. So if the user had had problems with her shift key in the previous example and submitted VIolEt eLIZaBeTH bOTt, our approach would not have done much to fix the string. We would have ended up with VIolEt ELIZaBeTH BOTt, which isn't much of an improvement. We can deal with this by making the submitted string lowercase with strtolower() before invoking ucwords():

```
$full_name = "VIolEt eLIZaBeTH bOTt";
$full_name = ucwords( strtolower($full_name) );
print $full_name; // prints "Violet Elizabeth Bott"
```

17

Breaking Strings into Arrays with explode()

The delightfully named explode() function is similar in some ways to strtok(). explode(), though, will break up a string into an array, which you can then store, sort, or examine as you want. explode() requires two arguments: the delimiter string that you want to use to break up the source string and the source string itself. The delimiter string can include more than one character, all of which will form a single delimiter (unlike multiple delimiter characters passed to strtok(), each of which will be a delimiter in its own right). The following fragment breaks up a date and stores the result in an array:

```
$start_date = "2000-01-12";
$date_array = explode("-", $start_date);
// $date[0] == "2000"
// $date[1] == "01"
// $date[2] == "12"
```

Summary

Strings are PHP's principal means of communication with the outside world and of storing information for later use. In this hour, you have covered some of the functions that enable you to take control of the strings in your scripts.

You learned how to format strings with printf() and sprint(). You should be able to use these functions both to create strings that transform data and lay it out. You learned about functions that investigate strings. You should be able to discover the length of a string with strlen(), determine the presence of a substring with strpos(), or extract a substring with substr(). You should be able to tokenize a string with strtok().

Finally, you learned about functions that transform strings. You can now remove white space from the beginning or end of a string with trim(), ltrim(), or chop(). You can change case with strtoupper(), strtolower(), or ucwords(). You can replace all instances of a string with str_replace().

Believe it or not, you are not finished with strings yet. PHP supports regular expressions that are an even more powerful means of working with strings than the functions already examined. Regular expressions are the subject of the next hour.

Q&A

Q Are there any other string functions that might be useful to me?

A Yes. PHP4 has about 60 string functions! You can read about them all in the PHP4 online manual at http://www.php.net/manual/ref.strings.php.

Q In the example that demonstrated printf(), we showed the formatting by wrapping our output in <PRE> tags. Is this the best way of showing formatted plain text on a browser?

A <PRE> tags can be useful if you want to preserve plain text formatting in an HTML context. If you want to output an entire text document to the browser, however, it is neater to tell the browser to format the entire output as plain text. You can do this with the header() function:

```
Header("Content-Type: Text/Plain");
```

Workshop

The Workshop provides quiz questions to help you solidify your understanding of the material covered. Try to understand the quiz answers before continuing to the next hour's lesson. Quiz answers are provided in Appendix A.

Quiz

1. What conversion specifier would you use with printf() to format an integer as a double? Write down the full syntax required to convert the integer 33.
2. How would you pad the conversion you effected in question 1 with zeroes so that the part before the decimal point is four characters long?

3. How would you specify a precision of two decimal places for the floating-point number we have been formatting in the previous questions?
4. What function would you use to determine the length of a string?
5. What function would you use to acquire the starting index of a substring within a string?
6. What function would you use to extract a substring from a string?
7. How might you remove white space from the beginning of a string?
8. How would you convert a string to uppercase characters?
9. How would you break up a delimited string into an array of substrings?

Activities

1. Create a feedback form that accepts a user's full name and an email address. Use case conversion functions to capitalize the first letter of each name the user submits and print the result back to the browser. Check that the user's email address contains the @ symbol and print a warning otherwise.
2. Create an array of doubles and integers. Loop through the array converting each element to a floating-point number with a precision of 2. Right-align the output within a field of 20 characters.

HOUR 18

Working with Regular Expressions

Regular expressions are a powerful way of examining and modifying text. They enable you to search for patterns within a string, extracting matches flexibly and precisely. Be warned that because they are more powerful, they are also slower than the more basic string function examined in Hour 17, "Working with Strings." You should use string functions, therefore, if you don't need the extra power afforded by the use of a regular expression function.

PHP supports two flavors of regular expression. It has a set of functions that emulate regular expressions as employed in Perl, and a set of function that support the more limited POSIX regular expressions. You will examine both.

In this hour, you will learn

- How to match patterns in strings using regular expressions
- The basics of regular expression syntax

- How to replace text in strings using regular expressions
- How to work with powerful Perl compatible regular expressions to match and replace patterns in text

POSIX Regular Expression Functions

POSIX regular expression functions make it possible for you to match and replace complex patterns in strings. They are commonly known simply as regular expression functions, but we refer to them as POSIX regular expression functions to distinguish them from the similar but more powerful Perl compatible regular expressions, and because they follow the POSIX definition for extended regular expressions.

A regular expression is a combination of symbols that match a pattern in text. Learning how to use regular expressions, therefore, is much more than learning the arguments and return types of PHP's regular expression functions. We will begin with the functions and use them to introduce regular expression syntax.

Using `ereg()` to Match Patterns in Strings

`ereg()` requires a string representing a pattern, a string representing the text to be searched, and an array variable into which the results of the search will be placed. `ereg()` returns an integer representing the number of characters matched if the pattern was discovered in the source string, or `false` otherwise. Let's search the string "Aardvark advocacy" for the letters "aa."

```
print ereg("aa","aardvark advocacy",$array);
print "<br>$array[0]<br>";
// output:
// 2
// aa
```

The letters "aa" exist in "aardvark," so `ereg()` returns `2`, which is the number of letters it matched. The first element of the `$array` variable is also filled with the matched string, which we print to the browser. This might seem strange given that we already know the pattern we are looking for is "aa". We are not, however, limited to looking for predefined characters. We can use a single dot (`.`) to match any character:

```
print ereg("d.","aardvark advocacy",$array);
print "<br>$array[0]<br>";
// output:
// 2
// dv
```

`d.` matches "d" followed by any character. We don't know in advance what the second character will be, so the value in `$array[0]` becomes useful.

Using Quantifiers to Match a Character More Than Once

When you search for a character in a string, you can use a quantifier to determine the number of times this character should repeat for a match to be made. The pattern `a+`, for example, will match at least one "a" followed by "a" zero or more times. Let's put this to the test:

```
if ( ereg("a+","aaaa", $array) )
   print $array[0];
// prints "aaaa";
```

Notice that this regular expression greedily matches as many characters as it can. Table 18.1 lists the quantifiers you can use to test for a recurring character.

TABLE 18.1 Quantifiers for Matching a Recurring Character

Symbol	*Description*	*Example*	*Matches*	*Does Not Match*
*	Zero or more instance	a*	xxxx	(Will match anything)
+	One or more instances	a+	xaax	xxxx
?	Zero or one instance	a?	xaxx	xaax
{*n*}	*n* instances	a{3}	xaaa	aaaa
{*n*,}	At least *n* instances	a{3,}	aaaa	aaxx
{,*n*}	Up to *n* instances	a{,2}	xaax	aaax
{*n*1,*n*2}	At least *n*1 instances, no more than *n*2 instances	a{1,2}	xaax	xaaa

The numbers between braces in Table 18.1 are called *bounds*. Bounds let you pinpoint exactly the number of times a character should repeat to be matched.

NEW TERM *Bounds* define the number of times a character or range of characters should be matched in a regular expression. You should place your upper and lower bounds between braces after the character you wish to match. For example,

```
a{4,5}
```

will match no fewer than 4 and no more than 5 instances of the character a.

Let's create an example. A club has allocated membership codes to its members. A valid code can be between one and four instances of the letter "y" followed by any number of alphanumeric characters, followed by the number 99. We have been requested by the club to parse a backlog, pulling out the membership codes where possible.

```
$test = "the code is yyXGDH99 -- have you received my sub?";
if ( ereg( "y{1,4}.*99 ", $test, $array ) )
   print "Found membership: $array[0]";
// prints "Found membership: yyXGDH99 "
```

In the previous code fragment, the membership code begins with two y characters, followed by four uppercase letters, followed by 99. y{1,4} matches the two y characters, and the four uppercase letters are matched by .*, which will match any number of characters of any type.

So that would seem to do the job. In fact, we have a long way to go yet. To ensure that the matched pattern ends at 99, we have required a space as the last character. This is returned when we match. Worse than this, if the string we were testing was

```
"my code is yyXGDH99 did you get my 1999 sub?"
```

the previous regular expression would match

```
"y code is yyXGDH99 did you get my 1999"
```

So what went wrong? The regular expression matched the y in my, and then matched any number of characters until it reached 99 followed by a space. Regular expressions are greedy; in other words, they match as many characters as they can. For this reason, we match all characters until the 99 of 1999 is reached, rather than the final 99 in our membership code. We might go some way towards fixing this if only we could make sure that the characters that we match between y and 99 are truly alphanumeric and contain no spaces. In fact, we can do this easily with a character class.

Matching Ranges of Characters with Character Classes

Until now we have either matched specified characters or used . to match any character. Character classes enable you to match any one of a group of characters. To define a character class, you surround the characters you want to match in square brackets.

[ab] will match "a" or "b." After you have defined a character class, you can treat it as if it were a character. So [ab]+ will match "aaa," "bbb," or "ababab."

You can also match ranges of characters with a character class: [a-z] will match any lowercase letter, [A-Z] will match any uppercase letter, and [0-9] will match any number. You can combine ranges and individual characters into one character class, so [a-z5] will match any lowercase letter or the number "5".

You can also negate a character class by including a caret (^) character after the opening square bracket: [^A-Z] will match anything apart from an uppercase character.

Let's return to the example from the previous section. We need to match "y" between one and four times, any alphanumeric character any number of times, and the characters "99."

```
$test = "my code is yyXGDH99 did you get my 1999 sub?";
if ( ereg( "y{1,4}[a-zA-Z0-9]*99 ", $test, $array ) )
   print "Found membership: $array[0]";
// prints "Found membership: yyXGDH99 "
```

We're getting closer. The character class that we have added will no longer match spaces, so the membership code is now returned. If we add a comma after the membership code in our test string, however, the regular expression fails again:


```
$test = "my code is yyXGDH99, did you get my 1999 sub?";
if ( ereg( "y{1,4}[a-zA-Z0-9]*99 ", $test, $array ) )
   print "Found membership: $array[0]";
// regular expression fails
```

This is because we have demanded a space at the end of the pattern to ensure that we are at the end of the membership code. So if a text includes a membership code in brackets, or before a hyphen or comma, the match will fail. We can amend our regular expression, so that we match anything other than an alphanumeric character, which will get us some way towards a solution:

```
$test = "my code is yyXGDH99, did you get my 1999 sub?";
if ( ereg( "y{1,4}[a-zA-Z0-9]*99[^a-zA-Z0-9]", $test, $array ) )
   print "Found membership: $array[0]";
// prints "Found membership: yyXGDH99,"
```

We're closer still, but there are still two problems. First, we have included the comma in our returned match, and second, the match will fail if the membership code is at the end of the string we are testing because it requires a character to exist after the membership code. We need, in other words, to find a reliable way of testing for a word boundary. We will return to this problem.

Working with Atoms

NEW TERM An *atom* is a pattern enclosed in brackets (often referred to as a *subpattern*). After you have defined an atom, you can treat it as if it were itself a character or character class. In other words, you can match the same pattern as many times as you want using the syntax described in Table 18.1.

In the next fragment, we define a pattern, enclose it in brackets, and require that the atom should match twice for the regular expression to succeed:

```
$test = "abbaxabbaxabbax";
if ( ereg( "([ab]+x){2}", $test, $array ) )
   print "$array[0]";
// prints "abbaxabbax"
```

`[ab]+x` will match "abbax", but `([ab]+x)2` will match "abbaxabbax".

The first element of the array variable that is passed to `ereg()` will contain the complete matched string. Subsequent elements will contain each individual atom matched. This means that you can access the component parts of a matched pattern as well as the entire match.

In the following code fragment, we match an IP address and access not only the entire address, but also each of its component parts:

```
$test = "158.152.55.35";
if ( ereg( "([0-9]+)\.([0-9]+)\.([0-9]+)\.([0-9]+)", $test, $array ) )
   {
   foreach ( $array as $val )
       print "$val<BR>";
   }
// Output:
// 158.152.1.58
// 158
// 152
// 1
// 58
```

Notice that we have used a backslash (\) to escape the dots in the regular expression. By doing this, we signal that we want to strip `.` of its special meaning and treat it as a specific character. You must do the same for any character that has a function in a regular expression if you want to refer to it.

Branches

You can combine patterns with the pipe (`|`) character to create branches in your regular expressions. A regular expression with two branches will match either the first pattern or the second. This adds yet another layer of flexibility to regular expression syntax. In the next code fragment, we match either `.com` or `.co.uk` in a string:

```
$test = "www.adomain.com";
if ( ereg( "\.com|\.co\.uk", $test, $array ) )
   print "it is a $array[0] domain<BR>";
// prints "it is .com domain"
```

Anchoring a Regular Expression

Not only can you determine the pattern you want to find in a string, you also can decide where in the string you want to find it. To test whether a pattern is at the beginning of a string, prepend a caret (^) symbol to your regular expression. `^a` will match "apple", but not "banana".

To test that a pattern is at the end of a string, append a dollar ($) symbol to the end of your regular expression. `a$` will match "flea" but not "dear".

The Membership Code Example Revisited

We now have the tools to complete our membership code examples. Remember that we are parsing emails to extract membership codes that consist of between one and four instances of the letter "y" followed by any number of any alphanumeric characters followed by "99". Our current problem is to determine when a matched pattern is on a word boundary. We can't use a space because a word can be bounded by punctuation. We can't require that a nonalphanumeric character bound the match because our pattern could begin or end a string.

Now that we can create branches and anchor patterns, we can require that the membership code be followed either by a nonalphanumeric character or the end of the string. We can use the same logic to determine a word boundary at the beginning of the code. We can also use brackets to recover the membership code shorn of any punctuation or spaces as follows:

```
$test = "my code is yyXGDH99, did you get my 1999 sub?";
if ( ereg( "(^|[^a-zA-Z0-9])(y{1,4}[a-zA-Z0-9]*99)([^a-zA-Z0-9]|$)", $test,
➥$array ) )
   print "Found membership: $array[2]";
// prints "Found membership: yyXGDH99"
```

As you can see, regular expressions are daunting at first glance. After you break them down into smaller chunks, however, they usually reveal their secrets quite easily. We have ensured that our matched pattern is on a word boundary (as we define it for these purposes). This means that it must either be preceded by a nonalphanumeric character or the beginning of the string. It must be also be followed by a nonalphanumeric character or the end of the string. We don't want to record any preceding or following characters, so we wrap the pattern we want to extract in brackets. We can then be sure to access it in the second element of the `$array` array.

`ereg()` is case sensitive. If you don't want to match case, you can use `eregi()`, which is not case sensitive but is the same as `ereg()` in all other respects.

Using `egrep_replace()` to Replace Patterns in Strings

Until now we have searched for patterns in a string, leaving the search string untouched. `egrep_replace()` enables you to find a pattern in a string and replace it with a new substring. `egrep_replace()` requires three strings: a regular expression, the text with which to replace a found pattern, and the text to modify. `egrep_replace()` returns a string, including the modification if a match was found or an unchanged copy of the original source string, otherwise. In the following fragment, we search for the name of a club official, replacing it with name of her successor:

```
$test = "Our Secretary, Sarah Williams is pleased to welcome you.";
print ereg_replace("Sarah Williams", "Rev. P.W. Goodchild", $test);
// prints "Our Secretary, Rev. P.W. Goodchild is pleased to welcome you."
```

Note that although `ereg()` will only match the first pattern it finds, `ereg_replace()` will find and replace every instance of a pattern.

Using Back References with `egrep_replace()`

Back references make it possible for you to use part of a matched pattern in the replacement string. To use this feature, you should use brackets to wrap any elements of your regular expression that you might want to use. The text matched by these subpatterns will be available to the replacement string if you refer to them with two backslashes and the number of the atom (`\\1`, for example). Atoms are numbered in order, outer to inner, left to right starting at `\\1`. `\\0` stores the entire match.

The following fragment converts dates in dd/mm/yy format to mm/dd/yy format:

```
$test = "25/12/2000";
print ereg_replace("([0-9]+)/([0-9]+)/([0-9]+)", "\\2/\\1/\\3", $test);
// prints "12/25/2000"
```

ereg_replace() is case sensitive. If you don't want to match case, you can use eregi_replace(), which is not case sensitive but is identical to ereg_replace() in all other respects.

Using split() to Break Up Strings

In Hour 17, you saw that you could split a string of tokens into an array using explode(). This is powerful but limits you to a single set of characters that can be used as a delimiter. PHP4's split() function enables you to use the power of regular expressions to define a flexible delimiter. split() requires a string representing a pattern to use as a delimiter and a source string. It also accepts an optional third argument representing a limit to the number of elements you want returned. split() returns an array.

The following fragment uses a regular expression with two branches to split a string on either a comma followed by a space or the word and surrounded by two spaces:

```
$text = "apples, oranges, peaches and grapefruit";
$fruitarray = split( ", | and ", $text );
foreach ( $fruitarray as $item )
    print "$item<BR>";
// output:
// apples
// oranges
// peaches
// grapefruit
```

Perl Compatible Regular Expressions (PCREs)

If you are migrating from Perl to PHP, you are likely to find the POSIX regular expression functions somewhat cumbersome. The good news is that PHP4 supports Perl compatible regular expressions. PCREs are even more powerful than the syntax that you have already examined. We will explore the differences in this section.

Matching Patterns with preg_match()

preg_match() accepts three arguments: a regular expression, a source string, and an array variable, which will store matches. preg_match() returns true if a match is found and false otherwise. The difference between this function and ereg_match() lies in the regular expression argument. Perl compatible regular expressions should be enclosed by delimiters. Conventionally, these delimiters are forward slashes, although you can use any character that isn't alphanumeric (apart from the backslash character). The following fragment uses `preg_match()` to match the character `p` followed by any character, followed by the character `t`:

```
$text = "pepperpot";
if ( preg_match( "/p.t/", $text, $array ) )
   print $array[0];
// prints "pot"
```

PCREs and Greediness

By default, regular expressions will attempt to match as many characters as possible. So,

```
"/p.*t/"
```

will find the first "p" in a string and match as many characters as possible until the last possible "t" character is reached. So, this regular expression matches the entire test string in the following fragment:

```
$text = "pot post pat patent";
if ( preg_match( "/p.*t/", $text, $array ) )
   print $array[0];
// prints "pot post pat patent"
```

By placing a question mark (`?`) after any quantifier, you can force a Perl compatible regular expression to be more frugal. So, whereas

```
"p.*t"
```

means "p followed by as many characters as possible followed by t,"

```
"p.*?t"
```

means "p followed by as few characters as possible followed by t."

The following fragment uses this technique to match the smallest number of characters starting with "p" and ending with "t":

```
$text = "pot post pat patent";
if ( preg_match( "/p.*?t/", $text, $array ) )
   print $array[0];
// prints "pot"
```

PCREs and Backslashed Characters

You can escape certain characters with Perl compatible regular expressions, just as you can within strings. `\t`, for example represents a tab character, and `\n` represents a newline. PCREs also define some escape characters that will match entire character types. Table 18.2 lists these backslash characters.

TABLE 18.2 Escape Characters That Match Character Types

Character	*Matches*
`\d`	Any number
`\D`	Anything other than a number
`\s`	Any kind of whitespace
`\S`	Anything other than whitespace
`\w`	Any word character (including the underscore character)
`\W`	Anything other than a word character

These escape characters can vastly simplify your regular expressions. Without them, you would be forced to use a character class to match ranges of characters. Compare the `ereg()` and `preg_match()` syntax for matching word characters:

```
ereg( "p[a-zA-Z0-9_]+t", $text, $array );
preg_match( "/p\w+t/, $text, $array );
```

PCREs also support a number of escape characters that act as anchors. *Anchors* match positions within a string, without matching any characters. These are listed in Table 18.3.

TABLE 18.3 Escape Characters That Act as Anchors

Character	*Matches*
`\A`	Beginning of string
`\b`	Word boundary
`\B`	Not a word boundary
`\Z`	End of string (matches before final newline or at end of string)
`\z`	End of string (matches only at very end of string)

Remember the problems we had matching word boundaries in our membership code example? PCREs make this job much easier. Compare the `ereg()` and `preg_match()` syntax for matching word characters and boundaries:

```
ereg( "(^|[^a-zA-Z0-9_])(p[a-zA-Z0-9_]+t)([^a-zA-Z0-9_]|$)", $text, $array );
preg_match( "\bp\w+t\b", $text, $array );
```

The `preg_match()` call in the previous fragment will match the character "p" but only if it is at a word boundary, followed by any number of word characters, followed by "t," but only if it is at a word boundary. The word boundary escape character does not actually match a character; it merely confirms that a boundary exists for a match to take place. For the `ereg_match()` call, you must construct a pattern for a nonword character and match either that or a string boundary.

You can also escape characters to turn off their meanings. To match a "." character, for example, you should add a backslash to it.

Finding Matches Globally with `preg_match_all()`

One of the problems with POSIX regular expressions is that it is difficult to match every instance of a pattern within a string. So, using `ereg()` to search for words beginning with "p" and ending with "s", we will match only the first found pattern. Let's try it out:

```
$text = "I sell pots, plants, pistachios, pianos and parrots";
if ( ereg( "(^|[^a-zA-Z0-9_])(p[a-zA-Z0-9_]+s)([^a-zA-Z0-9_]|$)",
             $text, $array ) )
   {
   for ( $x=0; is_string( $array[$x] ); $x++ )
       print "\$array[$x]: $array[$x]<br>\n";
   }
// output:
// $array[0]: pots,
// $array[1]:
// $array[2]: pots
// $array[3]: ,
```

As we would expect, the first match, "pots", is stored in the third element of the `$array` array. The first element contains the complete match, the second contains a space, and the fourth contains a comma. To get at every pattern match in our test string, we would have to use `ereg_replace()` in a loop to remove each match from the string before testing again.

We can use `preg_match_all()` to access every match in the test string in one call. `preg_match_all()` accepts a regular expression, a source string, and an array variable, and will return `true` if a match is found. The array variable is populated with a multidimensional array, the first element of which will contain every match to the complete pattern defined in the regular expression.

Listing 18.1 tests a string using `preg_match_all()`, using two `for` statements to output the multidimensional array of results.

LISTING 18.1 Using `preg_match_all()` to Match a Pattern Globally

```
 1: <html>
 2: <head>
 3: <title>Using preg_match_all() to match a pattern globally</title>
 4: </head>
 5: <body>
 6: <?php
 7: $text = "I sell pots, plants, pistachios, pianos and parrots";
 8: if ( preg_match_all( "/\bp\w+s\b/", $text, $array ) )
```

LISTING 18.1 continued

```
 9:     {
10:     for ( $x=0; $x< count( $array ); $x++ )
11:         {
12:         for ( $y=0; $y< count( $array[$x] ); $y++ )
13:             print "\$array[$x][$y]: ".$array[$x][$y]."<BR>\n";
14:         }
15:     }
16: // Output:
17: // $array[0][0]: pots
18: // $array[0][1]: plants
19: // $array[0][2]: pistachios
20: // $array[0][3]: pianos
21: // $array[0][4]: parrots
22: ?>
23: </body>
24: </html>
```

The first and only element of the `$array` variable that we passed to `preg_match_all()` has been populated with an array of strings. This array contains every word in the test string that begins with "p" and ends with "s".

`preg_match_all()` populates a multidimensional array to store matches to subpatterns. The first element of the array argument passed to `preg_match_all()` will contain every match of the complete regular expression. Each additional element will contain the matches that correspond to each atom (subpattern in brackets). So with the following call to `preg_match_all()`

```
$text = "01-05-99, 01-10-99, 01-03-00";
preg_match_all( "/(\d+)-(\d+)-(\d+)/", $text, $array );
```

`$array[0]` will store an array of complete matches:

```
$array[0][0]: 01-05-99
$array[0][1]: 01-10-99
$array[0][2]: 01-03-00
```

`$array[1]` will store an array of matches that corresponds to the first subpattern:

```
$array[1][0]: 01
$array[1][1]: 01
$array[1][2]: 01
```

`$array[2]` will store an array of matches that corresponds to the second subpattern:

```
$array[2][0]: 05
$array[2][1]: 10
$array[2][2]: 03
```

and so on.

Using `preg_replace()` to Replace Patterns

`preg_replace()` behaves in the same way as `ereg_replace()`, except that you have access to the additional functionality of Perl compatible regular expressions. `preg_replace()` requires a regular expression, a replacement string, and a source string. If a match is found, it returns a transformed string; otherwise, it returns a copy of the source string. The following fragment transforms dates in a string from dd/mm/yy to mm/dd/yy format:

```
$t = "25/12/99, 14/5/00";
$t = preg_replace( "|\b(\d+)/(\d+)/(\d+)\b|", "\\2/\\1/\\3", $t );
print "$t<br>";
// prints "12/25/99, 5/14/00"
```

Notice that we have used a pipe (|) symbol as a delimiter. This is to save us from having to escape the forward slashes in the pattern we want to match. `preg_replace()` supports back references in the same way as `ereg_replace()`.

Instead of a source string, you can pass an array of strings to `preg_match()`, and it will transform each string in turn. In this case, the return value will be an array of transformed strings.

You can also pass arrays of regular expressions and replacement strings to `preg_match()`. Each regular expression will be applied to the source string, and the corresponding replacement string will be applied. The following fragment transforms date formats as before, but also changes copyright information in the source string:

```
$text = "25/12/99, 14/5/00. Copyright 1999";
$regs = array( "|\b(\d+)/(\d+)/(\d+)\b|",  "/([Cc]opyright) 1999/" );
$reps = array( "\\2/\\1/\\3",              "\\1 2000" );
$text = preg_replace( $regs, $reps,  $text );
print "$text<br>";
// prints "12/25/99, 5/14/00. Copyright 2000"
```

We create two arrays. The first, `$regs`, contains two regular expressions, and the second, `$reps`, contains replacement strings. The first element of the `$reps` array corresponds to the first element of the `$reps` array, and so on.

If the array of replacement strings contains fewer elements than the array of regular expressions, patterns matched by those regular expressions without corresponding replacement strings will be replaced with an empty string.

If you pass `preg_replace()` an array of regular expressions but only a string as replacement, the same replacement string will be applied to each pattern in the array of regular expressions.

Modifiers

Perl compatible regular expressions allow you to modify the way that a pattern is applied through the use of pattern modifiers.

NEW TERM A *pattern modifier* is a letter that should be placed after the final delimiter in your Perl compatible regular expression. It will refine the behavior of your regular expression.

Table 18.4 lists the PCRE pattern modifiers

TABLE 18.4 Perl Compatible Regular Expression Modifiers

Pattern	*Description*
`/i`	Case insensitive.
`/e`	Treats replacement string in `preg_replace()` as PHP code.
`/m`	`$` and `^` anchors match the beginning and end of the current line.
`/s`	Matches newlines (newlines are not normally not matched by `.`).
`/x`	Whitespace outside character classes is not matched to aid readability. To match whitespace, use `\s`, `\t`, or `\ `.
`/A`	Matches pattern only at start of string (this modifier is not found in Perl).
`/E`	Matches pattern only at end of string (this modifier is not found in Perl).
`/U`	Makes the regular expression ungreedy—minimum number of allowable matches found (this modifier is not found in Perl).

Where they do not contradict one another, you can combine pattern modifiers. You might want to use the `x` modifier to make your regular expression easier to read, for example, and also the `i` modifier to make it match patterns regardless of case. `/ b \S* t /ix` will match "bat" and "BAT" but not "B A T", for example. Unescaped spaces in a regular expression modified by `x` are there for aesthetic reasons only and will not match any patterns in the source string.

The m modifier can be useful if you want to match an anchored pattern on multiple lines of text. The anchor patterns ^ and $ match the beginning and ends of an entire string by default. The following fragment uses the m modifier to change the behavior of $:

```
$text = "name: matt\noccupation: coder\neyes: blue\n";
preg_match_all( "/^\w+:\s+(.*)$/m", $text, $array );
foreach ( $array[1] as $val )
    print "$val<br>";
// output:
// matt
// coder
// blue
```

We create a regular expression that will match any word characters followed by a colon and any number of space characters. We then match any number of characters followed by the end of string ($) anchor. Because we have used the m pattern modifier, $ matches the end of every line rather than the end of the string.

The s modifier is useful when you want use . to match characters across multiple lines. The following fragment attempts to access the first and last words of a string:

```
$text = "start with this line\nand you will reach\na conclusion in the end\n";
preg_match( "/^(\w+).*?(\w+)$/", $text, $array );
print "$array[1] $array[2]<br>";
```

This code will print nothing. Although the regular expression will find word characters at the beginning of the string, the . will not match the newline characters embedded in the text. The s modifier will change this:

```
$text = "start with this line\nand you will reach\na conclusion in the end\n";
preg_match( "/^(\w+).*?(\w+)$/s", $text, $array );
print "$array[1] $array[2]<br>";
// prints "start end"
```

The e modifier can be particularly powerful. It allows you to treat the replacement string in `preg_replace()` as if it were PHP. You can pass back references to functions as arguments, for example, or process lists of numbers. In the following example we use the e modifier to pass matched numbers in dates to a function that returns the same date in a new format.

```
<?php
function convDate( $month, $day, $year )
 {
      $year = ($year < 70 )?$year+2000:$year;
 $time = ( mktime( 0,0,0,$month,$day,$year) );
 return date("l F Y", $time);
 }

$dates = "3/18/99<br>\n7/22/00";
```

```
$dates = preg_replace(  "/([0-9]+)\/([0-9]+)\/([0-9]+)/e",
   "convDate(\\1,\\2,\\3)", $dates);
print $dates;

// prints:
// Thursday 18 March 1999
// Saturday 22 July 2000
?>
```

We match any set of three numbers separated by slashes, using parentheses to capture the matched numbers. Because we are using the `e` modifier, we can call the user-defined function `convDate()` from the replacement string argument, passing the three back references to the function. `convDate()` simply takes the numerical input and produces a more verbose date which replaces the original.

Summary

Regular expressions are a huge subject, and we've really only scraped the surface of their power in this hour. Nevertheless, you should now be able to use regular expression functions to find and replace complex patterns in text.

You should be able to use the `ereg()` regular expression function to find patterns in strings and the `ereg_replace()` function to replace all instances of a pattern in a string. You should be able to find ranges of characters using character classes, multiple patterns using quantifiers, and alternative patterns using branches. You should be able to extract subpatterns and refer to them with back references. With the aid of Perl compatible regular expressions, you should be able to use escape characters to anchor patterns or to match character types. You should be able to use modifiers to change the way in which PCREs work.

Q&A

Q Perl compatible regular expressions seem very powerful. Is there anywhere I can find out more about them?

A The relevant section in the PHP manual at `http://www.php.net` will offer some information about regular expression syntax. You can also find some useful information at `http://www.perl.com`—in particular, an introduction to Perl regular expressions at `http://www.perl.com/pub/doc/manual/html/pod/perlre.html` and an article by Tom Christiansen at `http://www.perl.com/pub/doc/manual/html/pod/perlfaq6.html`.

Workshop

The Workshop provides quiz questions to help you solidify your understanding of the material covered. Try to understand the quiz answers before continuing to the next hour's lesson. Quiz answers are provided in Appendix A.

Quiz

1. Using POSIX regular expression functions, what function would you use to match a pattern in a string?
2. What regular expression syntax would you use to match the letter "b" at least once but not more than six times?
3. How would you specify a character range between "d" and "f"?
4. How would you negate the character range you defined in question 3?
5. What syntax would you use to match either any number or the word "tree"?
6. What POSIX regular expression function would you use to replace a matched pattern?
7. The regular expression

   ```
   .*bc
   ```

   will match greedily—that is, it will match "abc000000bc" rather than "abc". Using Perl compatible regular expressions, how would you make the preceding regular expression match only the first instance of a pattern it finds?
8. Using PCREs, what backslash character will match whitespace?
9. What PCRE function could you use to match every instance of a pattern in a string?
10. Which modifier would you use in a PCRE function to match a pattern independently of case?

Activity

1. Use regular expressions to extract email addresses from a file. Add them to an array and output the result to the browser. Refine your regular expression across a number of files.

Hour 19

Saving State with Cookies and Query Strings

HTTP is a stateless protocol. This means that every page a user downloads from your server represents a separate connection. On the other hand, Web sites are perceived by users and publishers alike as environments, as spaces within which a single page is part of a wider whole. It's not surprising, therefore, that strategies to pass information from page to page are as old as the Web itself.

In this hour, we will examine two methods of storing information on one page that can then be accessed on subsequent pages. In this hour, you will learn

- What cookies are and how they work
- How to read a cookie
- How to set a cookie
- How to use cookies to store site usage information in a database

- About query strings
- How to build a function to turn an associative array into a query string

Cookies

Netscape originated the "magic cookie" back in the days of Netscape 1. The origin of the name is the subject of some debate, though it seems reasonable to assume that the fortune cookie may have played a role in the thinking behind it. Since then, the standard has been embraced by other browser producers.

NEW TERM A *cookie* is a small amount of data stored by the user's browser in compliance with a request from a server or script. A host can request that up to 20 cookies be stored by a user's browser. Each cookie consists of a name, value, and expiry date, as well as host and path information. An individual cookie is limited to 4KB.

After a cookie is set, only the originating host can read the data, ensuring that the user's privacy is respected. Furthermore, the user can configure his browser to notify him of all cookies set, or even to refuse all cookie requests. For this reason, cookies should be used in moderation and should not be relied on as an essential element of an environment design without first warning the user.

Having said that, cookies can be an excellent way of saving small amounts of information about a user from page to page or even from visit to visit.

The Anatomy of a Cookie

Cookies are usually set in an HTTP header (although JavaScript can also set a cookie directly on a browser). A PHP script that sets a cookie might send headers that look something like this:

```
HTTP/1.1 200 OK
Date: Fri, 04 Feb 2000 21:03:38 GMT
Server: Apache/1.3.9 (UNIX) PHP/4.0b3
Set-Cookie: vegetable=artichoke; expires=Friday,
➥04-Feb-00 22:03:38 GMT; path=/; domain=zink.demon.co.uk
Connection: close
Content-Type: text/html
```

As you can see, the `Set-Cookie` header contains a name value pair, a GMT date, a path and a domain. The name and value will be URL encoded. The `expires` field is an instruction to the browser to "forget" the cookie after the given time and date. The `path` field defines the position on a Web site below which the cookie should be sent back to the server. The `domain` field determines the Internet domains to which the cookie should be sent.

The domain cannot be different from the domain from which the cookie was sent, but can nonetheless specify a degree of flexibility. In the preceding example, the browser will send the cookie to the server `zink.demon.co.uk` and the server `www.zink.demon.co.uk`. You can read more about HTTP headers in Hour 13, "Beyond the Box."

If the browser is configured to store cookies, it will then keep this information until the expiry date. If the user points the browser at any page that matches the path and domain of the cookie, it will resend the cookie to the server. The browser's headers might look something like this:

```
GET / HTTP/1.0
Connection: Keep-Alive
User-Agent: Mozilla/4.6  (X11; I; Linux 2.2.6-15apmac ppc)
Host: zink.demon.co.uk:1126
Accept: image/gif, image/x-xbitmap, image/jpeg, image/pjpeg, image/png, */*
Accept-Encoding: gzip
Accept-Language: en
Accept-Charset: iso-8859-1,*,utf-8
Cookie: vegetable=artichoke
```

A PHP script will then have access to the cookie in the environmental variable `HTTP-COOKIE` (which holds all cookie names and values), in the global variable `$vegetable`, or in the global array variable `HTTP_COOKIE_VARS["vegetable"]`:

```
print "$HTTP_COOKIE<BR>";                    // prints "vegetable=artichoke"
print getenv("HTTP_COOKIE")."<BR>";          // prints "vegetable=artichoke"
print "$vegetable<BR>";                      // prints "artichoke"
print "$HTTP_COOKIE_VARS[vegetable]<BR>";    // prints "artichoke"
```


Setting a Cookie with PHP

You can set a cookie in a PHP script in two ways. You can use the `header()` function to set the `Set-Cookie` header. You encountered the `header()` function in Hour 9, "Working with Forms." `header()` requires a string that will then be included in the header section of the server response. Because headers are sent automatically for you, `header()` must be called before any output at all is sent to the browser.

```
header ("vegetable=artichoke; expires=Friday, 04-Feb-00 22:03:38 GMT; path=/;
domain=zink.demon.co.uk");
```

Although not difficult, this method of setting a cookie would require you to build a function to construct the header string. Formatting the date as in this example and URL encoding the name/value pair would not be a particularly arduous task. It would, however, be an exercise in wheel reinvention because PHP provides a function that does just that.

setcookie() does what the name suggests—it outputs a Set-Cookie header. For this reason, it should be called before any other content is sent to the browser. The function accepts the cookie name, cookie value, expiry date in UNIX epoch format, path, domain, and integer that should be set to 1 if the cookie is only to be sent over a secure connection. All arguments to this function are optional apart from the first (cookie name) parameter.

Listing 19.1 uses setcookie() to set a cookie.

LISTING 19.1 Setting and Printing a Cookie Value

```
1: <?php
2: setcookie( "vegetable", "artichoke", time()+3600, "/",
3:             "zink.demon.co.uk", 0 );
4: ?>
5: <html>
6: <head>
7: <title>Listing 19.1 Setting and printing a cookie value</title>
8: </head>
9: <body>
10: <?php
11: if ( isset( $vegetable ) )
12:     print "<p>Hello again, your chosen vegetable is $vegetable</p>";
13: else
14:     print "<p>Hello you. This may be your first visit</p>";
15: ?>
16: </body>
17: </html>
```

Even though we set the cookie when the script is run for the first time, the $vegetable variable will not be created at this point. A cookie is only read when the browser sends it to the server. This will not happen until the user revisits a page in your domain. We set the cookie name to "vegetable" and the cookie value to "artichoke". We use the time() function to get the current time stamp and add 3600 to it (there are 3600 seconds in an hour). This total represents our expiry date. We define a path of "/", which means that a cookie should be sent for any page within our server environment. We set the domain argument to "zink.demon.co.uk", which means that a cookie will be sent to any server in that group (www.zink.demon.co.uk as well as dev.zink.demon.co.uk, for example). If you want the cookie returned only to the server hosting your script you can use the $SERVER_NAME environmental variable instead of hard coding the server name. The added advantage of this is that your code will work as expected even if you move it to a new server. Finally, we pass 0 to setcookie() signaling that cookies can be sent in an insecure environment.

Although you can omit all but the first argument, it is a good idea to include all the arguments with the exception of the domain and secure. This is because the path argument is required by some browsers for cookies to be used as they should be. Also without the path argument, the cookie will only be sent to documents in the current directory or its subdirectories.

Passing `setcookie()` an empty string ("") for string arguments or 0 for integer fields will cause these arguments to be skipped.

Deleting a Cookie

Officially, to delete a cookie you should call `setcookie()` with the name argument only:

```
setcookie( "vegetable" );
```

This does not always work well, however, and should not be relied on. It is safest to set the cookie with a date that has already expired:

```
setcookie( "vegetable", "", time()-60, "/", "zink.demon.co.uk", 0);
```

You should also ensure that you pass `setcookie()` the same path, domain, and secure parameters as you did when originally setting the cookie.

Creating Session Cookies

To create a cookie that only lasts as long as the user is running his or her browser, pass `setcookie()` an expiry argument of 0. While the user's browser continues to run, cookies will be returned to the server. The browser will not remember the cookie, however, after it has been quit and restarted.

This can be useful for scripts that validate a user with a cookie, allowing continued access to personal information on multiple pages after a password has been submitted. You will not want the browser to have continued access to these pages after it has been restarted because you can't be sure that it has not been booted by a new user.

```
setcookie( "session_id", "55435", 0 );
```

An Example—Tracking Site Usage

Imagine that we have been given a brief by a site publisher to use cookies and MySQL to gather statistics about visitors to the site. The client wants to get figures for the number of individual visitors to the site, average number of hits per visit for each visitor, and average time spent on the site for each user.

Our first duty will be to explain the limitations of cookies to the client. First, not all users will have cookies enabled on their browsers. If not passed a cookie by a browser, a cookie script is likely to assume that this is the user's first visit. The figures are therefore likely to be skewed by browsers that won't or can't support cookies. Furthermore, you cannot be sure that the same user will use the same browser all the time, or that a single browser won't be shared by multiple users.

Having done this, we can move on to fulfilling the brief. In fact, we can produce a working example in fewer than 90 lines of code!

We need to create a database table with the fields listed in Table 19.1.

TABLE 19.1 Database Fields

Name	*Type*	*Description*
`id`	integer	An autoincremented field that produces and stores a unique ID for each visitor
`first_visit`	integer	A time stamp representing the moment of the first page request made by a visitor
`last_visit`	integer	A time stamp representing the moment of the most recent page request made by a visitor
`num_visits`	integer	The number of distinct sessions attributed to the visitor
`total_duration`	integer	The estimated total time spent on the site (in seconds)
`total_clicks`	integer	The total number of requests made by the visitor

To create the MySQL table called `track_visit`, we need to use a `CREATE` statement:

```
create table track_visit (
                id INT NOT NULL AUTO_INCREMENT,
                PRIMARY KEY( id ),
                first_visit INT,
                last_visit INT,
                num_visits INT,
                total_duration INT,
                total_clicks INT
                );
```

Now that we have a table to work with, we need to write the code that will open a database connection and check for the existence of a cookie. If the cookie does not exist, we need to create a new row in our table, setting up the initial values for the fields we will maintain. We create this code in Listing 19.2.

LISTING 19.2 A Script to Add New User Information to a MySQL Database

```
 1: <?php
 2: $link = mysql_connect( "localhost", "harry", "elbomonkey" );
 3: if ( ! $link )
 4:     die( "Couldn't connect to mysqld" );
 5: mysql_select_db( "sample", $link ) or die ( mysql_error() );
 6: if ( ! isset ( $visit_id ) )
 7:     $user_stats = newuser( $link );
 8: else
 9:     print ''Welcome back $visit_id<P>";
10: function newuser( $link )
11:     {
12:     // a new user!
13:     $visit_data = array (
14:                 first_visit => time(),
15:                 last_visit => time(),
16:                 num_visits => 1,
17:                 total_duration => 0,
18:                 total_clicks => 1
19:                 );
20:     $query = "INSERT INTO track_visit ( first_visit,
21:                                         last_visit,
22:                                         num_visits,
23:                                         total_duration,
24:                                         total_clicks ) ";
25:     $query .= "values( $visit_data[first_visit],
26:                        $visit_data[last_visit],
27:                        $visit_data[num_visits],
28:                        $visit_data[total_duration],
29:                        $visit_data[total_clicks] )";
30:     $result = mysql_query( $query );
31:     $visit_data[id] = mysql_insert_id();
32:     setcookie( "visit_id", $visit_data[id],
33:                time()+(60*60*24*365*10), "/" );
34:     return $visit_data;
35:     }
36: ?>
```

We connect to the MySQL server in the usual way and select the database that contains our table (you can read more about working with MySQL in Hour 12, "Database Integration—MySQL"). We test for the presence of the variable `$visit_id`, which is the name of the cookie that identifies an individual user. If this variable does not exist, then we assume that we are dealing with a new user, calling a function that we have called `newuser()`.

`newuser()` requires a link identifier and will return an array of the values that we will add to our table. Within the function, we create an array called `$visit_data`. We set the first_visit and last_visit() elements to the current time in seconds. Because this is the first visit, we set the num_visits and total_clicks elements to 1. No time has elapsed in this visit, so we set total_duration to 0.

We use the elements of this array to create a new row in our table, setting each field to the value of the element of the same name. Because the id field autoincrements, this does not need to be defined. We can access the value set for id with the mysql_insert_id() function. Now that we have an ID for our new visitor, we add this to our $visit_data array, which then accurately reflects the visitor's row in the MySQL table.

Finally, we use setcookie() to set a visit_id cookie and return the $visit_data array to the calling code.

The next time our visitor hits this script, the $visit_id variable will have been populated with the value of the visit_id cookie. Because this variable is set, the user simply will be welcomed and no action will be taken.

In fact, we will need to update information in the track_visit table if we detect the return of a known visitor. We will need to test whether the current request is part of an ongoing visit or represents the beginning of a new visit. We will do this with a global variable that will define a time in seconds. If the time of the last request added to this interval is greater than the current time, then we will assume that the current request is part of a session in progress. Otherwise, we are welcoming back an old friend.

Listing 19.3 adds a new function, olduser(), to the code created in Listing 19.2.

LISTING 19.3 A Script to Track Users Using Cookies and a MySQL Database

```
 1: <?php
 2: $slength = 300; // 5 minutes in seconds
 3: $link = mysql_connect( "localhost", "harry", "elbomonkey" );
 4: if ( ! $link )
 5:     die( "Couldn't connect to mysqld" );
 6: mysql_select_db( "sample", $link ) or die ( mysql_error() );
 7: if ( ! isset ( $visit_id ) )
 8:     $user_stats = newuser( $link );
 9: else
10:     {
11:     $user_stats = olduser( $link, $visit_id, $slength );
12:     print "Welcome back $visit_id<P>";
13:     }
14:  function newuser( $link )
15:      {
16:      // a new user!
17:      $visit_data = array (
```

LISTING 19.3 continued

```
18:                  first_visit => time(),
19:                  last_visit => time(),
20:                  num_visits => 1,
21:                  total_duration => 0,
22:                  total_clicks => 1
23:                  );
24:      $query = "INSERT INTO track_visit ( first_visit,
25:                                          last_visit,
26:                                          num_visits,
27:                                          total_duration,
28:                                          total_clicks ) ";
29:      $query .= "values( $visit_data[first_visit],
30:                         $visit_data[last_visit],
31:                         $visit_data[num_visits],
32:                         $visit_data[total_duration],
33:                         $visit_data[total_clicks] )";
34:      $result = mysql_query( $query );
35:      $visit_data[id] = mysql_insert_id();
36:      setcookie( "visit_id", $visit_data[id],
37:                 time()+(60*60*24*365*10), "/" );
38:      return $visit_data;
39:      }
40: function olduser( $link, $visit_id, $slength )
41:     {
42:     // s/he's been here before!
43:     $query = "SELECT * FROM track_visit WHERE id=$visit_id";
44:     $result = mysql_query( $query );
45:     if ( ! mysql_num_rows( $result ) )
46:         // cookie found but no id in database -- treat as new user
47:         return newuser( $link );
48:     $visit_data = mysql_fetch_array( $result, $link );
49:     // there has been another hit so increment
50:     $visit_data[total_clicks]++;
51:     if ( ( $visit_data[last_visit] + $slength ) > time() )
52:         // still in session so add to total elapsed time
53:         $visit_data[total_duration] +=
54:                       ( time() - $visit_data[last_visit] );
55:     else
56:         // this is a new visit
57:         $visit_data[num_visits]++;
58:     // update the database
59:     $query  = "UPDATE track_visit SET last_visit=".time().",
60:                       num_visits=$visit_data[num_visits], ";
61:     $query .= "total_duration=$visit_data[total_duration],
62:                total_clicks=$visit_data[total_clicks] ";
63:     $query .= "WHERE id=$visit_id";
64:     $result = mysql_query( $query );
65:     return $visit_data;
```

LISTING 19.3 continued

```
66:     }
67: ?>
```

We added a new global variable to the script called `$slength`. This defines the interval after which we assume that a new visit is taking place. If the `$visit_id` variable is found, then we know that the cookie was in place. We call our new `olduser()` function, passing it the database link identifier, the `$visit_id` variable, and the `$slength` variable, which we have set to 300 seconds.

Within the `olduser()` function, we first query the database to acquire the information about the visitor that we have already stored. We look in the `track_visit` table for a row that has the same value in its `id` field as we have in our `$visit_id` variable. We can test the number of values returned by `mysql_query()` with `msql_num_rows()`, passing it a result identifier. If this function returns 0, then we know that there are no row matches the ID stored in the `visit_id` cookie, so we call `newuser()` and end execution of the function.

Assuming that we have located the row in our table that matches the `visit_id` cookie, we use `mysql_fetch_array()` to populate an array variable (`$visit_data`) with the row's field names and values. The current request represents a new hit, so we increment the `$visit_data[total_clicks]` element.

We test to see whether the value of the `$visit_data[last_visit]` element added to the interval stored in `$slength` is greater than the current time. If so, it means that less than `$slength` seconds have elapsed since the last hit, and we can assume that this request is part of a current session. We therefore add the time elapsed since the last hit to the `$visit_data[total_duration]` element.

If the request represents a new visit, we increment `$visit_data[num_visits]`.

Finally, we use the altered values in the `$visit_data` array to update the user's row in the `track_visit` table and return the `$visit_data` array to the calling code. Notice that we set the `last_visit` field to the current time.

Now that we've created the code, we should create a quick function to demonstrate it in action. The `outputStats()` function simply calculates the current user's averages and prints the result to the browser. In reality, you would probably want to create some analysis screens for your client, which would collate overall information. Listing 19.4 creates the `outputStats()` function. The code from previous examples is incorporated into this script using an `include()` statement.

LISTING 19.4 A Script to Output Usage Statistics Gathered in Listing 19.3

```
 1: <?php
 2: include("listing19.3.php"{);
 3: outputStats();
 4: function outputStats()
 5:     {
 6:     global $user_stats;
 7:     $clicks = sprintf( "%.2f",
 8:               ($user_stats[total_clicks]/$user_stats[num_visits]) );
 9:     $duration =  sprintf( "%.2f",
10:               ($user_stats[total_duration]/$user_stats[num_visits]) );
11:     print "<p>Hello! Your id is $user_stats[id]</p>\n\n";
12:     print "<p>You have visited
13:               $user_stats[num_visits] time(s)</p>\n\n";
14:     print "<p>Av clicks per visit: $clicks</p>\n\n";
15:     print "<p>Av duration of visit: $duration seconds</p>\n\n";
16:     }
17: ?>
```

Figure 19.1 shows the output from Listing 19.4. We use an `include()` statement to call the tracking code we have written. We will be including a similar line on every page of our client's site. The `outputStats()` function works with the global `$user_stats` array variable. This was returned by either `newuser()` or `olduser()` and contains the same information as our user's row in the `track_visit` table.

To calculate the user's average number of clicks, we divide the `$user_stats [total_clicks]` element by the number of visits we have detected. Similarly, we divide the `$user_stats[total_duration]` element by the same figure. We use `sprint()` to round the results to two decimal places. All that remains is to write a report to the browser.

We could, of course, extend this example to track user preference on a site, as well as to log browser types and IP addresses. Imagine a site that analyzes a user's movements and emphasizes content according to the links he chooses.

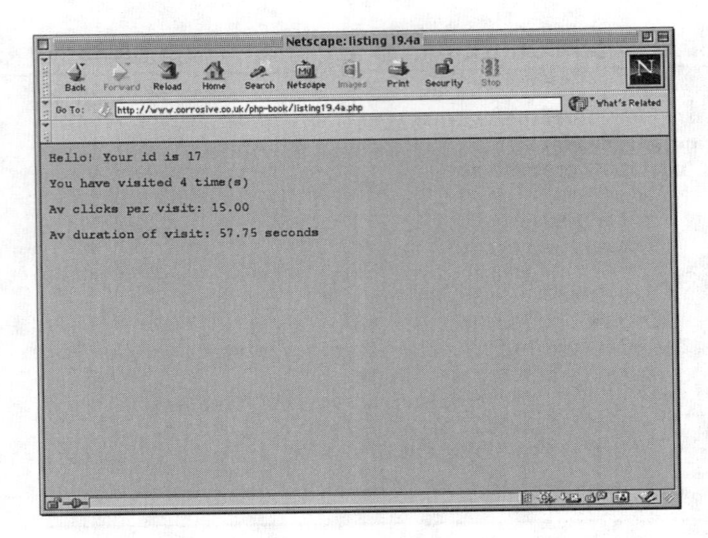

FIGURE 19.1
Reporting Usage Statistics

Working with the Query String

The great drawback of the cookie is its dependence on the client. Not only are you at the mercy of the user, who may choose not to allow cookies, you must also rely on the browser's implementation of the standard. Some browsers have documented bugs concerning the way that they deal with cookies. If you only want to save state for a single session, you might decide to use a more traditional approach.

When you submit a form using the `GET` method, its fields and values are URL encoded and appended to the URL to which the form is sent. They then become available to the server and to your scripts. Assuming a form with two fields, `user_id` and `name`, the query string should end up looking something like the following:

```
http://www.corrosive.co.uk/test5.php?name=344343&user_id=matt+zandstra
```

Each name and value is separated by an equals (=) sign, and each name/value pair is separated by an ampersand (&). PHP decodes this string and makes each of the pairs available in the `$HTTP_GET_VARS` associative array variable. It also creates a global variable for each name, populating with the corresponding value. So, to access the `user_id GET` variable, you could use either of the following variables:

```
$HTTP_GET_VARS[user_id];
$user_id;
```

You are not limited, however, to using forms to send query strings. You can build your own relatively easily and in so doing pass substantial amounts of information from page to page.

Creating a Query String

To create a query string, you need to be able to URL encode the keys and values you want to include. Assume that we want to pass a URL to another page as part of a query string. The forward slashes and the colon in a full URL would create ambiguity for a parser. We must therefore convert the URL into hexadecimal characters. We can do this using PHP's `urlencode()` function. `urlencode()` accepts a string and returns an encoded copy:

```
print urlencode("http://www.corrosive.co.uk");
// prints http%3A%2F%2Fwww.corrosive.co.uk
```

Now that you can URL encode text, you can build your own query string. The following fragment builds a query string from two variables:

```
<?php
$interest = "arts";
$homepage = "http://www.corrosive.co.uk";
$query = "homepage=".urlencode( $homepage );
$query .= "&interest=".urlencode( $interest );
?>
<A HREF="newpage.php?<?print $query ?>">Go</A>
```

The URL in the link will reach the browser including an encoded query string:

```
newpage.php?homepage=http%3A%2F%2Fwww.corrosive.co.uk&interest=arts
```

The `homepage` and `interest` parameters will become available within `newpage.php` as global variables.

This approach is clumsy, however. Because we have hard-coded variable names into the query string, we cannot reuse the code easily. To pass information effectively from page to page, we need to make it easy to embed names and values into a link and generate a query string automatically. This is especially important if we are to maintain the benefit of PHP that it is easy for a non-programmer to work around.

Listing 19.5 creates a function called `qlink()` that accepts an associative array and returns a query string.

LISTING 19.5 A Function to Build Query Strings

```
1: <html>
2: <head>
3: <title>Listing 19.5 A function to build query strings</title>
4: </head>
5: <body>
6: <?php
7: function qlink( $q )
```

LISTING 19.5 continued

```
8:      {
9:      GLOBAL $QUERY_STRING;
10:     if ( ! $q ) return $QUERY_STRING;
11:     $ret = "";
12:     foreach( $q as $key => $val )
13:         {
14:         if ( strlen( $ret ) ) $ret .= "&";
15:         $ret .= urlencode( $key ) . "=" . urlencode( $val );
16:         }
17:     return $ret;
18:     }
19: $q = array ( name => "Arthur Harold Smith",
20:              interest => "Cinema (mainly art house)",
21:              homepage => ''http://www.corrosive.co.uk/harold/"
22:              );
23: print qlink( $q );
24: // prints name=Arthur+Harold+Smith&interest=Cinema+%28mainly+art+house
25: //          %29&homepage=http%3A%2F%2Fwww.corrosive.co.uk%2Fharold%2F
26: ?>
27: <p>
28: <a href="anotherpage.php?<? print qlink($q) ?>">Go!</a>
29: </p>
30: </body>
31: </html>
```

`qlink()` expects an associative array, which it stores in the parameter variable `$q`. If `$q` is not set, we simply return the current script's query string as stored for us in `$QUERY_STRING`. In this way, `qlink()` can be used simply to pass on unchanged `GET` request data.

Assuming that `$q` has been set, we initialize a variable called `$ret` assigning an empty string to it. This will contain our query string.

A `foreach` statement is used to iterate through the `$q` array, placing each key in `$key` and each value in `$val`.

Key/value pairs are separated from one another by an ampersand (&) character, so if we are not on our first journey through the loop, we print this character. We know that the length of the string in `$ret` will be 0 for the first iteration, so we can use this fact to avoid prepending `&` to the string.

We use `urlencode()` to encode both the `$key` and `$val` variables and append them, separated by an equals (=) character to our `$ret` variable.

Finally, we return the encoded `$query` string.

Using this function, we can pass information between pages with the minimum of PHP code within HTML elements.

Summary

In this hour, we have looked at the two ways of passing information between requests. You can use these to create multiscreen applications and sophisticated environments that respond to user preferences.

You learned how to use the `setcookie()` function to set cookies on the user's browser. Developing this, you saw how a database could be used in conjunction with cookies to store information about a user between sessions. You learned about query strings and how to encode them, and developed a function to automate their creation.

Q&A

Q Are there any serious security or privacy issues raised by cookies?

A A server can only access a cookie set from its own domain. Although a cookie can be stored on the user's hard drive, there is no other access to the user's file system. It is possible, however, to set a cookie in response to a request for an image. So if many sites include images served from a third-party ad server or counter script, the third party may be able to track a user across multiple domains.

Q The query string looks ugly in the browser window. Would it be true to say that cookies are the neatest way of saving state?

A Unfortunately, it isn't that simple. At best, cookies are a transparent way of saving state. Some users, however, set their browsers to warn them every time a cookie is set. These users are likely to find a site that saves state information frequently somewhat frustrating.

Workshop

The Workshop provides quiz questions to help you solidify your understanding of the material covered. Try to understand the quiz answers before continuing to the next hour's lesson. Quiz answers are provided in Appendix A.

Quiz

1. What function is designed to allow you to set a cookie on a visitor's browser?
2. How would you delete a cookie?

3. What function could you use to escape a string for inclusion in a query string?
4. Which built-in variable contains the raw query string?
5. The name/value pairs submitted as part of a query string will become available as global variables. They will also be included in a built-in associative array. What is its name?

Activities

1. Create a user preference form in which a user can choose a page color and enter a name. Use a cookie to ensure that the user is greeted by name on subsequent pages and that the page is set to the color of her choice.
2. Amend the scripts you created in Activity 1 so that the information is stored in a query string rather than a cookie.

HOUR 20

Saving State with Session Functions

In the previous hour, we looked at saving state from page to page, using a cookie or a query string. Once again, PHP4 is one step ahead of us. With the release of PHP4, functions for managing user sessions were built into the language. These use techniques similar to those explored in the previous hour, but build them into the language, making saving state as easy as calling a function.

In this hour, you will learn

- What session variables are and how they work
- How to start or resume a session
- How to register variables with a session
- How to destroy a session
- How to unset session variables

What Are Session Functions?

Session functions implement a concept that you have already seen. That is the provision to users of a unique identifier, which can then be used from access to access to acquire information linked to that ID. The difference is that most of the work is already done for you. When a user accesses a session-enabled page, she will either be allocated a new identifier or reassociated with one that has already been established for her in a previous access. Any global variables that have been associated with the session will become available to your code.

Both the techniques for transmitting information from access to access that you looked at in the previous hour are automatically supported by PHP4's session functions. Cookies are used by default, but you can ensure success for all clients by encoding the session ID into all links in your session-enabled pages.

Session state is usually stored in a temporary file, though you can expect to see modules that support the more popular databases soon.

Starting a Session with `session_start()`

You need to explicitly start or resume a session unless you have changed your `php.ini` configuration file. By default, sessions do not start automatically. In `php.ini`, you will find a line containing the following:

```
session.auto_start = 0
```

By changing the value of `session.auto_start` to 1, you ensure that a session is initiated for every PHP document. If you don't change this setting, you need to call the `session_start()` function.

After a session has been started, you instantly have access to the user's session ID via the `session_id()` function. `session_id()` allows you to either set or get a session ID. Listing 20.1 starts a session and prints the session ID to the browser.

LISTING 20.1 Starting or Resuming a Session

```
1: <?php
2: session_start();
3: ?>
4: <html>
5: <head>
6: <title>Listing 20.1 Starting or resuming a session</title>
7: </head>
```

LISTING 20.1 continued

```
 8: <body>
 9: <?php
10: print "<p>Welcome, your session ID is ".session_id()."</p>\n\n";
11: ?>
12: </body>
13: </html>
```

When this script is run for the first time from a browser, a session ID is generated. If the page is later reloaded or revisited, then the same session ID is allocated to the user. This presupposes, of course that the user has cookies enabled on his or her browser. If you examine headers output by the script in Listing 20.1, you can see the cookie being set:

```
HTTP/1.1 200 OK
Date: Sun, 06 Feb 2000 13:50:36 GMT
Server: Apache/1.3.9 (UNIX) PHP/4.0b3
Set-cookie: PHPSESSID=2638864e9216fee10fcb8a61db382909; path=/
Connection: close
Content-Type: text/html
```

Because `start_session()` attempts to set a cookie when initiating a session for the first time, it is important to call it before you output anything else at all to the browser. Notice that no expiry date is set in the cookie that PHP sets for the session. This means that the session only remains current as long as the browser is active. When the user reboots his or her browser, the cookie will not be stored. You can change this behavior by altering the `session.cookie_lifetime` setting in your `php.ini` file. This defaults to 0, but you can set an expiry period in seconds. This causes an expiry date to be set for any session cookies sent to the browser.

Working with Session Variables

Accessing a unique identifier on each of your PHP documents is only the start of PHP4's session functionality. You can register any number of global variables with the session and then access them on any session-enabled page.

To register a variable with a current session, you must use the `session_register()` function. `session_register()` requires a string representing one or more variable names and returns `true` if the registration is successful. The syntax of the argument you must pass to this function is unusual in that you must pass only the name of the variable and not the variable itself.

Listing 20.2 registers two variables with a session.

LISTING 20.2 Registering Variables with a Session

```
 1: <?php
 2: session_start();
 3: ?>
 4: <html>
 5: <head>
 6: <title>Listing 20.2 Registering variables with a session</title>
 7: </head>
 8: <body>
 9: <?php
10: session_register( "product1" );
11: session_register( "product2" );
12: $product1 = "Sonic Screwdriver";
13: $product2 = "HAL 2000";
14: print session_encode();
15: print "The products have been registered";
16: ?>
17: </body>
18: </html>
```

The magic in Listing 20.2 will not become apparent until the user moves to a new page. Listing 20.3 creates a separate PHP script that accesses the variables registered in Listing 20.2.

LISTING 20.3 Accessing Registered Variables

```
 1: <?php
 2: session_start();
 3: ?>
 4: <html>
 5: <head>
 6: <title>Listing 20.3 Accessing registered variables</title>
 7: </head>
 8: <body>
 9: <?php
10: print "Your chosen products are:\n\n";
11: print "<ul><li>$product1\n<li>$product2\n</ul>\n";
12: ?>
13: </body>
14: </html>
```

Figure 20.1 shows the output from Listing 20.3. As you can see, we have access to the `$product1` and `$product2` variables in an entirely new page.

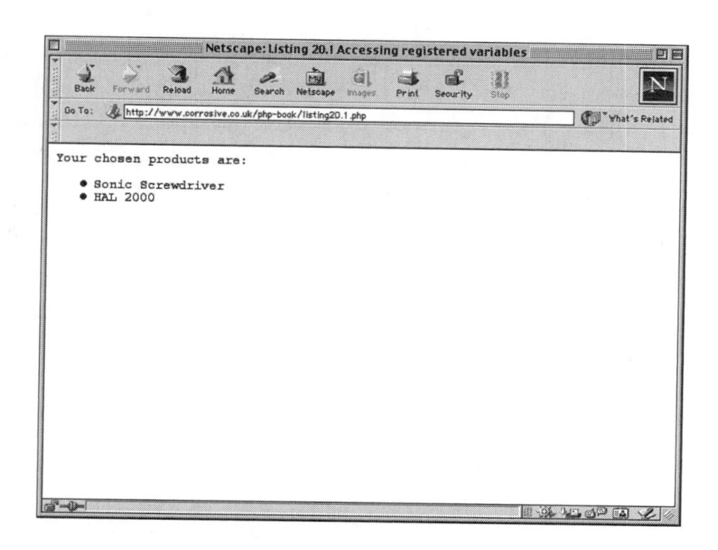

FIGURE 20.1
Accessing registered variables.

So how does the magic work? Behind the scenes, PHP4 is writing to a temporary file. You can find out where this is being written on your system with the `session_save_path()` function. `session_save_path()` optionally accepts a path to a directory and then writes all session files to this. If you pass it no arguments, it returns a string representing the current directory to which session files are saved. On my system,

```
print session_save_path();
```

prints `/tmp`. A glance at my `/tmp` directory reveals a number of files with names like the following:

```
sess_2638864e9216fee10fcb8a61db382909
sess_76cae8ac1231b11afa2c69935c11dd95
sess_bb50771a769c605ab77424d59c784ea0
```

Opening the file that matches the session ID I was allocated when I first ran Listing 20.1, I can see how the registered variables have been stored:

```
product1|s:17:"Sonic Screwdriver";product2|s:8:"HAL 2000";
```

When `session_register()` is called, PHP writes the variable name and value to a file. This can be read, and the variables resurrected, later.

20

When you register a variable using `session_register()`, you can still change its value at any time during the execution of your script, and the altered value will be reflected in the session file.

The example in Listing 20.2 demonstrates the process of registering variables with a session. It is not very flexible, however. Ideally, you should be able to register a varying number of values. You might want to let users pick products from a list, for example. Luckily, you can pass the name of an array variable to `session_register()`, and it will store and encode this data for you.

Listing 20.4 creates a form that allows a user to choose multiple products. You should then be able to use session variables to create a rudimentary shopping cart.

LISTING 20.4 Registering an Array Variable with a Session

```
 1: <?php
 2: session_start();
 3: ?>
 4: <html>
 5: <head>
 6: <title>Listing 20.4 Registering an array variable with a session</title>
 7: </head>
 8: <body>
 9: <h1>Product Choice Page</h1>
10: <?php
11: if ( isset( $form_products ) )
12:     {
13:     $products = $form_products;
14:     session_register( "products" );
15:     print "<p>Your products have been registered!</p>";
16:     }
17: ?><p>
18: <form method="POST">
19: <select name="form_products[]" multiple size=3>
20: <option> Sonic Screwdriver
21: <option> Hal 2000
22: <option> Tardis
23: <option> ORAC
24: <option> Transporter bracelet
25: </select>
26: </p><p>
27: <input type="submit" value="choose">
28: </form>
29: </p>
30: <a href="listing20.5.php">A content page</a>
31: </body>
32: </html>
```

We start or resume a session with `session_start()`. This should give us access to any previously set session variables. Within an HTML form, we set the `FORM` element's `ACTION` property to point to the current document. We then create a `SELECT` element named `form_products[]`, which contains `OPTION` elements for a number of products. Remember that HTML form elements that allow multiple selections should have square brackets appended to the value of their `NAME` arguments. This makes the user's choices available in an array.

Within the block of PHP code, we test for the presence of the `$form_products array`. If the variable is present, we can assume that the form has been submitted. We assign this variable to another called `$products` and then register this using `session_register()`. We do not directly register `$form_products` because this will then conflict with the `POST` variable of the same name if the form is resubmitted.

At the bottom of this page, there is a link to another, which we will use to demonstrate our access to the products the user has chosen. We create this new script in Listing 20.5.

LISTING 20.5 Accessing Session Variables

```
 1: <?php
 2: session_start();
 3: print session_encode();
 4: ?>
 5: <html>
 6: <head>
 7: <title>Listing 20.5 Accessing session variables</title>
 8: </head>
 9: <body>
10: <h1>A Content Page</h1>
11: <?php
12: if ( isset( $products ) )
13:     {
14:     print "<b>Your cart:</b><ol>\n";
15:     foreach ( $products as $p )
16:         print "<li>$p";
17:     print "</ol>";
18:     }
19: ?>
20: <a href="listing20.4.php">Back to product choice page</a>
21: </body>
22: </html>
```


Once again, we use `session_start()` to resume the session. We test for the presence of the `$products` variable. If it exists, we loop through it, printing each of the user's chosen items to the browser.

For a real shopping cart program, of course, you would keep product details in a database and test user input, rather than blindly storing and presenting it, but Listings 20.4 and 20.5 demonstrate the ease with which you can use session functions to access array variables set in other pages.

Destroying Sessions and Unsetting Variables

You can use `session_destroy()` to end a session, erasing all session variables. `session_destroy()` requires no arguments. You should have an established session for this function to work as expected. The following code fragment resumes a session and abruptly destroys it:

```
session_start();
session_destroy();
```

When you move on to other pages that work with a session, the session you have destroyed will not be available to them, forcing them to initiate new sessions of their own. Any variables that have been registered will have been lost.

However, `session_destroy()` does not instantly destroy registered variables. These will remain accessible to the script in which `session_destroy()` is called (until it is reloaded). The following code fragment resumes or initiates a session and registers a variable called `$test`, which we set to 5. Destroying the session does not destroy the registered variable.

```
session_start();
session_register( "test" );
$test = 5;
session_destroy();
print $test; // prints 5
```

To remove all registered variables from a session, you need to use the `session_unset()` function. This destroys all variables associated with a session, both in the session file and within your script. `session_unset()` is a blunt instrument; use it carefully.

```
session_start();
session_register( "test" );
$test = 5;
session_unset();
session_destroy();
print $test; // prints nothing. The $test variable is no more
```

Before destroying the session, we call `session_unset()`, which entirely removes the `$test` variable from memory and wipes any other registered session variables.

Passing Session IDs in the Query String

So far you have relied on a cookie to save the session ID between script requests. On its own, this is not the most reliable way of saving state because you cannot be sure that the browser will accept cookies. You can build in a failsafe, however, by passing the session ID from script to script embedded in a query string. PHP makes a name/value pair available in a constant called `SID` if a cookie value for a session ID cannot be found. You can add this string to any HTML links in session-enabled pages:

```
<a href="anotherpage.html?<? print SID; ?>">Another page</a>
```

will reach the browser as

```
<a href="anotherpage.html?PHPSESSID=08ecedf79fe34561fa82591401a01da1">Another
➥page</a>
```

The session ID passed in this way will automatically be recognized in the target page when `session_start()` is called, and you will have access to session variables in the usual way.

If PHP4 was compiled with the `--enable-trans-sid` option set, you will find that this query string is automatically added to every link in your pages. This option is disabled by default, however, so explicitly adding the `SID` constant to links will make your scripts more portable.

Encoding and Decoding Session Variables

You have already seen the way in which PHP encodes and saves (serializes) session variables when you peeked into a session file. You can in fact gain access to the encoded string at any time with `session_encode()`. This can be useful in debugging your session-enabled environments. You can use `session_encode()` to reveal the state of all session variables:

```
session_start();
print session_encode()."<br>";
// sample output: products|a:2:{i:0;s:8:"Hal 2000";i:1;s:6:"Tardis";}
```

From the sample output in the previous fragment, you can see the session variables that are stored. You can use this information to check that variables are being registered and updated as you expect. `session_encode()` is also useful if you need to freeze-dry session variables for storage in a database or file.

After having extracted an encoded string, you can decode it and resurrect its values using `session_decode()`. The following code fragment demonstrates this process:

```
session_start();
session_unset(); // there should now be no session variables
session_decode( "products|a:2:{i:0;s:8:\"Hal 2000\";i:1;s:6:\"Tardis\";}" );
foreach ( $products as $p )
    {
    print "$p<br>\n";
    }
// Output:
// Hal 2000
// Tardis
```

We start a session as usual. To ensure that we are working with a blank canvas, we use `session_unset()` to clear all session variables. We then pass an encoded string to `session_decode()`. Rather than returning values, `session_decode()` populates our name space with the unserialized variables. We confirm this by looping through the newly resurrected `$products` array.

Checking that a Session Variable Is Registered

As you have seen, you can test for the presence of a registered variable in a session-enabled script using `isset()`. You can, however, explicitly test that a variable has been registered with a session using the `session_is_registered()` function. This accepts a string representing a variable name and returns `true` if the variable has been registered.

```
if ( session_is_registered ( "products" ) )
    print "'products' is registered!";
```

This would be useful if you need to be sure of the source of a variable. You might want to make sure that the variable you are testing is available to you as a session variable as opposed to data passed to you as part of a `GET` request.

Summary

In this hour and the previous hour, you looked at different ways of saving state in a stateless protocol. All methods use some combination of cookies and query strings, sometimes combined with the use of files or databases. These approaches all have their benefits and problems.

A cookie is not intrinsically reliable and cannot store much information. On the other hand, it can persist over a long period of time.

Approaches that write information to a file or database involve some cost to speed that might become a problem on a popular site. Nonetheless, a simple ID can unlock large amounts of data stored on disk.

A query string is unlikely to persist as a cookie will. It looks ugly in the location window. Even so, it can pass relatively large amounts of information from request to request. The choice you make depends on the circumstances of your project.

In this hour, you learned how to initiate or resume a session with `session_start()`. Once in a session, you can register variables with it using `session_register()`, check that a variable is registered with `session_is_registered()`, and unset all registered variables with `session_unset()`. You should be able to destroy a session with `session_destroy()`.

To ensure that as many users as possible get the benefit of your session-enabled environment, you can now use the `SID` constant to pass a session ID to the server as part of a query string.

Q&A

Q Are there any pitfalls with session functions I should be aware of?

A The session functions are generally reliable. However, remember that cookies cannot be read across multiple domains, so if your project uses more than one domain name on the same server (perhaps as part of an e-commerce environment), you might need to consider disabling cookies for sessions by setting the

```
session.use_cookies
```

directive to `0` in the `php.ini` file.

Workshop

20

The Workshop provides quiz questions to help you solidify your understanding of the material covered. Try to understand the quiz answers before continuing to the next hour's lesson. Quiz answers are provided in Appendix A.

Quiz

1. Which function would you use to start or resume a session?
2. Which function contains the current session's ID?
3. How can you associate a variable with a session?

4. How would you end a session and erase all traces of it for future visits?
5. How would you destroy session variables both within the current script and the session?
6. What does the `SID` constant return?
7. How would you test whether a variable called `$test` is registered with a session?

Activities

1. In the previous hour's "Activities" section, you created a script that uses a cookie or query string to save user preferences from page to page. Each page in the environment should display a user-defined background color and greet the user by name. Recreate this using PHP4's session functions.
2. Create a script that uses session functions to remember which pages in your environment the user has visited. Provide the user with a list of links on each page to make it easy for her to retrace her steps.

HOUR 21

Working with the Server Environment

In previous hours, we have looked at techniques for communicating with remote machines and for gaining input from the user. In this hour, we look outward again, this time at some techniques for running external programs on our own machine. The examples in this hour are designed for the Linux operating system, but most of the principles hold true for Windows.

In this hour, you will learn

- How to pipe data to and from external applications
- Other ways of sending shell commands and displaying the results on the browser
- The security implications of interprocess communication from a PHP script

Opening Pipes to and from Processes with popen()

Just as you open a file for writing or reading with `fopen()`, you can open a pipe to a process with `popen()`. `popen()` requires the path to a command and a string representing a mode (read or write). It returns a file pointer that can be used similarly to the file pointer returned by `fopen()`. You can pass `popen()` one of two mode flags: `"w"` to write to the process and `"r"` to read from it. You cannot both read and write to a process in the same connection.

When you have finished working with the file handle returned by `popen()`, you must close the connection by calling `pclose()`, which requires a valid file handler.

Reading from `popen()` is useful when you want to parse the output from a process on a line-by-line basis. Listing 21.1 opens a connection to the GNU version of the `who` command and parses its output, adding a `mailto` link to each username.

LISTING 21.1 Using `popen()` to Read the Output of the UNIX `who` Command

```
 1: <html>
 2: <head>
 3: <title>Listing 21.1 Using popen() to read the
 4:         output of the UNIX who command</title>
 5: </head>
 6: <body>
 7: <h2>Administrators currently logged on to the server</h1>
 8: <?php
 9: $ph = popen( "who", "r" )
10:         or die( "Couldn't open connection to 'who' command" );
11:   $host="zink.demon.co.uk";
12: while ( ! feof( $ph ) )
13:     {
14:     $line = fgets( $ph, 1024 );
15:     if ( strlen( $line ) <= 1 )
16:         continue;
17:     $line = ereg_replace(     "^([a-zA-Z0-9_\-]+).*",
18:                 "<a href=\"mailto:\\1@$host\">\\1</a><BR>\n",
19:                 $line );
20:     print "$line";
21:     }
22: pclose( $ph );
23: ?>
24: </table>
25: </body>
26: </html>
```

We acquire a file pointer from `popen()` and then use a `while` statement to read each line of output from the process. If the output is a single character, we skip the rest of the current iteration. Otherwise, we use `ereg_replace()` to add an HTML link and table cells to the string before printing the line. Finally, we close the connection with `pclose()`. Figure 21.1 shows sample output from Listing 21.1.

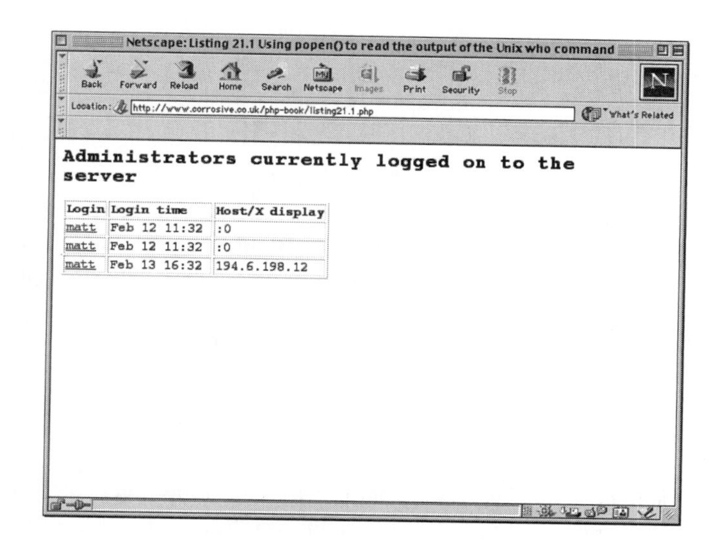

FIGURE 21.1
Reading the output of the UNIX `who` *command.*

You can also use a connection established with `popen()` to write to a process. This is useful for commands that accept data from standard input in addition to command-line arguments. Listing 21.2 opens a connection to the `column` application using `popen()`.

LISTING 21.2 Using `popen()` to Pass Data to the `column` Application

```
 1: <html>
 2: <head>
 3: <title>Listing 21.2 Using popen() to pass
 4:        data to the column command</title>
 5: </head>
 6: <body>
 7: <?php
 8: $products = array(
 9:         array( "HAL 2000", 2, "red" ),
10:         array( "Tricorder",  3, "blue" ),
11:         array( "ORAC AI", 1, "pink"  ),
12:         array( "Sonic Screwdriver", 1, "orange"   )
```

LISTING 21.2 continued

```
13:         );
14: $ph = popen( "column -tc 3 -s / > purchases/user3.txt", "w" )
15:     or die( "Couldn't open connection to 'column' command" );
16: foreach ( $products as $prod )
17:     fputs( $ph, join('/', $prod)."\n");
18: pclose( $ph );
19: ?>
20: </table>
21: </body>
22: </html>
```

The purpose of the script in Listing 21.2 is to take the elements of a multidimensional array and output them to a file as an ASCII table. We open a connection to the `column` command, adding some command-line arguments. `-t` requires that the output should be formatted as a table, `-c 3` determines the number of columns we require, and `-s /` sets the "/" character as the field delimiter. We ensure that the results will be written to a file called `user3.txt`. Note that the `purchases` directory must exist on your system and that your script must be able to write to it.

Notice that we are doing more than one thing with this command. We are calling the `column` command and writing its output to file. In fact, we are issuing commands to a noninteractive shell. This means that in addition to piping content to a process, we can initiate other processes as well. We could even have the output of the `column` command mailed on to someone:

```
popen( "column -tc 3 -s / | mail matt@zink.demon.co.uk", "w" )
```

This level of flexibility can open our system to a grave threat if we ever pass user input to a PHP function that issues shell commands. We will look at precautions you can take later in the hour.

Having acquired a file pointer, we loop through the `$product` array. Each value is itself an array, which we convert to a string using the `join()` function. Rather than joining on a space character, we join on the delimiter we established as part of our command-line arguments. Using the "/" character to join the array is necessary because the spaces in the product array would otherwise confuse the `column` command. Having joined the array, pass the resultant string and a newline character to the `fputs()` function.

Finally, we close the connection. Taking a peek into the `user3.txt` file, we should see the table neatly formatted:

```
HAL 2000            2  red
Tricorder           3  blue
```

```
ORAC AI             1  pink
Sonic Screwdriver   1  orange
```

We could have made the code more portable by formatting the text using the `sprintf()` function, but the approach you take is a matter of choice.

Running Commands with `exec()`

`exec()` is one of many functions that enable you to pass commands to the shell. The function requires a string representing the path to the command that you want to run. It also optionally accepts an array variable that will be populated with the command's output, and a scalar variable that will be populated with the command's return value.

To get a listing for the current working directory, for example, you might pass `exec()` the command `"ls -al ."`. We do this in Listing 21.3, printing the result to the browser.

LISTING 21.3 Using `exec()` to Produce a Directory Listing

```
 1: <html>
 2: <head>
 3: <title>Listing 21.3 Using exec() to produce a directory listing</title>
 4: </head>
 5: <body>
 6: <?php
 7: exec( "ls -al .", $output, $return );
 8: print "<p>Returned: $return</p>";
 9: foreach ( $output as $file )
10:     print "$file<br>";
11: ?>
12: </table>
13: </body>
14: </html>
```

Notice that the `ls` command returns `0` on success. If it were unable to find or read the directory passed to it, it would have returned `1`.

Once again, we have reinvented the wheel to a certain extent with this example. We could have used the `opendir()` and `readdir()` functions to acquire a directory listing. There will be times, however, when a command on your system can achieve an effect that would take a long time to reproduce using PHP's functionality. You might have created a shell or Perl script that performs a complex task. If speed of development is an important factor in your project, you might decide that it is worth calling the external script instead of porting it to PHP, at least in the short term. Remember, however, that calling an external process will always add an overhead to your script in terms of both time and memory usage.

Figure 21.2 shows the output from Listing 21.3.

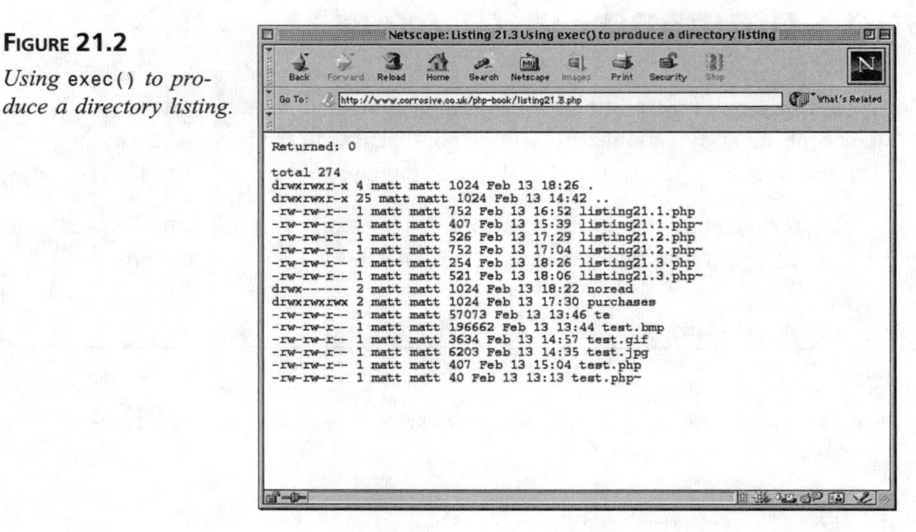
Netscape: Listing 21.3 Using exec() to produce a directory listing
Back
Forward
Reload
Home
Search
Netscape
Images
Print
Security
Stop
Go To:
http://www.corrosive.co.uk/php-book/listing21.3.php
What's Related
Returned: 0
total 274
drwxrwxr-x 4 matt matt 1024 Feb 13 18:26 .
drwxrwxr-x 25 matt matt 1024 Feb 13 14:42 ..
-rw-rw-r-- 1 matt matt 752 Feb 13 16:52 listing21.1.php
-rw-rw-r-- 1 matt matt 407 Feb 13 15:39 listing21.1.php~
-rw-rw-r-- 1 matt matt 526 Feb 13 17:29 listing21.2.php
-rw-rw-r-- 1 matt matt 752 Feb 13 17:04 listing21.2.php~
-rw-rw-r-- 1 matt matt 254 Feb 13 18:26 listing21.3.php
-rw-rw-r-- 1 matt matt 521 Feb 13 18:06 listing21.3.php~
drwx------ 2 matt matt 1024 Feb 13 18:22 noread
drwxrwxrwx 2 matt matt 1024 Feb 13 17:30 purchases
-rw-rw-r-- 1 matt matt 57073 Feb 13 13:46 te
-rw-rw-r-- 1 matt matt 196662 Feb 13 13:44 test.bmp
-rw-rw-r-- 1 matt matt 3634 Feb 13 14:57 test.gif
-rw-rw-r-- 1 matt matt 6203 Feb 13 14:35 test.jpg
-rw-rw-r-- 1 matt matt 407 Feb 13 15:04 test.php
-rw-rw-r-- 1 matt matt 40 Feb 13 13:13 test.php~

FIGURE 21.2
Using `exec()` *to produce a directory listing.*

Running External Commands with `system()` or the Backtick Operator

The `system()` function is similar to the `exec()` function in that it launches an external application. It requires the path to a command and, optionally, a variable, which will be populated with the command's return value. `system()` prints the output of the shell command directly to the browser. The following code fragment prints the manual page for the `man` command itself:

```
<?php
print "<pre>";
system(  "man man | col -b", $return );
print "</pre>";
?>
```

We print PRE tags to the browser to maintain the formatting of the page. We use system() to call man, piping the result through another application called col, which reformats the text for viewing as ASCII. We capture the return value of our shell command in the $return variable. system() returns its output.

You can achieve a similar result by using the backtick operator. This involves surrounding a shell command in backtick (`) characters. The enclosed command will be executed, and any output returned. You can print the output or store it in a variable.

We can re-create the previous example using backticks:

```
print "<pre>";
print `man man | col -b`;
print "</pre>";
```

Note that we have to explicitly print the return value from the backtick operator.

Plugging Security Holes with escapeshellcmd()

Before looking at escapeshellcmd(), let's examine the danger it guards against. We want to allow users to type in the names of manual pages and view output online. Now that we can output one manual page, it is a trivial matter to output any available page. Do not install the code in Listing 21.4; we are deliberately leaving a major security gap unplugged.

LISTING 21.4 Calling the man Command

```
 1: <html>
 2: <head>
 3: <title>Listing 21.4 Calling the man command.
 4:         This script is not secure</title>
 5: </head>
 6: <body>
 7: <form>
 8: <input type="text" value="<?php print  $manpage; ?>" name="manpage">
 9: </form>
10: <pre>
11: <?php
12: if ( isset($manpage) )
13:     system(  "man $manpage | col -b" );
14: ?>
15: </pre>
16: </table>
17: </body>
18: </html>
```

We extend our previous examples a little by adding a text field and including the value from the form submission to the shell command we pass to the `system()` function. We are being trusting, however. On a UNIX system, a malicious user would be able to add his own commands to the `manpage` field, thus gaining limited access to the server. Figure 21.3 shows a simple hack that could be applied to this script.

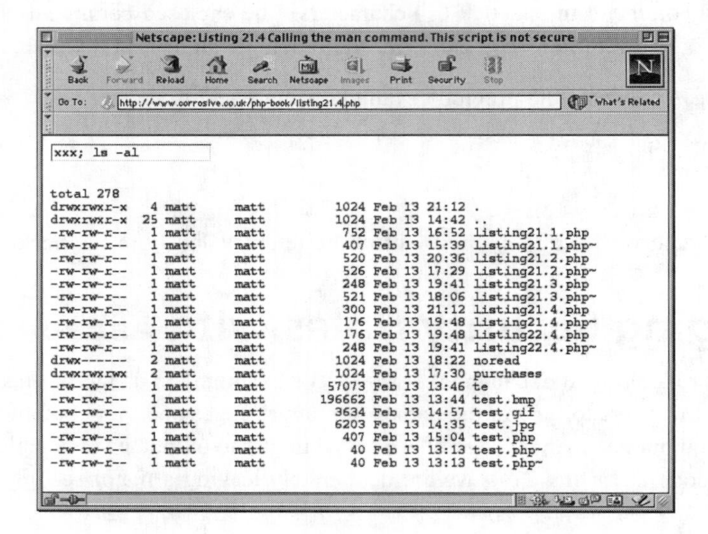
Netscape: Listing 21.4 Calling the man command. This script is not secure
Back Forward Reload Home Search Netscape Images Print Security Stop
Go To: http://www.corrosive.co.uk/php-book/listing21.4.php
What's Related
xxx; ls -al
total 278
drwxrwxr-x 4 matt matt 1024 Feb 13 21:12 .
drwxrwxr-x 25 matt matt 1024 Feb 13 14:42 ..
-rw-rw-r-- 1 matt matt 752 Feb 13 16:52 listing21.1.php
-rw-rw-r-- 1 matt matt 407 Feb 13 15:39 listing21.1.php~
-rw-rw-r-- 1 matt matt 520 Feb 13 20:36 listing21.2.php
-rw-rw-r-- 1 matt matt 526 Feb 13 17:29 listing21.2.php~
-rw-rw-r-- 1 matt matt 248 Feb 13 19:41 listing21.3.php
-rw-rw-r-- 1 matt matt 521 Feb 13 18:06 listing21.3.php~
-rw-rw-r-- 1 matt matt 300 Feb 13 21:12 listing21.4.php
-rw-rw-r-- 1 matt matt 176 Feb 13 19:48 listing21.4.php~
-rw-rw-r-- 1 matt matt 176 Feb 13 19:48 listing22.4.php
-rw-rw-r-- 1 matt matt 248 Feb 13 19:41 listing22.4.php~
drwx------ 2 matt matt 1024 Feb 13 18:22 noread
drwxrwxrwx 2 matt matt 1024 Feb 13 17:30 purchases
-rw-rw-r-- 1 matt matt 57073 Feb 13 13:46 te
-rw-rw-r-- 1 matt matt 196662 Feb 13 13:44 test.bmp
-rw-rw-r-- 1 matt matt 3634 Feb 13 14:57 test.gif
-rw-rw-r-- 1 matt matt 6203 Feb 13 14:35 test.jpg
-rw-rw-r-- 1 matt matt 407 Feb 13 15:04 test.php
-rw-rw-r-- 1 matt matt 40 Feb 13 13:13 test.php~
-rw-rw-r-- 1 matt matt 40 Feb 13 13:13 test.php~

FIGURE 21.3
Calling the `man` *command.*

The malicious user has submitted the value `xxx; ls -al` via the form. We have stored this value in the `$manpage` variable. After we combine this text with the shell command string we pass to `system()`, we end up with the following string:

```
"man xxx; ls -al | col -b"
```

This instructs the shell to fetch the manual page for `xxx`, which doesn't exist. It then performs a full directory listing, running the output through the `col` command. If you think that this is as bad as it gets, think again. An unfriendly visitor can list any readable directory on your system. He or she can even read your `/etc/passwd` file by adding the following line to the form field:

```
xxx; cat /etc/passwd
```

Fortunately, our encrypted passwords are stored in a file called `/etc/shadow`, which can only be read by the root user, but this still represents a grave breach in security. We clearly cannot allow this to happen. The safest way of protecting against this is never to pass user input directly to a shell. You can make yourself a little safer, though, by using the `escapeshellcmd()` function to add backslashes to any metacharacters that the user might submit. `escapeshellcmd()` requires a string and returns a converted copy. We can now amend our code, making our script a little safer, As shown in Listing 21.5.

LISTING 21.5 Escaping User Input with the `escapeshellcmd()` Function

```
 1: <html>
 2: <head>
 3: <title>Listing 21.5 Escaping user input with
 4:        the escapeshellcmd() function</title>
 5: </head>
 6: <body>
 7: <form>
 8: <input type="text" value="<?php print  $manpage; ?>" name="manpage">
 9: </form>
10: <pre>
11: <?php
12: if ( isset($manpage) )
13:     {
14:     $manpage = escapeshellcmd( $manpage );
15:     system(  "man $manpage | col -b" );
16:     }
17: ?>
18: </pre>
19: </table>
20: </body>
21: </html>
```

If the user attempts to enter `"xxx; cat /etc/passwd "` now, it will be amended to `"xxx\; cat /etc/passwd "`, preventing a new command from being issued. In fact, she will be presented with the manual page for the `cat` command rather than our password file!

Although you can improve security by using `escapeshellcmd()`, avoid passing user-submitted content to the shell. We could make our script even safer by compiling a list of all valid manual pages on our system and testing user input against this before calling `system()`. We do something similar in the next section.

Running External Applications with `passthru()`

`passthru()` is similar to `system()` except that any output from the shell command you send will not be buffered. This makes it suitable for running commands that produce binary as opposed to text data. passthru() accepts a shell command and an optional variable. The variable will be filled with the return value of the command.

Let's construct an example. We want to create a script that outputs images as thumbnails and that can be called from HTML or PHP pages. We are going to let external applications do all the work so that our script will be simple. Listing 21.6 shows the code that locates the image and outputs the data to the browser.

LISTING 21.6 Using passthru() to Output Binary Data

```
1: <?php
2: if ( isset($image) && file_exists( $image ) )
3:     {
4:     header( "Content-type: image/gif" );
5:    passthru( "giftopnm $image | pnmscale -xscale .5 -yscale .5 | ppmtogif" );
6:     }
7: else
8:     print "The image $image could not be found";
9: ?>
```

Notice that we have not used escapeshellcmd(). Instead, we have tested the user input against our file system using the file_exists() function. We will not pass the $image variable to the shell if the image requested does not exist. We could make the script safer still if we restrict the file extension we will accept and the directory that can be accessed.

In the call to passthru(), we issue a command that calls three applications. Note that for this script to work on your system, you must have these applications installed, and they must be available in your path. First, we call giftopnm, passing it the $image variable. This reads a GIF image and outputs data in portable anymap format. This output is piped to pnmscale, which scales the image to 50 percent of its original size. The output from pnmscale is in turn piped to ppmtogif, which converts the data to GIF format. This data is finally output to the browser.

We can now call this script from any Web page.

```
<img src="listing21.6.php?image=<?php print urlencode("/path/to/image.gif") ?>">
```

Calling an External CGI Script with the `virtual()` Function

If you are converting a site from plain HTML to PHP-enabled pages, you may have noticed that your server-side includes no longer work. If you are running PHP as an Apache module, you can use the `virtual()` function to call CGI scripts, such as Perl or C Web counters, and include their output in your pages. Any CGI script you write must output HTTP headers.

Let's write a simple Perl CGI script. If you don't know Perl, don't worry about this. It simply outputs an HTTP header and all the environmental variables available to it:

```
#!/usr/bin/perl -w
print "Content-type: text/html\n\n";
foreach ( keys %ENV ){
    print "$_: $ENV{$_}<br>\n";
}
```

Assuming that this script is saved in an executable file called `test.pl` in a `cgi-bin` directory, you can now call it with the `virtual()` function, including its output in your PHP document:

```
<?php
virtual("/cgi-matt/test.pl");
?>
```

Summary

In this hour, you learned how to communicate with the shell and through it with external applications. PHP is a powerful language, but it sometimes will be faster to call on an application than it will be to create similar functionality yourself.

You learned how to pipe data to and from a command using the `popen()` function. This approach is useful for applications that accept data on standard input and when you want to parse data as it is sent to you by an application.

You learned how to use `exec()`, `system()`, and the backtick operator to pass commands to the shell and to acquire user input. You learned about the dangers of passing user input to the shell and examined the `escapeshellcmd()` function, which will afford you some protection from malicious input. You learned how to use the `passthru()` function to accept binary data resulting from a shell command. Finally, you learned how to emulate server-side includes with the `virtual()` function.

Q&A

Q You've mentioned security a lot in this hour. Where can I go to get more information about security on the Web?

A Probably the most authoritative introduction to Web security is the Frequently Asked Questions document by Lincoln Stein (author of the famous Perl module, `CGI.pm`). You can find this at `http://www.w3.org/Security/Faq/`.

Q When should I consider calling an external process rather than re-creating its functionality in a script?

A The issues you should consider when weighing this are portability, speed of development, and efficiency.

If you build functionality into your script instead of relying on an external process, your script should run easily on different platforms or on systems that don't include the third-party application you would be calling. For simple tasks (such as obtaining a directory listing, for example), it is likely to be more efficient to handle the problem within your code, saving you the overhead of spawning a second process every time your script is called.

On the other hand, some tasks may be difficult to achieve in PHP or slow to complete (`grepping` a large file, for example). In these cases, it may be advisable to use a tool specifically designed for the job.

Workshop

The Workshop provides quiz questions to help you solidify your understanding of the material covered. Try to understand the quiz answers before continuing to the next hour's lesson. Quiz answers are provided in Appendix A.

Quiz

1. Which function would you use to open a pipe to a process?
2. How would you read data from a process after you have opened a connection?
3. How can you write data to a process after you have opened a connection to it?
4. Will the `exec()` function print the output of a shell command directly to the browser?
5. What does the `system()` function do with the output from an external command it executes?
6. What does the backtick operator return?

7. How can you escape user input to make it a little safer before passing it to a shell command?
8. How might you execute an external CGI script from within your script?

Activities

1. Create a script that uses the UNIX `ps` command to output the currently running processes to the browser. Given that knowledge is power, it might not be good idea to make this script available to your users!
2. Check the `ps` man page for command-line arguments for the `ps` command. Add a form to your script to allow users to choose from a range of command-line arguments to `ps` so that they can change the information output. Do not send *any* user input directly to the command line.

HOUR 22

Debugging

At the time of this writing, support for the PHP debugger has been removed from PHP4. Debugging features such as stack traces are promised for the future, so it is likely that a more advanced debugger will become available in the near future, if it is not already part of your release. For now, we will examine some of the simple techniques you can use to track down bugs in your code.

In this hour, you will learn

- How to find out about PHP's configuration
- How to find out about the variables automatically made available by PHP
- How to write error messages to a log file
- How to keep track of data in your code
- How to spot common errors

Getting Information About PHP and Your Script

When a script is not working as it should, one of your first steps should be to check your configuration. You will also want to know more about the variables that your script has available to it. If you're still puzzled, you might want to take a fresh look at your source code using syntax coloring to pinpoint potential problem areas. This section looks at two techniques you can use to get more information about your distribution of PHP and your script in particular.

`phpinfo()`

`phpinfo()` is one of the most powerful debugging tools at your disposal. It is a function that when included in a script gives you information about PHP, your server environment, and the variables in your script. It requires no arguments. `phpinfo()` returns only a boolean, but it outputs neatly formatted HTML to your browser window. You can see the output of `phpinfo()` in Figure 22.1.

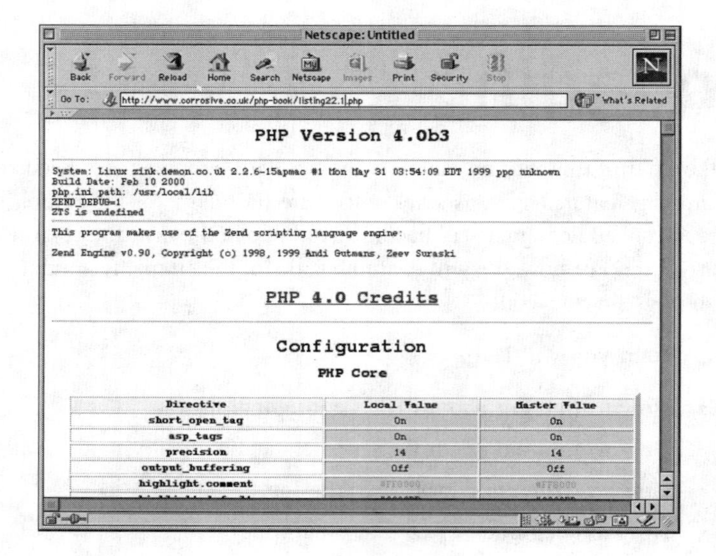

FIGURE 22.1
Printing PHP information.

The page begins with information about the PHP version that you are running, the server you are running it with, your system, and credits. You then see a table detailing the PHP configuration settings. You can change these settings in your `php.ini` file.

Imagine that you have a form field called "user," but for some reason your script never has access to a defined `$user` variable. A look at the PHP configuration settings might tell you what is going on. You notice the following settings:

```
track_vars   On
gpc_globals  Off
```

You have located your problem. `track_vars` defines whether to store `GET` variables in the `$HTTP_GET_VARS[]` array, `POST` variables in the `$HTTP_POST_VARS[]` array, and cookie variables in the `$HTTP_COOKIE_VARS[]` array. `gpc_globals` defines whether to make each individual variable acquired from `POST`, `GET`, and cookies available as individual global variables. Both are on by default, but in your configuration file, you have disabled `gpc_globals`. You now have two possible solutions. First, you can find your `php.ini` file and change the setting for `gpc_globals`. Don't know where it is? Well the output from `phpinfo()` tells you that as well! Second, you could change your code to access `$HTTP_POST_VARS[user]` rather than `$user`.

You will also find a table giving you information about your session configuration. If this table is absent, you do not have session support compiled into PHP. Within this table, you can find information that will help you track down problems with your session code. You might have created sessions that you want to persist over time, for example. If sessions are lost when your user closes her browser and you see the following setting

```
session.cookie_lifetime       0
```

you have located your problem. You will need to set the `session.cookie_lifetime` value in `php.ini` to the number of seconds you want a session to persist.

You may even see something like

```
session.use_cookies       0
```

which means that cookies are disabled for sessions. In this case, you would need to rely on the query string, or to change this setting in `php.ini`.

You will also find a lot of information about your server and its environment, especially if you are running Apache. In particular, you can see a listing of the entire request and response HTTP headers associated with your script, as well as Apache environment variables such as `HTTP_REFERER`.

If you have support for a database compiled into PHP, you will see configuration information relating to this. In particular, you may be able to check settings such as the default user, host, and port for the database.

Finally, and perhaps most important, you can see a list of all the global variables that PHP makes available to your script, complete with their values. Let's test this. Listing 22.1 creates a simple script that contains an HTML form and sets a cookie.

LISTING 22.1 A Script to Test `phpinfo()`

```
 1: <?php
 2: setcookie( "id", "2344353463433", time()+3600, "/" );
 3: ?>
 4: <html>
 5: <head>
 6: <title>Listing 22.1 A script to test phpinfo()</title>
 7: </head>
 8: <body>
 9: <form action="<?php print "$PHP_SELF" ?>" METHOD="get">
10: <input type="text" name="user">
11: <br>
12: <select name="products[]" multiple>
13: <option>Potatoes
14: <option>Cheese
15: <option>Bread
16: <option>Poultry
17: </select>
18: <br>
19: <input type="submit" value="test!">
20: </form>
21: <p></p>
22: <hr>
23: <p></p>
24: <?php
25: phpinfo();
26: ?>
27: </body>
28: </html>
```

When the form in Listing 22.1 is submitted, the script will have access to the values entered by the user. A cookie will also have been set. We call `phpinfo()` so that we can see these variables. You can see the relevant portion of the output from `phpinfo()` in Figure 22.2.

As you can see, the cookie and `$HTTP_GET_VARS` variables are visible. We included a multiple choice form element called `products[]`, and the entire array is formatted.

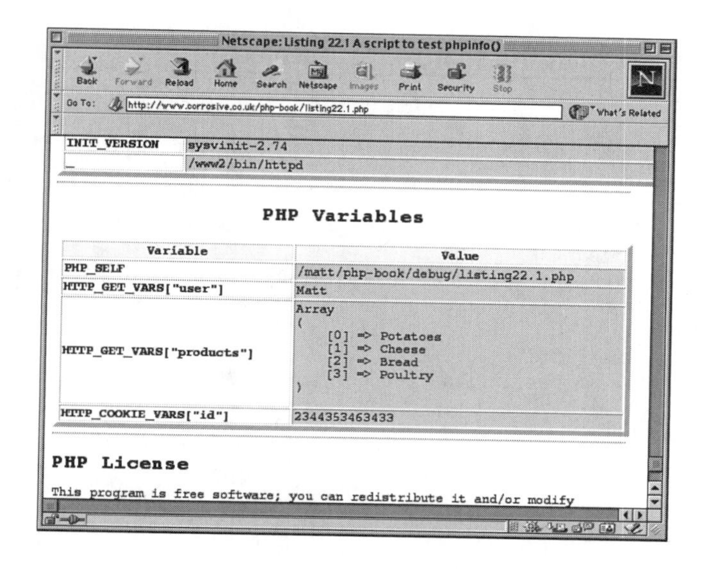

FIGURE 22.2
Accessing global variables.

It can sometimes be difficult to keep track of form submissions and cookies in larger projects, which makes `phpinfo()` an invaluable debugging tool.

Viewing Source with Syntax Coloring

If you can't find your problem using `phpinfo()`, your configuration might not be to blame. It is a good idea to take a look at your code again. PHP provides a mechanism by which you can view the source of a script, even coloring keywords, comments, strings, and HTML for you.

If you are running Apache, you can change your configuration file (usually `httpd.conf`) to include a line that maps an extension to syntax coloring mode.

```
AddType application/x-httpd-php-source .phps
```

After you have added this line, any file with a `.phps` extension will be displayed as syntax-colored source. If you cannot change your server's configuration files, you can still take advantage of this feature using the `show_source()` function. `show_source()` requires the path to a file and outputs its contents to the browser in syntax coloring mode.

Listing 22.2 builds a simple script that you can use to view the source of your projects.

LISTING 22.2 Viewing the Source of a Document

```
 1: <html>
 2: <head>
 3: <title>Listing 22.2 Viewing the source of a document</title>
 4: </head>
 5: <body>
 6: <form action="<?php print $PHP_SELF ?>" method="get">
 7: Enter file name:
 8: <input type="text" name="file" value="<?php print $file; ?>">
 9: <p></p><hr><p></p>
10: <?php
11: if ( isset( $file ) )
12:     show_source( $file ) or print "couldn't open \"$file\"";
13: ?>
14: </body>
15: </html>
```

Figure 22.3 shows Listing 22.2 in operation.

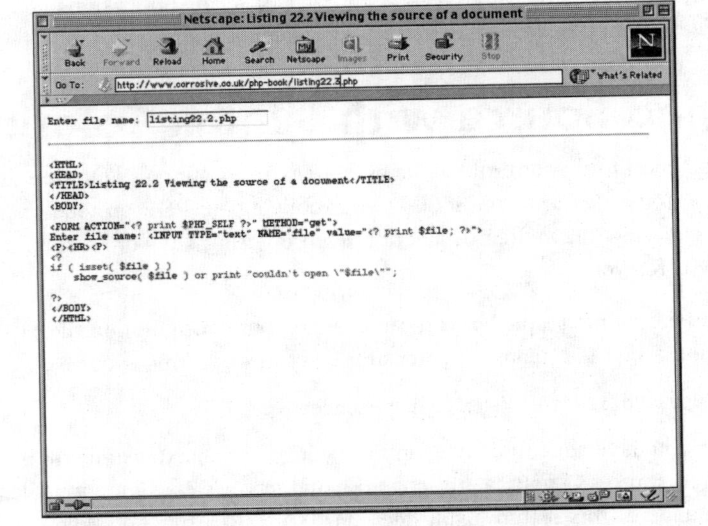

FIGURE 22.3
Showing syntax coloring.

Why would you want to use this feature? After all, you can view the source in your usual editor. The benefit lies in the syntax coloring. The fact that many keywords are highlighted means that a misspelling will be rendered in the default color.

Another common problem that can be difficult to track down is the failure to close a set of quotation marks. Because the PHP interpreter treats all text after the first set of quotation marks as a string, it often reports an error in the wrong place. Quoted strings are highlighted, however, so syntax coloring mode enables you to see the entire run-on string.

Table 22.1 shows the different aspects of your code that will be highlighted.

TABLE 22.1 Syntax Coloring

`php.ini` *Setting*	*Default Color*	*Code*	*Highlights*
`highlight.string`	Red	#DD0000	Quotation marks and quoted text.
`highlight.comment`	Orange	#FF8000	PHP comments.
`highlight.keyword`	Green	#007700	Many built-in functions. Language constructs. Operators.
`highlight.default`	Blue	#0000BB	All other PHP.
`highlight.html`	Black	#000000	HTML code.

PHP Error Messages

As you've worked through this book, you might have come across PHP error messages occasionally. You might have forgotten to end a statement with a semicolon, for example, or misspelled a function name. These messages are useful in debugging your code. You can ensure that errors are printed to the browser by setting the `display_errors` option in `php.ini` to "On." Don't forget that you can use `phpinfo()` to check that this option is enabled.

When you are sure that your scripts output error information to the browser, you can decide how strict you want the messages to be. If you want to set a default level, you can do so in `php.ini` by assigning a number to the `error_reporting` option. Fortunately, error reporting numbers are stored in constant variables, which makes it easy to choose the level you require. Table 22.2 lists the different levels that you can apply.

TABLE 22.2 Levels of Strictness for Error Reporting

Variable	*Name*	*Description*	*Action*
`E_ALL`	All	Every kind of error	Dependent on error encountered
`E_ERROR`	Errors	Fatal errors (memory allocation problems, for example)	Notify and end script execution

TABLE 22.2 continued

Variable	Name	Description	Action
`E_WARNING`	Warnings	Nonfatal errors (such as malformed function arguments)	Notify of problem but do not end execution
`E_PARSE`	Parser errors	Parser does not understand syntax.	Notify and end script execution
`E_NOTICE`	Notices	Potential problem (uninitialized variables, for example)	Notify and continue
`E_CORE_ERROR`	Start-up errors	Fatal errors encountered during start-up	Abort start-up
`E_CORE_WARNING`	Start-up warnings	Nonfatal errors encountered during start-up	Notify and continue

You cannot use these settings to change the action taken when an error is found; you only have control over whether the error is reported to the browser.

You are likely to want to combine two or more of these error reporting levels. You can do this by separating the constants you would like to apply with a pipe (|) symbol. For example,

```
error_reporting = E_ERROR|E_WARNING
```

will set the error reporting to include both errors and warnings.

If you wish to include all error types, you can use `E_ALL`. What would you do if you would like to report all error types apart from one?

```
error_reporting = E_ALL & ~E_NOTICE
```

will set error reporting to all errors apart from notices. `E_ERROR | E_WARNING` and `E_ALL & ~E_NOTICE` are binary arithmetic expressions that produce a new number that defines the level of error reporting. Binary arithmetic is beyond the scope of this book, but the procedure should be clear enough.

You can override the `error_reporting` option in `php.ini` with a function unsurprisingly called `error_reporting()`. This requires an integer representing the level of error reporting you want set for the execution of your script, and returns the previous error reporting setting. Once again you can use the constants that PHP provides for you. Let's look at an example where changing the level of error reporting can help you. See if you can spot the deliberate mistake in Listing 22.3.

LISTING 22.3 A Deliberate Error

```
1: <?php
2: error_reporting( E_ERROR|E_WARNING|E_PARSE );
3: $flag = 45;
4: if ( $flg == 45 )
5:     print "I know that \$flag is 45";
6: else
7:     print "I know that \$flag is NOT 45";
8: ?>
```

As you can see, we are testing the `$flag` variable, but we have misspelled it. There is no fatal error in this script, so it will always run. At an error reporting level of `E_ERROR | E_WARNING | E_PARSE` (which resolves to 7), there will be no warning, and your code might find its way into a production environment, where it will wait until the worst possible moment to manifest itself. If we change the value passed to `error_reporting()` to `E_ERROR | E_WARNING | E_PARSE | E_NOTICE` (which resolves to 15 and includes notices), however, this script will generate the following output:

```
Warning: Undefined variable: flg in
➥ /home/matt/htdocs/php-book/debug/listing22.3.php on line 4
I know that $flag is NOT 45
```

Not only do we now know that there is a problem, we also know the line number at which it was found. We could achieve the same effect by setting the error reporting level to `E_ALL`.

Setting the error reporting level to include notices can have less fortunate side effects, though. You might occasionally want to work with an undefined variable. Consider the following code fragment:

```
<INPUT TYPE="text" NAME="user" VALUE="<? print $user; ?>">
```

We have taken advantage of the fact that printing an undefined variable has a similar effect to printing an empty string (no effect at all). The `"user"` field in the preceding form will include a previously submitted value for `$user`, or nothing at all. If we were to call `error_reporting()` with an argument of 15, we would get an error message.

Writing Error Messages to a Log File

The bugs that we have been chasing so far are immediate problems for the most part. In other words, they are caught as you write your code. Some bugs, though, occur later on, perhaps as a result in changes to a script's environment. Imagine a script that writes data to a text file when a user submits a form. You test your script, monitor its performance for a while in a production environment, and then leave it to get on with its job. A few weeks later, you mistakenly remove the directory that contains the file to which the script is programmed to write. The error caused by this could go unrecorded.

PHP provides `error_log()`, a built-in method of logging errors to the server's error log or to a file of your choosing. `error_log()` requires two arguments: the error message itself and an integer representing an error type. Depending on the value of the error type argument, `error_log` will also accept an additional two arguments: a path to a file or an email address and additional headers for a mail message.

Table 22.3 lists the available error types.

TABLE 22.3 Error Type Arguments for the `error_log()` Function

Value	*Description*
0	Write error to error log defined by `php.ini` `error_log` option
1	Send error as mail to address in destination argument
3	Append error to file in destination argument

To write an error message to an error log, a destination must be set for the `error_log` option in `php.ini`. You can check whether this has been done by running a script containing a `phpinfo()` function call. If it hasn't, you can edit `php.info` so that errors are logged to a file of your choice:

```
error_log = /home/matt/logs/php_errors
```

If you are running NT or UNIX, you can alternatively assign the string "syslog" to `error_log`. Calls to `error_log()` that include an error type 0 argument will then be written to the system log for UNIX or the event log for NT. The following code fragment calls `error_log()` when we cannot open a file for reading:

```
fopen( "./important.txt", "a" )
      or error_log( __FILE__." line ".__LINE__.":
➥ Couldn't open important.txt", 0 );
```

We build an error message that includes the constant `__FILE__`, which gives us the path to the currently running script, the constant `__LINE__`, which holds the current line, and a description of the problem. We opt to write to the default error log by passing a 0 as our error type argument. We might get an error looking like this:

```
/home/matt/htdocs/php-book/debug/test5.php line 4:
➥ Couldn't open important.txt
```

If we need to write an error message to a specific file, we must pass `error_log()` an argument of 3:

```
if ( ! $did = mysql_connect( "localhost", "matt", "pumpkin" ) )
   {
   error_log( date("d/m/Y H I")." Couldn't connect to database",
              3, "dberrors.txt" );
   return false;
   }
```

When we output an error type of 3, we must also supply a destination argument so that the function knows where to write the error message.

We can also set `error_log()` to mail its error. This requires an error type of 1:

```
if ( ! file_exists( "crucial.txt" ) )
   error_log( "Oh no! crucial.txt is gone!", 1, "matt@corrosive.co.uk" );
```

When we output an error of type 1, we need to supply a destination argument containing the address to which the message should be sent.

Getting the Error String

When you are writing an error message to a file or email, it can be useful to have access to the error message produced by PHP. To do this, you must set the `track_errors` option in your `php.ini` file to "On." You can then access the most recent error in the variable `$php_errormsg` (much like Perl's `$!` variable).

This can make your error messages more informative. The following code produces an error message that tells more about the error than our previous messages:

```
fopen( "./important.txt", "a" )
       or error_log( __FILE__." line ".__LINE__.": $php_errormsg", 0 );
```

The full message might now be something like the following:

```
/home/matt/htdocs/php-book/debug/test5.php line 21:
fopen("./important.txt","a") - Permission denied
```

Manual Debugging

The simplest way of debugging a script is to scatter it with print statements, outputting the status of any variables that you are interested in to the browser. It is always difficult to pin down a bug that does not generate an error message. Often a variable in your script will contain an unexpected value.

A typical debug print statement might look like this:

```
print "<p>yep -- $val</p>";
```

This is the sort of quick test that you might add to a project to check that a function or loop has been reached and to confirm the value of the `$val` variable.

You might be neater and better organized than I am, however, and create your own convention.

```
print "<p>".__LINE__.": test is $test</p>";
```

You could even create a function to help with outputting debug messages, perhaps using `include()` to make it available to your script during development. Listing 22.4 writes a function that enables us to create structured debug messages.

LISTING 22.4 A Function to Format Debugging Messages

```
 1: <?php
 2: function debug( $line, $msg  )
 3:     {
 4:     static $calls = 1;
 5:     print "<P><HR>\n";
 6:     print "DEBUG $calls: Line $line: $msg<br>";
 7:     $args = func_get_args();
 8:     if (  count( $args ) % 2 )
 9:         print "Odd number of args<BR>";
10:     else
11:         {
12:         for ( $x=2; $x< count($args); $x += 2 )
13:             {
14:             print "   \$$args[$x]: ".$args[$x+1];
15:             print " .... (".gettype( $args[$x+1] ).")<BR>\n";
16:             }
17:         }
18:     print "<hr><p></p>\n";
19:     $calls++;
20:     }
21: $test = 55;
22: debug( __LINE__, "First message", "test", $test );
23: $test = 66;
```

LISTING 22.4 continued

```
24: $test2 = $test/2;
25: debug( __LINE__, "Second message", "test", $test, "test2", $test2 );
26: ?>
```

The `debug()` function requires a line number and a message. Thereafter, you can pass it any number of name/value pairs, and it will output these in a list. Printing the line number and the message is the easy part. We then take advantage of a feature of PHP4 that allows functions to accept variable numbers of arguments. No matter how many arguments the calling code includes, we can get them all by using the `func_get_args()` function, which returns an array of all the arguments sent to our function. We assign this array to the variable `$args`. We are expecting name/value pairs, so we print a warning to the browser if we have been passed an odd number of arguments. Otherwise, we loop through the arguments (starting with the third) printing each name value pair, as well as the data type of each variable.

Figure 22.4 shows the output of Listing 22.4.

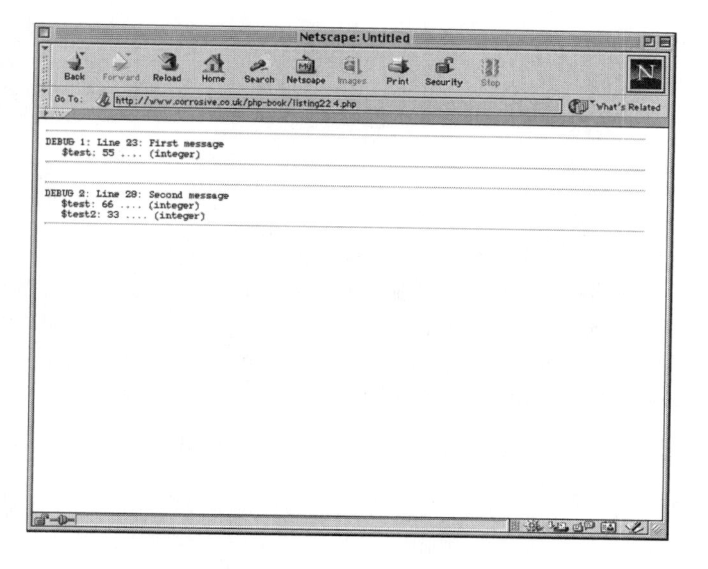

FIGURE 22.4
Using the `debug()` *function.*

Common Errors

We all make mistakes, especially as a deadline looms. There are some traps that most coders fall into sooner or later. As you become more used to coding, you tend to pay less attention to your fingers as they clatter away on the keyboard. This means that you code faster but also that subtle mistakes creep in as your mind rushes ahead to the next problem.

Can you spot the error in the next fragment of code?

```
$var=0;
while ( $var < 42 );
        {
        print "$var<BR>";
        $var++;
        }
```

You will get so used to typing a semicolon after each statement that it is easy to add one where it does not belong. By placing a semicolon after the test expression of the `while` statement, we ended the `while` statement. The `$var` variable will never be incremented, so the loop will never end.

How about this?

```
$val = 1;
while ( $val != 50 )
        {
        print $val;
        $val+=2;
        }
```

`while` statements depend on an expression evaluating to false to end their execution. In the preceding example, our test expression will only return false when `$val` is equivalent to 50. We initialize `$val` to 1 and then increment it by 2 for each iteration of the loop. `$val` is therefore never equivalent to 50. Just as common, but more obvious, is to omit the statement that increments a counter variable altogether.

The error in the following fragment is common and quite insidious:

```
if ( $test = 4 )
   {
   print "$test is 4<P>\n";
   }
```

We have assigned 4 to `$test` rather than testing for equivalence between the two. The assignment operator returns the value of its right-hand operand, so this test will always resolve to `true`, as well as overwrite the original value stored by `$test`. Errors of this kind are difficult to spot on the page and won't prevent your code from executing.

Strings present their own problems. I am particularly prone to the next mistake:

```
$test = "Today's date is . date('d/m/Y H I');
print $test;
```

Because we did not close the quotation marks after opening our string, the PHP interpreter has no idea where the string ends. This will almost always cause an error, but can be difficult to track down because the interpreter will often give you the wrong line number. The failure to close brackets of any kind can cause similar problems.

The final error we will look at is easy to track down:

```
print "You are logged in as "$user" at $domain";
```

You must escape quotation marks in a string if it is surrounded by quotation marks of the same kind. The previous fragment should be rewritten as follows:

```
print "You are logged in as \"$user\" at $domain";
```

So, the common errors discussed in this section include the following:

- Prematurely ending a loop statement by including a semicolon after the test expression
- Failure to create the condition that will allow a `while` statement to end execution
- Using an assignment operator instead of an equivalence operator
- Failure to close quotation marks or brackets
- Using unescaped quotation marks within a string enclosed by quotation marks of the same type

Summary

Debugging is probably the most frustrating part of the development process. You can make your life easier by being systematic about your approach.

In this hour, you learned about the `phpinfo()` function and how it can give you information about your configuration and the environmental variables available to you. You learned about the `error_log()` function and the ways in which you can use it to write error messages to a file or to an email. You learned about manual debugging using print statements or a function to output the value of variables to the browser. If you know about the data that your script is manipulating, you can track down bugs quickly and easily.

Finally, you learned about some of the errors that occasionally blight even the most experienced programmer's code.

Q&A

Q Is there a technique for minimizing bugs and errors in my code?

A Stay vigilant! In fact, it is all but impossible to create code that runs perfectly the first time. Write code that is as modular as possible so that an error can be isolated easily. Test as often as possible. Don't write a script and then run it. Write a few lines, test your script, and then write a few more lines. Test your assumptions and prepare for the worst. If your script depends on the existence or writability of a file, for example, be prepared to handle the possibility of the file's absence.

Workshop

The Workshop provides quiz questions to help you solidify your understanding of the material covered. Try to understand the quiz answers before continuing to the next hour's lesson. Quiz answers are provided in Appendix A.

Quiz

1. What function outputs useful information about your PHP configuration to the browser?
2. What function could you use to include a syntax-colored source listing of a PHP script?
3. Which `php.ini` directive enables you to control the strictness of error messages?
4. What function can be used to override this directive?
5. Which function allows you to log errors?
6. What built-in variable will contain the error message if the `php.ini` `track_errors` option is allowed?

Activity

1. By now, you should be considering your own projects. Review your code or planning in light of the techniques and issues discussed in this hour.

Part IV

Bringing It All Together

Hour

HOUR 23

An Example (Part 1)

If you've stayed the course all the way through this book, you should now have a good basis in the nuts and bolts of PHP. In this hour and the next, we will build a complete working example that draws on many of the techniques that we discussed in previous hours.

In this hour, you will learn

- How to create a project plan
- How to use `include()` to create function libraries and flexible navigation elements
- How to maintaining state with query strings, databases, and session functions
- How to separate HTML from PHP to enable non-technical designers and builders to work with dynamic environments
- How to use the `header()` function to redirect the user
- How to build a strategy for password protecting user accounts within a service

The Brief

Suppose that a community portal has asked us to build a small interactive events diary for the small town that it serves. Clubs and bands should be able to register with the service to publicize their events. Users can then check the event database to see what's going on. Users should be able to narrow their search according to the type of club or event, as well as the area in which an event is taking place.

In this hour and the next, we will work on a preliminary version of this application.

The Structure

Before we write a single line of code, we must decide exactly how the script will work. How will the user navigate the environment? What screens will we include?

The project naturally divides itself into two environments. First, a members' space that will be used to maintain club information and add new events to the diary. Second, a users' space for browsing the database.

Figure 23.1 shows the structure of the application.

New members will join up from a page called `join.php`, where they can set a name/password pair. Assuming that the name they choose is not already taken, they will be redirected to a form at `updateclub.php` where they can add information about their club. Until this form is completed, members will not be able to add events. After club data has

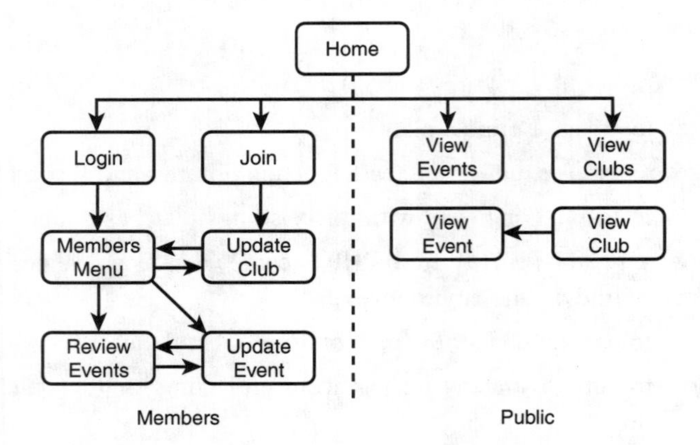

FIGURE 23.1
Application structure.

been added, the member will be sent to a members menu page (`membersmenu.php`) from where all member utilities can be reached.

An existing member will begin at a login screen (`login.php`). After the name and password have been checked, the member will be redirected straight to `membersmenu.php`.

From the menu page, members will be able to add new events (`updateevent.php`) and see a list of their currently set events (`reviewevents.php`). They will also be able to change their club details at any time (`updateclub.php`).

All users will be able to view a list of events by month, year, type, and area from a single PHP page, `viewevents.php`. They will also be able to view a list of clubs according to location or type from `viewclubs.php`. Users will be able to click a club or event name to see more detailed information on `viewevent.php` and `viewclub.php`, respectively.

Designing the Database

We will create a database called `organizer` and add four tables: `clubs`, `events`, `areas`, and `types`. We clearly need to keep data about clubs and events in separate tables because one club will link to multiple events. We will build separate tables to define event types and areas because this will make it easy to build pull-down menus for searching and adding data. We will create the tables manually. First, the `clubs` table:

```
create table clubs ( id INT NOT NULL AUTO_INCREMENT,
                     PRIMARY KEY( id ),
                     name VARCHAR(50),
                type CHAR(3),
                area CHAR(3),
                     mail VARCHAR( 50 ),
                     description BLOB,
                login VARCHAR(8),
                     password VARCHAR(8)
                     );
```

The member will add data for the `name`, `mail`, `description`, `login`, and `password` fields. `type` and `area` will hold identifiers that will link to the `types` and `areas` tables, respectively.

The events table will store information about every event belonging to each club:

```
create table events( id INT NOT NULL AUTO_INCREMENT,
                     PRIMARY KEY( id ),
                     type CHAR(3),
                     area CHAR(3),
                     edate INT,
                     ename VARCHAR(100),
                     evenue VARCHAR(100),
                     eaddress VARCHAR( 255 ),
                     ezip VARCHAR(20),
                     edescription BLOB,
                     eclub INT NOT NULL
                     );
```

Notice that this table, too, has type and area fields. A club may be based in the north of the city but hold an event in the south. A social club might hold an educational seminar or a political meeting. The eclub field will hold the ID of the club that owns the event. We can use this to list all events belonging to a club or to access club data from an event listing.

The types and areas fields are simple:

```
create table areas( id CHAR(3), area VARCHAR( 30 ) );
create table types( id CHAR(3), type VARCHAR( 30 ) );
```

The member will not be able to amend data in these tables. Instead, we will add our own category information, using SQL INSERT statements, and the member will be given these values as options to choose from:

```
INSERT INTO types ( id, type ) VALUES("COM", "Community");
```

Tables 23.1 and 23.2 list the data that we will insert.

TABLE 23.1 Data Added to the type Table

ID	*Types*
MUS	Music
FAM	Family
SOC	Social
COM	Community

TABLE 23.2 Data Added to the area Table

ID	*Areas*
NOR	North
SOU	South

TABLE 23.2 continued

ID	*Areas*
EAS	East
WES	West

Design Choices

You have already seen the choices that we have made in structuring this project. We have opted to build a separate page per screen rather than a monolithic application that serves different pages according to circumstances. This choice has both advantages and disadvantages.

Building a dynamic environment that uses multiple pages can involve some duplication of code structures and can make a project more difficult to maintain as it grows. On the other hand, we will be able to hand on our completed prototype to designers and page builders who can develop our pages almost as they would with standard HTML pages.

The Members Environment

It's time at last to start coding! For the rest of this hour, we will be constructing the members section of the application. It's a good idea to build this section first to make it easy to start adding sample data. Before we can do this, however, we must be able to create an account for ourselves.

`join.php` and `dblib.inc`

`join.php` will hold the form that allows the new member to submit a new username and password. To test for login name duplications and to add the member data, we must first open the database. This will be such a common need that it is a good idea to create a function for this purpose, which we will store in a separate document. This can then be added to every page we create using an `include()` statement. In fact, we will use this document, which we will call `dblib.inc`, to store an entire library of functions that work with the database. This will keep our PHP pages clear of SQL queries.

Keeping functions that talk to a database separate from your main code, can make it easier to amend your scripts to work with different data storage applications. You may have to rewrite the functions themselves at some point, but the calling code should continue to work as expected.

Let's create the function that will connect to the database:

LISTING 23.1 An Extract from `dblib.inc`

```
 1: $link;
 2:  connectToDB();
 3:  function connectToDB()
 4:      {
 5:      global $link;
 6:      $link =  mysql_connect( "localhost", "harry", "elbomonkey"  );
 7:      if ( ! $link )
 8:          die( "Couldn't connect to MySQL" );
 9:      mysql_select_db( "organizer", $link )
10:          or die ( "Couldn't open organizer: ".mysql_error() );
11:      }
```

The `connectToDB()` function declares a global variable, `$link`, that will store the database identifier returned by `mysql_connect()`. We have declared `$link` as global so that other database query functions will have access to it. Not only do we connect to the `mysql` daemon in the `connectToDB()` function, we also attempt to select the `organizer` database. Because the success of these operations is crucial to the working of the environment as a whole, we end execution if either `mysql_connect()` or `mysql_select_db()` fails.

We will create a further library that all pages will share. This will be called `clublib.inc` and will contain functions that help with session management and authentication. We will be using the session functions to store an associative array called `$session`. In `clublib.inc`, then, we use `session_start()` to initiate or resume a session and `session_register()` to associate our variable with it:

LISTING 23.2 An Extract from `clublib.inc`

```
1: session_start();
2: session_register( "session" );
```

Remember that any PHP code in included files must be surrounded by PHP start (`<?php`) and end tags (`?>`). It may seem needlessly confusing to store functionality in separate files, but it will save us a lot of duplication across the many pages in this project. We are now ready to create the `join.php` page. We do this in Listing 23.3.

LISTING 23.3 `join.php`

```
1: <?php
2: include("dblib.inc");
3: include("clublib.inc");
4: $message="";
5: if ( isset( $actionflag ) && $actionflag=="join")
```

LISTING 23.3 continued

```
 6:     {
 7:     if ( empty( $form[login] ) ||
 8:            empty( $form[password] ) ||
 9:            empty( $form[password] ) )
10:         $message .= "you must fill in all fields<BR>\n";
11:     if ( $form[password] != $form[password2] )
12:         $message .= "Your passwords did not match<BR>\n";
13:     if ( strlen( $form[password] ) > 8 )
14:         $message .= "Your password must be less than
15:                       8 characters<BR>\n";
16:     if ( strlen( $form[login] ) > 8 )
17:         $message .= "Your login must be less than
18:                       8 characters<BR>\n";
19:     if ( getRow( "clubs", "login", $form[login] ) )
20:         $message .= "Login \"$form[login]\" already exists.
21:                       Try another<BR>\n";
22:     if ( $message == "" ) // we found no errors
23:         {
24:         $id = newUser( $form[login], $form[password] );
25:         cleanMemberSession( $id, $form[login], $form[password] );
26:         header( "Location: updateclub.php?".SID );
27:         exit;
28:         }
29:     }
30: ?>
31: <html>
32: <head>
33: <title>Join!</title>
34: </head>
35:
36: <body>
37: <?php
38: include("publicnav.inc");
39: ?>
40: <p>
41: <h1>Join</h1>
42: <?php
43: if ( $message != "" )
44:     {
45:     print "<b>$message</b><p>";
46:     }
47: ?>
48: <p>
49: <form action="<?php print $PHP_SELF;?>">
50: <input type="hidden" name="actionflag" value="join">
51: <input type="hidden" name="<?php print session_name() ?>"
52:         value="<?php print session_id() ?>">
53: Login: <br>
54: <input type="text" name="form[login]"
```

LISTING 23.3 continued

```
55:         value="<?php print $form[login] ?>" maxlength=8>
56: </p>
57: <p>
58: Password: <br>
59: <input type="password" name="form[password]" value="" maxlength=8>
60: </p>
61: <p>
62: Confirm password: <br>
63: <input type="password" name="form[password2]" value="" maxlength=8>
64: </p>
65: <p>
66: <input type="submit" value="update">
67: </p>
68: </form>
69:
70: </body>
71: </html>
```

We first `include()` our library files, so we should instantly have a database connection and an active session. We initialize a variable called `$message`. This variable will be found on many pages in our project. It has a dual purpose. We will fill it with error information when we test submitted data. This can then be written to the browser. We can also use it as a flag to tell us whether problems have been encountered. If `$message` remains an empty string, we can assume that all the tests that we have performed have been successful.

We test for the presence and contents of a variable called `$actionflag`. This is another pattern that you will see repeating. We set a hidden field called `actionflag` in every form we create and give it a relevant value. If the corresponding variable `$actionflag` is present and filled with the expected value, then we can be sure that the form has been submitted, and we can proceed to check the input. If the variable is not present, we know that the member has arrived via a link or bookmark and is not submitting data yet.

Let's skip to the HTML section for now. Within the `BODY` element, we first `include()` yet another file. This will contain global navigation. It's a good idea to include navigation from an early stage. It will make it easier to test the environment as we go along. We will add navigation elements to an include file called `publicnav.inc`. For now this will only contain navigation for the publicly available pages.

LISTING 23.4 An Extract from `publicnav.inc`

```
1: <a href="viewclubs.php?<?php print SID ?>">Browse clubs</a> |
2: <a href="viewevents.php?<?php print SID ?>">Browse events</a> |
3: <a href="join.php?<?php print SID ?>">Join</a> |
```

LISTING 23.4 continued

```
4: <a href="login.php?<?php print SID ?>">Login</a> |
5: <a href="index.php?<?php print SID ?>">Home</a>
```

By including the navigation elements in a separate file, we can update the look and feel of the entire site's navigation with a single change.

After writing the title of the page, we test the `$message` variable. If it does not hold an empty string, we write its contents to the browser. This is the mechanism by which we can send feedback to the member if we can't work with his or her input.

The HTML form defines three visible fields. `form[login]`, `form[password]`, and `form[password2]`. We use this strange naming technique because PHP will convert these names, and their corresponding values, into a single associative array called `$form`. This will help to protect us from namespace pollution. We will be keeping all session variables in an array called `$session`, and all form variables in an array called `$form`. This will help to protect us against clashes. It is a good idea to keep your global variables to a minimum, to avoid confusion in projects of this size. We will use a `$form` array for every script that contains a form.

We also create one hidden element called `actionflag`, and another one that will store the session name and variable. Throughout this project, we will always pass the session ID from page to page, so that we will not lose clients who cannot or will not use cookies.

> If you are testing a session-enabled script, it is a good idea to disable cookies on your browser first. You will then know whether you have failed to pass the session ID from request to request.

Now that we have looked at the HTML form, we can examine the code we use to test input. We check that the member has filled in all fields, that none of them contain more than eight characters. We then call a new function called `getRow()`, this is one of the functions that we include in the `dblib.inc` file. It requires a table name, field name, and field value. It then uses these to attempt to find a corresponding row in the database, returning it in an array.

LISTING 23.5 An Extract from `dblib.inc`

```
1: function getRow( $table, $fnm, $fval )
2:      {
3:      global $link;
4:      $result = mysql_query( "SELECT * FROM $table WHERE $fnm='$fval'", $link );
5:      if ( ! $result )
6:          die ( "getRow fatal error: ".mysql_error() );
7:      return mysql_fetch_array( $result );
8:      }
```

We pass the function the table name `clubs`, the field name `login`, and the value given to us by the member in `$form[login]`. If `mysql_fetch_array()` returns a populated array, we know that a member with this login already exists, so we set an error message.

If the `$message` variable still contains an empty string, we can go ahead and create our new member. There are two stages to this. First, we must update the database. We create a new `dblib.inc` function called `newUser()` to handle this:

LISTING 23.6 An Extract from `dblib.inc`

```
1: function newUser( $login, $pass )
2:      {
3:      global $link;
4:      $result = mysql_query( "INSERT INTO clubs (login, password)
5:                 VALUES('$login', '$pass')", $link);
6:      return mysql_insert_id( $link );
7:      }
```

This function accepts login and password values. It uses these to insert a new row into the `clubs` table. It uses `mysql_insert_id()` to return the automatically incremented `id` field.

Now that we have a value for the member's ID, we can call another library function. `cleanMemberSession()` lives in `clublib.inc`. It accepts an ID, a login name, and a password, and stores these in the `$session` array. These values will now be available to every session-enabled page the member visits. We will be able to use them to authenticate the member on each screen.

LISTING 23.7 An Extract from `clublib.inc`

```
1: function cleanMemberSession( $id, $login, $pass )
2:      {
3:      global $session;
4:      $session[id] = $id;
5:      $session[login] = $login;
```

LISTING 23.7 continued

```
6:      $session[password] = $pass;
7:      $session[logged_in] = true;
8:      }
```

As well as setting id, login, and password elements, we also set a flag element called `logged_in`.

Finally, in `join.php`, having updated the session and the database, we can send the member on her way. We call the `header()` function, redirecting her browser to `updateclub.php` where she must add more information about the club she is registering.

You can see the output from `join.php` in Figure 23.2.

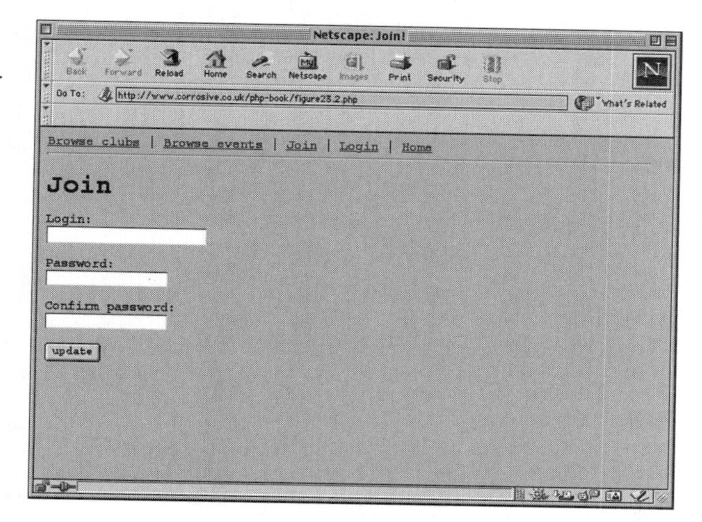

FIGURE 23.2
Output from `join.php`.

`updateclub.php`

This screen performs the dual purpose of allowing a new member to add club information and an established member to make changes to his or her data.

You can see `updateclub.php` in Listing 23.8.

LISTING 23.8 updateclub.php

```
1: <?php
2: include("dblib.inc");
3: include("clublib.inc");
4: $club_row = checkUser();
5: $message = "";
6: if ( isset( $actionflag ) && $actionflag=="update" )
7:     {
8:     if ( empty( $form[name] ) )
9:         $message .="Your club must have a name<br>\n";
10:    if ( ! getRow( "areas", "id", $form[area] ) )
11:        $message .= "PANIC: That area code can't be found<br>";
12:    if ( ! getRow( "types", "id", $form[type] ) )
13:        $message .= "PANIC: That type code can't be found<BR>";
14:    if ( $message == "" )
15:        {
16:        updateOrg( $session[id], $form[name], $form[area],
17:                   $form[type], $form[mail], $form[description] );
18:        header("Location: membersmenu.php?".SID);
19:        exit;
20:        }
21:    }
22: else
23:     {
24:     $form = $club_row;
25:     }
26: ?>
27: <html>
28: <head>
29: <title>Update your club listing</title>
30: </head>
31:
32: <body>
33: <?php
34: include("publicnav.inc");
35: ?>
36: <h1>Amend club information</h1>
37: <?php
38: if ( $message != "" )
39:     {
40:     print "<b>$message</b><p>";
41:     }
42: ?>
43: <form action="<?php print $PHP_SELF;?>">
44: <input type="hidden" name="actionflag" value="update">
45: <input type="hidden" name="<?php print session_name() ?>"
46:        value="<?php print session_id() ?>">
47: <p>
48: Club name: <br>
49: <input type="text" name="form[name]"
```

LISTING 23.8 continued

```
50:         value="<?php print stripslashes($form[name]) ?>">
51: </p>
52: <p>
53: Club area: <br>
54: <select name="form[area]">
55: <?php writeOptionList( "areas", $form[area] ) ?>
56: </select>
57: </p>
58: <p>
59: Club type: <br>
60: <select name="form[type]">
61: <?php writeOptionList( "types", $form[type] ) ?>
62: </select>
63: </p>
64: <p>
65: Contact e-mail: <br>
66: <input type="text" name="form[mail]"
67:         value="<?php print stripslashes($form[mail]) ?>">
68: </p>
69: <p>
70: Club description: <br>
71: <textarea name="form[description]" rows=5 cols=30 wrap="virtual">
72: <?php print stripslashes($form[description]) ?>
73: </textarea>
74: </p>
75: <p>
76: <input type="submit" value="update">
77: </p>
78: </form>
79: </body>
80: </html>
```

Once again, we include `dblib.inc` and `clublib.inc`, saving us from having to write code to open the database and resume a session all over again. We call a new function called `checkUser()`, which resides in the `clublib.inc` library. The function checks the member's session data against the database.

LISTING 23.9 An Extract from `clublib.inc`

```
1:  function checkUser( )
2:      {
3:      global $session, $logged_in;
4:      $session[logged_in] = false;
5:      $club_row = getRow( "clubs", "id", $session[id] );
6:      if (     ! $club_row ||
7:          $club_row[login] != $session[login] ||
```

LISTING 23.9 continued

```
 8:          $club_row[password] != $session[password] )
 9:          {
10:          header( "Location: login.php" );
11:          exit;
12:          }
13:      $session[logged_in] = true;
14:      return $club_row;
15:      }
```

`checkUser()` is relatively strict. It uses the `$session[id]` element array in conjunction with `getRow()` to extract the relevant row from the database. It stores this associative array in the variable `$club_row` and tests its login and password elements against those stored in the `$session` variable. If these don't match, it sends the user back to the login page `login.php`.

Why do we go to the expense of a database request for authentication? Could we not simply check the `logged_in` element of the `$session` variable? This would be open to abuse because a malicious user could simply add something like

```
session%5Blogged_in%5D=1&session%5Bid%5D=1
```

to a query string. PHP would transform this into a `$session` array made up of `GET` parameters, which could fool a less vigorous test. A user could use a similar trick to fool the test in `checkUser()`, but because we are testing the login and password against the values in the database, the fake `$session` variable would have to contain valid data to be accepted.

A byproduct of the test in `checkUser()` is the fact that it returns all data associated with the club in question. Pages that need to authenticate a member can work with this data.

When we call `checkUser()` in `updateclub.php`, the return value is stored in the variable `$club_row`. Skipping ahead once again to the HTML body, we begin by including the navigation file `publicnav.inc` once again. We have moved on a little, however, and can extend this document to include members navigation elements as well:

LISTING 23.10 An Extract from `publicnav.inc`

```
1:  <p>
2:  <a href="viewclubs.php?<?php print SID ?>">Browse clubs</a> |
3:  <a href="viewevents.php?<?php print SID ?>">Browse events</a> |
4:  <a href="join.php?<?php print SID ?>">Join</a> |
5:  <a href="login.php?<?php print SID ?>">Login</a> |
6:  <a href="index.php?<?php print SID ?>">Home</a>
7:  </p>
8:  <?php
```

LISTING 23.10 continued

```
 9:  if ( $session[logged_in] )
10:      {
11:      ?>
12:      <p>
13:      <A HREF="updateclub.php?<?php print SID ?>">Your details</A> |
14:      <A HREF="reviewevents.php?<?php print SID ?>">Your events</A> |
15:      <A HREF="updateevent.php?<?php print SID ?>">New event</A> |
16:      <A HREF="membersmenu.php?<?php print SID ?>">Members home</A>
17:      </p>
18:      <?
19:      }
20:  ?>
21:  <hr>
```

If the `$session[logged_in]` flag is set to `true`, then links that should only be available to members will also be printed. Notice that we include the `SID` constant in all our links. This will ensure that session ID is passed from page to page, even if cookies are disabled.

The form in `updateclub.php` is unremarkable. We include both `actionflag` and session ID hidden elements. We provide text entry elements for the club's name, description, and a contact email address. To produce the pull-down menus for the club area and type, however, we call a new function, `writeOptionList()`. This function is stored in our database library, `dblib.inc`. It accepts the name of a table, (either `areas` or `types`), and a string value.

LISTING 23.11 An Extract from `dblib.inc`

```
 1:  function writeOptionList( $table, $id )
 2:      {
 3:      global $link;
 4:      $result = mysql_query( "SELECT * FROM $table", $link );
 5:      if ( ! $result )
 6:          {
 7:          print "failed to open $table<p>";
 8:          return false;
 9:          }
10:      while ( $a_row = mysql_fetch_row( $result ) ){
11:          print "<option value=\"$a_row[0]\"";
12:          if ( $id == $a_row[0] )
13:              print "SELECTED";
14:          print ">$a_row[1]\n";
15:          }
16:      }
```

The function uses the `$table` parameter variable to select every row from either the `areas` or `types` table. It then loops through each of the rows in the resultset, writing an HTML `OPTION` element to the browser. If the second element in the array returned by `mysql_fetch_row()` matches `$id`, the second parameter argument, the string `"SELECTED"` is added to the element. This technique ensures that the correct element in the pull-down remains selected if the form is represented.

The PHP code that checks the input ensures that the `form[name]` field has been filled in. It also checks that `form[area]` and `form[type]` contain legal values. If the `$message` variable contains an empty string, we know that our criteria for the user-submitted data have been met. We pass the user input to a function calledupdateOrg(), which will populate the relevant row of the `clubs` table. `updateOrg()` requires a club's ID, in addition to values for the `name`, `area`, `type`, `mail`, and `description` fields in the `clubs` table.

LISTING 23.12 An Extract from `dblib.inc`

```
 1: function updateOrg( $id, $name, $area, $type, $mail, $description )
 2:     {
 3:     global $link;
 4:     $query = "UPDATE clubs set name='$name', area='$area',
 5:               type='$type', mail='$mail', description='$description'
 6:               WHERE id='$id'";
 7:     $result = mysql_query( $query, $link );
 8:     if ( ! $result )
 9:         die ( "updateOrg update error: ".mysql_error() );
10:     }
```

After the row has been updated, the member can be sent on to the member's menu page, `membersmenu.php`.

If the member reached `updateclub.php` via a link or bookmark, the `$actionflag` variable will not be set, and the testing and updating code will be skipped. There is still work to be done, however. The `$club_row` associative array variable was populated when we called `checkUser()`. It contains the field names and values for the current club's row in the database. We assign this array to the `$form` variable, thereby ensuring that the update form will be populated with the current information for the club.

Figure 23.3 shows the output of Listing 23.8.

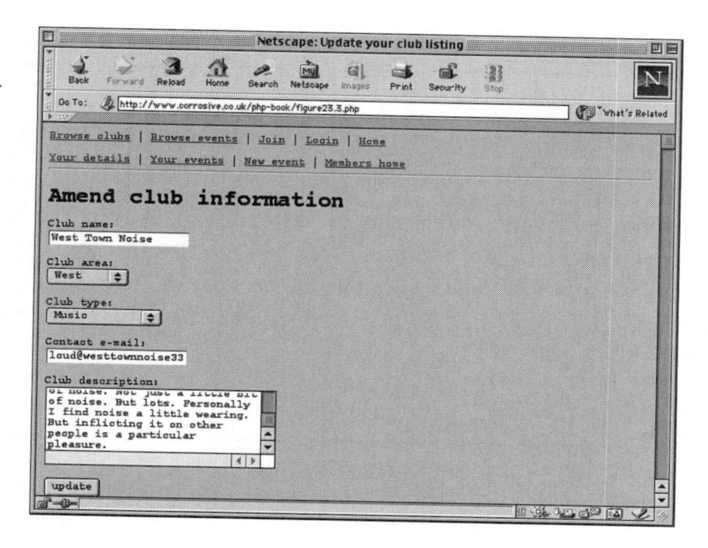

FIGURE 23.3
Output of Listing 23.8.

membersmenu.php

membersmenu.php is the heart of the members area. Essentially a list of links, it would eventually be populated by news and offers that might be interesting to members. You can see this page in Listing 23.13.

LISTING 23.13 membersmenu.php

```
 1: <?php
 2: include("dblib.inc");
 3: include("clublib.inc");
 4:
 5: $club_row = checkUser();
 6: checkClubData( $club_row );
 7: ?>
 8:
 9: <html>
10: <head>
11: <title>Welcome</title>
12: </head>
13:
14: <body>
15: <?php
16: include("publicnav.inc");
17: ?>>Members menu</h1>
18:
19: <a href="updateclub.php?<?php print SID ?>">Review your club details</a><br>
20: <a href="reviewevents.php?<?php print SID ?>">Review your events</a><br>
21: <a href="updateevent.php?<?php print SID ?>">New event</a><br>
```

LISTING 23.13 continued

```
22:
23: </body>
24: </html>
```

There's one new feature on this page. After we call `checkUser()` to ensure that the user is a member, we pass the array it returns to another function that we keep in `clublib.php`. The `checkClubData()` function ensures that the member has already created a club profile. We do not want members to create events unless they have fully defined their club. The minimum we require is a club name.

LISTING 23.14 An Extract from `clublib.inc`

```
1: function checkClubData( $clubarray  )
2:     {
3:     if ( ! isset( $clubarray[name] ) )
4:         {
5:         header( "Location: updateclub.php?".SID );
6:         exit;
7:         }
8:     }
```

login.php

Before we move onto the pages that members can use to maintain their events, we must look at `login.php`. This script enables a registered member to return to the environment. You can see it in Listing 23.15.

LISTING 23.15 `login.php`

```
 1: <?php
 2: include("dblib.inc");
 3: include("clublib.inc");
 4:  $message="";
 5:  if ( isset( $actionflag ) && $actionflag == "login" )
 6:      {
 7:      if ( empty( $form[login] ) || empty( $form[password] )  )
 8:          $message .= "you must fill in all fields<br>\n";
 9:      if ( ! ( $row_array =
10:              checkPass( $form[login], $form[password] ) ) )
11:          $message .= "Incorrect password try again<br>\n";
12:      if ( $message == "" ) // we found no errors
13:          {
14:          cleanMemberSession( $row_array[id], $row_array[login],
15:                              $row_array[password] );
```

LISTING 23.15 continued

```
16:             header( "Location: membersmenu.php?".SID );
17:             }
18:         }
19: ?>
20: <html>
21: <head>
22: <title>Login</title>
23: </head>
24: <body>
25: <?php
26: include("publicnav.inc");
27: ?>
28: <h1>Login</h1>
29: <?php
30: if ( $message != "" )
31:     {
32:     print "<p><b>$message</b></P>";
33:     }
34: ?>
35: <p>
36: <form action="<?php print $PHP_SELF;?>">
37: <input type="hidden" name="actionflag" value="login">
38: <input type="hidden" name="<?php print session_name() ?>"
39:        value="<?php print session_id() ?>">
40: </p><p>
41: Login: <br>
42: <input type="text" name="form[login]"
43:        value="<?php print $form[login] ?>">
44: </p><p>
45: Password: <br>
46: <input type="password" name="form[password]" value="">
47: </p><p>
48: <input type="submit" value="update">
49: </form>
50: </body>
51: </html>
```

The structure of this page should now be familiar. We use `dblib.inc` and `clublib.inc` to initialize a database connection and resume a session.

If an `$actionflag` variable has been set, we test the form fields. We use a new `dblib.inc` function to check the `$form[login]` and `$form[password]` elements.

Listing 23.16 An Extract from dblib.inc

```
 1:  function checkPass( $login, $password )
 2:      {
 3:      global $link;
 4:      $result = mysql_query( "SELECT id, login, password FROM clubs
 5:                  WHERE login='$login' and password='$password'",
 6:                  $link );
 7:      if ( ! $result )
 8:          die ( "checkPass fatal error: ".mysql_error() );
 9:      if ( mysql_num_rows( $result ) )
10:          return mysql_fetch_array( $result );
11:      return false;
12:      }
```

`checkPass()` accepts a login and password and sends a simple `SELECT` query to the `clubs` table.

If no errors have been found, we call `cleanMemberSession()`, which initializes the `login`, `password`, and `id` elements of the `$session` variable. We then redirect the member to `membersmenu.php`

updateevent.php

Now that members can join or log in to our service and amend their club details, we need to make it possible for them to create and edit events. You can see the whole of `updateevent.php` in Listing 23.17.

Listing 23.17 updateevent.php

```
 1: <?php
 2: include("dblib.inc");
 3: include("clublib.inc");
 4: include("date.inc");
 5: $club_row = checkUser();
 6: checkClubData( $club_row );
 7: $date = time();
 8: $message = "";
 9: if ( ! empty( $event_id ) )
10:     $event_row = getRow( "events", "id", $event_id );
11: else
12:     $event_id = false;
13: if ( isset( $actionflag ) && $actionflag=="update_event" )
14:     {
15:     if ( empty( $form[ename] ) )
16:         $message .="The venue must have a name<br>\n";
17:     if ( ! getRow( "areas", "id", $form[area] ) )
```

LISTING 23.17 continued

```
18:         $message .= "PANIC: That area code can't be found<br>";
19:     if ( ! getRow( "types", "id", $form[type] ) )
20:         $message .= "PANIC: That type code can't be found<br>";
21:     foreach ( array( "months", "years", "days", "minutes" )
22:             as $date_unit )
23:         {
24:         if ( ! isset( $form[$date_unit] ) )
25:             {
26:             $message .= "PANIC: Can't make sense of that date";
27:             break;
28:             }
29:         }
30:     $date =  mktime( $form[hours], $form[minutes], 0, $form[months],
31:                      $form[days], $form[years] );
32:     if ( $date < time() )
33:         $message .= "You've chosen a date in the past!";
34:     if ( $message == "" )
35:         {
36:         insertEvent(     $form[ename], $form[evenue], $form[area],
37:                 $form[type], $form[eaddress], $form[ezip],
38:                 $form[edescription], $session[id], $date,
39:                 $event_id );
40:         header( "Location: reviewevents.php?".SID );
41:         }
42:     }
43: elseif ( $event_id )
44:     {
45:     //foreach( $event_row as $key=>$value )
46:     //    $form[$key] = $value;
47:     $form = $event_row;
48:     $date =  $event_row[edate];
49:     }
50: else
51:     {
52:     $form[area] = $club_row[area];
53:     $form[type] = $club_row[type];
54:     }
55: ?>
56: <html>
57: <head>
58: <title>Add/amend event</title>
59: </head>
60: <body>
61: <?php
62: include("publicnav.inc");
63: ?>
64: <h1>Amend event</h1>
65: <?php
66: if ( $message != "" )
```

LISTING 23.17 continued

```
67:     {
68:     print "<b>$message</b>";
69:     }
70: ?>
71: <p>
72: <form action="<?php print $PHP_SELF;?>">
73: <input type="hidden" name="actionflag" value="update_event">
74: <input type="hidden" name="<?php print session_name() ?>"
75:         value="<?php print session_id() ?>">
76: <input type="hidden" name="event_id"
77:         value="<?php print $event_id ?>">
78: Event Name: <br>
79: <input type="text" name="form[ename]"
80:         value="<?php print stripslashes($form[ename]) ?>">
81: </p>
82: <p>
83: Date and time: <br>
84: <select name="form[months]">
85: <?php writeMonthOptions( $date ) ?>
86: </select>
87:  <select name="form[days]">
88:  <?php writeDayOptions( $date ) ?>
89:  </select>
90: <select name="form[years]">
91: <?php writeYearOptions( $date ) ?>
92: </select>
93: <SELECT NAME="form[hours]">
94: <? writeHourOptions( $date ) ?>
95: </SELECT>
96: <SELECT NAME="form[minutes]">
97: <? writeMinuteOptions( $date ) ?>
98: </SELECT>
99: </p>
100: <p>
101: Event area: <br>
102: <select name="form[area]">
103: <?php writeOptionList( "areas", $form[area] ) ?>
104: </select>
105: </p>
106: <p>
107: Event type: <br>
108: <select name="form[type]">
109: <?php writeOptionList( "types", $form[type] ) ?>
110: </select>
111: </p>
112: <p>
113: Describe the event: <br>
114: <textarea name="form[edescription]" wrap="virtual" rows=5 cols=30>
115: <?php print stripslashes($form[edescription]) ?>
```

LISTING 23.17 continued

```
116: </textarea>
117: </p>
118: <p>
119: Venue name: <br>
120: <input type="text" name="form[evenue]"
121:        value="<?php print stripslashes($form[evenue]) ?>">
122: </p>
123: <p>
124: Venue address: <br>
125: <textarea name="form[eaddress]" wrap="virtual" rows=5 cols=30>
126: <?php print stripslashes($form[eaddress]) ?>
127: </textarea>
128: </p>
129: <p>
130: Venue zip code: <br>
131: <input type="text" name="form[ezip]"
132:        value="<?php print stripslashes($form[ezip]) ?>">
133: </p>
134: <p>
135: <input type="submit" value="update">
136: </p>
137: </form>
138: </body>
139: </html>
```

This page creates a form that matches the field names in the `events` table. As usual, we need to test these values and update the database. However, we must also retrieve a listing if the form is to amend an event rather than add a new one. The `$event_id` variable will be passed to this page in a query string if we are to work with an existing listing. If the `$event_id` variable is not empty, we use `getRow()` to populate a variable called `$event_row` with the event's data. If the `$event_id` variable is absent or empty, we initialize it to `false`.

If the form has been submitted, we test that all essential data has been provided. We also test that the date and time chosen have not already passed. In so doing, we set a global variable called `$date` to a time stamp based on the previous input.

If the submitted data checks out to our satisfaction, we call another `dblib.inc` function called`insertEvent()`. As you can see, this requires all the fields in the `events` table. The final field required is an ID for the event. This will be used by `insertEvent()` to determine whether it should be updating or inserting data. Notice that the ID of the club is stored in the `$session[id]` variable. This will be placed in the `eclub` field of the `events` table. We are using a time stamp to store date information in the database.

LISTING 23.18 An Extract from `dblib.inc`

```
 1: function insertEvent( $name, $venue, $area, $type, $address,
 2: $zip, $desc, $club_id, $timestamp, $event_id )
 3:     {
 4:     global $link;
 5:     if ( ! $event_id )
 6:         {
 7:         $query = "INSERT INTO events (ename, evenue, area, type,
 8:               eaddress, ezip, edescription, eclub, edate )
 9:                 VALUES( '$name', '$venue', '$area', '$type', '$address',
10:                         '$zip', '$desc', '$club_id', '$timestamp')";
11:         }
12:     else
13:         {
14:         $query = "UPDATE events SET ename='$name', evenue='$venue',
15:                   area='$area', type='$type', eaddress='$address',
16:                   ezip='$zip', edescription='$desc', eclub='$club_id',
17:                   edate='$timestamp' WHERE id='$event_id'";
18:         }
19:     $result = mysql_query( $query, $link );
20:     if ( ! $result )
21:         die ( "insertEvent error: ".mysql_error() );
22:     }
```

As you can see, the `insertEvent()` function tests the `$event_id` argument. If this resolves to false, then an `INSERT` statement will be built. Otherwise, `$event_id` will be used as the condition in an `UPDATE` statement.

After the database has been updated, we redirect the member to `reviewevents.php` where she can see her entire schedule.

If the member has not yet submitted data, we will have skipped the data check and database amendment code. If we have an `$event_id` variable, however, we have cached event data from the database that we need to present in our form. We do this by assigning `$event_row` to the `$form` variable. We also set the global `$date` variable to the `edate` element of `$event_row`.

If the form has not been submitted and there is no `$event_id`, we set the `$form[area]` and `$form[type]` elements to their equivalents for the club data we have stored in `$club_row`. Remember that `$club_row` contains a row from the `clubs` table. This causes the respective pull-down menus to default to the values the member set for her club's area and type.

Within the HTML form, the only code of any note is the code that writes the pull-down menus for event date and time. These menus would be easy enough to hard-code, but we need them to automatically select either the current time, the time that the member last chose, or the time stored in the `events` table. We have already stored this in the `$date` variable. This is initialized to the current time stamp at the beginning of the script. If user input is detected, we build a new time stamp based on these choices and assign it to `$date`. Otherwise, if we are amending an existing event, we populate `$date` with the value from the `edate` field in the `events` table.

Each of the pull-downs passes the time stamp in `$date` to a relevant function stored in yet another library file called `date.inc`. You can see these in Listing 23.19.

LISTING 23.19 `date.inc`

```
 1: <?php
 2: function writeMonthOptions( $d )
 3:     {
 4:     $d_array = getDate( $d );
 5:     $months = array( "Jan","Feb","Mar","Apr","May","Jun",
 6:                      "Jul","Aug","Sep","Oct","Nov","Dec" );
 7:     foreach ( $months as $key=>$value )
 8:         {
 9:         print "<OPTION VALUE=\"".($key+1)."\"";
10:         print ( ( $d_array[mon] == ($key+1) )?"SELECTED":"" );
11:         print ">$value\n";
12:         }
13:     }
14: function writeDayOptions( $d )
15:     {
16:     $d_array = getDate( $d );
17:     for ( $x = 1; $x<=31; $x++ )
18:         {
19:         print "<OPTION VALUE=\"$x\"";
20:         print ( ( $d_array[mday] == $x )?"SELECTED":"" );
21:         print ">$x\n";
22:         }
23:     }
24: function writeYearOptions( $d )
25:     {
26:     $d_array = getDate( $d );
27:     $now_array = getDate(time());
28:     for ( $x = $now_array[year]; $x <= ($now_array[year]+5); $x++ )
29:         {
30:         print "<OPTION VALUE=\"$x\"";
31:         print ( ( $d_array[year] == $x )?"SELECTED":"" );
32:         print ">$x\n";
33:         }
```

LISTING 23.19 continued

```
34:         }
35: function writeHourOptions( $d )
36:         {
37:         $d_array = getDate( $d );
38:         for ( $x = 0; $x< 24; $x++ )
39:             {
40:             print "<OPTION VALUE=\"$x\"";
41:             print ( ( $d_array[hours] == $x )?"SELECTED":"" );
42:             print ">".sprintf("%'02d",$x)."\n";
43:             }
44:         }
45: function writeMinuteOptions( $d )
46:         {
47:         $d_array = getDate( $d );
48:         for ( $x = 0; $x<= 59; $x++ )
49:             {
50:             print "<OPTION VALUE=\"$x\"";
51:             print ( ( $d_array[minutes] == $x )?"SELECTED":"" );
52:             print ">".sprintf("%'02d",$x)."\n";
53:             }
54:         }
55: ?>
```

All these functions accept a time stamp and write a list of HTML `OPTION` tags. They use `getDate()` to acquire an index for the relevant portion of the date stamp (year, month, day of month, hour, minute). They can then compare this number with each of the numbers within their range (1 to 31 for months, or 0 to 59 for minutes). If a match is found, they add the string `SELECTED` to the `OPTION` element that they write to the browser.

Figure 23.4 shows the output from Listing 23.17.

reviewevents.php

Finally, we must provide members with a way of reviewing all the events they have set up. They should see a list of all events and be able to edit or delete any one of them.

`reviewevents.php` is relatively simple. You can see it in Listing 23.20.

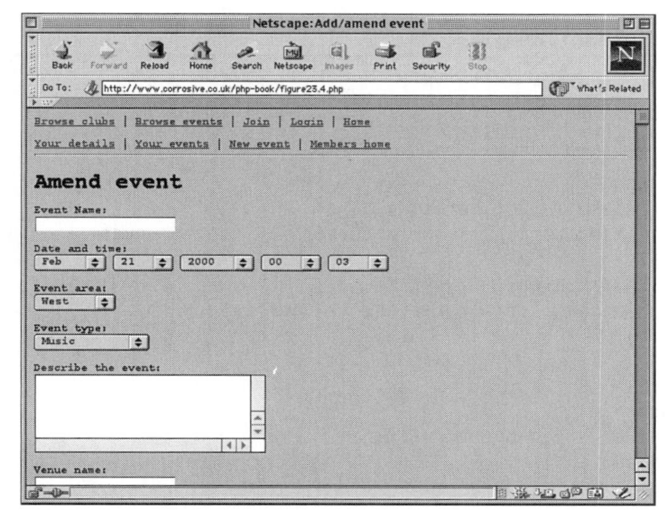

FIGURE 23.4
Output of Listing 23.17.

LISTING 23.20 reviewevents.php

```
 1: <?php
 2: include("dblib.inc");
 3: include("clublib.inc");
 4: $club_row = checkUser();
 5: checkClubData( $club_row );
 6: function writeEvents()
 7:     {
 8:     global $club_row;
 9:     $events = getEvents( $club_row[id] );
10:     if ( ! $events )
11:         {
12:         print "You have no events in your schedule<P>";
13:         return;
14:         }
15:     print "<table border=1>\n";
16:     print "<td><b>Date</b></td>\n<td><b>Name</b></td>\n
17:             <td><b> </b></td>\n";
18:     foreach ( $events as $row )
19:         {
20:         print "<tr>\n";
21:         print "<td>".date("j M Y H.i", $row[edate])."</td>\n";
22:         print "<td><a href=\"updateevent.php?event_id=$row[id]&".SID."\">".
23:                 html($row[ename])."</a></td>\n";
24:         print "<td><a href=\"$GLOBALS[PHP_SELF]?event_id=$row[id]";
25:         print "&actionflag=deleteEvent&".SID."\"";
26:         print "onClick=\"return window.confirm('Are you sure you
27:                 want to delete this item')\">";
28:         print "delete</a><br></td>\n";
```

LISTING 23.20 continued

```
29:         print "</tr>\n";
30:         }
31:     print "</table>\n";
32:     }
33: $message="";
34: if ( isset( $actionflag ) &&
35:      $actionflag == "deleteEvent" && isset( $event_id ) )
36:     {
37:     deleteEvent( $event_id );
38:     $message .= "That event is now history!<br>";
39:     }
40: ?>
41: <html>
42: <head>
43: <title>Review events</title>
44: </head>
45: <body>
46: <?php
47: include("publicnav.inc");
48: ?>
49: <h1>Review event schedule</h1>
50: <?php
51: if ( $message != "" )
52:     {
53:     print "<b>$message</b>";
54:     }
55: ?>
56:
57: <?php
58: writeEvents();
59: ?>
60: </body>
61: </html>
```

Having used `dblib.inc` to start the database connection and `clublib.inc` functions to resume the session and refuse access to unregistered users, we create a function called `writeEvents()`. This can be called from anywhere in the body of the HTML and directly outputs event information to the browser. We already have club information stored in `$club_row`, which contains the information returned by `checkUser()`. We can use the club ID stored in `$club_row[id]` as the key to unlock all the events associated with the member's club. To do this, we use a `dblib.inc` function called `getEvents()`. We will cover this function in more detail in the next hour. However, it accepts a club ID and returns a multidimensional array containing every event row associated with the club.

We store the return value from getEvents() in a variable called $events. In fact, we are retrieving more information than we need, but the getEvents() function is flexible, so we should use it unless we experience performance problems with our script. If the value contained in $events resolves to false, we print a message to the browser and end the function. Otherwise, we build an HTML table. Looping through the $events array, we print some of the elements from each of its subarrays.

We output a formatted date by passing the edate element of each subarray to the date() function. We also create an HTML link using each found event's id and ename fields. The id field is used with the SID constant to create a query string that can be passed to updateevent.php and then used to retrieve the event for editing. Finally, within our loop, we create a link for each element that points back to the current page. For this, we construct a query string that combines the event's ID and an actionflag parameter with the value deleteEvent. This will be used to delete the given event, so we also build a JavaScript event handler that will prevent the link from activating if the member changes her mind.

Having created the writeEvents() function, we must handle the possibility that the member has chosen to delete an event. We can do this by testing the $actionflag and $event_id variables. If these check out, we call a dblib.inc function called deleteEvent() passing it the $event_id variable.

LISTING 23.21 An Extract from dblib.inc

```
1: function deleteEvent( $id )
2:     {
3:     global $link;
4:     $query = "DELETE FROM events WHERE id='$id'";
5:     $result = mysql_query( $query, $link );
6:     if ( ! $result )
7:         die ( "deleteEvent fatal error: ".mysql_error() );
8:     return ( mysql_affected_rows($link) );
9:     }
```

You can see sample output from reviewevents.php in Figure 23.5.

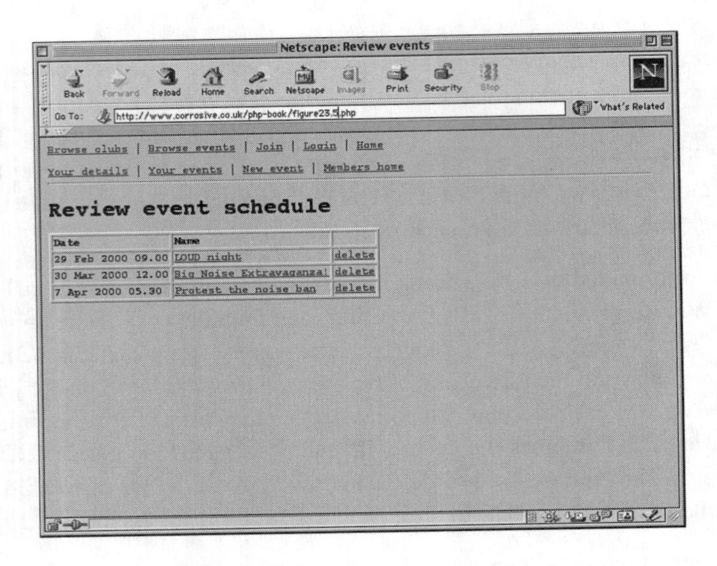

FIGURE 23.5
Output of `review-events.php`.

Summary

We now have a complete working members environment for our events script. By putting as much code as possible into libraries, we have made it possible for Web designers to work effectively around our code. We have used the `header()` function to move the user on to new pages when input is acceptable. We have used session functions to store login information and database queries to authenticate our member with every request.

In the next hour, we will use similar techniques to build the public face of our environment.

Q&A

Q I find projects spread across multiple pages difficult to visualize and control. Is there a secret?

A We have used a model based on a single script for most examples in this book. When a project grows beyond a single script, you need to think of the entire environment as a single application. Individual pages are just points of interaction with the user. Keep any code used by more than one page in a function in a library file.

If you would prefer to create a more centralized script, you could create a single page that contains only basic HTML templating. All other elements can then be generated dynamically by your script. You will need to pass an action flag of some kind to the script for every request so that the correct output is generated. This can make your code much neater and avoids the need for the less than elegant `Location` header solution. On the other hand, it will also involve embedding much more HTML in your PHP code.

Workshop

The Workshop provides quiz questions to help you solidify your understanding of the material covered. Try to understand the quiz answers before continuing to the next hour's lesson. Quiz answers are provided in Appendix A.

Quiz

1. What PHP function do we use to make our connection to the MySQL database server?
2. What PHP function do we use to initiate or resume a session?
3. Which function do we use to include library files in our project's pages?
4. What PHP function do we use to send SQL queries to the MySQL database?
5. What constant do we use to add a session ID to an HTML link?
6. How do we move the user on to a new page?
7. What function do we use to format date information?

Activity

1. Review the code introduced in this hour. Are there any techniques or issues that might have relevance for your own projects?

Hour 24

An Example (Part 2)

In Hour 23, "An Example (Part 1)," we built an environment that allows users to subscribe to a service and to add club and event information to it. Now we will create the scripts necessary to allow the general user browse this information.

In this hour, you will learn

- How to create functions that extract data from multiple tables with a single request
- How to create functions that vary the structure of a SQL query according to the parameters that they are passed
- How to save user search options using session functions
- How to prepare plain text data for presentation in an HTML environment

The Events Diary Public Screens

Now that members can register their clubs and events with our database, we must build screens that will allow the general user to access this information. These screens will enable the user to browse rather than search for information, although it wouldn't be difficult to add further functionality.

In this section, we will build four screens that will enable a user to see listings that match his area or interest for any given month.

`viewevents.php`

The `viewevents.php` screen allows the user to browse entered events. It is similar in some ways to the `reviewevents.php` screen covered in the preceding hour but allows the user greater range and flexibility in viewing, if not editing, data. You can see the code for this screen in Listing 24.1

LISTING 24.1 `viewevents.php`

```
 1: <?php
 2: include("dblib.inc");
 3: include("date.inc");
 4: include("clublib.inc");
 5:
 6: if ( isset($actionflag) && $actionflag == "showEvents" )
 7:     $session[viewevents] = $form;
 8: elseif ( $session[viewevents] )
 9:     $form = $session[viewevents];
10: else
11:     {
12:     $d_array = getDate( time() );
13:     $session[viewevents][area] = "ANY";
14:     $session[viewevents][type] = "ANY";
15:     $session[viewevents][months] = $d_array[mon];
16:     $session[viewevents][years] = $d_array[year];
17:     }
18:
19: $range = getDateRange( $session[viewevents][months],
20:                        $session[viewevents][years] );
21: function displayEvents(  )
22:     {
23:     global $range, $session;
24:
25:     $events = getEvents( 0, $range, $session[viewevents][area],
26:                          $session[viewevents][type] );
27:     if ( ! $events )
28:         {
```

LISTING 24.1 continued

```
29:             print "No events yet for this combination<p>";
30:             return;
31:             }
32:         print "<table border=1>\n";
33:         print "<td><b>Date</b></td>\n";
34:         print "<td><b>Event</b></td>\n";
35:         print "<td><b>Club</b></td>\n";
36:         print "<td><b>Area</b></td>\n";
37:         print "<td><b>Type</b></td>\n";
38:         foreach ( $events as $row )
39:             {
40:             print "<tr>\n";
41:             print "<td>".date("j M Y H.i", $row[edate])."</td>\n";
42:             print "<td><a href=\"viewevent.php?event_id=$row[id]&".SID."\">".
43:                   html($row[ename])."</a></td>\n";
44:             print "<td><a href=\"viewclub.php?club_id=$row[eclub]&".SID."\">".
45:                   html($row[name])."</a></td>\n";
46:             print "<td>$row[areaname]</td>\n";
47:             print "<td>$row[typename]</td>\n";
48:             print "</tr>\n";
49:             }
50:         print "</table>\n";
51:         }
52: ?>
53:
54: <html>
55: <head>
56: <title>View events</title>
57: </head>
58: <body>
59: <?php
60: include("publicnav.inc");
61: ?>
62: <h1>View Events</h1>
63: <p>
64: <form action="<?php print $PHP_SELF;?>">
65: <input type="hidden" name="actionflag" value="showEvents">
66: <input type="hidden" name="<?php print session_name() ?>"
67:        value="<?php print session_id() ?>">
68: <select name=form[months]>
69: <?php writeMonthOptions( $range[0] ); ?>
70: </select>
71:
72: <select name=form[years]>
73: <?php writeYearOptions( $range[0] ); ?>
74: </select>
75:
76: <select name=form[area]>
77: <option value="ANY">Any Area
```

24

LISTING 24.1 continued

```
78: <?php writeOptionList( "areas", $form[area] ) ?>
79: </select>
80:
81: <select name=form[type]>
82: <option value="ANY">Any type of event
83: <?php writeOptionList( "types", $form[type] ) ?>
84: </select>
85:
86: <input type = "submit" value="Change">
87: </form>
88: </p>
89:
90: <?php
91: displayEvents( );
92: ?>
93:
94: </body>
95: </html>
```

We begin the code by including the library files `dblib.inc`, `date.inc`, and `clublib.inc`. As well as giving access to the functions contained in these files, including `dblib.inc` and `clublib.inc` ensures that we open a database connection and that we start or resume a session.

We then check whether the user has submitted a form on the page by testing a variable called `$actionflag`. The equivalent field `actionflag` is embedded as a hidden variable in the page's form. If the user has submitted a form, her choices must take precedence over any options we have previously saved. In the preceding hour, you saw how we registered an associative array variable with our user session to store login details. In this hour, we will add new elements to the same array that will keep track of the user's preferences.

The `$session` variable was registered with the user session when we included the `clublib.php` file.

```
session_start();
session_register( "session" );
```

We now turn the `$session` variable into a multidimensional array by assigning associative array elements to an element called `$session[viewevents]`. In doing this, we keep option variables categorized as belonging only to this screen. The options that the user can choose on this page are area, type, months, and years. We assign the form choices that the user has made to `$session[viewevents]` elements of the same name.

If the user has not submitted the form on this page, she might have done so in the past. In which case, the `$session[viewevents]` array will be set, but the `$actionflag` variable will not. If so, we set the `$form` array to the same values. This will ensure that the form shows the correct settings.

If the user has not submitted the screen's form and the `$session[viewevents]` element is empty, then we must construct the array based on default values. We use the `getDate()` function to build an array of date indices. This array is used to set the `$session[viewevents][months]` element to the current month index and the `$session[viewevents][years]` to the current year.

We now know that the `$session[viewevents][months]` and `$session[viewevents][years]` elements contain the correct month and year values, whether they derive from form submission, a user session, or the default of the current date. We pass these values to a new function in `date.inc` called `getDateRange()`. This function accepts values for month and year and returns an array of two time stamps, marking the beginning and end of the month.

LISTING 24.2 An Extract from `date.inc`

```
1: function getDateRange( $mon, $year )
2:     {
3:     $start = mktime( 0, 0, 0, $mon, 1, $year );
4:     $end = mktime( 0, 0, 0, $mon+1, 1, $year );
5:     $end--;
6:     return array( $start, $end );
7:     }
```

The array returned by this function is stored in the global variable `$range`.

We create a function called `displayEvents()` that will write the chosen event summaries to the browser. This will be called from the body of the HTML document.

To get an array of event summaries, we call the `getEvents()` function, which is stored in the `dblib.inc` file we included earlier. We encountered this function in the preceding hour, but exploited little of its flexibility.

LISTING 24.3 An Extract from `dlib.inc`

```
1: function getEvents( $club_id=0, $range=0, $area=0, $type=0 )
2:     {
3:     global $link;
4:     $query  = "SELECT clubs.name, events.*, areas.area as areaname,
5:                 types.type as typename ";
```

LISTING 24.3 continued

```
 6:     $query .= "FROM clubs, events, areas, types WHERE ";
 7:     $query .= "clubs.id=events.eclub
 8:             AND events.area=areas.id
 9:             AND events.type=types.id ";
10:     if ( ! empty( $club_id ) && $club_id !="ANY"  )
11:         $query .= "AND events.eclub='$club_id' ";
12:     if ( ! empty($range) )
13:         $query .= "AND events.edate >= '$range[0]' AND
14:                     events.edate <='$range[1]' ";
15:     if ( ! empty($area) && $area != "ANY" )
16:         $query .= "AND events.area='$area' ";
17:     if ( ! empty($type) && $type != "ANY" )
18:         $query .= "AND events.type='$type' ";
19:     $query .= "ORDER BY events.edate";
20:      $result = mysql_query( $query, $link );
21:     if ( ! $result )
22:         die ( "getIDevents fatal error: ".mysql_error() );
23:     $ret = array();
24:     while ( $row = mysql_fetch_array( $result ) )
25:         array_push( $ret, $row );
26:     return $ret;
27:     }
```

Although this function is called `getEvents()`, it gets a lot more than that. As you can see, it accepts four arguments: a club ID, a date range in the form of an array of two time stamps, an area code, and a type code. All these arguments are optional and could be replaced by either 0 or false if you don't want them to form part of a SQL query.

The bulk of the function dynamically builds a SQL query based on the arguments passed to it. The core query joins all the tables in the database, ensuring that the club name, area name (as opposed to its code), and type name will be included in the resultset.

```
$query  = "SELECT clubs.name, events.*, areas.area as areaname,
            types.type as typename ";
$query .= "FROM clubs, events, areas, types WHERE ";
$query .= "clubs.id=events.eclub
        AND events.area=areas.id
        AND events.type=types.id ";
```

Thereafter, additional conditions are added to the query depending on whether the corresponding function arguments are set to empty values. The `$type` and `$area` parameter variables will also be ignored if they contain the string `"ANY"`.

In practice, this means that the more arguments this function receives, the narrower the resultset it returns. Given no arguments, it will return every event in the events table. Given a `$club_id` argument, it will only return events associated with a particular club. Given a `$range` array, it will only return events whose time stamps fall within that period, and so on.

Finally, the query is submitted and a multidimensional array containing the resultset returned.

Having acquired this array as a result of a call to `getEvents()`, we only need to loop through it. We use each `edate` field to format a date in conjunction with the `date()` function. We then build a link to `viewevent.php`, which will provide more information about the event. For this, we construct a query string containing the event's ID and the `SID` constant. In this loop, we also create an HTML hyperlink to `viewclub.php`, creating a query string that contains the club ID for the event and the `SID` constant.

Finally, we print the names of the event's type and area.

You may have noticed in the preceding hour, that we used a function called `html()` when we output member event data in summary form. As we loop through event data in the `writeEvents()` function, we call `html()` again. This function is user-defined and lives in the `clublib.inc` library. It accepts a string and returns a transformed version that's suitable for printing to the browser. Special characters are converted to HTML entities, and newlines have `BR` tags added to them.

LISTING 24.4 An Extract from `clublib.inc`

```
 1: function html( $str )
 2:     {
 3:     if ( is_array( $str ) )
 4:         {
 5:         foreach ( $str as $key=>$val )
 6:             $str[$key] = htmlstr( $val );
 7:         return $str;
 8:         }
 9:     return htmlstr( $str );
10:     }
11: function htmlstr( $str )
12:     {
13:     $str = htmlspecialchars( $str );
14:     $str = nl2br( $str );
15:     return $str;
16:     }
```

As you can see, this is not one but two functions. `html()` accepts either a string or an array. If the parameter variable contains an array, we loop through it, converting each value. Otherwise, the conversion is applied directly to the parameter variable. The actual conversion is affected in another function `htmlstr()`, which applies two built-in functions to the given string. `htmlspecialcharacters()` converts any character that might not display well in an HTML environment to its HTML entity equivalent. `nl2br()` adds `BR` tags to the string where appropriate.

Having set default data and created a function to output event information, all that is left is to build a form to allow the user to choose how she wants to browse the events.

The user choice form is easy to build using the functions explored in the preceding hour, which dynamically output HTML `OPTION` elements.

Figure 24.1 shows sample output from `viewevents.php`.

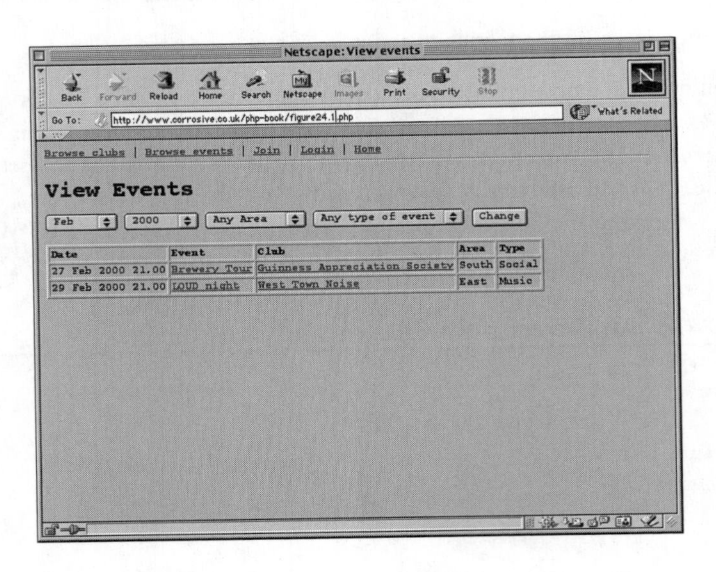

FIGURE 24.1
Output from `viewevents.php`.

viewclubs.php

The user might want to view the database according to the clubs it contains rather than its events, narrowing the found set according to a club's type and area. The `viewclubs.php` screen allows her to do this. You can see this script in Listing 24.5.

LISTING 24.5 viewclubs.php

```
 1: <?php
 2: include("dblib.inc");
 3: include("date.inc");
 4: include("clublib.inc");
 5: if ( isset($actionflag) && $actionflag == "showClubs" )
 6:     $session[viewclubs] = $form;
 7: elseif ( $session[viewclubs] )
 8:     $form = $session[viewclubs];
 9: else
10:     {
11:     $session[viewclubs][area] = "ANY";
12:     $session[viewclubs][type] = "ANY";
13:     }
14: function displayClubs(  )
15:     {
16:     global $session;
17:     $clubs = getClubs( $session[viewclubs][area],
18:                        $session[viewclubs][type] );
19:     if ( ! $clubs )
20:         {
21:         print "No clubs yet that fit these conditions<p>\n";
22:         return;
23:         }
24:     print "<table border=1>\n";
25:     print "<td><b>Club</b></td>\n";
26:     print "<td><b>Area</b></td>\n";
27:     print "<td><b>Type</b></td>\n";
28:     foreach ( $clubs as $row )
29:         {
30:         print "<tr>\n";
31:         print "<td><a href=\"viewclub.php?club_id=$row[id]&".SID."\">".
32:               html($row[name])."</a></td>\n";
33:         print "<td>$row[areaname]</td>\n";
34:         print "<td>$row[typename]</td>\n";
35:         print "</tr>\n";
36:         }
37:     print "</table>\n";
38:     }
39: ?>
40: <html>
41: <head>
42: <title>View clubs</title>
43: </head>
44: <body>
45: <?php
46: include("publicnav.inc");
47: ?>
48: <P>
49: <h1>View Clubs</h1>
```

LISTING 24.5 continued

```
50: <p>
51: <form action="<?php print $PHP_SELF;?>">
52: <input type="hidden" name="actionflag" value="showClubs">
53: <input type="hidden" name="<?php print session_name() ?>"
54:        value="<?php print session_id() ?>">
55: <select name=form[area]>
56: <option value="ANY">Any Area
57: <?php writeOptionList( "areas", $form[area] ) ?>
58: </select>
59: <select name=form[type]>
60: <option value="ANY">Any type of club
61: <?php writeOptionList( "types", $form[type] ) ?>
62: </select>
63: <input type = "submit" value="Change">
64: </form>
65: </p>
66: <?php
67: displayClubs( );
68: ?>
69: </body>
70: </html>
```

As you can see, this script is similar in structure and logic to the previous example. We store session variables for this page in `$session[viewclubs]`. If the user has submitted the page's form, we update the session variables. If the user has not submitted the form but session variables are available, we assign `$session[viewclubs]` to the `$form` variable. If all else fails, we populate the `$session[viewclubs]` array with default values.

We create a function called `displayClubs()`. Within this function, we call a new `dblib.inc` function called `getClubs()`. This function will optionally accept values for either the type or area fields in the `clubs` table:

LISTING 24.6 An Extract from `dlib.inc`

```
 1: function getClubs( $area="", $type="" )
 2:     {
 3:     global $link;
 4:     $query  = "SELECT clubs.*, areas.area as areaname,
 5:                types.type as typename ";
 6:     $query .= "FROM clubs, areas, types WHERE ";
 7:     $query .= "clubs.area=areas.id AND clubs.type=types.id ";
 8:     if ( $area != "ANY" && ! empty( $area ) )
 9:         $query .= "AND clubs.area='$area' ";
10:      if ( $type != "ANY" && ! empty( $type ) )
11:          $query .= "AND clubs.type='$type' ";
```

LISTING 24.6 continued

```
12:     $query .= "ORDER BY clubs.area, clubs.type, clubs.name";
13:      $result = mysql_query( $query, $link );
14:     if ( ! $result )
15:         die ( "getIDevents fatal error: ".mysql_error() );
16:     $ret = array();
17:     while ( $row = mysql_fetch_array( $result ) )
18:         array_push( $ret, $row );
19:     return $ret;
20:     }21:
```

getClubs() builds a dynamic SQL query based on the arguments it is passed. By default, it joins the clubs, areas, and types tables. If it is passed anything other than an empty string, or the string "ANY" for its $type and $area arguments, it will further narrow the WHERE condition according to these values. Once again, it will return a multidimensional array.

We loop through the array returned by getClubs() writing name, areaname, and typename fields to the browser. As before, the club name forms part of a hyperlink pointing to viewclub.php.

viewclub.php

The viewclub.php screen displays all information associated with a club. It can be reached via hyperlinks in either viewevents.php or viewclubs.php. In terms of its code, it combines the logic and many of the functions that you have seen in previous examples. You can see the code for this screen in Listing 24.7.

LISTING 24.7 viewclub.php

```
 1: <?php
 2: include("dblib.inc");
 3: include("clublib.inc");
 4: if ( ! isset($club_id) )
 5:     header( "Location: viewclubs.php?".SID );
 6: $club = getClubJoined( $club_id );
 7: $club = html( $club );
 8: if ( $club[mail] != "" )
 9:     $club[mail] = "<A HREF=\"mailto:$club[mail]\">$club[mail]</A>";
10: function displayEvents()
11:     {
12:     global $club_id;
13:     $events = getEvents( $club_id );
14:     if ( ! $events )
15:         {
```

LISTING 24.7 continued

```
16:          print "No events yet for this club<P>";
17:          return;
18:          }
19:      print "<table border=1>\n";
20:      print "<td><b>Date</b></td>\n";
21:      print "<td><b>Event</b></td>\n";
22:      print "<td><b>Area</b></td>\n";
23:      print "<td><b>Type</b></td>\n";
24:      foreach ( $events as $row )
25:          {
26:          print "<tr>\n";
27:          print "<td>".date("j M Y H.i", $row[edate])."</td>\n";
28:          print "<td><a href=\"viewevent.php?event_id=$row[id]&".SID."\">".
29:                 html($row[ename])."</a></td>\n";
30:          print "<td>$row[areaname]</td>\n";
31:          print "<td>$row[typename]</td>\n";
32:          print "</tr>\n";
33:          }
34:      print "</table>\n";
35:      }
36: ?>
37: <html>
38: <head>
39: <title>View clubs</title>
40: </head>
41: <body>
42: <?php
43: include("publicnav.inc");
44: ?>
45: <p>
46: <h1>View club details</h1>
47: <h4><?php print $club[name] ?></h4>
48: <p>
49: Area: <b><?php print $club[areaname] ?></b>
50: <br>
51: Type: <b><?php print $club[typename] ?></b>
52: <BR>
53: Mail: <b><?php print $club[mail] ?></b>
54: </p>
55: Description:<br>
56: <b><?php print $club[description] ?></b>
57: <hr>
58: <?php
59: displayEvents();
60: ?>
61: </body>
62: </html>
```

This script requires a `$club_id` parameter. We test for this and return the user to the `viewclubs.php` screen if we don't find it. To get club information, we call the `dblib.inc` function `getClubJoined()`. This accepts a club ID and returns an array:

LISTING 24.8 An Extract from `dlib.inc`

```
 1: function getClubJoined( $id )
 2:     {
 3:     global $link;
 4:     $query  = "SELECT clubs.*, areas.area as areaname, types.type as typename
➥";
 5:     $query .= "FROM clubs, events, areas, types WHERE ";
 6:     $query .= "clubs.area=areas.id
 7:             AND clubs.type=types.id
 8:             AND clubs.id='$id'";
 9:      $result = mysql_query( $query, $link );
10:     if ( ! $result )
11:         die ( "getClubJoined fatal error: ".mysql_error() );
12:     return mysql_fetch_array( $result );
13:     }
```


We call this function rather than `getRow()` (which could also return club data) because the SQL query it builds includes the names associated with the `area` and `type` fields. It does this by performing a join between the `clubs`, `areas`, and `types` tables producing additional elements in the return array called `areaname` and `typename`, respectively.

We store the array returned by `getClubJoined()` in a variable called `$club`. The `$club` array is written to the browser in the body of the document. We also define a function called `displayEvents()`, which acquires a list of events associated with the club by passing the `$club_id` variable to the `getEvents()` function.

Figure 24.2 shows typical output from `viewclub.php`.

viewevent.php

`viewevent.php` is the final screen in our script. It provides complete information about any individual event and can be reached via hyperlinks from any public pages that list event summaries. You can see the code for this page in Listing 24.9.

LISTING 24.9 `viewevent.php`

```
1: <?php
2: include("dblib.inc");
3: include("clublib.inc");
4: if ( ! isset($event_id) )
```

Listing 24.9 continued

```
 5:     header( "Location: viewevents.php?".SID );
 6: $event = getEvent( $event_id );
 7: html( $event );
 8: ?>
 9: <html>
10: <head>
11: <title>View event details</title>
12: </head>
13: <body>
14: <?php
15: include("publicnav.inc");
16: ?>
17: <P>
18: <h1>View event details</h1>
19: <h4><?php print $event[ename] ?></h4>
20: <p>
21: Club:
22: <b>
23: <?php print "<a href=\"viewclub.php?club_id=$event[eclub]&".SID."\">
24: $event[clubname]</a>"
25: ?>
26: </b>
27: <br>
28: Area: <b><?php print $event[areaname] ?></b>
29: <br>
30: Type: <b><?php print $event[typename] ?></b>
31: </p>
32: Description:<br>
33: <?php print $event[edescription] ?>
34: </body>
35: </html>
```

As you can see, this screen is simple. We acquire an array from the events table using the `dblib.inc` function `getEvent()`, passing it the variable `$event_id` that should contain the ID value passed to us via a query string. After we have this array, it is simply a matter of writing it to the browser.

You can see the `getEvent()` function in Listing 24.10. It consists of a relatively simple SQL statement that joins the `clubs` and `events` tables.

Listing 24.10 An Extract from `dlib.inc`

```
1: function getEvent( $event_id )
2:  {
3:  global $link;
4:
```

LISTING 24.10 continued

```
 5: $query  = "SELECT clubs.name as clubname, events.*,
 6:                  areas.area as areaname, types.type as typename ";
 7: $query .= "FROM clubs, events, areas, types WHERE ";
 8: $query .= "clubs.id=events.eclub
 9:     AND events.area=areas.id
10:     AND events.type=types.id
11:     AND events.id='$event_id'";
12:  $result = mysql_query( $query, $link );
13: if ( ! $result )
14:  die ( "getEvent fatal error: ".mysql_error() );
15: return mysql_fetch_array( $result );
16: }
```


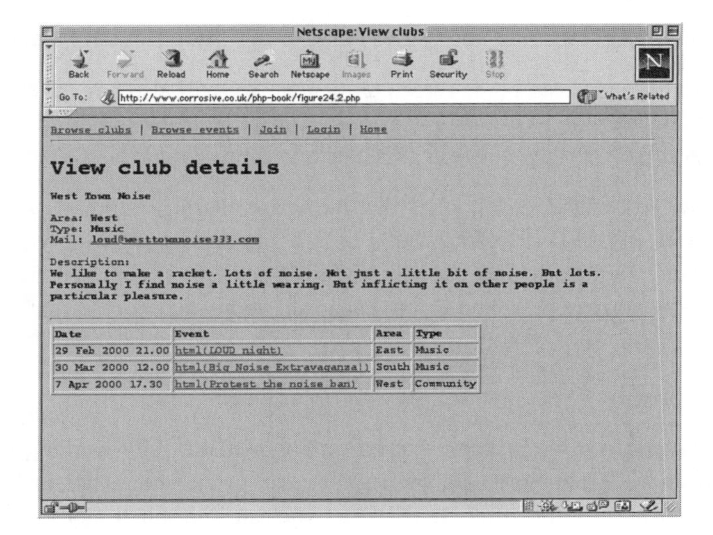

FIGURE 24.2
Output from `viewclub.php`.

The Future

We have now worked through the entire events diary script. I hope that it has given you some feel for the dynamics of a small real-world project and a sense of what is possible with PHP.

In particular, notice how easy PHP's session functions make it to save user preferences from page to page. If our user returns to the `viewevents.php` screen at any time within a single session, she will see the same choices that she made on her previous visit to this screen. Without the session functions, we would probably have to pass much more information from request to request using URL query strings.

Although the events diary is complete in some senses, it nonetheless represents a prototype, enough to show to a client as work in progress. It would benefit from a few more features, most notably a keyword search. It would also be nice to allow visitors to comment on the events listed. This could add an entirely new dimension to the script, making it a compulsive environment to visit.

We might want to allow club administrators to include links to images that can be incorporated in club summaries. We could even allow administrators to upload images via the browser.

Members might also be allowed to clone events and to make events recurring.

Before the script can be delivered to a client, we will also have to build an administration environment, with tools to allow a non-technical producer to edit and remove both accounts and events as well as add and edit area and type categories.

Finally, you might have noticed that the script output is currently somewhat spartan. We will need to hand our work on to a design and build team who will add branding, slick navigation, and additional content. Luckily, most of our code will be easy to work around, although we may be called on to amend the loops that output summary information.

Summary

In this hour and the preceding hour, we completed a fully working multi-screen Web application. We explored techniques for saving state, authenticating users, manipulating and presenting information stored in a database, and much more.

A multi-screen code example is not easy to work through in a book, but it is worth persevering. We have addressed issues that you will encounter time and time again in your projects. Almost any script you write will have to handle more than one request, so you will need to build strategies for maintaining state information.

Q&A

Q Well, that's it. What next?

A Now it's over to you. This book contains enough information for you to build your own sophisticated scripts and environments. Armed with this and with the wealth of information available online, there should be no stopping you!

Workshop

The Workshop provides quiz questions to help you solidify your understanding of the material covered. Try to understand the quiz answers before continuing to the next hour's lesson. Quiz answers are provided in Appendix A.

Quiz

1. What function do you use to add an element to the end of an array?
2. Is it possible to add an element to an array without using a function?
3. Which function do you use to translate special characters into HTML format?
4. Which function do you use to translate newline characters into `<BR>` tags?
5. You can use the `SID` constant to pass the session ID to another page via an HTML link. How do you achieve the same effect with a form?

Activities

1. Review the code presented in this hour. Are there any techniques or issues that might have relevance for your own projects?
2. Flip back through the book and through your notes if you have been making them. If you have followed the book as a course, remember that you should revisit your notes a few times to get the full benefit from the work you have done.

APPENDIX A

Answers to the Quiz Questions

This appendix provides answers to the quiz sections at the end of each chapter.

Hour 1

Quiz

1. What did the initials PHP originally stand for?

   PHP originally stood for personal home page, forming a suite of macros called the Personal Home Page Tools.

2. Who created the original version of PHP?

   The original version of PHP was written by Rasmus Lerdorf.

3. What is the name of the new scripting engine that powers PHP?

   Sitting below PHP4 is an entirely new scripting engine called Zend.

4. Name a new feature introduced with PHP4?

   PHP4 introduces (among other things) new array functions, a new statement to loop through arrays called `foreach`, a `boolean` data type, enhanced support for objects, session functions, new built-in variables, and Java and XML support.

Hour 2

Quiz

1. Where can you find the PHP online manual?

   The manual for PHP4 is available at `<http://www.php.net>`.

2. From a UNIX operating system, how would you get help on configuration options (the options that you pass to the `configure` script in your PHP distribution)?

   You can get help on configuration options by calling the `configure` script in the PHP distribution folder and passing it the `-help` argument:

```
./configure --help
```

3. What is Apache's configuration file typically called?

   The Apache configuration file is called `httpd.conf`.

4. What line should you add to the Apache configuration file to ensure that the `.php` extension is recognized?

   The line

```
AddType application/x-httpd-php .php
```

   ensures that Apache will treat files ending with the `.php` extension as PHP4 scripts.

5. What is PHP's configuration file called?

   PHP's configuration file is called `php.ini`.

Hour 3

Quiz

1. Can a user read the source code of PHP script you have successfully installed?

   No, the user will only see the output of your script.

2. What do the standard PHP delimiter tags look like?

```
<?php
// your code here
?>.
```

3. What do the ASP PHP delimiter tags look like?

```
<%
// your code here
%>.
```

4. What do the script PHP delimiter tags look like?

```
<script language="php">
// your code here
</script>.
```

5. What function would you use to output a string to the browser?

```
Print()
```

Hour 4

Quiz

1. Which of the following variable names is not valid?

```
$a_value_submitted_by_a_user
$666666xyz
$xyz666666
$_____counter_____
$the first
$file-name
```

The variable name `$666666xyz` is not valid because it does not begin with a letter or an underscore character. The variable name `$the first` is not valid because it contains a space. `$file-name` is also invalid because it contains a nonalphanumeric character.

2. How could you use the string variable created in the assignment expression

```
$my_var = ''dynamic'';
```

to create a “variable” variable, assigning the integer 4 to it. How might you access this new variable?

You can set a “variable” variable using a dollar sign followed by a string variable. You can access a “variable” variable directly, or by using a string variable.

```
$my_var = ''dynamic'';
$$my_var = 4;

print $dynamic;
print ''${$my_var}'';
```

A

3. What will the following statement output?

```
print gettype(''4'');
```

The statement will output the string "string".

4. What will be the output from the following code fragment?

```
$test_val = 5.4566;
settype( $test_val, ''integer'' );
print $test_val;
```

The code will output the value 5. When a double is converted to an integer, any information beyond the decimal point is lost.

5. Which of the following statements does not contain an expression?

```
4;
gettype(44);
5/12;
```

They are all expressions because they all resolve to values.

6. Which of the statements in question 5 contains an operator?

The statement 5/12; contains a division operator.

7. What value will the following expression return?

```
5 < 2
```

What data type will the returned value be?

The expression will resolve to false, which is a boolean value.

Hour 5

Quiz

1. How would you use an `if` statement to print the string "`Youth message`" to the browser if an integer variable, `$age`, is between 18 and 35? If `$age` contains any other value, the string "`Generic message`" should be printed to the browser.

```
$age = 22;

if ( $age >= 18 && $age <= 35 )
    print ''Youth message<BR>\n'';
else
    print ''Generic message<BR>\n'';
```

2. How would you extend your code in question 1 to print the string `"Child message"` if the `$age` variable is between 1 and 17?

```
$age = 12;

if ( $age >= 18 && $age <= 35 )
    print ''Youth message<BR>\n'';
elseif ( $age >= 1 && $age <= 17 )
    print ''Child message<BR>\n'';
else
    print ''Generic message<BR>\n'';
```

3. How would you create a `while` statement that prints every odd number between 1 and 49?

```
$num = 1;
while ( $num <= 49 )
    {
    print ''$num<BR>\n'';
    $num += 2;
    }
```

4. How would you convert the `while` statement you created in question 3 into a `for` statement?

```
for ( $num = 1; $num <= 49; $num += 2 )
    print ''$num<BR>\n'';
```

A

Hour 6

Quiz

1. True or False: If a function doesn't require an argument, you can omit the parentheses in the function call.

   The statement is false. You must always include the parentheses in your function calls, whether you are passing arguments to the function or not.

2. How do you return a value from a function?

   You must use the `return` keyword.

3. What would the following code fragment print to the browser?

```
$number = 50;

function tenTimes()
    {
    $number = $number * 10;
```

```
    }

tenTimes();
print $number;
```

It would print 50. The `tenTimes()` function has no access to the global `$number` variable. When it is called, it will manipulate its own local `$number` variable.

4. What would the following code fragment print to the browser?

```
$number = 50;

function tenTimes()
    {
    global $number;
    $number = $number * 10;
    }

tenTimes();
print $number;
```

It would print 500. We have used the `global` statement, which gives the `tenTimes()` function access to the `$number` variable.

5. What would the following code fragment print to the browser?

```
$number = 50;

function tenTimes( $n )
    {
    $n = $n * 10;
    }

tenTimes( $number );
print $number;
```

It would print 50. When we pass an argument to the `tenTimes()` function, it is passed by value. In other words, a copy is placed in the parameter variable `$n`. Any changes we make to `$n` have no effect on the `$number` variable.

6. What would the following code fragment print to the browser?

```
$number = 50;

function tenTimes( &$n )
    {
    $n = $n * 10;
    }

tenTimes( $number );
print $number;
```

It would print 500. By adding the ampersand to the parameter variable `$n`, we ensure that this argument is passed by reference. `$n` and `$number` point to the same value, so any changes to `$n` will be reflected when you access `$number`.

Hour 7

Quiz

1. What function can you use to define an array?

   You can create an array with the `array()` function.

2. What is the index number of the last element of the array defined below?

   ```
   $users = array(''Harry'', ''Bob'', ''Sandy'');
   ```

   The last element is `$users[2]`. Remember that arrays are indexed from 0 by default.

3. Without using a function, what would be the easiest way of adding the element "Susan" to the `$users` array defined previously?

   ```
   $users[] = ''Susan'';
   ```

4. Which function could you use to add the string "Susan" to the `$users` array?

   ```
   array_push( $users, ''Susan'' );
   ```

5. How would you find out the number of elements in an array?

   You can count the number of elements in an array with the `count()` function.

6. In PHP4, what is the simplest way of looping through an array?

   You can loop through an array using the `foreach` statement.

7. What function would you use to join two arrays?

   You can merge arrays with the `array_merge()` function.

8. How would you sort an associative array by its keys?

   You can sort an associative array by its keys with the `ksort()` function.

A

Hour 8

Quiz

1. How would you declare a class called `emptyClass()` that has no methods or properties?

   You can declare a class with the `class` keyword:

   ```
   class emptyClass
       {

       }
   ```

2. Given a class called `emptyClass()`, how would you create an object that is an instance of it?

   You should use the `new` operator to instantiate an object:

   ```
   $obj = new emptyClass();
   ```

3. How can you declare a property within a class?

   You can declare a property using the `var` keyword:

   ```
   class Point
       {
       // properties
       var $x = 0;
       var $y = 0;
       }
   ```

4. How would you choose a name for a constructor method?

   You can't choose the name of a constructor. It must take the name of a class that contains it.

5. How would you create a constructor method in a class?

   You can create a constructor by declaring a method that has the same name as the class that contains it. The constructor will be called automatically when an object is instantiated from the class.

   ```
   class Point
       {
       // properties
       var $x = 0;
       var $y = 0;
   ```

```
    // constructor
    function Point( $x, $y )
        {
        // set up code goes here
        }
    }
```

6. How would you create a regular method within a class?

   A method is a function of any name declared within a class:

```
class Point
    {
    // properties
    var $x = 0;
    var $y = 0;

    // constructor
    function Point( $x, $y )
        {
        // set up code goes here
        }

    // method
    function moveTo( $x, $y )
        {

        }
    }
```

7. How can you access and set properties or methods from within a class?

   Within a class, you can access a property or method by combining the `$this` variable and the `->` operator:

```
class Point
    {
    // properties
    var $x = 0;
    var $y = 0;

    // constructor
    function Point( $x, $y )
        {
        // calling a method
        $this->moveTo( $x, $y );
        }

    // method
```

A

```
function moveTo( $x, $y )
    {
    // setting properties
    $this->x = $x;
    $this->y = $y;
    }
}
```

8. How would you access an object's properties and methods from outside the object's class?

   You can call an object's methods and access its properties using a reference to the object (usually stored in a variable) in conjunction with the -> operator:

```
// instantiating an object
$p = new Point( 40, 60 );

// calling an object's method
$p->moveTo( 20, 200 );

// accessing an object's property
print $p->x;
```

9. What should you add to a class definition if you want to make it inherit functionality from another class?

   For a class to inherit from another it must be declared with the `extends` keyword and the name of the class from which you want to inherit:

```
class funkyPoint extends Points
    {
    }
```

Hour 9

Quiz

1. Which environment variable could you use to determine the IP address of a user?

   The variable `$REMOTE_ADDR` should store the user's IP address.

2. Which environment variable could you use to find out about the browser that called your script?

   Browser type and version, as well as the user's operating system, are usually stored in a variable called `$HTTP_USER_AGENT`.

3. What should you name your form fields to access their submitted values from an array variable called `$form_array`?

Creating multiple fields with the name `form_array[]` creates a populated array called `$form_array` when the form is submitted.

4. Which built-in associative array contains all values submitted as part of a `GET` request?

   The built-in array `$HTTP_GET_VARS` contains all values submitted as part of a `GET` request.

5. Which built-in associative array contains all values submitted as part of a `POST` request?

   The built-in array `$HTTP_POST_VARS` contains all values submitted as part of a `POST` request.

6. What function would you use to redirect the browser to a new page? What string would you pass it?

   You can redirect a user by calling the `header()` function. You should pass it a `Location` header:

   ```
   Header(''Location: anotherpage.html'');
   ```

7. How must you limit the size of a file that a user can submit via a particular upload form?

   When creating upload forms in PHP4, you should include a hidden field called `MAX_FILE_SIZE`:

   ```
   <INPUT TYPE="hidden'' NAME="MAX_FILE_SIZE'' VALUE="51200">
   ```

8. How can you set a limit to the size of upload files for all forms and scripts?

   The php.ini option `upload_max_filesize` determines the maximum size of an upload file that any script will accept. This is set to 2 megabytes by default.

Hour 10

Quiz

1. What functions could you use to add library code to the currently running script?

   You can use the `require()` or `include()` functions to incorporate PHP files into the current document.

2. What function would you use to find out whether a file is present on your file system?

   You can test for the existence of a file with the `file_exists()` function.

3. How would you determine the size of a file?

   The `filesize()` function returns a file's size in bytes.

4. What function would you use to open a file for reading or writing?

   The `fopen()` function opens a file. It accepts the path to a file and a character representing the mode. It returns a file pointer.

5. What function would you use to read a line of data from a file?

   The `fgets()` function reads data up to the buffer size you pass it, the end of the line, or the end of the document, whichever comes first.

6. How can you tell when you have reached the end of a file?

   The `feof()` function returns `true` when the file pointer it is passed has reached the end of the file.

7. What function would you use to write a line of data to an open file?

   You can write data to a file with the `fputs()` function.

8. How would you open a directory for reading?

   The `opendir()` function enables you to open a directory for reading.

9. What function would you use to read the name of a directory item after you have opened a directory for reading?

   The `readdir()` function returns the name of a directory item from an opened directory.

Hour 11

Quiz

1. What function would you use to open a DBM database?

   You can open a DBM database with the `dbmopen()` function.

2. What function would you use to insert a record into a DBM database?

   The `dbminsert()` function adds a record to a DBM database.

3. What function would you use to replace a record in a DBM database?

   The `dbmreplace()` function replaces a record in a DBM database.

4. How would you access a record from a DBM database by name?

   The `dbmfetch()` function returns an element given a DBM pointer and the element's name.

5. How would you get the name (as opposed to the value) of the first element in a DBM database?

   dbmfirstkey() returns the name of the first element in a DBM database.

6. How would you get subsequent element names?

   After calling dbmfirstkey(), you can get subsequent element names by calling dbmnextkey().

7. How would you delete a named element from a DBM database?

   You can delete an element with dbmdelete().

Hour 12

Quiz

1. How would you open a connection to a MySQL database server?

   You can connect to a MySQL daemon using the mysql_connect() function.

2. What function would you use to select a database?

   The mysql_select_db() function attempts to select a database.

3. What function would you use to send a SQL query to a database?

   You can send a SQL query to the database server with the mysql_query() function.

4. What does the mysql_insert_id() function do?

   mysql_insert_id() returns the value of an automatically incrementing field after a new row has been added to a table.

5. Assuming that you have sent a successful SELECT query to MySQL, name three functions that you might use to access each row returned.

   You can use the mysql_fetch_row(), mysql_fetch_array(), or mysql_fetch_object() functions to access each row of a found set.

6. Assuming that you have sent a successful UPDATE query to MySQL, what function might you use to determine how many rows have been updated?

   You can discover the number of rows altered by a SQL statement with the mysql_affected_rows() function.

7. What function would you call if you want to list all databases available from a MySQL server?

The `mysql_list_dbs()` function returns a result pointer that can be used to list all the databases available.

8. What function would you use to list all tables within a database?

   The `mysql_list_tables()` function returns a result pointer that can be used to list all the tables within a database.

Hour 13

Quiz

1. What environmental variable might give you the URL of the referring page?

   You can often find the URL of the referring page in the `$HTTP_REFERRER` variable.

2. Why can you not rely on the `$REMOTE_ADDR` variable to track an individual user across multiple visits to your script?

   Many service providers allocate a different IP address to their users every time they log on, so you cannot assume that a user will return with the same address.

3. What does HTTP stand for?

   HTTP stands for hypertext transfer protocol.

4. What client header line tells the server about the browser that is making the request?

   A client might send a `User-Agent` header, which tells the server about the client version and operating system that are running.

5. What does the server response code 404 mean?

   The server response 404 means that the requested page or resource cannot be found on the server.

6. Without making your own network connection, what function might you use to access a Web page on a remote server?

   The `fopen()` function can be used for Web pages on remote machines as well as files on your file system.

7. Given an IP address, what function could you use to get a hostname?

   The `gethostbyaddr()` function accepts an IP address and returns a resolved hostname.

8. What function would you use to make a network connection?

   The `fsockopen()` function will establish a connection with a remote server.

9. What PHP function would you use to send an email?

   You can send email with the `mail()` function.

Hour 14

Quiz

1. What header should you send to the browser before building and outputting a GIF image?

   To output a GIF image, you should use the `header()` function to send the line `"Content-type: image/gif"` to the browser.

2. What function would you use to acquire an image identifier that you can use with other image functions?

   The `imagecreate()` function returns an image identifier.

3. What function would you use to output your GIF after building it?

   You can output a GIF with the `imagegif()` function.

4. What function could you use to acquire a color identifier?

   You can acquire a color identifier with the `imagecolorallocate()` function.

5. With which function would you draw a line on a dynamic image?

   The `imageline()` function will draw a line.

6. What function would you use to fill an area in a dynamic image?

   The `imagefill()` function will fill an area with color.

7. What function might you use to draw an arc?

   You can draw an arc with the `imagearc()` function.

8. How might you draw a rectangle?

   You can draw an outline rectangle with the `imagerectangle()` function. If you want to draw a filled rectangle, you can use `imagefilledrectangle()`.

9. How would you draw a polygon?

   You can draw a polygon with either `imagepolygon()` or `imagefilledpolygon()`.

10. What function would you use to write a string to a dynamic image (utilizing the FreeType library)?

    You can write a string to a dynamic image with the `imageTTFtext()` function.

Hour 15

Quiz

1. How would you acquire a UNIX time stamp representing the current date and time?

   The `time()` function returns the current date in time stamp format.

2. What function accepts a time stamp and returns an associative array representing the given date?

   The `getdate()` function returns an associative array whose elements contain aspects of the given date.

3. What function would you use to format date information?

   The `date()` function is used to format a date.

4. How would you acquire a time stamp for an arbitrary date?

   Given arguments representing the hour, minute, second, month, day of month, and year, the `mktime()` function returns a UNIX time stamp.

5. What function could you use to check the validity of a date?

   You can check a date with the `checkdate()` function.

Hour 16

Quiz

1. What single function could you use to convert any data type to any other data type?

   You can convert data types with the `settype()` function.

2. Could you achieve the same thing without a function?

   You can also change type using a cast—that is, by placing the name of a data type in brackets in front of the value to be converted.

3. What will the following code print?

   ```
   print ''four'' * 200;
   ```

   Strings that don't begin with numbers will resolve to 0 (zero) in expressions, so

   ```
   print ''four'' * 200
   ```

   will output `0`.

4. How would you determine whether a variable contains an array?

   To test whether a variable is an array, you could use the `is_array()` function. Alternatively, you could test the return value of `gettype()`.

5. Which function is designed to return the integer value of its argument?

   The `intval()` function returns the integer value of the argument it is passed.

6. How would you test whether a variable has been set?

   The `isset()` function tells you whether a variable has been set.

7. How would you test whether a variable contains an empty value, such as 0 or an empty string?

   The `empty()` function returns `true` if the variable passed to it is unset, or if it contains an empty value.

8. What function would you use to delete an array element?

   You can delete an array element with the `unset()` function.

9. What function could you use to custom sort a numerically indexed array?

   You can custom sort an array using the `usort()` function.

A

Hour 17

Quiz

1. What conversion specifier would you use with `printf()` to format an integer as a double? Write down the full syntax required to convert the integer 33.

   The conversion specifier `f` is used to format an integer as a double:

```
printf(''%f'', 33 );
```

2. How would you pad the conversion you effected in question 1 with zeroes so that the part before the decimal point is four characters long?

   You can pad the output from `printf()` with the padding specifier—that is, a space or a zero followed by a number representing the number of characters you want to pad by.

```
printf(''%04f'', 33 );
```

3. How would you specify a precision of two decimal places for the floating-point number we have been formatting in the previous questions?

The precision specifier consists of dot (.) followed by a number representing the precision you want to apply. It should be placed before the conversion specifier:

```
printf(''%04.2f'', 33 );
```

4. What function would you use to determine the length of a string?

   The `strlen()` function returns the length of a string.

5. What function would you use to acquire the starting index of a substring within a string?

   The `strstr()` function returns the starting index of a substring.

6. What function would you use to extract a substring from a string?

   The `substr()` function extracts and returns a substring.

7. How might you remove white space from the beginning of a string?

   The `ltrim()` function removes white space from the start of a string.

8. How would you convert a string to uppercase characters?

   The `strtoupper()` function converts a string to uppercase characters.

9. How would you break up a delimited string into an array of substrings?

   The `explode()` function will split up a string into an array.

Hour 18

Quiz

1. Using POSIX regular expression functions, what function would you use to match a pattern in a string?

   The `ereg()` function can be used to find a pattern in a string.

2. What regular expression syntax would you use to match the letter "b" at least once but not more than six times?

   You can use braces containing the minimum and maximum instances (the bounds) of a character to match:

   ```
   b{1,6}
   ```

3. How would you specify a character range between "d" and "f"?

   You can specify a character range using square brackets:

   ```
   [d-f]
   ```

4. How would you negate the character range you defined in question 3?

   You can negate a character range with the caret symbol:

   ```
   [^d-f]
   ```

5. What syntax would you use to match either any number or the word "tree"?

   You can match alternative branches with the pipe (¦) character:

   ```
   [0-9]¦tree
   ```

6. What POSIX regular expression function would you use to replace a matched pattern?

   The `ereg_replace()` function can be used to replace a matched pattern with a given alternative.

7. The regular expression

   ```
   .*bc
   ```

   will match greedily—that is, it will match "abc000000bc" rather than "abc". Using Perl compatible regular expressions, how would you make the preceding regular expression match only the first instance of a pattern it finds?

   By adding a question mark to a quantifier, you can force the match to be non-greedy when using PCREs:

   ```
   /.*?bc/
   ```

8. Using PCREs, what backslash character will match whitespace?

   `\w` will match whitespace in a PCRE.

9. What PCRE function could you use to match every instance of a pattern in a string?

   The `preg_match_all()` function will match every instance of a pattern in a string.

10. Which modifier would you use in a PCRE function to match a pattern independently of case?

    The `/i` modifier will make a PCRE function match independently of case.

Hour 19

Quiz

1. What function is designed to allow you to set a cookie on a visitor's browser?

   The `setcookie()` function allows you to set a cookie (although you could also output a `Set-Cookie` header using the `header()` function).

2. How would you delete a cookie?

   You can delete a cookie by calling `set-cookie()` with a date that has already passed.

3. What function could you use to escape a string for inclusion in a query string?

   The `urlencode()` function translates a string so that it can be included in a query string.

4. Which built-in variable contains the raw query string?

   The entire query string is made available to you in the `$QUERY_STRING` variable.

5. The name/value pairs submitted as part of a query string will become available as global variables. They will also be included in a built-in associative array. What is its name?

   The `$HTTP_GET_VARS` variable will contain the name/value pairs submitted as part of a query string.

Hour 20

Quiz

1. Which function would you use to start or resume a session?

   You can start a session with the `session_start()` function.

2. Which function contains the current session's ID?

   You can access the session's ID with the `session_id()` function.

3. How can you associate a variable with a session?

   The `session_register()` function associates the given variable with the current session.

4. How would you end a session and erase all traces of it for future visits?

   The `session_destroy()` function removes all traces of a session for future requests.

5. How would you destroy session variables both within the current script and the session?

   The `session_unset()` function removes session variables from the current script as well as the session.

6. What does the `SID` constant return?

   If cookies are not available, the `SID` constant contains a name/value pair that can be incorporated in a query string. This will pass the session ID from script request to script request.

7. How would you test whether a variable called `$test` is registered with a session?

   You can use the `is_registered()` function to check that a variable is associated with the current session.

   ```
   is_registered(''test'')
   ```

Hour 21

Quiz

1. Which function would you use to open a pipe to a process?

   You open a connection to a process with the function `popen()`.

2. How would you read data from a process after you have opened a connection?

   You can read from a process that you have opened with `popen()` as you would from a file. In other words, you can use functions such as `feof()` and `fgets()`.

3. How can you write data to a process after you have opened a connection to it?

   You can write to a process as you could with a file, usually with the `fputs()` function.

4. Will the `exec()` function print the output of a shell command directly to the browser?

   The `exec()` function accepts an array variable, which it fills with the output of the shell command it makes. Output is not sent directly to the browser.

5. What does the `system()` function do with the output from an external command it executes?

   The `system()` function prints the output of the external command directly to the browser.

6. What does the backtick operator return?

   The backtick operator returns the output of the external command that it calls. This can be stored, parsed, or printed.

7. How can you escape user input to make it a little safer before passing it to a shell command?

You can escape user input to make it safer using the `escapeshellcmd()` function. The safest way to execute shell commands, though, is to refrain from passing user input at all.

8. How might you execute an external CGI script from within your script?

   The `virtual()` function will call an external CGI script.

Hour 22

Quiz

1. What function outputs useful information about your PHP configuration to the browser?

   The `phpinfo()` function will output information about your version of PHP, its configuration, and any environmental variables available to the current script.

2. What function could you use to include a syntax-colored source listing of a PHP script?

   The `show_source()` function accepts a path to a PHP script and includes a syntax-colored listing in the current script.

3. Which `php.ini` directive enables you to control the strictness of error messages?

   The `error_reporting` `php.ini` directive controls how strict PHP will be in reporting errors.

4. What function can be used to override this directive?

   The `error_reporting()` function allows you to override the `php.ini` setting of the same name.

5. Which function allows you to log errors?

   You can log errors with the `error_log()` function.

6. What built-in variable will contain the error message if the `php.ini` `track_errors` option is allowed?

   The `$php_errormsg` will hold the most recent error message.

Hour 23

Quiz

1. What PHP function do we use to make our connection to the MySQL database server?

The `mysql_connect()` function attempts to make a connection to the MySQL daemon.

2. What PHP function do we use to initiate or resume a session?

   The `session_start()` function initiates a session.

3. Which function do we use to include library files in our project's pages?

   The `include()` function incorporates a library file in the current script.

4. What PHP function do we use to send SQL queries to the MySQL database?

   The `mysql_query()` function passes a SQL query to the database.

5. What constant do we use to add a session ID to an HTML link?

   The `SID` constant contains a name/value pair suitable for adding to a query string. The name is the name of the session, and the value is the session ID.

6. How do we move the user on to a new page?

   You can redirect a user to a new script with the `header()` function. You must include a `Location` header.

```
header(''Location: membersmenu.php?''.SID);
```

7. What function do we use to format date information?

   The `date()` function accepts formatting flags and a date in time stamp format. It returns a formatted date string.

A

Hour 24

Quiz

1. What function do you use to add an element to the end of an array?

   The `array_push()` function adds an element to an array.

2. Is it possible to add an element to an array without using a function?

   You can add an element to an array by assigning it to the array variable followed by empty square brackets:

```
$array[] = $new_element
```

3. Which function do you use to translate special characters into HTML format?

   The `htmlspecialcharacters()` function translates special characters into HTML entities so that they will be properly displayed on the browser.

4. Which function do you use to translate newline characters into `<BR>` tags?

   The `nl2br()` function transforms newlines into `<BR>` tags.

5. You can use the `SID` constant to pass the session ID to another page via an HTML link. How do you achieve the same effect with a form?

   To embed a session ID in an HTML form, you can use a hidden field. You should name it according to the string returned by the `$session_name()` function and give it the value returned by the `$session_id()` function.

```
<input type=''hidden'' name=''<?php print session_name() ?>''
       value=''<?php print session_id() ?>''>.
```

INDEX

Symbols

E

F

I

J-K

L

M

N

O

P

Q

T

U

X-Z